# BINDING MEDIA

STANFORD
TEXT TECHNOLOGIES

**Series Editors**

Ruth Ahnert

Roopika Risam

Elaine Treharne

**Editorial Board**

Benjamin Albritton

Caroline Bassett

Lori Emerson

Alan Liu

Elena Pierazzo

Andrew Prescott

Matthew Rubery

Kate Sweetapple

Heather Wolfe

# BINDING MEDIA

*Hybrid Print-Digital Literature
from across the Americas*

ÉLIKA ORTEGA

Stanford University Press
Stanford, California

Stanford University Press
Stanford, California

© 2025 by Élika Ortega. All rights reserved.

No part of this book may be reproduced or transmitted in any form or by any means, electronic or mechanical, including photocopying and recording, or in any information storage or retrieval system, without the prior written permission of Stanford University Press.

Printed in the United States of America on acid-free, archival-quality paper

Library of Congress Cataloging-in-Publication Data
Names: Ortega, Élika, author.
Title: Binding media : hybrid print-digital literature from across the Americas / Élika Ortega.
Other titles: Text technologies.
Description: Stanford, California : Stanford University Press, 2025. | Series: Stanford text technologies | Includes bibliographical references and index.
Identifiers: LCCN 2024028690 (print) | LCCN 2024028691 (ebook) | ISBN 9781503641785 (cloth) | ISBN 9781503641952 (ebook)
Subjects: LCSH: Literature and technology—America. | Books and reading—Technological innovations—America. | Publishers and publishing—Technological innovations—America.
Classification: LCC PN56.T37 O775 2025 (print) | LCC PN56.T37 (ebook) | DDC 070.5/3—dc23/eng/20240724
LC record available at https://lccn.loc.gov/2024028690
LC ebook record available at https://lccn.loc.gov/2024028691

Cover design: Hollis Duncan

**CONTENTS**

*Acknowledgments* vii

Introduction 1

**1** Binding Media: 31
Negotiating (Un)Boundedness

**2** From the Digital Revolution in Publishing 71
to a Material History of Hybrid Books

**3** Divergent Temporalities in Binding Media 127

**4** Media Hybridity and Cultural Hybridity 175

**Conclusion** From Computer-Generated Books 217
to NFT Publishing

**Appendix** Binding Media Corpus 251

*Notes* 257
*Bibliography* 291
*Index* 313

## ACKNOWLEDGMENTS

This book owes its existence to three institutions: the Maryland Institute for Technology in the Humanities (MITH) at the University of Maryland, the Electronic Literature Lab (ELL) at Washington State University Vancouver, and the Media Archaeology Lab (MAL) at University of Colorado (CU) Boulder. I'm grateful to Matthew Kirschenbaum and Dene Grigar, who supported and guided my work during my time at MITH and ELL in spring 2018. I have had the enormous luck to share a campus with and be within walking distance of MAL. I'm thankful to MAL managing director, libi striegl, whose minute knowledge of everything at the lab expanded and illuminated every aspect of my research. Vital for the book was the encouragement, advice, mentorship, and friendship of Lori Emerson, who provided critical feedback, support, and guidance for the manuscript at every stage of writing and revision.

I'm thankful for the help, advice, and support of a multitude of people: Erica Wetter and Caroline McKusick and the Text Technologies Series editors Ruth Ahnert, Roopika Risam, and Elaine Treharne. I'm also thankful to the entire Stanford University Press production, design, and marketing team. My colleagues at the Department of Spanish and Portuguese at CU Boulder, especially Tracy Quan, Esther Brown, Tania Martuscelli, and Mary Long, have offered valuable support and encouragement. Past colleagues at Northeastern University were some of the first audiences of this project: José Buscaglia, Moya Bailey, and the members of the NULab and the CSSH. Other friends and colleagues who directly and indirectly helped shape my work are Alan Liu, Brian Rosenblum, Juan Luis Suárez, Jen Giuliano, Jacque Wernimont, Liz Losh, Ali Pearl, Kathi Berens, Kim Martin, Ryan Cordell, Hannah Alpert-Abrahams, Magalí Rabasa, Rita Raley, Paul Benzon, Nick Montfort, Zach Whalen, Claudia Kozak, Leo Flores, Tina Escaja, Matthew Gold, Marcy Schwartz, Nickoal Eichmann-Kalwara, Anna Ferris, Alyssa Arbuckle, Janneke Adema, Matt Schneider, Whitney Trettien, Cecily Raynor, Gabriela Baeza Ventura, Carolina Villarroel, Isabel Galina, Irene Artigas, Nair Anaya, Adela Ramos, Roberto Cruz Arzabal, Cynthia García Leyva, María Andrea Giovine, Susana González Aktories, Ana Cecilia Medina, Mónica Nepote, Ernesto Priani, Miriam Peña, and Marina Garone.

I want to thank the writers, artists, and publishers whose work I examine in these pages and who took the time to talk to me about their creations: Cristina Rivera Garza, Vega Sánchez Aparicio, Vivian Abenshushan, Verónica Gerber Bicecci, Canek Zapata, Carlos Bergen, J. R. Carpenter, Stephanie Strickland, Amaranth Borsuk, Ian Hatcher, Kate Durbin, Belén Gache, Luis Correa-Díaz, David Stairs, Allison Parrish, James Ryan, Maurits Montañez, Ernesto Miranda, Ricardo Domínguez, Amy Sara Carroll, Felicia Rice, and Ana María Caballero.

During summer 2020, I was lucky to be part of the Junior Faculty of Color Writing Group at CU Boulder, an amazing group of scholars who supported one another during the weirdest of times for writing. In particular I'm grateful to Natalie Avalos, Maria Windell, Kristie Soares, Yesika Ordaz, René Espinoza, Nishant Appadurai, and Azita Ranjbar. Meeting in parks and other outdoor spaces as we churned ideas has been one of my favorite writing experiences despite the circumstances that forced such conditions.

Two pillars sustained and, quite literally, lived through the process of writing this book. The "compound," a remote space for friendship, support, humor, and, when needed, anger that I share with Alex Saum and Nora Benedict. My husband, Erik Radio, encouraged, animated, and supported me through the entire process; our dogs Baxter, Bruna, and Elvis always ensured I went out for walks and fresh air.

My family is, and has always been, the foundation of everything I do. This book is for my moms, Guille y Pita.

**INTRODUCTION**

**I MUST HAVE BEEN ON** social media when sometime in 2012 I came across the literary work that gave rise to this study: the augmented-reality poetry collection *Between Page and Screen* (*BPaS*). Created by the poet and programmer duo Amaranth Borsuk and Brad Bouse, and published by Los Angeles–based Siglio Press, *BPaS* is made up of a print book with no text aside from paratexts and an augmented-reality (AR) web application. In the predominantly white pages of the codex are geometrical figures resembling QR codes, which can be read through the AR web application that unlocks the words hidden in them. To read *BPaS*, the reader must hold the open book in front of a computer's webcam, ensure the page isn't warped, and carefully look at the text popping up on the screen. The unlocked poetry collection is the correspondence between P(age) and S(creen), and, in addition to their letters, there are animated concrete poems about the relationship between these two media characters. More than a decade after its publication, *BPaS* has become an essential reference for contemporary book studies, poetry, and digital literature. Until recently, when Adobe Flash was discontinued at the end of 2020, readers could still experience how effectively *BPaS* forces a "binding" of its two media objects: there is no way *just to read* the book or *just to play* with the digital application.[1] To fully appreciate the poetics of the work, readers must use both objects simultaneously, and, as we do so, *BPaS* prompts us to observe how its meaning is created in a matrix of human and machine languages, print and digital media objects, and crucially, the reader's role in handling the many pieces. The seemingly empty space *between* book and computer turns out to be the very material holding those items together—or, as I argue, the *binding* of the work.

I open this introduction with *BPaS* as a paradigm of what I call "binding media": the literary practice in which authors fasten together codex and electronic or digital applications to create a single literary work. Fastening together print and digital objects brings about the creation and production of hybrid media objects that circulate, operate, read, and mean differently than print or digital literature alone. Thus, "binding media," as a compound noun, refers to the resulting hybrid media objects. Further, binding media are a form of "media poetics" in which authors engage in material practices of signification to fulfill their literary purposes.[2] I resort to the notion of "binding," more readily associated with print culture, to characterize the strategies for joining book and digital media objects, and the expressive physical, conceptual, and metaphorical qualities that emerge from such fastening. In this way, binding media evidence how specific media are more than holders of "content" and foster particularized modes of reading, writing, and meaning-making alone or in tandem. Further, binding media enact an apparent paradox between the stability of the codex and its media protocols, and the rapidly changing landscape of digital technologies where acid-free paper—or even acid-free bits—does little to counter the regime of digital presentism based on planned obsolescence.[3]

In the decade I have devoted to this book, I have amassed a collection of about a hundred titles encompassing four decades starting in the early 1980s, seven countries across the Americas, and three languages (English, Spanish, and Portuguese). During this time, I have uncovered a history of binding media that turned out to be longer than I first anticipated and have witnessed an ongoing increase in the creation and publication of binding media. In this way, binding media open a window into the changes the publishing industry, literary creation, and reading practices have undergone in the last few decades. The corpus of binding media shows how, despite economic limitations, independent and institutional publishers have been responsible for bringing forth innovations to the book form through digital technologies. Most interesting in binding media is how the tensions at the heart of their media objects, writing, reading, production, and distribution work congruously, though not seamlessly, to produce what I argue are materially complex single works rather than editions, adaptations, or attachments of each other. Although these frameworks could also be used to read the literary works I call binding media, they would yield distinct insights with regard to those I'm interested in. By considering them to be fastened, I seek to highlight how the relationship of print and digital objects does not consist of a variation in format alone, nor are they tied in a dynamic of source-target texts. Instead, binding media offer unique configurations of print and digital objects at the levels of text, book design and production, and technical compositions that serve as the binding mechanisms holding the pieces of a work together. In binding media, print books and digital applications may seem like discrete facets, but as I argue, they are, in fact, coconstitutive.

Simultaneously, I have observed the decay and obsolescence of many of the examples that prompted this investigation. Looked at all together, the corpus of binding media lays bare the effects of technological innovation and obsolescence on cultural objects, literary scholarship, and memory-making. Central to binding media are divergent temporalities wherein digital applications are prone to obsolescence only a few years after release. At the same time, most print facets continue to inhabit bookshelves decades after publication. This paradox prompts an interrogation of the methodologies of contemporary literary inquiry that rely on various degrees of fixity and consistency. Instead, as storage media become discontinued, new operating systems stop supporting various softwares, and websites go offline, the corpus of binding media constitutes an archive of remains that signal what used to be there. In this way, binding media force a reckoning with how we write their history, focusing less on their "contents" and more on their contexts of creation and production, including those of their obsolescence. In a media archaeological fashion, binding media prompt a history that runs counter and adds friction to the dominant histories of technology in publishing, focused mainly on the industry developments and less so on material and literary affectations.

**A Hybrid Media Landscape**

Throughout this book, I consider the materiality of binding media to be a hybrid of print and digital objects and their affordances, industries, and temporalities, and I argue that the shifts in the media landscape of the last few decades are so profound that they have fostered and furthered cultural changes as well. Therefore, in these pages, I aim to bridge the notions of media hybridity and cultural hybridity. The hermeneutic conceptualization of hybridization put forward by the Argentinian Mexican anthropologist Néstor García Canclini informs my use of the term. Viewing it as a process rather than a finished outcome, I use "hybridization" to characterize the "processes in which discrete structures or practices, previously existing in separate form, are combined to generate new structures, objects, and practices."[4] Moreover, although notions of hybridization need to start with and from discrete or stable units—in this case, print and digital media—I in no way argue for the purity of either. Instead, I take binding media as one link in a long chain of media shifts that have included hybridization processes and have often responded to dramatic cultural shifts. Binding media, then, are the material substrate of the two concomitant processes of media and cultural hybridization as they express hybridity in more than one way: by fastening print and digital media objects; by concretizing the cultural changes brought about by the popularization of digital media; by precipitating transitional creative, publishing, and reading practices; and by manifesting the cultural encounters provoked by late capitalist transnational communications and markets.

The scope of the intersections or hybridizations between media in cultural production can be observed in the heterogeneity of critical and theoretical foci devoted to them: everything from bibliographic and artistic experimentation to publishing, media objects, markets, and even, as British artist James Bridle would have it, "ways of seeing the world."[5] However, each of these perspectives alone can only say so much about the systemic influence of the digital in culture at large. To grasp this larger dimension, I aim to consider media changes in an ecological fashion inspired by media theorist Neil Postman's thesis that "technological change is neither additive nor subtractive. It is ecological . . . One significant change generates total change."[6] For Postman, these changes have economic, political, historical, and even cognitive dimensions useful for framing the larger significance of a phenomenon like binding media. Similar ecological approaches have been proposed by electronic literature scholar Katherine Hayles in *Writing Machines* (2002)[7] and by the team of twenty-two scholars known as the Multigraph Collective in *Interacting with Print* (2018).[8] As technological changes modify what we think about and the tools we think with, they both abstract previous changes and further them.

Creative endeavors such as binding media allow us to describe distinct processes of hybridization involving the material processes of creation, production, and reception. Additionally, the materiality of binding media allows us to go further than a simple characterization of hybridity and serves to explain the "relations of meaning that are reconstructed through mixing."[9] Among these reconstructed relations of meaning, we can list the place of the print book in an expanded media ecology; the staying role of literature, not just technology, in pushing innovation; shifting reading habits fostered by the culture and tech industries, and others. Moreover, these media changes emerge from and yield what comparatist Mary-Louise Pratt termed a zone of contact, "the space and time where subjects previously separated by geography and history are copresent, the point at which their trajectories now intersect."[10] I expand Pratt's theorization to consider the zone of contact as the landscape where media changes and hybridization generate heterogeneous, nonstandardized, and experimental media objects. The intersections of trajectories outlined have produced new forms of textual media in which we can observe, to use the words of media theorist Lisa Gitelman, "the novelty years, transitional states, and identity crises of different media [that] stand to tell us much."[11] Simultaneously, the zone of contact is also the locus where globalization processes carried out through digital communications, a shifting media ecology, and human movement prompt the emergence of similar cultural practices—such as binding media—in distant contexts and present a challenge to the national, regional, and linguistic demarcation that still reign in literary studies.

Characteristic of a landscape like the one depicted above, with so much variety, are diverse forms and processes of hybridization. Therefore, although my investigation of binding media is primarily an inquiry into literary and textual media, I draw knowledge and insights from a wealth of scholarly fields, including book history and publishing studies, media theory and media archaeology, and history and cultural studies. Far from being a prescriptive exercise in interdisciplinarity, the hybridity of binding media has imposed a methodology of "ands" that *bind* the extremes of what could be considered binary realms and yield, instead, comparative insights. Binding media are books *and* digital applications; they are phenomena of the publishing industry *and* the tech industry; they are future-looking endeavors *and* objects of the recent past; they are obsolescent *and* stable media; they are bespoke literary and media objects *and* recurrent phenomena. The trope of hybridity has allowed me to show these domains as coconstitutive and to observe how, for instance, an interrogation of the book form is concurrently a subversion and a reification of its bounds. Moreover, the scholarly history of hybridity and hybridization allows me to spotlight power differences—technological, economic, and cultural—in the distinct contexts of Latin America, the United States, and Canada.

Although hybridity is a better trope to tangle and untangle such coconstitutive relationships in binding media, my methodology is also informed by formulations more commonly used in literary studies, such as transmediality, intermediality, and other adjacent concepts that have a history of problematizing the interactions between media objects. The dichotomy of print and digital media in literary studies was already heavily contested from different theoretical perspectives by the time I began this investigation. In their introduction to *Comparative Textual Media: Transforming the Humanities in the Postprint Era* (2013), Katherine Hayles and Jessica Pressman explain that "so intermixed are digital and print media through modern printing and publishing machines that they must be considered comparatively to make sense of their production at all."[12] Their approach favors a much more extended and integrated media landscape that considers installations, SMS texting, and others that, just like digital literature, have transformed the role and place of print and text. A few years earlier, in 2006, media scholar Henry Jenkins had established the basis of convergence culture and transmedia storytelling where stories or "media content" circulate "across different media systems, competing media economies, and national borders."[13] Intermediality studies, more common in the European academy, similarly focus on the mixture of media with "heightened awareness of the materiality and mediality of artistic practices and of cultural practices in general."[14] Although this branch of intermediality studies comes from a longer (predigital) tradition of interarts practice, it was also in the 2010s that the work of German comparatist Irina Rajewsky, for instance, gained much attention within studies of digital literary production.

This burgeoning of critical approaches to the intersection of literature and electronic and digital media should not mislead us into thinking that these phenomena are all that recent. As a matter of fact, there has been no shortage of instances in which literary creation and forms of computation meet since around the mid-twentieth century. A central figure in digital literary studies, Matthew Kirschenbaum has explored the adoption of personal computers by various writers and the impact of this shift on literary production in *Track Changes* (2016), thus opening a window into the early history of this intersection.[15] In the 1990s, Brazilian media poet Eduardo Kac posited that the print medium had become insufficient for the poetic endeavors of the turn of the century that necessitated technological developments to continue innovating.[16] The first decade of the 2000s, once the initial overenthusiasm and overresistance toward digital media had passed, was a period in literary scholarship with much interest in examining the myriad existing relationships between print and digital media. Theorizations like poetry scholar Marjorie Perloff's "differential texts" remind us, as my corpus confirms, that writers were producing print, digital, and installation versions of their works before the turn of the twenty-first century. For Perloff, differential texts are "neither single nor autonomous but a set of variants" of a work that has resulted in "a poetry in which no single version necessarily has priority."[17] However, unlike binding media, this notion considers the print, digital, and installation versions of such texts separately and not producing meaning jointly. Perloff's conceptualization also seems to subscribe to a view where a medium can be examined in isolation from others rather than in a comparative fashion—a view that I contest throughout this book. Similarly, Americanist Alan Golding's concept of "transitional materialities" deals with what could be considered adaptations of print texts to online environments and the "points of reciprocity" between them or how each medium entails unique expressive affordances.[18] Hayles made a similar claim through her conceptualizations of "media specificity" and "technotexts," but one much more powerful and relevant to binding media because it considers medium, "the literary work as physical artifact," as the space of analysis.[19] Within the multidisciplinary lineage of literary studies of print and digital media, Hayles's enduring notion continues to be relevant as the relationships between these media and the artifactuality of literary works along with them change. Currently, the instances in which print and digital media inform and illuminate each other at all stages in the lifespan of a literary work, from its writing to its reviewing, are even more intricate. As print and electronic literature scholar Jessica Pressman notes, "we face something far more complex and interesting" than a separation of print and digital.[20] Far from causing the "death of the book," as many wrongly feared in the 1990s and early 2000s, the irruption of various digital technologies has entailed equally varied reinvestments in print. The intersections between print and digital media have yielded a heterogeneous media landscape where new models of creation, production, and consumption have flourished and dwindled around the world. However, despite this exciting heterogeneity, we should not look at this moment as exceptional when, in fact, moments of radical media change have abounded throughout history.[21] As I examine in these pages, though relatively short and recent, there is already a history of binding media to excavate.

Binding media appeal to familiar sensibilities of the early twenty-first century—a cultural moment when our day-to-day media habits constantly take our hands, eyes, and attention around a plethora of screens of all sizes, apps, and print matter. Transmedia commercial practices of conglomerate franchises, developed across a multitude of platforms and business models that were novel in the early 2000s, have become the norm of distribution and consumption in many contexts. For this readjustment to happen, the relationships between media had to undergo a shift "where a particular medium assumes a newly found dominance."[22] Intermedia contexts like those theorized by Rajewsky offer a broad spectrum of media affectations as digital technologies have touched all other media realms, from books to television and education. Therefore, as Rajewsky acknowledges, intermediality as a category can refer to too many different phenomena and is, thus, useful when deployed critically for analyzing specific individual media products or configurations.[23] Certainly, among these products and configurations, we can situate binding media. More recently, Latin Americanist scholar Gianna Schmitter has sought to bridge some of the varied approaches mentioned above through the über-term "transliteratures"— literary works that are transnational, transmedia, and transitional (in domains as varied as historical, bodily, media, authorial, or literary).[24] The breadth of Schmitter's conceptualization might be capacious, but it encompasses so many possible features that it risks encompassing everything.

Binding media, as I hope to show, don't quite fit critical and theoretical models like transmedia, intermediality, or even transliteratures.

While it would be possible to read them as such, I find that such frameworks can be simultaneously too broad and too narrow for the types of analysis I conduct. I'm interested in examining what the objectual configuration of binding media does to how literary works are written, published, distributed, valued, and read. More expansively, I'm interested in reading binding media to test what a specifically demarcated phenomenon can tell us about its larger and more general cultural moment. Thus, my approach to binding media is not a study of their transmediality or their intermediality. This methodological departure does not negate that these works exist in a *trans-* or *inter-* media fashion. Instead, my focus underscores how, within the capacious realms and industries of literary creation and publishing and software development, print and digital media are so intricately woven together that the leap *across* media or platforms still assumed to be different is barely a leap anymore. The process of binding is the process of hybridization entailing a synthesis that does not resolve tensions and contradictions but highlights and benefits from them. In the critical ecological landscape formed at the intersection of literary, book, media, and cultural studies, the fundaments of my analysis are the bespoke mechanisms authors use to bind print and digital media. They are the probeable strategies of meaning-making, the marks of creativity and inventiveness, the emergent practices of publishing, and the evidence of fraught cultural changes. Studying them in this manner draws binding media away from their categorization as products of intermediality and, instead, enables their consideration as developments in the history of the book, as products of the publishing industry, as works of digital literature, as cultural remains or media archaeological objects, and, ultimately, as the material substrate of media-cultural hybridity.

With some exceptions, concerted attention to binding media as "bound" print and digital objects has been lacking in the scholarship of electronic literature. Digital works like American poet and book artist Paul Zelevansky's *Swallows* (1986),[25] Argentinian concrete poet María Uribe's *Anipoemas* (1997), and American poet and pianist Oni Buchanan's *The Mandrake Vehicles* (2006)[26] are all well studied and even anthologized. Nevertheless, aside from pointing out that they have been published along with a print book, little attention is paid to the hybrid materiality of the works as a whole and the meaning-making potential of such configurations. American poet Stephanie Strickland's *V: Vniverse* (2002), read under *trans-* and *inter-* media paradigms, might be the exception proving the rule.[27] In their extended essay "Making the *Vniverse*," Strickland and her coauthor programmer Cynthia Lawson-Jaramillo explicitly stated, "Though either the book or the *Vniverse* can be read alone, the richest meanings will occur to people who are reading between them."[28] American novelist Mark Z. Danielewski's *House of Leaves* (2000) offers an example of the opposite consideration, a "networked novel," as Jessica Pressman calls it, that is often read as "just a book." In Danielewski's work, Pressman explains, the book is "the central node in a network of multimedia, multi-authored forms that collectively comprise its narrative: The *House of Leaves* website (www.houseofleaves.com), *The Whalestoe Letters* (an accompanying book by Danielewski containing a section from the novel's Appendix), and the musical album *Haunted* by the author's sister, the recording artist Poe."[29] Instead of the metaphor of the network used by Pressman entailing connections among separate nodes, I use the notion of binding to underscore the coconstitutiveness of a work's distributed objects and the emergent media hybridity. This consideration forces a reckoning with the poetics emerging out of that hybridity, particularly in works like *Between Page and Screen*, *Vniverse*, and before them, novelist William Gibson's *Agrippa (A Book of the Dead)* (1992), whose print-digital configuration cannot be overlooked no matter how hard one tries.

    The vast majority of binding media are published in small print runs by independent presses that offer more room for authors to participate in the design and production processes.[30] The earliest exemplars of binding media, however, were published by software companies. Large commercial publishers have also tried their hand at hybrid publishing, seeking to streamline their production processes, but have been unsuccessful in most cases. The exception most of us will recognize is textbooks, which for decades have included digital content to enhance their courses of study. Even with this precedent, it's clear that binding media inhabit a more specific realm than expanded or augmented publishing. It's not just that digital literature still struggles to enter the literary canons and the world of book apps, but also that there isn't an industry around digital literature that authors or readers can rely on for production, distribution, cultural capital, and business models. In contrast, binding media have partially benefited from the infrastructures of print culture for its study, production, and preservation. Nevertheless, it has also become clear that protocols designed for print media (preservation, accessibility, cataloging) do not fit the material specificities of binding media and entail considerable challenges to remediate their dwindling.

As this introductory review of theorizations on the interactions between books and literature and digital media shows, the scholarly focus has been primarily on the observable shifts in technological developments, whether in publishing or literary practices. None of these approaches, however, treats in detail (although some seem to intuit) the larger cultural dimension that technological developments have both fostered and furthered. In fact, in my readings of binding media, I aim to show that in the world of globalized and accelerated communications, emerging markets, rapid technological innovation, human movement, and forced displacement, there is much to learn by theorizing cultural and media hybridization processes as a continuum. Thus, the heterogeneity in the manifestations of media hybridity is suggestive of underlying processes of cultural hybridization. Moreover, the hemispheric and multilingual scope of the corpus of binding media demands that, in addition to approaches focused on book and publishing studies and media, we pay attention to the technocultural differences between Latin America and North America. In particular, I consider the implications for the Latin American region, which, rather than being a center of technological innovation, has been the origin of raw materials extraction and cheap labor that sustains the transnational free market. Further, this approach should also alert us to the fact that the cultural and media changes taking place at the turn of the twenty-first century are not restricted to an economic, linguistic, or literary region. Over this basis, a contribution I hope to make through the hemispheric and multilingual approach is to counterbalance the existing bias in media studies and digital literature toward the Global North.

**Building the Corpus**
Once I had identified binding media as recurrent phenomena across the Americas, the process of building the corpus demanded an excavation of the phenomenon toward the past and away from the US publishing world alone. This has taken me from an initially identified set of titles published in the 2010s in the United States by American authors, such as *Vniverse* by Stephanie Strickland in its second edition (2014), Nick Montfort's *#!* (2014), and Jacob Garbe and Aaron Reed's *Ice-Bound* (2015), into works published thirty years earlier. Former poet laureate Robert Pinsky created *Mindwheel: An Electronic Novel* in collaboration with programmers Steve Hales and Cathryn Mataga; the work was published in 1984. The year 1986 seems to be a turning point for print-digital publications: Thomas Disch's *Amnesia*, Paul Zelevansky's *The Case for the Burial of Ancestors. Book 2. Genealogy*, and Judy Malloy's *Uncle Roger* were all published that year. William Gibson's *Agrippa (A Book of the Dead)* came out to instant fame in 1992. This male-heavy list of American pioneers of binding media might give the impression that this is a phenomenon proper to the Anglo-American region. Likely, the role and influence of the innovative technological prowess of the United States, and the quick adoption of personal computers and word processors by authors in this country, are the reasons for it. However, when considering this apparent insularity, it is equally important to acknowledge that in the 1980s, the market for personal computers was nascent, and the global reach of their distribution cannot even begin to be compared to today. Likewise, prohibitively high currency exchange rates and a pre–free market agreements world where high tariffs were imposed on the importation of electronics are the basis for the lack of early examples of binding media outside the United States.[31]

A broader map of the phenomenon emerges at the turn of the century. Works that were in the making through the mid- and late 1990s, such as *Árbol veloZ* (1990–98) by Uruguayan artist Luis Bravo, Brazilian writer and artist Giselle Beiguelman's *O Livro depois do Livro* (1999/2003), and *El libro del fin del mundo* (2002) by Argentinian writer Belén Gache, were published by various presses around the Southern Cone. Notably, Brazilian poet Augusto de Campos's *Não (poemaxerox)* from 1990 was reissued in 2003 in a print collection of his concrete poetry, including his clip-poems, in a CD-ROM. Though some identified exemplars are outside the geographic scope of this book, they are worth mentioning as they offer a broader perspective to my study. Czech-born Brazilian philosopher Vilém Flusser's hypertextual version of his novel *Die Schrift* was published by Immatrix in 1987. Responsible for both the print and digital editions, the publisher indicated in a paper insert: "you decided to take part in an experiment of developing new dimensions of communication. In front of you lies the first real no-longer-a-book."[32] Other instances are Italian electronic literature writer Lorenzo Miglioli's *RADIO* (1993); Swiss artist Camille Scherrer's *Souvenirs du monde des montagnes* (2008); Japanese artist and musician Yuri Suzuki's *The Barcode Book* (2010); Polish poet Zenon Fajfer's *dwadzieścia jeden liter* (2010) and *Powieki* (2013); and British digital artist Richard A. Carter's *Waveform* (2020), *Signals* (2022), *Orbital Reveries* (2021–2023), among others. As the corpus has expanded in every direction, it has become evident that binding media are not as radically contemporary as they might have seemed at first—certainly not just "postdigital"—and that their features are widely varied. Ultimately, the entire corpus demonstrates that this kind of recurrent experimentation manifests in strikingly similar ways at different moments in a dimension we can consider global.

Binding media are not the kind of "books" that one finds in booksellers' displays; they are not even easily found in specialized bookstores and archives; and there is no cataloging category that distinguishes them from other books of "poetry," "essay," or "fiction," or other nomenclature like "computer game" or "software." During the course of this research, one constant I encountered was the lack of a standard cataloging procedure that could accurately and regularly account for the objects that make up binding media exemplars and, more importantly, make them discoverable. Regular library bibliographic catalogs might include a mention of a CD-ROM or a diskette in the book's physical description or the notes section. Special collections often provide more detail and useful tags like "production format," used at the Joan Flasch Artists' Book Collection at the School of the Art Institute of Chicago. Some libraries physically catalog print and digital media separately, not as a bundle. But cataloging categories can vary widely. For example, search results in WorldCat identify the format of Stephanie Strickland's *Zone : Zero*, predictably, as a print book, but much more surprisingly, also as a "kit" and as "downloadable archival material." The lack of established cataloging standards, symptomatic of the emergent and nonstandardized quality of hybrid publishing, has proved challenging for my research, which has consisted in no small part of collecting the corpus itself. This excavatory labor has been surprising and fulfilling, and has taken many turns through word-of-mouth recommendations, chance encounters, ancillary documentation, and visits to media and humanities labs and library special collections. Countless colleagues have also pointed me to a wealth of adjacent print-digital objects, from augmented newspaper articles and magazines to roleplaying games, bicycle manuals, and music scores.

Undoubtedly, one of the most intriguing works I came across in the years spanning this research was American writer Holly Franking's *Negative Space CVN®. A Computerized Video Novel,* published by Diskotech Inc. Software in 1995 and held in the Electronic Literature Lab (ELL) collection. This intriguing artifact is made up of a print manual that includes an introduction to the work, reviews, and exact instructions and software specifications to run the accompanying CD-ROM on a Windows 3.1 operating system. The copy at the ELL, however, was the second edition of the work, published five years earlier, which, according to the manual, "combined three media—print, software, and video—to create a new form of the novel for this postmodern era."[33] The description continues: "that first edition contained one documentation manual, two 5.25 [inch] and one 3.5 [inch] computer diskettes, and one VHS videotape ... *Negative Space CVN®* is not a printed text scrolling on a computer screen; it is not interactive fiction; it is not a video game. It is a literary novel that combines print, software and video to create a new form of the novel."[34] When I found this work on the ELL shelves during a visit in 2018, *Negative Space CVN®* was sitting among dozens of other items in the queue to be cataloged by the lab's team. Still, no one was aware of its existence or its material characteristics binding print and digital media.

While I can't say that *Negative Space CVN®* is a great, transformative work of literature akin to *Between Page and Screen* (the ELL team and I were, ultimately, unable to make it run on any of the myriad computers available at the ELL), I remain curious about how its weirdness and over-the-top-ness did not prevent it from going unnoticed in the last three decades. The plot, described in the manual, concerns a university English professor and his wife who are undergoing a variety of fertility procedures and might not sound like the stuff of best sellers. Nevertheless, Franking's insistence on the hybrid character of the novel, one in which trying to "reduce it to its various parts—text, video, software, print, music, voice-overs, etc.—would be like trying to separate the peach from the plum in a nectarine," is indicative of a heightened awareness of the intersections between print and digital media that were happening in the early and mid-1990s (and before then) and would continue to the present.[35] The handling of this work is highly suggestive of the reading media landscape, too. As one reviewer of the first edition explains, "in the package there is a 3.5 inch diskette, a video tape and a user's guide. The video can be viewed in the Media Center. The diskette must be carried up to the Computer Lab on the third floor."[36] This seemingly innocuous set of instructions reveals how the conditions of reading have not always been self-evident and entail a multitude of devices, gestures, and locations. While one may be skeptical of how much that "counts" as reading, a central argument of this book is that in binding media, the suite of handling and reading instructions is constitutive of a work's meaning as a literary object. Further, an obscure work like *Negative Space CVN®* highlights, more than any other, the challenges of researching experimental and nonstandardized materials. Even highly specialized places like the ELL are unable to stock every possible hardware-software configuration that will read these unique works—something that invites us to reflect on the challenges digital media might pose to literary scholarship. The need for robust institutional infrastructure to study works like this was evident to Franking's reviewer, and it should be for us, too.

To say that the variety of items I have examined in the course of my research is heterogeneous would be an understatement. Nevertheless, the very heterogeneity of the phenomenon has helped me pinpoint the distinguishing qualities of binding media. Indeed, as will become apparent through the following chapters, the heterogeneity of the corpus in terms of themes, technology, genre, language, and so on is bridged by two unifying principles. First, in contrast to publications like print and digital travel guides, cookbooks, manuals, and even scholarship, binding media are creative literary endeavors. Second, although on certain occasions other materials (cassette tapes, postcards, and performances) are part of a work's makeup, binding media have a material configuration comprising print objects and digital applications constitutive of its literary effects and aesthetics.

A multitude of examples of scholarly binding media came to my attention, too. Perhaps not unexpectedly, one of the foundational texts of hypertextual writing, Jay David Bolter's *Writing Space* (1991), binds media. In the preface, Bolter argues that the print book could be about the electronic book, but not be such electronic book. The media scholar further explains that he had "added an electronic shadow: a diskette that contains a hypertextual version of *Writing Space*."[37] The disk is not bound to the print book but could be "obtained by sending in the order form enclosed in this book."[38] The spring 1991 issue of the journal *Writing on the Edge (WOE)* included a 3.5-inch "Special Hypertext Section Disk" guest-edited by electronic literature scholar and writer Stuart Moulthrop. The disk included the hypertexts "WOE" by Michael Joyce and "Izme Pass" by Carolyn Guyer and Martha Petry. Interestingly, the editors of *WOE* include a thank-you to Apple Computer Inc. "for financing the purchase and duplications of the disks provided in this issue."[39] Three years later, literary scholar Richard A. Lanham published *The Electronic Word: Democracy, Technology and the Arts* (1994) also as a print book and "in a hypertext edition for your Macintosh© computer."[40] Katherine Hayles's *Writing Machines* (2002), a central critical work in my research, came with a "Web Supplement" designed by Anne Burdick that included "the lexicon linkmap, notes, index, bibliography, errata, and source material."[41] More important than the supplemental material was the interface allowing the exploration of the work, which "grew to include alternative mappings of the book's conceptual terrain in a manner specific to the web—as any good technotext should—with additional functionalities unavailable in print."[42] *The New Media Reader* (2003), edited by artists and scholars of computational literature Noah Wardrip-Fruin and Nick Montfort, similarly had an accompanying CD-ROM that contained "examples of early games, digital art, independent literary efforts, software created at universities, and home-computer commercial software."[43] Brazilian scholar of electronic literature Jorge Luiz Antonio published *Poesía digital: Teoría, história, antologías* in 2010 with a DVD of accompanying materials. On the disk, it is possible to read, "This DVD is part of the print book *Poesia digital: Teoria, história, antologias* and can't be sold separately."[44] The statement signals the hybrid character of the work and alludes to the commercial implications of such hybridity. *Remix the Book* (2011) by artist and theorist Mark Amerika relies on print and digital media to expand on the concept of theory writing through remixing and performance. Novelist Steve Tomasula, in his recently published anthology *Conceptualisms* (2022), declares, "To experience the full range, readers should have both the printed book and this website in hand."[45] Other instances include Manifold books published by the University of Minnesota Press, among them book and literary scholar Whitney Trettien's *Cut, Copy, Paste* (2021) and media theorists Lori Emerson, Darren Wershler, and Jussi Parikka's *The Lab Book* (2021). This parallel trajectory of hybrid publishing offers additional context to this volume, even when not examined here.

Readers familiar with the field of electronic literature will notice that I chose not to investigate the corpus published by Eastgate Systems Inc., founded by American poet and scholar Charles Bernstein. Except for the three specific cases of Robert DiChiara's *Hardboiled / A Sucker in Spades* (1985/1988), John McDaid's *Uncle Buddy's Phantom Funhouse* (1992), and Stephanie Strickland's *True North* (1997), I have not included the majority of the dozens of works published under the imprint in my corpus even though they incorporate print matter—most commonly in the form of booklets—in their hypertexts. The reason for this is that the booklets encased with the disks are mainly ancillary to the hypertext itself: software license agreements, advertising for Storyspace, Eastgate's authoring software, and instructions to run the works on Mac and PC. Sometimes, one will find a short introduction to the work, an author bio, a dedication, or a table of contents, but not constitutive parts of the work. The now iconic folios that gave these hypertexts the look and feel of books have made the distinction much more challenging since they are the actual physical binding of hypertext novels offering a wealth of paratextual information. Nevertheless, when compared to DiChiara's and Strickland's works, which were also published as print books, or to McDaid's, whose "box of chocolates" contained essential parts of the narrative in print, the majority of Eastgate titles can hardly be seen as binding media. Nonetheless, they make up the broader contexts of electronic and expanded publishing in the United States during the 1990s.

As many of the examples in my corpus emerge out of the world of experimental literature and independent publishing, it would be easy to cast them aside as amusing or gimmicky novelties in all the realms touched by binding media—literature, literary art, and publishing—and to look at them as separate from popular or mainstream phenomena. Indeed, Alexander Provan, editor of the experimental literature magazine *Triple Canopy*, has put forward such a position. Speaking of hypertext novels like Mark Amerika's *GRAMMATRON*, Provan, derisively, and likely provocatively, asks, "In 50 years, how many people will think of such works as anything but technological novelties?"[46] Aside from the fundamental role that technological innovations have had in shaping print-based literary canons, Provan's assertion that "traditional narrative forms can represent contemporary experience just fine" seems to be overlooking how contemporary experience is very much shaped and mediated by ongoing technological developments and practices to collate content across platforms. In fact, I would argue that a central experience of the contemporary world is that of nonstop upgrading, obsolescence, newness, and the proliferation of writing, publishing, and reading surfaces.

Ultimately, one last consideration of the corpus is its hemispheric perspective along the Americas from Argentina to Canada. The geographic boundaries, however, remain unfixed and reveal processes of human movement: Chilean-born author Luis Correa-Díaz has worked in the United States for decades; Canadian-born J. R. Carpenter is based in the United Kingdom. This pattern is not uncommon among the authors studied in these pages, and it is one that I share as a Mexican living and working in the United States. Similarly, the places of print publication do not always coincide with the authors' current location or place of origin. On the web, location might not even be a helpful consideration. The extent and indeterminacy of the geographic scope of my corpus resonate with electronic literature scholar Leonardo Flores's question: "What if digital technologies bring about a parading shift so radical and foreign to traditional literary movements that we can talk about an international, and even postnational, literary movement?"[47] In the context of binding media, the question includes but goes beyond the affectations to book-based literature and the idea of electronic literature as a movement, to help us think about the zone of contact, including transnational publishing, migration, globalized communications, and other cultural changes acting as the context and material basis for this kind of hybrid creation. The hemispheric scope of this research is a deliberate intervention I make in the book, one that responds to the processes of hybridization brought about by globalization that underlie the entirety of the project. This scholarly innovation, as an exercise in interdisciplinarity, has presented challenges to weave together literary traditions and scholarly trajectories from, mainly, Latin America and

Anglo America. One difficulty is "translating" the traditions and trajectories back and forth to readers who might know only one. To facilitate this process, I have added brief introductory phrases for authors, scholars, literary works, and presses to locate and contextualize them. I hope that the book itself will enable a zone of contact where these literary and scholarly realms negotiate their mutual relevance.

As a collection of bibliographic objects, binding media constitute analogous manifestations of a hybrid media trope in trajectories across geographic and linguistic regions, literary traditions, publishing sectors, and so on. Binding media follow parallel trajectories along developments in each of these realms. Thus, this study aims to be a transversal approximation that follows these trajectories to locate their points of intersection. As such, I contend that binding media can be taken to be the archaeological remains of an elongated present and its recent past produced by the accelerated technocultural changes of the last four decades that, due to the irruption of ever new electronic and digital technologies, have taken place in literary creation, in publishing, media, and in culture at large.

Before moving on to the overview of the book's chapters, I think it opportune to offer a synthesis of the many definitions of the polysemic conceptualization of "binding media." At the basis of the term is a McLuhanian understanding that medium and message are inseparable, just as form and content are considered equally inseparable in literature. Rather than a conduit or a channel through which literary content traverses, I think of media as the materials that concretize meaning and aesthetics specific to their properties and affordances. I use the plural "media" to underscore the tension entailed in the action of joining two seemingly discrete print and electronic/digital objects. Binding, conversely, denotes synthesis, the action of fastening together previously separate materials. Together, "binding media" alludes to the processes of media hybridization where tension and synthesis are two sides of the same phenomenon.

More concretely, as a singular noun, "binding media" *is* a literary form where meaning and aesthetic effects manifest in the space created by fastening print and electronic/digital objects. Consequently, "binding media" refers to the varied strategies or mechanisms (visual, textual, metaphorical) devised to join print and digital objects. As such, "binding media" are also the hybrid media objects produced through the processes of distinct individuals or industries and, often, sold or distributed via specific infrastructural channels. Because print books and digital applications are bound, we can also think of "binding media" as a contemporary form of the book resulting from nonstandardized yet recurrent publishing practices. Following the media ecological thread in the book, the term "binding media" serves to outline the technological and cultural period that has made possible the development of these literary and bookish phenomena. Ultimately, as I wrap up the book's writing, I realize that "binding media" has also been the methodological framework informing the critical stance I take. Rather than looking for instances of rupture or dramatic change, I seek the continuities, intersections, and encounters. I'm cognizant of the proliferation of meanings behind "binding media," from the concrete to the theoretical and methodological. But rather than trying to resolve the terminological tension, I hope such polysemy is productive in making the phenomenon legible as an object of study with many layers of signification.

**The Chapters**
In chapter 1, I build the notion of binding media as a development in the contemporary history of the book. Through the notion of binding media, I seek to expand our understanding of binding as not just "the casing used to secure the folded and sewn sheets, together with its accompanying endpapers and binder's leaves," as Fredson Bowers has defined.[48] I rely on studies devoted to artists' books for the theoretical foundation to take a book's binding as a structural and semantic feature. Moreover, in the unstable media ecology of the turn of the twenty-first century, where the bound book is still central to the publishing industry and the literary world, but not the exclusive form, the consideration of binding aims to reflect on how "content" is collated across distributed media objects. Therefore, in this chapter, I bridge bibliographic stud-

ies with those centered on artists' books. This juncture allows me to underscore bookbinding as evidence of a book's production within an industry and as part of the meaning-making mechanisms in literary works. Consequently, binding media negotiate the tension between the unboundedness of works that exist across distributed print and digital objects, and the boundedness of how these separate objects create meaning together as a single literary media object. To consider them so, instead of as editions, adaptations, or attachments to each other, I argue that the "binding" in binding media must be thought of as a remediation or a transfer of the affordances of a book's binding onto bespoke literary, book, and publishing strategies to collate, attach, and fasten together two or more objects.

Lastly, I mark a division in my corpus between titles that rely on physical bindings and those based on "loose bindings." As can be gleaned from the expression, physical bindings are structural features that materially fasten print matter and digital media, such as envelopes in back covers to fasten disks *inside* the book. Examples examined in this section include Belén Gache's *El Libro del fin del mundo* (2002) and Augusto de Campos's *Não poemas* (2003). In contrast, "loose binding" works are those where the mechanisms joining together print and digital objects are predominantly metaphorical, conceptual, narrative, or visual; these works are often published at different times, but their poetics and design bring them together. Instances examined under this perspective are J. R. Carpenter's *This is a Picture of Wind* (2020) and Vivian Abenshushan's *Permanente obra negra* (2019).

Chapter 2 tells a history of expanded and augmented publishing as the larger landscape that informed and yielded the production of binding media. To approach this understudied area and period in contemporary book history, I draw from John B. Thompson's exploration of the digital revolution in publishing since the mid-1980s to establish a basis for the many radical changes surrounding binding media. This basis allows me to investigate comparatively how this revolution happened in Latin America later and at a slower pace. Despite marked differences, common across the continent is a series of cycles of enthusiasm and retrenchment toward expanded and augmented publishing. Through these cycles, it is possible to observe that binding media was initially a practice in software development companies seeking to acquire cultural capital by being more literary. From this period, I examine Synapse & Brøderbund's Electronic Novel series published in the United States from 1984 to 1986. Later, the emphasis on binding digital technologies and publishing seems to have shifted to propose a renewal of the book through expansion and augmentations, as was the case of American media visionary Bob Stein's Voyager and the Expanded Books Project/Toolkit. While separated by a few years, these two initiatives allow us to observe how more affordable computers pushed publishers into an arms race for digital strategies that could be deployed widely and profitably.[49] They also reveal how, from the early years, issues of cash flow, lengthy production times, and a lack of standardization have afflicted hybrid publishing projects. More contemporary instances, such as the collaboration between the Mexican Council for Culture and the Arts and the cultural tech company Manuvo around 2010 to create a repertoire of national digital heritage applications, reveal that, even with public funding and involving state projects, digital and hybrid publishing are still extremely fragile propositions. Similarly, attempts to augment books as a sales strategy, such as those used by Melville House's HybridBook project and Penguin English Library, suggest that simply adding digital content to print books does little to ensure the success, significance, or sustainability of hybrid publishing.

In contrast to the challenges experienced by these historical initiatives, I show how binding media have found a niche in the vibrant scenes of independent publishing across the Americas. The seeming impossibility of standardization at the heart of binding media, the close collaboration between editors and authors, and the need to build their own public have been suitably met by practices already built into independent publishing. To illustrate these issues, I examine Amaranth Borsuk, Kate Durbin, and Ian Hatcher's *ABRA* (2015), which sheds light on the ties between grant-funded projects, institutional and independent publishing, and app stores. The two editions of Stephanie Strickland's *Vniverse* (2002/2016) similarly reveal the differences between commercial and independent publishing, as well as the shift in platform from the web to the iPad. Lastly, Luis Correa-Díaz's *clickable poem@s* (2018) and *metaverse* (2021) offer the opportunity to observe how editors put forward new literacies through binding media.

In chapter 3, I examine how the hybrid materiality of binding media causes them to be ephemeral cultural objects. Contrary to the previous chapters, here I make the case for considering print matter and digital applications as two distinct material media objects with distinct temporalities that impact the lifespan and cultural valuation of binding media. Particularly, I query the ways in which the temporalities of print and digital facets are exercises in power: the imperative of innovation and obsolescence of the tech industry over the preservation of memory of the cultural sector and the construction of a canon in literary scholarship. The broader context of these divergences is the linear, progressivist, omniscient sense of the present that French historian François Hartog has theorized as "presentism"—the current regime of historicity characterized by ephemerality, real time, and acceleration that reigns particularly in digital and globalized communications.[50] I argue that due to their hybrid materiality, binding media prompt us to step out of the linearity of presentism and to historicize obsolescent literary and artistic works not as exemplars of the recent past but as latent objects documenting histories with various origin points and moving in different directions. One objective of the chapter is to mark a methodological shift in our consideration of digital literature that is not precluded by obsolescence but made possible by it. In order to do that, I examine how digital media manifest their temporal divergences not as part of their aesthetic project but due to the temporality of their materiality and their conditions of possibility. Over this basis, and relying on the work of Giselle Beiguelman,[51] Nelly Richard,[52] and Cristina Rivera Garza,[53] I propose a historical materialist/media archaeological approach that considers the remains of obsolescent and obsolescing digital literature as indexes that insist on the presence of what was there. This approach allows us to move away from the generally ruinous landscape left by the history of digital literature and into a media archaeological reorganization of its temporalities. Moreover, I underscore how the lifespan of digital literature is at odds with the literary methodologies used to interpret it and with the technological developments that are the conditions of possibility of digital literature.

In this chapter, I read Ian Bogost's *A Slow Year* (2010), J. R. Carpenter's *The Gathering Cloud* (2016–17), and Verónica Gerber Bicecci and coauthors' "La máquina distópica" / *La compañía* (2018–19) to investigate the authors' concern with how distinct media temporalities are embedded in ideologies of progress and modernization, and also serve to erase, oppress, and damage. I further examine how Bogost, Carpenter, Gerber Bicecci, and others relate to the history of technology and advance distinct proposals to look at the complexity of this history and its embedded temporalities through writing techniques, palimpsestic composition, documentation, and fastening media objects together. Moreover, the analyses of *A Slow Year, The Gathering Cloud,* and "La máquina distópica" / *La compañía* reveal specific treatments of the temporalities of the media used by the authors. Bogost expertly reconstructs an obsolete technology in minute detail, seeking to bring back a moment in time right *as it was*, rather than in the ways *it continues to be*. In contrast, Carpenter and Gerber Bicecci build palimpsests of archival materials, fragments, ruins, and remains from different moments in time to complicate the linearity of histories of technology and industrialization. They both suggest that nothing is of the past alone to add depth to the present.

Although specific conceptualizations of hybridity cross the entire book, chapter 4 tackles the theoretical and literary juncture of cultural and media hybridity. I propose binding media as a material substrate of processes of cultural hybridization happening under globalized culture and tech industries. Far from celebrating a coming together of the world through real-time digital technologies, I emphasize that processes of cultural hybridization take place under dynamics of oppression in which power is negotiated along changing identities, usually through discursive representations in literature and media. At the turn of the twenty-first century, these dynamics are instigated by the neoliberalization of the market economies, the movement of goods and monetary resources around the world, neocolonial extractivism of natural resources that includes overt and covert military intervention, and the globalization and expediency of digital communications with military origins. Their results, forced migration, environmental displacement, and economic migration, are the dynamics fostering cultural "encounter" and processes of hybridization. To consider the multifaceted understanding of the cultural encounter, I weave together the work of Mary Louise Pratt[54] and Alan Liu[55] to re-elaborate the contact zone as a space where both media and cultural hybridity are concomitant. This basis allows me to query the use of "hybrid" and "hybridity" in media and publishing theorizations to consider not just the effect of technology on culture but the effect of culture on technology as well.

To attend to these interlocking considerations surrounding globalized technocultural processes of hybridization, I examine three works that, like all binding media, have a hybrid print-digital configuration and, in addition, thematically address migration and transnationality as a matter of survival, identity healing, and historical documentation. *The Transborder Immigrant Tool / La herramienta transfronteriza para inmigrantes* by the Electronic Disturbance Theatre 2.0 / b.a.n.g. lab (2010/2014); Guillermo Gómez-Peña, Felicia Rice, and coauthors' *DOC/UNDOC* (2014/2017); and Cristina Rivera Garza's "@EstacionCamaron"/ *Autobiografía del algodón* (2016/2020). Together, these examples of binding media foreground how thinking about processes of hybridization is helpful to describe not only the formal material composition of literary works that bind print and digital media objects but also to address the geographic movement, identity healing, and historical representation of vulnerable bodies in the region of the Mexican–US border. Moreover, the three works I examine lay bare the contradictory status of hybridity by showing both the reparatory potential of blurring the lines between supposedly stable realms like Mexico/United States, here/there, documented/undocumented, and History/history, and the limitations to depict the conflicts arising from it. As I explain in my analyses, where these cultural negotiations appear synthetical, they are only so in their aesthetic roundedness. Conceptually and politically, however, there is ample evidence of the tensions and contradictions of mixing in these works.

In my conclusion, I focus on two recent developments in the history of binding media. On the one hand, I examine the burgeoning of computer-generated books through publishing initiatives like the Using Electricity series edited by Nick Montfort for Counterpath Press and James Ryan's Aleator Press. I then discuss my theorizations on how computer-generated books have specific binding mechanisms. Namely, they bind computational and print media through a transformation of the algorithmic procedure, its data, and its output, mediated by a process of selection, editing, layout, and production into a print codex. Additionally, I argue that computer-generated books are "bound" because they are books with a spine and covers, and also "bound" because the edition process sets limits to the often gigantic generative potential of the systems. Books like Lillian-Yvonne Bertram's *Travesty Generator* (2019), *Subcutanean* (2020) by Aaron Reed, and *ReRites* (2018) by David (Jhave) Johnston reveal how even these seemingly straightforward mechanisms of binding media can yield radically different aesthetic projects and approaches to publishing. Almost impossible not to mention, the release of OpenAI's ChatGPT in November 2022 has raised heterogeneous takes on computer-generated literature. Palpable misunderstandings and raging confusion in literary and other writerly circles feeling the threat of automation have yielded a wholesale rejection of computer-generated literature. Conversely, for others, the generic and parasitic workings of corporate large language models (LLMs) serve to underscore the radically creative and careful ethical approaches of poets like Alison Parrish and the capacity of poetry to offer a counterweight.

Lastly, the gold rush of eight-figure sales of computer-generated art minted on the blockchain as nonfungible tokens (NFTs) via galleries like Open Sea and auction houses like Christie's 3.0 has led to the second development I investigate, the emergence of literary NFTs.

Proponents of minting literary works on the blockchain present NFTs as a medium to empower writers to take advantage of the technology to increase their earnings by participating in a market that manufactures scarcity. As NFT publishers begin to pop up, literary groups like theVERSEverse incorporate the blockchain as part of their aesthetic projects, changing the nature of poetry into that of art. More than a shift in nomenclature alone, theVERSEverse proposes a turn where all poetry seeks to approximate the visual attractiveness and unicity of art NFTs. I take a critical stance on these endeavors as the proposed shift appears to underscore the objectual dimension and signification mechanisms of visual, concrete, and computational poetry, less as a poetic or conceptual investigation, and more as a deliberate strategy to gain access to and capitalize from the speculative transactional value of the crypto art market. I term these strategies the "aesthetic of transactionality." Nevertheless, this latest development lays bare the fact that writers and publishers will continue to invest in print objects and fasten them to digital ones. Not surprisingly, like other technological developments before, literary NFTs promise to revolutionize how literature is valued and how it is possible to have an unintermediated relationship between poets and readers. Yet, like other developments in binding media, if these endeavors follow the same trajectory of art NFTs, as is expected, they are likely to join the ranks of all those projects now constituting the recent past.

This book has never intended to project the future of hybrid publishing. If anything, in the process of writing, I have been engaged in a constant game of catching up with new publications, applications and software being discontinued and sunsetted, and the release of new platforms used to create binding media. This process, which I have gone through live as it unfolds, more than likely mimics all the other moments I have studied now as historical. Perhaps because of the unstandardized nature of the phenomenon I set out to study, it is quite impossible to offer conclusions. Instead, I aim to identify a handful of recurrences, such as the ongoing cycles of enthusiasm and retrenchment, the always surprising ways in which authors and publishers continue to bind print and digital media, the role of presentism foreshortening the accrual of cultural value of literary works like those examined here, and the staying power of print books. As the material conditions of writing, reading, publishing, sharing, and buying literature, knowledge, and information have rapidly shifted within our lifespans, so have our ways of experiencing the world through them.

Many more examples of binding media than just the ones examined closely in each chapter made these reflections possible. The book's appendix presents the corpus of works I collected. Others that didn't fit within the confines of "binding media" sedimented the phenomenon at hand. Indeed, a whole universe of print-digital forms of literary expression and publishing is in need of detailed studies. This book can only hope to offer an opening into the head-spinning media shifts in literature, publishing, and the book form at the turn of the twenty-first century. As the reader traverses these pages, I hope they join me in wondering what the place of binding media will be in ten, fifty, or a hundred years and what they will have taught us about the last few decades.

ONE

# BINDING MEDIA: NEGOTIATING (UN)BOUNDEDNESS

**BEFORE WE CAN BEGIN READING** American poet Robert Pinsky's electronic novel *Mindwheel* on a Commodore 64 computer, our attention shifts from the computer screen to the book. Until then, it could appear that the book is an elaborate packaging for the disks containing the famous interactive fiction. "ATTENTION! ATTENTION!" we read on the screen, prompting us to type the codeword—a word found in a given position, line, and page of the book.[1] With this gesture, though transactional at this point, Pinsky and his collaborators, programmers Steve Hales and Cathryn Mataga, establish how the reader must traverse both electronic application and print book to make it to the end of the work. Far from being a set of directions alone, the back-and-forth between the two media illuminates the characters, or the "minds," in the novel, offers solutions to puzzles, and showcases the complex world imagined by Pinsky. An electronic novel like *Mindwheel* is an early instance of "binding media."

"Binding media" refers to the literary practice in which a codex and electronic media are fastened together. Out of this creative process emerge hybrid media objects that circulate, operate, read, and mean differently than print or electronic literature alone. Historically, binding media have emerged over intense technological innovations in computing power, storage capabilities, widespread internet adoption, the proliferation of smartphones, and other such advances. Prompted by these developments, authors and publishers have made room, quite literally, in their books for electronic and digital media since the early 1980s. In my theorization of binding media, I follow Katherine Hayles's assertion that "to change the material artifact is to transform the context and circumstances for interacting with the words, which inevitably changes the meaning of the words as well."[2] Consequently, the creative and material strategies through which books and digital media accommodate each other radically impact the meaning-making mechanisms of literary works. Reciprocally, literary experimentations across media have pushed the boundaries of book design and publishing. Therefore, the term "binding media" refers to the process of meaning-making at the intersection of print and digital materials, and the hybrid media objects created from such interactions.

In this chapter, I look at binding media as a development in the history of the book in the twenty-first century. I theorize how, through creative and material innovations, fastening together codex and electronic and digital media has yielded a distinctly contemporary form of the book where we can appreciate a continuum spanning trade publishing, software development, poetry and narrative, and artists' books. I understand and propose "binding" as an expansion of the notion of bookbinding, which commonly refers to the materials (case, endpapers, stitches) that hold together and protect the pages of a book, into a theoretical framework that queries what is inside and outside of a book, how print-digital structures can be considered a form of the book, and how meaning is produced at the intersection of two material objects. The binding in "binding media" is, therefore, not a fixed quality but one in a constant tension between what is physically or conceptually bound or unbound, what is form, and what is content. In this way, examining print-digital works allows me to underscore the importance of a feature like binding to our notion of what a book is and how it creates meaning—two aspects challenged and reified in binding media through its interactions with digital media.

As a concept, binding media is a conduit to study jointly the seemingly discrete objects—print book and digital media—that, under a different framework, could be seen as editions, adaptations, or companions. Synapse & Brøderbund, the American software development company that published early binding media examples like *Mindwheel*, insisted on how "electronic novels" were not "'computer versions' of existing novels—they're stories conceived especially for this new medium."[3] In this way, the concept of binding media allows us to explore the complexity of the interactions between a work's print and digital parts. Moreover, the examinations afforded by binding media are useful to theorize what makes distributed textual media cohere physically and conceptually. As the marker of a book's physical and conceptual bounds, binding negotiates the contours of dispersed or distributed objects. Therefore, despite comprising a single work, as I argue, binding media constitutively question the idea of wholeness and boundedness. In this way, a codex's binding elements, like stitches, glue, covers, and endpapers, in binding media become instructions for reading across media, running software, visual design, and the overall aesthetic project. What's more, by going beyond the codex and joining it with digital applications, binding media test the very capaciousness and variations of the book form. Thus, the binding strategies I analyze here signal an overflowing of the book (unboundedness) and its capaciousness and flexibility (boundedness).

While my conceptualization of binding media relies on Hayles's media-specific analysis, I also base my examination on bibliography and artists' book studies to fully appreciate these works as book objects that create meaning through material strategies. This interdisciplinary theoretical gathering allows me to think about the book form as the accelerated development of digital technologies has come into contact with and modified it. My readings of Belén Gache's *El libro del fin del mundo*, Augusto de Campos's *Não poemas*, J. R. Carpenter's *This is a Picture of Wind*, and Vivian Abenshushan's *Permanente obra negra* show how, as process and as hybrid media objects, binding media rely on bespoke strategies and mechanisms for fastening codex and digital media together. These vary from one example to another but generally are of two types: those with physical binding structures, such as disks held in back cover pockets, and those whose binding mechanisms are visual, conceptual, or metaphorical. Further, whether physical or conceptual, binding mechanisms operate in three main realms: literary, bibliographic, or technological. In all cases, however, the poetics of individual works emerge from binding both objects. Thus, binding media require an examination that does not treat them as print literary works or digital ones alone. Binding media is, therefore, a theoretical framework to study the various layers touched by print-digital works: binding media as a form of the book within bibliographic studies; as a media object that underwent processes of innovation and experimentation along with softwares, storage media, and computers; and as a structure supporting the creation of literary meaning.

## Bookbinding, the Structure of the Codex

In his classic text *Principles of Bibliographical Description*, the American textual scholar Fredson Bowers refers to a book's binding as "the casing used to secure the folded and sewn sheets together with its accompanying end-papers and binders' leaves, which are not part of the original sheets as they emerged from the printing press."[4] While in bibliography, bookbinding has been relegated to the outer surfaces of a codex, here I want to reconsider it as an organizing structure facilitating the volume's handling, storing, reading, and, as I argue in the next section, its meaning-making.[5] Obscured by its ubiquity, bookbinding encompasses a series of painstaking activities, such as sheet folding and trimming, collating, sewing, pasting, and covering. For centuries, these tasks were done by hand in workshops where tradespeople were responsible for each stage. Starting in the nineteenth century, mechanization slowly turned each of the once artisanal processes into the industrial procedures of contemporary bookmaking.[6] Whether done manually or industrially, binding is constitutive to our notion of what a book is. For the Multigraph Collective, "books are fundamentally the creation of binders ... Only in the act of folding printed sheets into folios or quartos or octavos or other formats, and then attaching those folded sheets to one another, do we get a book."[7] Indeed, the invention of binding marks the birth of the codex.[8] The earliest acts of binding loose leaves are synonymous with the earliest codices.[9] Moreover, like all other features of the book, throughout history, bindings have changed in myriad ways depending on book uses, availability of materials, developments in binding techniques and technologies, aesthetic sensibilities, trade practices, and, for a long time, the preferences of book owners. In short, throughout the history of the book, bindings have never been static features.

While industrial bookbinding ensures uniformity in editions and standardization of formats for optimal reading, storing, transportation, and displaying, bespoke bindings constructed at the request of individual book owners or booksellers were the norm until the 1800s.[10] Bindings used to be so variable that, more often than not, two copies of the same book bound in the same workshop would show variation.[11] Before mechanization, bookbinding proved a trade difficult to scale up. Monetary and production imperatives dictated the sewing technique, type of covering, and decoration used for individual books or, at best, small batches of them. Along with structural differences involving supports, sewing, and materials, bookbinding decorations shifted according to contemporaneous artistic ideas.[12] Materials and techniques, moreover, changed along with the growth in readership and readers' preferences.[13] Operationally, different binding structures and features developed throughout history have profoundly shaped how specific types of books are handled. For instance, the European girdle binding allowed medieval book owners to attach small volumes to their belts for portability. Coptic books are, to this day, the structure best suited for books that need to stay open over tables or lecterns. In addition to ornamentation, clasps ensure that the leaves of a codex keep their flatness, and post binding allows for the later addition of leaves to a volume. As the recent edition and marketing of the Flipback book suggests, even in our day when the form of the book is largely standardized through industrial processes, bindings continue to evolve to respond to new reader habits and sensibilities.[14]

From the Roman polyptychs and the early Coptic bindings to the ubiquitous perfect binding in present-day paperbacks to the metadata collating the "assemblages of digital assets" that makeup e-books,[15] bindings function as the physical structures and the organizing principles facilitating the operations of a book. Admittedly, however, bookbinding is not a feature of books that receives much attention except to study ornamentation or provenance. Nonspecialists rarely stop to reflect on the mere presence of a binding structure holding pages together. For most people, an awareness of bookbinding comes in terms of format: hardbacks and paperbacks. However, even in this marginal way, a book's binding encodes a series of meanings: an established cycle of publishing and marketing, the expected commercial success of a book, its past success. The lack of attention to this structural feature might be attributed to overfamiliarity with the codex and the consequent prioritization of the text or content over the object, as Amaranth Borsuk has proposed.[16] Developments in printing, design, and book production technologies, such as dust jackets and illustrated covers, have also played a role in the obfuscation of bookbinding.[17] Still, a book's binding is always there holding together the bundle of pages that readers flip through or turn over individually with care and attention.

Bookbinding has also been central to our conceptions of literature. Fastened together and encased by covers, a text block of printed text, images, music notation, slips, and so on is joined together beyond physical proximity. It is also fastened together conceptually: as a complete fictional or historical narrative; a collection of poems, recipes, or images; a series of lectures or treatises; or a course of study. Jeffrey Todd Knight, a Shakespeare scholar, has demonstrated how, in Renaissance Britain, binding together several literary works and including additions or supplements was a common occurrence. In addition to being a pragmatic approach, these practices fashioned notions of what a literary work was during that historical period and up to today.[18] Throughout history, a book's binding, as the structure of an object through which we access information, has shaped meaning through "the presentation and collation of the leaves it encloses" and its affordances.[19]

The expanded consideration of bookbinding that I propose allows me to locate "binding media" within the spectrum of contemporary developments of the codex. In binding media, it is possible to see how bookbinding practices accommodate the ever new electronic and digital technologies with which the book has come into contact in the last four decades. Though brief, this diachronic revision of bookbinding allows us to glean coincidences between earlier book practices and the current landscape of textual media—as moments of both great diversity and nonstandardized practices. If exact analogies among distinct historical moments might be impossible, the rapidly changing forms of binding media and, for example, the variety in bindings before the nineteenth century are evidence of impermanent structures and practices developing alongside newer technologies, tastes, and cultural changes. Furthermore, the changes to binding structures have resulted from a changing trade and changing technocultural attitudes that have influenced the role of the book within specific cultures. Ultimately, it is possible to observe that, as structures, bookbindings organize the content of a book as they outline the book's affordances and how readers can use and handle it.

**Bookbinding as Meaning-Maker**

As structural features, bookbindings can also be potent meaning-makers. For a book, the fact of being bound or not renders it an object beyond the ideas it contains. A book's physical features guide how it is handled, read, cataloged, and even sold; therefore, these tactile details offer a wealth of possible ways to make meaning and transmit ideas. In binding media, the implications of the structural possibilities multiply due to the conjunction of print and digital objects, their individual affordances, and those emerging from the junction of both. Binding media, therefore, are hybrid structures signaling an overflowing of the book (a tendency toward unboundedness) and simultaneously the book's capaciousness and flexibility (the proclivity to boundedness). The physical form of binding media encodes their hybridity as objects emerging from a rapidly and constantly moving media landscape. It also codifies the provisional space they occupy between print and digital cultures. Lastly, it interrogates the bounds of the book as object and as content. Even on the surface, the form of binding media produces meaning, but the examination of individual works in the following pages brings these characteristics to the fore.

The centrality of a book's form in creating meaning has been a concern in theories of artists' books. Book artists like Mexican Ulises Carrión and American Keith A. Smith, who extensively theorized how meaning can be made through the physical features of the codex, approach binding as a structure that first and foremost produces aesthetic meaning. For these artists, there must be a reciprocity between binding structure and content.[20] For Smith, particularly, the structure of a book cannot be arbitrarily chosen without influencing the development of the ideas it contains.[21] Even outside the realm of artists' books, in bibliographic studies, the meaningfulness of the form of the book has come to the forefront, most famously with D. F. McKenzie's call to "be concerned to show that forms effect meaning."[22] Although coming from two subfields of book studies, theorizations on artists' books and from bibliographic studies both indicate that a book's structure, in particular its binding, draws the contours of the ideas presented and bolsters them as well. These considerations illuminate how binding media, in part, function as artists' books. Ultimately, Carrión's and Smith's approaches to print matter echo Hayles's literary notion of material metaphors as the "traffic between words and physical artifacts."[23] The palpable attention to a book's affordances and operations in binding media, like that in artists' books, communicates poetic interests, medium interrogations, and narrative worlds.

The relationship between binding media and artists' books can be best observed through a paradigmatic example. American artist David Stairs's *Boundless* (1983) is a humorous and even puzzling take on how even the simplest binding—a metal spiral—facilitates the reading of a book (or not), readers' interaction with it, its pagination (or lack thereof), and the form of the object. In Figure 1, it is possible to see how contradictorily *Boundless* is bound all around by a metal spiral that appears to have no beginning or end. Artists' books, like Stairs's, offer a context and a theoretical base to study the deliberate use of structural features and their meaning-making dimension, one that serves as a starting point to examine and understand binding media.

Similar to artists' books, binding media rely on bespoke mechanisms to make meaning and fasten their distributed print and digital objects together. If one of the primary functions of bookbinding materials—stitches, glue, covers—is to keep leaves and sections together in a deliberate order, in binding media these functions are transferred into alternative materials, processes, or marks, which nevertheless retain this intent. Instructions for reading between objects or running soft-

FIGURE 1. David Stairs, *Boundless* (1983). The spiral binding shapes the book and the possibility of interactions. Reproduced with permission of the artist.

ware, paratextual information, and "content" (narrative, visual) become the fasteners. Further, since this expanded conceptualization of bookbinding makes this structural feature critical to the creation of meaning and the demarcation of a work's bounds, the dispersion of the objects that make up binding media does not imply an absence of meaning or a lack of boundedness. Instead, binding media produce their meaning and establish their limits through the tension between a work's boundedness and unboundedness. These kinds of creative explorations of the codex in trade edition books have been facilitated by shifts in printing and binding technologies, offering writers a more expansive space of experimentation with the book form. While the bespoke mechanisms used in binding media resemble the practices used in artists' books, binding media are produced most generally as trade edition books and distributed by independent or institutional publishers. Thus, binding media occupy a bibliographic space situated in the midst of artistic and literary creation and their publication as trade edition books. I would even argue that the material qualities, in addition to the limited print runs in which they appear, make binding media ready-made rare books.

Throughout her many writings on artists' books, the American scholar and book artist Johanna Drucker has identified a handful of processes central to artists' books that are particularly relevant for binding media. First, the characterization of artists' books as "productions rather than creations" that make meaning through "attention to materials [and] their interactions."[24] As literary works not consisting of a single object, binding media have an emergent and cumulative way of making meaning that demands the reader's consideration of both print and digital facets. Further, Drucker also explores the "conceptual constructs" emerging in hybrid forms where print book and digital media are mutually modified.[25] These constructs, sequence, finitude, and boundedness, are structural features of the codex that go beyond its affordances. Indeed, she suggests that the limited human capacity to understand data meaningfully is tied to editing, selection, and exclusion—principles already built into the book. For Drucker, there is a concern about how digital artists' books have a way of "resisting bookness," of going out of the book's bounds.[26] The resistance to bookness is an intriguing proposition for binding media. On the one hand, the discreteness of the codex is void by the overall hybridity of the literary objects, yet the presence of the book remains. Here, the resistance to bookness brings forth a series of questions that go beyond versioning and iteration and even the artistic precedent of the multiple. Instead, because binding media are only like artists' books to some extent, what looks like resistance to bookness is a manifestation of the changing form of the book and its place in the current media ecology. On the other hand, binding media also resist the features of the digital medium and rely on bookish operations and modes of production and distribution.

The expansion of the concept of binding proposed thus far helps us better study binding media. Bibliographic studies highlight the wealth of information that can be gleaned from the unique physical binding of a book and the specific technocultural contexts that favored changes to binding practices. Artists' book studies emphasize the meaning-making dimension of book structures and the interrogations to the form of the book itself. When viewed together, bibliographic studies, artists' book studies, and media-specific analysis of literature demonstrate that the form of the book and its objectual features tell us much about the sensibilities of authors, readers, and publishers. These characteristics also reveal how specific book forms are sustained by equally specific media moments. In that sense, the practices of binding print and digital objects that I investigate here, recurrent throughout the four decades since the popularization of home computers and across the Americas, are suggestive not so much of individual artistic choices casually taking place at various points in time and place, but of significant cultural shifts in writing, reading, communicating, publishing, and consuming.

Binding media would not have emerged had digital technologies not become ubiquitous in readers' homes early on and in pockets nowadays. Additionally, the history of the book, and particularly the developments in bookbinding, have demonstrated that these are ever-shifting technologies and media, too. These literary works serve as reminders that books (as objects, commodities, and literary works) are made not just of words and paper but also of a plethora of changing materials shaping their content. This view of binding media compels a recognition of their cultural significance beyond the literary, to include the material dimension—as aspects of the form of the codex and its implications for the publishing industry. The most salient result of this approach is that digital applications are not a surplus or an attachment to the codex, but integral to the literary works and to the book as an object published and distributed by a press and sold in bookstores. This foundation also allows us to observe that hybrid or augmented publishing is a rich, yet understudied area of contemporary book history, one that has involved commercial publishing and independent presses with widely different expectations and outcomes. This history is the focus of chapter 2.

In the following sections of this chapter, I embark on a detailed reading of binding media examples. In particular, I seek to theorize the physical, visual, and aesthetic relationships of coconstitutiveness between print and digital media. How are disks and books bound together? How do physical binding features contribute to the creation of a work's meaning? How are individual works bound or unbound? And similarly, are "loose" or nonphysical binding mechanisms possible? How do they operate? As the examples of physical binding show, physical features don't preclude the presence of other binding mechanisms; in parallel, binding as a nonphysical feature depends on fastening mechanisms like software, and narrative, visual, and other forms of "content."

## Physical Binding Media

At first look, it might be easy to consider binding media that rely on physical bindings as the ultimate examples of this phenomenon. A great majority of these examples come from the pre-web and early web era when it was common for digital applications to circulate in their storage medium as diskettes and CD-ROMs. US artists and writers published some of the first instances of this phenomenon, including

Paul Zelevansky's *The Case for the Burial of Ancestors II* (1984), William Gibson's *Agrippa (A Book of the Dead)* (1992), and John McDaid's hypermedia novel *Uncle Buddy's Phantom House* (1993). In the first example, a disk is bound to the codex in a back cover pocket. Gibson's legendary deluxe edition had several pages in the back of the book hollowed out and glued together to nest the 3.5-inch diskette. McDaid's novel had a special case binding, a "chocolate box sourced from a confectionary supplier" and explicitly designed to hold together the disks, cassette tapes, and print matter constituting his work.[27]

A collective instance deserving a more detailed examination consists of the four "electronic novels" published by Synapse & Brøderbund between 1984 and 1986, using software developed by Steve Hales and Cathryn Mataga: Robert Pinsky's *Mindwheel* (1984), Bill Darrah's *Essex* (1985), James Paul's *Brimstone* (1985), and Rod Smith's *Breakers* (1986). In these four works, the diskettes were placed in protective sleeves inside the covers of the book, but the sleeves were not glued to the back cover. Instead, the binders in charge of these works experimented with the features of the spine to make room for the disks at the back of the codex. As can be observed in Figure 2, in the earliest of these works, Pinsky's *Mindwheel*, the binder added a couple of extra gatherings of blank pages to the text block and then cut off these pages, leaving only their stubs, which were then hidden between endpapers glued together. As a result, a few millimeters of extra space are created by the oversized spine that accommodate the two disks and the reference card.

Figure 3 shows how in later works, such as *Essex* and *Brimstone*, the binders designed a spine with asymmetrical joints where the endpapers go deeper toward the spine and reach the end of the case's gutter. This modification makes it possible for the back cover to fold further back and open a small gap into which the disks fit. In addition to making room for the disks, this binding strategy is subtler and cleaner than the earlier one, and unlikely to draw attention to itself. These ingenious binding media strategies suggest that, in these early works, the emerging norm of keeping disks in back cover pockets was not entirely standardized, and yet publishers were well aware of the

FIGURE 2. A view of the spine in Robert Pinsky's *Mindwheel* (1984) shows the unglued endpapers and the pages cut off to make room to hold two 5.25-inch diskettes and a reference card. Print copy from the author's collection.

need to have a protective space for the more fragile 5.25-inch diskettes for the Apple IIe and the Commodore 64. These strategies underscore how the electronic media were as much a part of the book as its other, more common, features. Moreover, the developments in the bindings of these electronic novels, separated in their publication by only a year or two, punctually illustrate a period of experimentation and try-outs. Ultimately, though the Synapse & Brøderbund binding strategy is the exception in an emerging media ecology that quickly adopted the back cover pocket, it is also a literalization of the very idea of binding media—a mechanism by which book designers and binders fastened together the distributed objects making up these works.

FIGURE 3. A view of the asymmetrical joint in an electronic novel's case binding (Bill Darrah's *Essex* [1985]) meant to make a gap in the spine to hold two 5.25-inch diskettes and a reference card. Print copy from the Media Archaeology Lab Printed Matter Collection.

Whether they were held in an envelope glued to the back cover or ensconced at the back of the book instead of pages, in physical binding media the disks are physically joined to the complementary print materials. Their binding is a function of their production as books, and both media objects are published, distributed, and sold simultaneously. As a result, in works where a physical binding is present, the disk is an undeniable part of the "book," understood as content, and the book as a published object is considered incomplete if no disk is present. In fact, many of these examples display legends indicating that disks are not stand-alone products and cannot be sold separately. For instance, in several electronic novel examples, we find the following text: "This product, both printed material and software, is copyrighted by Synapse Software."[28] Paradoxically, in several cases, because of the computing challenges due to access or obsolescence to read the disks, works like Luis Bravo's *Árbol veloZ,* published in Uruguay, and Augusto de Campos's *Não poemas,* published in Brazil, are better known and studied as poetry collections without their digital applications. And due to the small editions of binding media, "Swallows," the electronic chapter of Zelevansky's *The Case for the Burial of Ancestors II,* and *Wordtoys,* the web instance of the digital applications of the Argentinian writer Belén Gache's *El libro del fin del mundo,* have been widely studied as digital literature alone.

Further, the use of a recurrent structure of physical binding does not mean that this form of binding is the only fastening method in these works. Although there may be overlaps among them, the physical binding does not determine or direct the literary and aesthetic relationships between the two objects. A comparison of physically bound binding media is critical to appreciate how seemingly identical binding strategies can yield distinct literary and media effects. Among those works where a physical binding is present, I will focus on Gache's *El libro del fin del mundo* (2002) and de Campos's *Não poemas* (2003). Both these works are collections of texts: Gache's is a collection of short narratives, visual poems, and digital pieces, and de Campos's is a collection of concrete poems and "clip-poems." They also share the use of the CD-ROM as the storage medium for their digital pieces, which are held in back cover pockets. Moreover, their publication dates are separated only by a year. The two works are also particularly useful for examining how physical binding is only one among many features holding together codex and CD-ROM. Instead, they point us to other literary, visual, bibliographic, and conceptual features that equally contribute to the coherence of the two media.

### Interrogations to the Book Form in *El libro del fin del mundo*
*El libro del fin del mundo (LFM)* tells the story of book destruction and recovery. In the opening pages, Gache presents *LFM* as a metafictional narrative where Roberto el Intempestivo, the ruler of a Babelian land,

has ordered the burning of all the books written before his reign. The recovery, led by Roberto's successor, yields *LFM*, which is the collection in our hands: "With the limited loose fragments he found, little by little he put together *El libro del fin del mundo*."[29] Binding print and digital media, *LFM* gathers seventy-five "found" fragments, seven of which are digital pieces in a CD-ROM. As a collection, *LFM* is meticulously organized in subject sections, including "Bestiary," "Famous Men and Women," and "Cartography."[30] This ordering is key to understanding the complementarity of the two media objects. The found texts, whether print or digital, are not randomly juxtaposed or separated by medium but belong in specific sections. In this way, Gache prompts her readers to follow the given order and move from the codex to a computer playing the CD-ROM sequentially through the different sections and the various fragments. In fact, the table of contents in *LFM* lists the fragments in sequence without distinguishing what medium they're on. Figure 4 illustrates how, procedurally, in the codex, the reader is directed to the digital fragments through the interleaving of placeholder pages for them. This purposeful process of collation between the print fragments and the digital ones guides the reader's traversal of the collection across both media and makes it possible for Gache to build the sense of unicity and coherence that a distributed media object could interrogate. Thus, collation in *LFM* produces meaning by ordering the fragments and scripting the reader's actions. The clip art icon of a hand holding a compact disk found in the placeholder pages further encourages the reader to follow the established order. This digital "manicule" is a succinct bibliographic mark that serves as the stitches holding the various fragments together across media.

Additionally, the visual design of the codex is maintained in the digital application. The seven digital fragments are presented as leaves unbound from the book. The application launches with the codex's front cover design, and the navigation interface displays a small album of loose leaves identical to the placeholder pages except for the added digital manicule. Most surprising is that the loose leaves include and follow the pagination from the codex—a design gesture that further ties the digital fragments to the print book as shown in the table of contents. At

FIGURE 4. A placeholder page in Gache's *El libro del fin del mundo* shows the distinctive digital manicule instructing readers to proceed to this fragment in the CD-ROM. Reproduced with permission of the artist.

the same time, the digital fragments play with the unit of the page. In many cases, they keep a single interface as a stand-in for a single page. In other instances, the digital fragments include notes and hyperlinks that take the reader to a different interface while keeping the illusion that it's the same page. The fragment that most challenges the page unit is "El increíble viaje de Don Pedro de Alfaroubeira," shown in Figure 5.

FIGURE 5. Screen captures of "El increíble viaje de Don Pedro de Alfaroubeira" show two of the many different screens inhabiting page 113. Reproduced with permission of the artist.

There we can appreciate how Gache plays with the scope of the page and recombines numerous screens over the background of page 113. In a note, we learn how Gache used keywords in the text to search the web for images tagged with it and produce new rendering of the same page, thus amplifying the possible number of screens presented in the space of a single page.

As can be seen, the scope of strategies that bind together print and digital media in *LFM* profoundly complement the joining effect of the physical binding. The metanarrative of the collection, the page design crossing the entirety of the book and the digital application, the collation of fragments across media, the scripting of the reader's actions, and the table of contents all contribute to the sense that the two facets of *LFM* are not stand-alone but tightly bound into a single work. A legend in the README file included in the CD-ROM declares: "This CDRom accompanies the paper edition, and it cannot be distributed independently."[31] Considering how much work goes into binding print and digital media in *LFM*, it's not hard to imagine how, without the overarching narrative and collation, the seven digital fragments would seem to be missing the pages around them. Ultimately, the meticulous design of *LFM* owes to the fact of being published by Fin del Mundo

Ediciones, Gache's imprint based in Buenos Aires and, initially, an online platform dedicated to publishing net art in Spanish.

The binding strategies used by Gache come even more to the forefront when compared with *Wordtoys*, a fully digital work deriving from *LFM*. In addition to the seven digital fragments from *LFM*, *Wordtoys* includes seven more pieces created between 2002 and 2006. This expanded collection, however, uses visual aesthetics different from the ones found in *LFM*, which, in contrast to the CD-ROM pieces, makes it a stand-alone work. Some echoes remain, nevertheless. In the absence of a print book, the navigation interface is that of a codex, enclosed by front and back covers, and whose pages we turn by clicking on the bottom right corner. The book-like characteristics are emphasized through the inclusion of a table of contents in the back of the "book." Furthermore, in *Wordtoys*, we find the author's explicit intent to "deconstruct the standards of the print book—a seemingly paradoxical statement given that the digital pieces are bound in a suite of bookish elements."[32] Despite the apparent attachment to the codex, it is undeniable that, in both *LFM* and *Wordtoys*, Gache exceeds the bounds of the book, physically and metaphorically. In this way, *Wordtoys* clarifies how Gache repeatedly negotiates the bounds and standards of the print book through the use of the codex as a structuring principle—a space constantly flooded with elements that surpass it. In *Wordtoys*, she achieves this through writing techniques like recombination, randomness, animation, and interactivity, against the backdrop of a bound book. But in *LFM*, while those writing techniques are also present, the interrogation of the book as form is predominantly done by staging the tension between that which is bound and that which is unbound—a questioning key to binding media.

### *Não poemas:* Binding Media Outside the Bounds of the Book
Another illuminating example of physically bound binding media is *Não poemas* by Brazilian concrete poet Augusto de Campos. Published in 2003 by Editora Perspectiva in São Paulo, *Não poemas* should not be mistaken for a second edition of the title poem "Não." The sole poem

"Não" was originally published as an artist's book in 1990 in a small (6 × 6 cm), fifteen-page, photocopied, numbered edition. This self-published edition circulated casually at its time of publication. Making this distinction is important both because it illuminates the volume's publication history and because the 2003 volume, *Não poemas* (meaning, literally, "not poems"), serves as an anthology of sorts that includes the earlier title. As a collection of poems previously created and exhibited either as artists' books, banners, objects, or installations, *Não poemas* brings together a period of the poet's creative output. The timeframe of the collection encompasses primarily the period from the early 1990s to the early 2000s, during which de Campos experimented with computational graphic technologies. However, during this period, the Brazilian author also reworked some of his older poems, such as "Cidadecitycité" (1963), "Rever" (1972), "Caos" (1974), and others, through animation— at the time, a newfound way to enact the sense of movement key to his concrete poetry. Indeed, for de Campos, the remaking of static poems into animated "clip-poems" constitutes not a process of adaptation but rather a rematerialization of the creative impulses that inspired them from the outset. In addition to gathering the new "versions" of old poems, the CD-ROM includes two instances of the "clip-poems," the 1997 "cut" made up of sixteen poems including "Cidadecitycité," "Rever," and "Poesia é risco;" and the much briefer 2003 cut with only half as many poems including, again, "Cidadecitycité," "Rever," and "Sem saída." The presence of these two digital cuts created in newly emerging multimedia application authoring platforms such as Macromedia Director and Adobe Flash, underscores how de Campos constantly sought to amplify the kinetics of his poems as new software developments with distinct animation capabilities became available.

In this way, *Não poemas* serves as a window to observe de Campos's creative, iterative practice. As the volume itself presents several iterations of the same poems, we can speculate that an ultimate final form is not the goal for de Campos. Instead, by fastening together different iterations, the volume appears to focus on the very practice of remaking. For Eduardo Ledesma, de Campos's constant reworking of his poems, such as "Tensão" and "Viva Vaia," is a process of "transcreation," that is, a process of remaking the older poems through the utilization of newly available technologies that actualize the originary kinetic poetic ambitions.[33] De Campos makes a similar declaration in the notes to the 1997 collection of clip-poems: "Since I acquired my own personal computer, in the early nineties, I've seen that the poetical practice I'm involved with, which emphasizes the materiality of words and their interrelationships with non-verbal signs, has a lot to do with the computer."[34] That animation software, in a way, actualized the kinetic interests of concrete poetry is one way of reading de Campos's digital transcreations. But missing from that interpretation is his keen interest in the book as a form palpable in the preface to the collection. In it, we see de Campos's reflections on the (un)boundedness at play in putting this collection together.

In *Não poemas*, the ordering of print and digital leaves is not the only important aspect; gathering previously separate texts and several iterations of the same poems into a single volume is key to understanding the operations of this example of binding media. First, we must consider how de Campos perceives the deliberate act of creating a book with these characteristics. In his "NÃOfácio," the "(not) preface" to the volume, he acknowledges that "these poems would perhaps fit better in an exhibition, proposed as paintings, than in a book. But the book, even bombarded by new technological means, is an inescapable package."[35] Further, in the book as a medium, de Campos sees a way to "arrumar" (arrange, package) the poems created and reworked during a period of about nine years. The wide variety of poems included in *Não poemas* seems to only fit within the (contested) bounds of a book. It benefits from the affordances of trade publishing in terms of the lifespan of the codex in contrast with a temporary exhibition, and in terms of cost when compared with paintings and objects. Similarly, there may have been a pragmatic dimension of publishing *Não poemas* as a trade edition book relating to circulation. While de Campos's clip-poems had been shown and performed in exhibitions such as "Arte Suporte Computador" in São Paulo in 1997 and on his website, the release of the book amplified the potential audience for these clip-poems. The second printing of *Não poemas*, published in 2009, attests to the popularity and wide circulation of the volume.[36] Lastly, de Campos believes that computational tools make the poems "palatable to paper and the book," an intriguing assertion that might signal how, once movement is actualized in the animated poems, it sticks to the print poems, illustrating the kinetics that were only suggested through visual metaphors on the page.[37] The brief "NÃOfácio" thus offers a series of musings on the intersections of print book and digital technologies that prompt us to further examine the implications of binding the collected print and digital poems that make up *Não poemas* as, in Drucker's words, a resistance to bookness—a "Não livro," or a "not-book."

Despite being a volume in which binding print and digital media shapes our understanding of it as an anthology of "transcreation," *Não poemas* can be understood as a book reaching toward unboundedness, too. The most obvious way this occurs is that there are two CD-ROM sub-collections. The clip-poems of, for instance, "Caos," "Criptocardiograma," and "Pérolas para cummings" break the unit of the page by making the poems jump out on the interactive applications. However, it is the strikingly colorful visual poem "Sem saída" that best illuminates the jump from page to screen. In the clip-poem, we are initially faced with a black screen, but moving the cursor around reveals, one by one, several verses in different colors winding over the background. In contrast, "Sem saída" in print form displays the seven verses all at once, entangled with one another over a black background. This distinction makes the two readings quite distinct: on the screen, the independence of each thread is emphasized, whereas on the page, the total visual effect is prioritized. The fact that, in the digital application, the whole poem comes into full view only after all the threads have been clicked on detracts from the feeling of labyrinth-ness that makes the static iteration so spectacular.

Still, much more telling of how this poem advances a feeling of unboundedness is its location in the volume itself. "Sem saída" (No Exit) is the last poem of the print book and the back cover art—in a way, it is the exit out of the book. De Campos characterizes it as "almost outside the book, right out of it," and this placement has the effect of making the binding of the book the content of the book as well. It is both page and cover, inside and outside.[38] Therefore, while the digital labyrinthine clip-poem of "Sem saída" does question the unit of the page, this interrogation is taken one step further to the very bounds of the cover. Altogether, the multiple facets of "Sem saída" stage the tension between what is bound inside the book and what exceeds its limits.

Other characteristics of the codex complement the patent interrogation of the book as a bound form in *Não poemas*. The pagination, for example, appears on the bottom right corner of the verso page and lists both the verso—a primarily blank page throughout the book that includes the poems' titles and dates—and the recto page where the visual poems appear. This design creates a designated space for each print visual poem to stand on its own on a single page. Here, "Sem saída" stands out again. The poem is located on page 124, where its title and date are printed, but instead of appearing on the corresponding recto page like the other poems, it jumps outside to the back cover. The same listing appears in the table of contents where the "contracapa" is included as part of the content. The negotiations of (un)boundedness seen in "Sem saída" constitute interrogations to conventional units of meaning: page, book, poetry, and cover art. The insistence on negation evident in the title, *Não poemas*, and the preface, "NÃOfácio," and the resistance to bookness implied by the fastening together of print and digital media, suggest a contested relationship with the book and its meaning-making affordances—one that, nonetheless, becomes fundamental to how de Campos's collection makes sense in book form.

It is clear that both Gache and de Campos are invested in interrogating the form of the book, and both resort to the inclusion of digital applications to surpass the bounds of the book. These two works also use the same physical binding strategy of a sleeve on the back cover to hold the CD-ROMs. Interestingly, in both works, it is possible to observe an intent to gather loose, disarranged fragments or poems. Gache thematizes and fictionalizes this intent, while for de Campos, these groupings allow for a reflection on his recent creative practice. Visually, both works use graphic cues to take the reader outside the codex and into the digital application (Gache) or onto the back cover (de Campos). The parallels, however, end there, and we can see different uses of binding media strategies with creative agendas particular to each work. For example, unlike the bookishness of the digital application seen in Gache's work, de Campos does not attempt to remediate the codex in either of the clip-poem cuts. In lieu of digital page design and flipping animations, we find the dissolve transition effect ubiquitous in the animations produced with the multimedia application authoring platform Director. In the first case, the digital application seems to reach out to the book; in the latter, the digital application moves away from it. Similarly, the all-encompassing table of contents in Gache's work becomes three lists in de Campos's volume: one for the poems in the book and two for each digital application. The intent of challenging units of meaning cuts through de Campos's volume: from the poems to the cover-content and from the movements afforded by the codex to those possible through animation softwares. In contrast, while Gache challenges the page unit as well, as seen in "El increíble viaje," she relies on its bounds to do so.

It is worth noting how, in both cases, we see affectations to elements of the codex other than the physical binding. The table of contents, in which materials outside of the bounds of the book are listed, is the clearest example of this phenomenon. It also directly negotiates what is part of the work or is bound in binding media. Furthermore, the physical bindings of *LFM* and *Não poemas* are heavily complemented by other conceptual, visual, and narrative fastening strategies. The complementary binding mechanisms evidence how binding media are not only a development in publishing practices and emerging media but also an indication of the changing sensibilities of creators, publishers, and readers who are increasingly more attuned to collecting and collating content distributed across objects and media. As digital content distribution has moved away from stand-alone storage media and onto the web and smartphone applications, these sensibilities have become critical and serve as the basis for binding media. Although not yet fully, binding media have increasingly shed their physical binding forms and relied on those other "loose" strategies that fasten together the parts of a single aesthetic work.

**Loose Bindings**

The paradoxical notion of "loose binding" refers to the textual, visual, and conceptual mechanisms that fasten together the distributed objects that constitute a single literary work of literature. As Gache's and de Campos's works show, physical bindings work together with loose bindings, whether tangible (visual and textual) or nontangible (conceptual and metaphorical). Physical bindings underscore the unicity of literary works like *El libro del fin del mundo* and *Não poemas*. In contrast, examples of binding media that rely primarily on loose bindings lack the physical features seen in the works examined in the previous sections. Generally speaking, loose-binding examples are recently created works spanning the first two decades of the twenty-first century. As the storage, availability, and distribution of digital applications have almost entirely moved to the web and the cloud, the physical pairing of print and digital media seen in earlier years has shifted. Creators interested in the artistic encounters facilitated by binding media have resorted to fastening strategies that may seem less obvious than back cover pockets, but which, nonetheless, are equally compelling. The lack of a physical binding in loose-binding instances raises at least two questions: how can they be understood as bound together rather than as stand-alone works in their own right? And what do we gain by reading them together? Admittedly, it is possible to consider the print or digital facets of loose-binding media as separate versions or iterations and engage with only one of their elements. A comparative reading of works like these where no version has priority has been proposed in Marjorie Perloff's notion of "differential texts."[39] However, as I argue here, these works' poetic and aesthetic ambitions are more fully realized when both print and digital facets are considered to be bound. Furthermore, loose bindings often reveal how digital and print components have followed different production paths, one as a trade edition book and one as a digital application typically found on the web or as a mobile app. Unlike a physical binding, a loose binding does not designate a particular order or reveal its "stitches" quite as clearly. Without a physical binding, the job of fastening together seemingly discrete parts falls to mechanisms as varied as book/web design and book/web production; conceptual, narrative, and visual elements; technological operations; and reading affordances. Therefore, it is up to the reader to navigate the features left by the authors that signal the relation between the print and digital objects, and to unearth the ways they mean together.

Among loose-binding works we can find Giselle Beiguelman's *O livro depois do livro*, Stephanie Strickland's *V: WaveSon.Nets / Losing L'una*, Carlos Cociña's *Plagio del afecto*, Jason Edward Lewis and co-authors' *Poetry for Excitable [Mobile] Media*, Amaranth Borsuk, Kate Durbin, and Ian Hatcher's *ABRA*, and Vivian Abenshushan's *Permanente obra negra*. J. R. Carpenter stands out in this portion of the corpus with a handful of works: *GENERATION[S]*, *The Gathering Cloud*, *An Ocean of Static*, *This is a Picture of Wind*, and *The Pleasure of the Coast*.[40] An older example indicates that loose binding is not exclusive to the last two decades. Stephanie Strickland's *True North* (1997) is an earlier work where print and digital facets are unbound. Similar to the physical binding examples where other fastening strategies come into play, loose-binding media rely on visual, literary, and conceptual fasteners to keep print and digital objects together. A look into Carpenter's *This is a Picture of Wind* (2018/2020) and Abenshushan's *Permanente obra negra* (2019) shows that, though seemingly more tenuous, the binding of these works' objects is constitutive of their overall poetics. Further, if physical bindings operated in myriad ways, loose bindings offer an even greater variety of relations among media.

### *This is a Picture of Wind:* Meaning-Making across Distributed Book Objects

J. R. Carpenter's *This is a Picture of Wind (TPW)* explores a multitude of written representations of the wind and its effects through short poetic texts inspired by the 2014 floodings in the United Kingdom and based on historical descriptions of the weather. The author describes it as "part poetic almanac, part private weather diary, and part live wind report."[41] At the center of *TPW* is an interest in how forces like the wind, "which we can only see indirectly through its effect," can be represented by language.[42] Carpenter first created *TPW* as a limited-edition zine around 2015, then launched it as a digital application commissioned by the IOTA Institute in Canada in 2018, and published it with Longbarrow Press in 2020. In total, *TPW* includes six groupings of texts: four series of twelve poems, one for each month of the year; a series made up of descriptions of wind or its effects; and a series of weather and seasonal events, also organized by month. While most of the textual content of the work does not change from print to digital, Carpenter has progressively added two more sets of monthly poems to the digital app since it was first launched. The third set was added as production of the print book was under way, and a fourth set was included for the Digital Storytelling exhibition at the British Library in summer 2023.[43] A second edition of the print book, including all four sets of the monthly poems, is scheduled to launch in 2024. This iterative process suggests how Carpenter takes advantage of the specificity of each medium to enhance her exploration of changing weather and climate through language. It also reveals how changes to one facet of *TPW* produce changes to the other.

Carpenter designed the digital app to be viewed in smartphone browsers, although it is also functional on web browsers. It presents the monthly poems statically in a horizontally scrolling grid that centers the current month's poems on the lower half of the phone's (or the computer's) screen. While in Figure 6 only the first of the monthly poems is visible, it sits atop a stack of three other poems, one per year, placed below it. To the right and left are the stacks of poems for the rest of the months. Further, juxtaposed as a background to the monthly poems are weather and seasonal events for each month, dynamically recombining every few seconds. October, for example, includes "lightning and hail," "travel moon," and "first frost," among other events. April depicts seasonal occurrences such as "cherry blossoms," "sprouting grass moon," and "sparrows nesting."[44] Other months' descriptions are consistent

BINDING MEDIA: NEGOTIATING (UN)BOUNDEDNESS    59

with the seasons in the Northern Hemisphere. Two more dynamic lines on the top half of the screen complete the picture of the current conditions. The third line from the top is another instance of the monthly seasonal occurrences, while the fourth, in smaller font size, uses the descriptions of wind and its effects: "a breeze raises dust and loose paper," "smooth sailing," and so on.[45] Altogether, the static poems and the dynamic lines work together to create a sense of ever-changing yet recurrent weather conditions.

As a digital facet, *TPW* relies on the conventions readers would recognize from mobile weather forecasting applications, such as location services and a quick-view summary of the current conditions. Carpen-

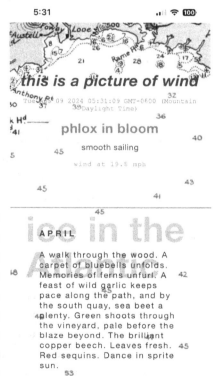

FIGURE 6. A screenshot of "This is a Picture of Wind" on a smartphone shows the static month poem at the bottom with the dynamic lines as the background and a fragment of the Beaufort scale poems on the upper part of the image. Reproduced with permission of the author.

ter establishes this resemblance using the browser's location services and her poetic series. As seen in Figure 6, the digital application displays one's device date, time, and time zone at the top of the screen—a suite of information that contributes to the illusion that *TPW* works in real time and corresponds to each user's location. Furthermore, instead of the expected quick-view conditions of weather apps, such as "sunny," "overcast," "clear," or "partly cloudy," Carpenter employs descriptions such as "little rain," "elder in flower," and "green salt grass," among others, from the series of weather and seasonal occurrences.[46] This poetic characterization of the weather radically changes our relationship to climate as it infuses its measuring scales and controlled vocabularies with affective observations.

As with most combinatorial and dynamic works of digital literature, it is practically impossible to read the digital facet of *TPW* in its entirety as a text or to know that we've read it thoroughly. This is where the bounds of the print book help us navigate the digital application, grasp the scope of the work, and observe where the digital application surpasses them. In its print form, *TPW* reveals the inside workings of the digital application and simultaneously shifts the illusion that the reader is dealing with current localized information. In contrast to the current version of the digital app, the book comprises only five collections, which are the same variable lines and poems from the digital application. Three of them are organized as calendar years ("A Year at Tottenham," "A Year at Sissinghurst," and "A Year at Sharpham"), which map onto the first three rows of monthly poems seen in the digital application.[47] The poems in these three collections derive from Luke Howard's *Barometrographia* (1847), Vita Sackville-West's writing on gardening (1946), and @theriverdart's Twitter posts, respectively.[48] The two other collections, "The Beaufort Poems" and "The Month Arrays," contain the phrases that permutate in the dynamic lines. While in the digital application all five collections appear simultaneously distributed throughout the screen, the affordances of the codex make them static and linear. Instead of seeing the three monthly poems in a column, each month is separated by year. Nevertheless, despite the seemingly static nature of the codex, Carpenter suggests dynamics and variability in the print book too. "The Month Arrays," for example, are presented as .js lists, the digital file format used to populate the dynamic lines in the digital app. Similarly, as Figure 7 illustrates, in "The Beaufort Poems," the author evokes the scale of wind intensity invented by Sir Francis Beaufort visually through the use of various size fonts going from a teeny-tiny "quiet" to a large "dreadful," and from a very small "lull" to a big "torment."[49] The visual effect of this scale concretizes the tiers of intensity and, in so doing, reveals the affective differences that the digital application may insinuate but not fully realize.

The two years between the release of the digital application (2018) and the publication of the print book by Longbarrow Press (2020) might give the impression that these two literary objects don't make a single work but rather are a first edition and a second edition, or an adaptation. In a fashion resembling de Campos's practice, Carpenter refers to them

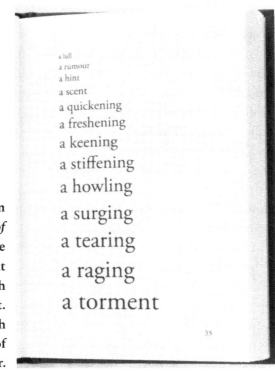

FIGURE 7. A page from *This is a Picture of Wind* shows the dynamics of print language through visual layout. Reproduced with permission of the author.

as *iterations,* which suggests a repetition of the *same* work rather than a remaking. Indeed, although the print book constitutes an iteration out of the digital app, the origin of *TPW* as a zine demonstrates that "there was always a consideration of the page" and that the project was never tied to a single material form but to a poetic exploration.[50] The iterative addition of more poems to the digital app and the second edition of the print book further confirm this. Ultimately, the temporal distance between the two facets, in addition to being the result of revising the poetics of the work, can be attributed to different production flows, timeframes in publishing and artistic commissions, and interruptions due to the COVID-19 pandemic in early 2020. Unlike Gache's and de Campos's works, reading *TPW* in either the print book or the digital application is possible. Unlike other authors of binding media, Carpenter doesn't separate sequential sections across the two objects, and there is no complementary content between the two. Instead, the author takes advantage of the sequentiality of the codex to emphasize how the passage of time, three years in weather observations, is represented and collated. The timeframe of *TPW,* which in the digital application appears compacted in a column encompassing four years simultaneously, in print offers a contrasting way of representing weather and climate through linear order. What is more, the codex and the digital application illuminate the reading of one another and, in a way, serve as mutual reading guides. "The Beaufort Poems" seem more dynamic than they are due to the impression left by the changing lines in the digital application. Similarly, read in their entirety, "The Month Arrays" remind us that the monthly lists do not work cumulatively but are constantly changing. When placed in tension with one another, the affordances of each medium become apparent as they recall and rewrite each other. Considering print book and digital application together allows us to see how Carpenter plays with technical (.js lists), scientific (Beaufort's scale), and poetic language structures. This is true in each facet but comes to the forefront more clearly when they are read side by side.

In her foreword to the print facet of *TPW,* Johanna Drucker characterizes the digital application as "formatted with the small screen in mind, the personal device, phone, where our intimate ongoing check-in with news, weather, communications, updates occurs."[51] This intimate smallness is replicated in the format of the print book: a 6 × 4.5 inch hardback. These dimensions remind us of the smartphone on which the work was designed to be viewed. As stated by Carpenter, Brian Lewis's design of the book "preserved the shape of the text from the app, which in turn was borrowing the shape from the zine."[52] Given that Carpenter's stated interest was "weather in all its written forms," it is not surprising that she carries out this exploration in both dynamic combinatorial language and static print language through visual poetics.[53] In this way, the two facets illuminate each other not just by revealing the affordances of one another but also by showing the representations of wind through various writing techniques and inscription technologies.

## The Poetics of Unfinishedness in *Permanente obra negra*

This cumulative way of meaning-making across distributed objects is also key to understanding Mexican writer and editor Vivan Abenshushan's *Permanente obra negra (PON)*.[54] Abenshushan's novel is a complex gathering of four book objects: a trade edition book, a die-cut book, a card catalog, and a web application. The four facets share almost identical textual and visual content, which is divided into six series or narrative threads, and presented in short fragments. Relying on the fragmentariness of her text and the four deftly designed material objects, Abenshushan builds a device through which her readers engage in processes of selection, collation, and combination of short passages yielding countless reading paths and modes. The author deliberately suggests this form of engagement. Early in the work, readers find Abenshushan's recurrent musings asking them to consider the overall scope of the work: "What are the bounds of this ~~book~~?"[55] She also nudges readers to adjust their reading expectations, "If this is not a ~~book~~ and neither is it a novel, then what is it? An archive? A card catalog? An artifact? An unfolded ~~book~~ as Mallarmé imagined?"[56] More than instructions for reading the four facets, these questions become a guide to consider the work in its entirety.

As the title in Spanish indicates, this is a work in a constant process of becoming: *obra negra* refers to an unfinished construction, a "rough-in." This metaphor enables Abenshushan to suggest from the beginning that her text is permanently being made due to the number of possible combinations among fragments. The distinct ways of reading each facet and the small but meaningful differences in content among them amplify the motif of unfinishedness. However, the more than one thousand fragments are not totally uncollated and disorganized. They are grouped into six autonomous though connected series and distinguished by their own typeface and narrative thread: "Baskerville 1st series → Permanent Rough-In," "Bodoni 2nd series → Archive of black writing," "Corbel 3rd series → The non-expert novel [Provisional Title]," "Adobe Caslon Pro 4th series → The Book of Epigraphs," "Franklin Gothic Medium 5th series → The Index Card Artists," and "Eurostile 6th series → User Manual." *PON* stages the tension between boundedness and unboundedness across its four facets and the six narrative series through typographic and narrative strategies. Features like paratextual information, reading affordances of each facet, and the self-reflexive narrative content in *PON* loosely hold together the pieces in the work.

Figure 8 shows that the unusual copyright page includes paratextual information illuminating the production history of the whole work: the funding institution, the multinational banking group BBVA, the printers and binders in charge of each print facet, the developers of the web application; book and interface designers; the Mexican independent publisher Sexto Piso, and so on. The creative network that emerges from this information displays Abenshushan's original concept, which is reiterated in the making of each facet. The many participants listed demonstrate that *PON* required dedicated involvement from various experts for its execution and, perhaps more important, that its production occurred outside the regular publishing and web development workflows. Crucially, unlike *TPW* and most loose-binding examples, all four facets of *PON* were released simultaneously—a feat of coordination among many actors that Abenshushan attributes to the funding available for the project.

BINDING MEDIA: NEGOTIATING (UN)BOUNDEDNESS 65

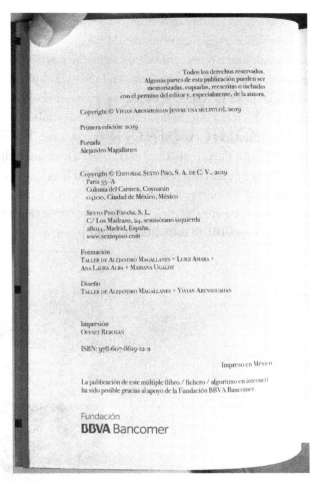

FIGURE 8. The copyright page in *Permanente obra negra* clearly lists the network of collaborators in charge of different aspects of the book's design and production. Reproduced with permission.

Additionally, the possible ways to order and read the series across the four facets of *PON* are unique to the specific book object, which creates cumulative yet fragmentary meanings to finish the "rough-in." To do this, Abenshushan takes full advantage of the affordances and conventions of each book object, shown in Figure 9. While the unifying design and conceptualization binds them, their individual mechanisms, structure, and afforded reading practice are specific to each facet. The trade edition book underscores and challenges the possibility of linear and sequential reading. The die-cut book and the web application insist on combinatorial poetics. The card catalog hints at the autonomy of each fragment, which is nonetheless related to the whole.

A short examination of the threads woven among the narrative series illustrates how, despite its tendency toward unboundedness and dispersion, *PON* is bound through self-referential fragments scattered throughout each of its parts. For example, in Series 6, one finds an abundance of references to the different facets of *PON* that are essentially identical but specific to each object. For instance:

FIGURE 9. The three print objects of *Permanente obra negra*. Photograph by Vivian Abenshushan. Reproduced with permission.

NOTE

This ~~book~~ is many ~~books~~, never the same. For that reason, it has several material forms: a print ~~book~~ with a montage fixed in time and a die-cut book. Look for them.⁵⁷

NOTE

This ~~book~~ is many ~~books~~, never the same. For that reason, it [also!] has other material forms: a card catalog with interchangeable cards and a die-cut book. They circulate in numbered copies. Look for them.⁵⁸

NOTE

Permanente obra negra is many ~~books~~, never the same. For that reason, it adopts several forms: an algorithm / card catalog / a book. Look for them.⁵⁹

Fragments such as these have two effects: they reiterate the specificity of the object being read among the four possible ones, and once this specificity has been highlighted, they resignify the place that it occupies in the work as part of a whole. Furthermore, these passages serve to amplify *PON*'s poetics of unfinishedness not just as a function of the proliferation of objects but also through their relations. That is to say, they cause the bounds of the facet at hand to come undone, and each object becomes partial yet fastened to the others, prompting readers to encounter the rest.

The central motif of the unfinishedness of the rough-in relies on the myriad possible readings of *PON*. This excess of possibilities is the basis of the combinatorial poetics through which the work tends to dispersion. The patent tension between what is bound in the specificity of each object, its reading practices, and the unboundedness possible through the combination of fragments serves "to contain the dispersion ⇄ to amplify it."⁶⁰ On the one hand, the work is not constrained to one of its facets since it overflows the specificities of a single object. On the other hand, it also surpasses the affordances of each object's functioning. All of these features contribute to the poetics of unfinishedness, of the permanent rough-in. Abenshushan's use of the strikethrough when referring to "the ~~book~~" is also telling of the author's approximation to "the ~~book~~" and the many book objects making up her work. Through this seemingly simple gesture, one can also observe the tension inherent in "loose binding," a tension that prevents Abenshushan from disregarding the notion of the book altogether and simultaneously signals a sense of interrogation. In *PON*, it is clear that for Abenshushan, the book forms employed explore the very capaciousness, flexibility, and variations of the book. Her exploration, moreover, unveils a fascination with print objects but one that wonders about their roles in an expanded media ecology.

Carpenter's and Abenshushan's works evidence how, in the absence of physical binding features, conceptual, visual, paratextual, and narrative or poetic elements take up the function of keeping distributed elements together. Although a specific ordering is not indicated in either of these works, their relationships come to the forefront and amplify the poetic ambitions of the authors, whether it is an exploration of the representation of weather or one concerned with the meanings specific book forms make.

---

Based on the material and literary features of works by Gache, de Campos, Carpenter, and Abenshushan, in this chapter I have elaborated the central conceptualization of this book: binding media are creative, literary, and publishing practices in which print and digital objects are fastened together into a single distributed work. Binding media are also the resulting hybrid media objects. Moreover, I have proposed that "binding media" is a development in the contemporary history of the book, whose unstandardized yet recurrent structural features are indications of a rapidly changing media landscape. Among these are alterations to case bindings as in Synapse & Brøderbund's "electronic novels"; disk pockets attached to back covers as in Gache's and de Campos's works; and expanding the information contained in copyright pages as in *Permanente obra negra*. However, I don't see bookbinding as a structural feature alone. Instead, I propose it as a framework to explore media intersections and encounters. Following Hayles's notion of material metaphor, I have discussed and shown how the features of binding media, whether physical, visual, or aesthetic, are part of the meaning-making mechanisms of each work examined. My analyses lead me to argue that, in the reciprocal transfer of meaning from artifact to text taking place in binding media, an expansion of our considerations of bookbinding is warranted as a central feature of a work's aesthetic project. While common for artists' books, this expanded theorization of binding comes to the forefront when examining the symbolic dimensions of seemingly inert structural features in codices produced as trade edition books. It also allows us to theorize how literary expression is not found on the page alone but crucially in the media that actualize it.

As can be seen from the examples, in binding media, there is an implicit and sometimes explicit interrogation of what a book is and what its bounds are, a tension between boundedness and unboundedness. This tension is fundamental not only for the unique aesthetic purposes of works like *El libro del fin del mundo*, *Não poemas*, *This is a Picture of Wind*, and *Permanente obra negra*, but also one that suggests the constancy and innovation of the codex in a media landscape that repeatedly has been purported to entail its demise. Conversely, each instance of binding media is a reinvestment in the print book, one where deep and concerted engagements with it confirm its flexibility and capaciousness. The four works analyzed, and binding media more generally, reveal a complex landscape where interactions among media are varied and abundant. Both physical and loose bindings enact literary, bibliographic, and technological ways of fastening print and digital media together where the negotiation of (un)boundedness can be more clearly appreciated. Ultimately, binding media bring to the forefront changes in the creative, publishing, and reading sensibilities taking place over the last four decades. Though this chapter is not a history of every development in binding media, a diachronic understanding of its mechanisms and their effects paves the way for a historicized view of phenomena that tend to be treated as ever new trends (see chapter 3).

Binding media are radically contemporary, as they would certainly not have emerged had digital technologies not become ubiquitous in readers' homes (early on) and in their pockets (nowadays). Studies in the history of the book, and particularly of the developments in bookbinding, have demonstrated that these are ever-shifting technologies and media that respond to economic, technological, and cultural changes. Binding media serve as reminders that books (as objects, commodities, and literary works) are made not just of words and paper but of a plethora of changing materials that shape their content. This view of binding media requires recognizing their cultural significance beyond the literary to include their material dimensions and developments in the publishing industry.

While the bespoke literary, bibliographic, and media mechanisms used in binding media resemble artists' book practices, binding media are, in most cases, produced and distributed as trade edition books, albeit most commonly from independent or institutional publishers. Binding media occupy a bibliographic and literary space between their publication as trade edition books and their material, artistic production. As I have argued, the most salient result of the materiality of binding media is that the digital application is not a surplus or an attachment to the codex but rather integral to the work as an object that, once published and distributed by a press, enters a market. Therefore, the concept of binding media also allows us to pay attention to how hybrid, print-digital publishing has been approached in commercial and independent presses. The unique results that emerge from these overlaps will be the focus of chapter 2.

TWO

# FROM THE DIGITAL REVOLUTION IN PUBLISHING TO A MATERIAL HISTORY OF HYBRID BOOKS

**THE POPULARIZATION OF DIGITAL MEDIA** has prompted a complex and abundant set of interactions with the print book. This reconfigured media landscape has proven to be an inviting space for creative projects that take advantage of the blurred boundaries between cultural industries and media objects. In the literary realm, authors have, for decades now, experimented with and adopted hybrid print-digital book forms. As I argued in chapter 1, the work of these authors, found throughout the Americas, forces a reconsideration of the bounds and the form of the print book and how print-digital literary creations overflow it. As much as there is to learn from studying exemplars of binding media as both unique literary creations and contemporary forms of the book, it is also crucial to investigate the publishing landscape that has made these endeavors possible. Even the terminology used to denominate publishing initiatives adjacent to binding media allows us to appreciate the many intersections between print and digital media, literature and software, and the projections to "improve" upon the codex via digital technologies. Sometimes referred to as "expanded," "enhanced," or "augmented" books because of features deemed "extra" to the codex, "hybrid" publishing offers a window into the many changes that have taken place in the industry. Starting in the 1970s, the burgeoning of software development companies and the changing publishing industry fostered "hybrid" publishing initiatives. A look into instances in the history of the fusion of publishing and tech industries that have facilitated the publishing of binding media is key to outlining the characteristics of this bookish phenomenon from the editorial perspective.

Few have written as much about these changes as British sociologist of media industries J. B. Thompson. For him, these changes have constituted a "technological revolution" in publishing: a long and still ongoing process of intersecting media ecologies that include markets, production processes, audiences' literacies, the pull and push between these two industries, and the profound ongoing impacts of their collaborations and encounters.[1] Thompson's conceptualization is helpful to synthesize many different stories and trajectories at distinct levels of the publishing industry, for specific book forms and formats, and in various genres. Moreover, even as it is helpful to think about the technological revolution in publishing as a phenomenon that has impacted the entirety of the industry and taken place around the world, we must also consider how technological developments haven't been even or concurrent in all sectors of the publishing industry. The technological revolution in print has taken many shapes, depending on factors as diverse as free trade agreements, the role of the state in publishing, the rates of computer adoption, and a market accelerated by rapid tech developments.

In her study of early e-book web stores in Latin America, Argentinian sociologist Daniela Szpilbarg explains that the adaptations to digital media generated and catalyzed a variety of changes everywhere in the publishing industry, first in the English-speaking world, and later in the Spanish-speaking one.[2] For Szpilbarg, a fundamental shift in the publishing industry in Latin America is the changeability of the roles of editor, reader, author, and distributor.[3] Similarly, formal changes have taken place, giving way to new paradigms of practice, production, and public building in publishing, and yielded a plethora of possible material configurations: print, digital, print and digital, multimedia, expanded or augmented, and so on.[4] The long period encompassed by the digital revolution is one full of formal experimentation and what many could consider "failed" attempts to reinvent the book. Most notably, "hybrid," "expanded," or "augmented" books (terms that I use largely as synonymous) have a compelling, yet understudied history that intersects with binding media. As they have failed to become established, profitable, and sought after, we can now see various instances of expanded books as the material vestiges of the messy media landscape of the last four decades, the technocultural bets placed by publishers and software developers alike, the results of creative imaginations trying out new materials, and the incipience of a public for artifacts of this kind.

In this chapter, I build a history of "hybrid" publishing since the 1980s as the background developments in the publishing industry generating binding media. I investigate some of the motivations that have made experimentations with the form of the book possible and how they have achieved various levels and forms of success. I propose a reading of binding media across industries and modes of publishing that does justice to these complex material objects within the cultural systems that have produced them. First, I consider Thompson's digital revolution in publishing as the backdrop to elaborate and discuss the underappreciated role of literary endeavors in developing new book forms. Then, I examine a handful of historical publishing initiatives that sought to establish models of creation, production, and distribution for digital, expanded, and hybrid books in the 1980s (Synapse Software) and 1990s (The Voyager Company's Expanded Books). A few more initiatives from the early 2010s (CONACULTA iPad apps, Melville House's HybridBooks project, and the AR Penguin English Library) demonstrate how, as a topos recurrent since the early 1980s, "hybrid" and "expanded" publishing repeats in short-lived cycles of enthusiasm and retrenchment up until the present. I then delve into the production and publication history of three binding media titles: *ABRA* by the American poets Amaranth Borsuk, Kate Durbin, and Ian Hatcher (2011), Stephanie Strickland's multipart work *V* (2002, 2016), and the poetry collections *clickable poem@s* (2016) and *metaverse* (2021) by US-based Chilean poet Luis Correa-Díaz. These examples of binding media reveal how institutional support and independent publishing help produce this type of aesthetic, poetic, and bookish experimentation in a way that commercial endeavors do not. On this basis, I theorize why built-in principles of independent publishing, such as close collaborations with authors, the creation of publics, and the launch of experimental catalogs, have been favorable for this type of work. Increasingly, however, as the precarity of digital media has become more and more problematic for presses, authors have stepped into the role of secondary publishers in charge of releasing and maintaining the digital facets of their work. In the last section of the chapter, I review recent legislation concerning books and publishing. This survey is critical in order to observe how ongoing shifts in the media and publishing landscapes have already forced changes in our understanding and definitions of the book up to a legal framework.

These shifts show that while book objects like binding media continue to be experimental and not the "new" form of the book, the plethora of bookish phenomena launched in the last few decades have already had deep and lasting cultural repercussions. The hemispheric geographical approach of the book highlights how, despite marked differences and specificities, these phenomena have emerged from similar challenges and produced analogous outcomes. Ultimately, the recurrence of hybrid publishing across locales signals that, even as an experimental form and practice, it is already an established, albeit highly variable, publishing approach.

## Binding Media and the Cycles of the Technological Revolution in Publishing

The technological changes the publishing industry has undergone in the last few decades have been so profound that they have become part of the popular collective imagination. Big-budget movies, documentaries, series, and profiles have been devoted to changes in the publishing industries, such as corporatization, book deals, and celebrity writers and editors.[5] While the production processes of a book's writing, editing, printing, and distribution have all undergone a profound though "hidden" revolution, changes to the publishing industry have had little visible and lasting impact on the form of the codex, as Thompson would have it. For the British sociologist, rather than birthing new forms of the book, the revolution in publishing has transformed the notion of where and what the book is. Reconstituted as a digital file, "the symbolic content of the book is no longer tied to the physical print-on-paper object in which it was traditionally embedded."[6] The media shifts might have stripped a book's salable and copyrightable content from its paper substrate, facilitating its sale in various formats, print and digital. Nevertheless, literary and other artistic experimentations that rely on their physical objects to be concretized offer nuances to these shifts.

As American writer and technologist Craig Mod has pointedly stated, the newfound fluidity of a book's content affects primarily the "dregs of the publishing world: disposable books." It makes room for books "defined by content," books where the form of the book matters.[7] Meaningful material approaches to the form of the book have become common owing to digitally enhanced processes of design, production, and packaging. Two instances are *Tree of Codes* by Jonathan Safran Foer (2010) and the hugely successful *S* by Doug Dorst and J. J. Abrahams (2013). In these two titles, the book design follows the authors' content and aesthetic project, and their bookish concretization owes to the creative vision as much as to the availability of digital printing and die-cutting technologies.[8] Despite examples like these and many others, in *Book Wars*, Thompson suggests that a new form of the book has not yet been created. And yet, his account of initiatives "re-inventing the book" offers extensive evidence of new forms of the book being invented by editors, writers, and publishers, though these have failed to become established as business models and industry practices despite various degrees and manners of success.[9] Indeed, Thompson appears to be looking for a new form that serves as a "container" to shape the liquid content in digital files. In Thompson's diagnosis, we can appreciate that "success"—meaning economic viability and formal standardization and replicability—in the publishing industry is not the same as literary, aesthetic, or technical success. Binding media are located at a complex juncture: they are new forms of the book with material contours used recurrently, yet despite such replicability and literary success, they are not a standardized creative practice in publishing. Even at their small scale, we can see how binding media prove that Thompson's focus on industry-level developments misses the contributions that literary endeavors have made to the reinvention of the form of the book. As seen in the previous chapter, in binding media, the creation of literary works and the publishing process are often simultaneous and intimately tied to producing the final physical form, both as paper objects and as digital ones. And it is the practices of independent publishers that have promoted the invention and reinvention of these new book forms. I will come back to this later in this chapter.

Admittedly, Thompson may be right that a new, stable form of the book viable under the standards of the existing commercial imperatives of the publishing industry does not yet exist. However, from a historical, literary, and bibliographic viewpoint, the dismissal of a plethora of bookish phenomena demands to be addressed. Thus, I propose to shift from Thompson's focus on the industry viability of new book forms to an emphasis on the signification of hybrid, augmented, and expanded publishing for literary studies and the bibliographic wellspring found in these "failed" bookish experiments. Whereas the individual analysis of these objects and initiatives offers precise synchronic access over about forty years, in the diachronic consideration of the history of expanded publishing, we can see their value outside of their newness and the monetary concerns of the industry. The study of hybrid publishing reveals a phenomenon that has not gone away despite "failing" repeatedly, and that already has a long history that both precedes and follows the technological revolution in publishing. As anthropologist Catherine Alexander explains in her study of the temporalities and traces of failure, "shifting temporal scales may radically alter whether or not something is perceived as a failure."[10] Consequently, in the following pages, I elaborate how failure—economic failure, in most cases—in the short term must not preclude the valorization of publishing initiatives and/or individual exemplars of binding media as key instances of literary and bibliographic history. Along with expanded books, book apps, and digital shorts, binding media are instances of a "non-hidden" revolution developed in parallel yet on the industry's margins.

Over these bases, I argue that literary hybrid publishing is already a fairly well-established publishing practice even when a single form or approach may be impossible and, in fact, undesirable. The cultural, literary, and bibliographic relevance of book artifacts that never reached standardization might seem dwarfed by the exciting histories of mergers and acquisitions leading up to the consolidation of big corporate publishing, the just-opened possibilities of new modes of distribution and commercialization, and the rags-to-riches stories of authors thriving in online publishing platforms and later achieving commercial success. It is precisely because they are understudied and underappreciated that hybrid publishing and binding media stand to tell us much about the contemporary history of the book.

Despite their largely experimental features, binding media are embedded in, and are another manifestation of, the changes observed in the more sensational stories of the publishing industry. They are material historical instances of the same shifts brought about by the hidden revolution and a nonhidden one. While not representative of all the changes digital technologies have brought about in publishing, the corpus serves as a microcosm of the cycles of enthusiasm and retrenchment regarding the potential of digital technologies that have cut across the industry. Further, the history of binding media reveals the speculation created by the rise of electronic technologies and, later, the internet, which led major publishers to engage in rapid and costly experimentation with formats, making book content digital and augmenting print books. As we know, however, this initial impetus toward digital publishing did not immediately translate to wide adoption of digital formats, not even e-books.[11] A stable business model for digital publishing remains elusive to this day. This short-lived cycle repeats itself every time a renewed excitement for the revolutionary possibilities of digital technologies produces new, promising books and literary artifacts that rapidly dwindle toward extinction.[12] The "retrenchment," as Thompson calls it, serves as an incubation period for the next big idea and the cycle to begin again. Since the early 1980s and until now, the digital future of books forecast and feared is still an unfulfilled success for the publishing industry at large. But we shouldn't be too quick to diagnose these projects as failures. The apparent ruins of extinct hybrid publishing initiatives have a "residual future potential" that reappears every time the cycle begins.[13] Moreover, along the way, we have been left with exciting bookish artifacts with great literary, bibliographic, and historical value.

The expanded or augmented book model, though an imperfect fit for binding media, advances a genealogy beyond just literary works that includes most commonly children's books, reference books, and textbooks. Further, expanded books have come in formats ranging from the fully digital to the hybrid. Interestingly, many instances of expanded books negotiate the hybridity of published titles with assurances of "options" where print or digital are not complementary but stand-alone[14] or companions and expansions,[15] rather than exploiting such hybridity. Moreover, "hybrid" publishing has taken many nonliterary forms. In 1996, Macmillan Digital Reference launched four Frommer's Interactive Travel Guides. As journalist James A. Martin explains, "each CD was packaged with its paperback guidebook counterpart and sold for about $30."[16] Only a couple of years later, the tech manuals press Jamsa launched Kids Interactive, a line of children's books accompanied by CD-ROMs.[17] Simon & Schuster Interactive put out an edition of *The Joy of Cooking* with an accompanying CD-ROM in 1998.[18] The ubiquity of digital companions in textbooks is the most representative case.[19] Individual instances of print-digital literary works, like Iain Pears's *Arcadia*, have enjoyed tremendous critical success and media enthusiasm due to their digital innovations, even when the author himself acknowledged the difficulties in development and publishing.[20] What, then, makes binding media different from both textbooks and other reference titles?

The answer I put forward considers binding media as a publishing practice that is, on the one hand, keen on highlighting the value of the book as a cultural object in a changing media landscape and, on the other, interested in putting out books for which the physical book form is meaningful and one where digital applications are equally meaningful. Publishing aims such as these are commonly found in small and independent presses. Editor Abril Castillo of the Mexican imprint Alacraña explains her interest in books "that one can read from their design to their content. Books in which everything means."[21] Based in Los Angeles, Eli Horowitz and Russell Quinn put this editorial impulse into practice by producing print and iOS book apps in their press and media company, Sudden Oak. Indeed, examining the presses behind binding media publishing reveals several trajectories across various publishing sectors and situates our object of study away from the major houses, their multimillion-dollar mergers, and their absorption into media and entertainment conglomerations in all the countries represented in the corpus. The burgeoning world of independent publishing throughout the Americas has proved to be the most welcoming space for binding media. The distribution of binding media titles by type of publisher is displayed in Figure 10.

As can be readily seen, the definitive majority of the corpus of binding media has been published well outside the world of transnational conglomerates.[22] Only a handful of items in the corpus, including Stephanie Strickland's *V: WaveSon.Nets/Losing L'una* (2002) and Eli Horowitz's *The Pickle Index* (2015), *The Silent History* (2014), and *The New World* (2015), were published by a major commercial publisher or its subsidiary (Penguin and Macmillan's FSG, respectively). Likewise, Penguin Random House is the publisher of *Autobiografía del algodón*

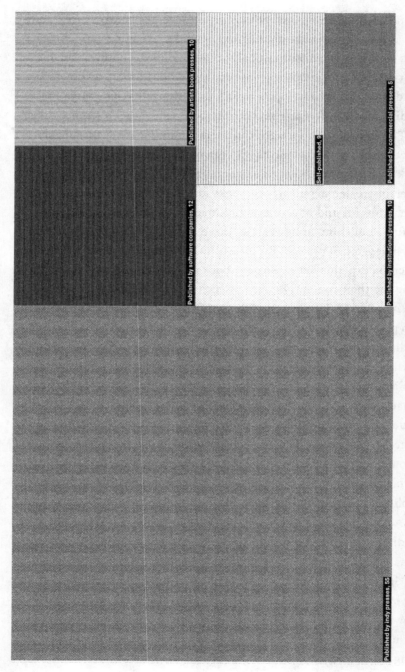

FIGURE 10. Distribution of the binding media corpus in print by type of publisher. (See the appendix.) Figure by the author.

(2020) by Mexican writer Christina Rivera Garza. This distribution is both predictable and surprising. It is predictable because minor genres, particularly experimental literature, are one of the primary foci of independent, institutional, and self-publishing. But it is surprising that the technological and financial prowess and transnational reach of the Big Five publishers, namely Penguin Random House, HarperCollins, Hachette, Macmillan, and Simon & Schuster, would appear to be a more propitious environment for the publication of these works than the small budgets and teams of independent publishers, or even more so the crowdfunded efforts of self-publishing.

Independent publishers that have been welcoming to experimental forms of publishing have been outspoken about waiting for commercial presses to take some of the financial risks of innovation in digital publishing before undertaking it themselves.[23] Thompson confirms this position, claiming that "mainstream publishers have been much more proactive about experimenting with new forms."[24] Multimedia storytelling scholar Lyle Skains, similarly, lists a series of book adaptations into book apps by Faber/Faber, Penguin, and Random House, among other publishers, that were launched with success but have not been maintained.[25] Nevertheless, for publishers, there are clear counterarguments to engage in innovations to the book, such as book apps. As Random House digital publishing executive Lisa McCloy-Kelley commented around 2020, "we're finding that the effort behind these types of books is a magnitude of somewhere between seven and fifteen times as much effort as a typical illustrated ebook."[26] Challenges such as expensive maintenance and resource-intensive production have caused publishers to drop these types of experimentation in book form.[27] In the case of binding media, there is no question that independent publishers have undertaken, at least, a significant portion of the risks. As I explain later in the chapter, more recently, some of these risks have been offloaded onto the authors themselves. This seemingly contradictory scenario signals the complexity of binding media as niche literary endeavors that, despite their modesty, run parallel and push toward an imaginary and elusive future of the book and publishing.

A chronological consideration of binding media publishing, as shown in Figure 11, is helpful to observe the cycles of enthusiasm and retrenchment; it also reveals the different trajectories that converge in the publication of print and digital books in distinct sectors of the industry. Upon first look, one can observe the crucial role of software development companies in the origins of binding media as text adventures. This publishing trajectory stops early in the period I consider due to the consolidation of software companies' own industry practices away from publishing models. Moreover, institutional presses (university and government-funded presses), artists' book presses, and self-publishing run throughout the period of the corpus. Lastly, the most remarkable feature in the timeline is the growing preponderance of independent publishers in the corpus since the 1990s. This shift, which coincides with the burgeoning of independent presses all along the continent, indicates that the feasibility of binding media as a publishing practice depends on principles that have distinguished independent publishing, namely, literary and material risk-taking, literary and material hybridity, interrogations of the form of the book, and public-building.[28] As the list in the appendix shows, few publishers have undertaken multiple binding media titles—a fact suggestive of the production challenges these bespoke projects entail.[29] The production of singular binding media titles by independent presses is also symptomatic of a cautious approach of editors for whom a rush toward widespread digital publishing could prove devastating.

Central to this study is how binding media and these cycles have taken place all over the Americas. Despite stark digital divides and distinct publishing/literary cultures, it is possible to observe strikingly similar phenomena at different times across borders. Writing about the publishing industry in contexts as different as the United States and Latin America is no small challenge, especially when the technological development of the last few decades is fundamental to this investigation. In the United States, the period from the mid-1980s to the 1990s saw the beginning of widespread collaborations between tech companies and publishing firms, conglomeration, and the establish-

FIGURE 11. Timeline of binding media publishers. In the years considered in the corpus, there have been shifts in who dominates the publishing of binding media. Initially, it was software companies and, later, independent publishers. Figure by the author.

ment of new "digital strategy" departments in many houses. While the landscape of digital approaches to publishing in Latin America didn't take off until the early 2000s, the decade of the 1990s already saw some incipient initiatives.[30]

The areas of emphasis have been different as well. In the United States, early technological innovations were happening at the level of industry operations. A digital arms race among large publishers seeking to shape the future of publishing was taking place, too. In Latin America, the spread of digital technologies has favored access to culture and knowledge, and touched on state plans for education, modernization, and democratization.[31] While in the United States, cookbooks, travel guides, children's books, and textbooks were proposed as new consumer, reference, and entertainment products in the form of floppy disks and CD-ROMs in the 1990s, instances like the Venezuelan Biblioteca Ayacucho founded by Uruguayan literary scholar Ángel Rama—a collection of Latin American classics operating in print since 1974—was launched online with funding from the Venezuelan government to distribute its titles freely since 2009. Monetary backing of digital publishing has been radically different in the two regions. In Latin American countries, public funding for education and culture has driven some of the most productive initiatives, whereas in the United States it has been the realm of investors, corporate publishers, and some publishing grants. Nevertheless, as the corpus suggests, across the Americas, individual writers and small publishers were persuaded by the availability of computers and their prospective capacity to revolutionize publishing. In spite of the patent digital divide between these two areas, the specific publishing and book cultures, and the distinct publishing ecologies, similar processes of binding media in literary works along with their resulting publication have taken place.

From Argentina to Canada, the technological revolution that started in the 1980s has had specific features and followed particular visions about the role of the book within an industry and even a society. Yet, it is undeniable that technological developments have prompted writers to test the creative possibilities of digital writing, seeking to revamp ways to narrate, explore new poetic forms, and interrogate the bounds of the book all along the continent. The cyclical histories of digital publishing, from software to independent publishing, punctuate the varied landscape underlying hybrid publishing and binding media. In the next section, a review of hybrid and expanded book publishing initiatives helps us get close to the moments that have made binding media possible and exciting, and to appreciate how those precise junctures have foreshortened their durability as market and cultural objects.

**Cycles of Hybrid and Expanded Publishing**

The growing popularization of electronic technologies for home and entertainment usage in the 1980s triggered two trajectories relevant to binding media: one within the burgeoning world of software development and a second one in the publishing industry.[32] As noted by Szpilbarg, these trajectories began in the English-speaking world; thus, most of the early instances I discuss in this section are from authors and companies based in the United States. Entertainment software companies sought to gain cultural capital by producing complex computer games that would resemble literary works. Interest had been growing in game development companies like Infocom, Electronic Arts, and Synapse to produce interactive narrative games that could equal the textual and literary qualities of print literature. This ambitious undertaking led software companies to collaborate with already renowned writers and titles to recast literary classics in the public domain (Shakespeare's *Macbeth*, Bram Stoker's *Dracula*) as well as to produce new titles (Stephen King's *The Mist*) into interactive fictions. The impetus yielded terminological ideations like "compunovels," "literature of the future," "living literature," "living books," and, most evocatively, "bookware."[33] Some of these early endeavors focused on using the text of literary works to migrate or adapt them into interactive fiction. Other games, such as Danielle Bunten Berry's *The Seven Cities of Gold* and Thomas Disch's *Amnesia* (Electronic Arts), and *A Mind Forever Voyaging* by Steve Meretzky (Infocom), were made more complex by the inclusion of print manuals and other paper matter that provided contextual and complementary gameplay information. Yet others sought to participate in the market of books and similarly showed interest in having their literary games look (and thus be distributed and sold) like books.

In parallel, pushed by speculation about the future of the book, the publishing industry underwent a short but accelerated period of technologization. Publishers sought to gain an edge through rapid and costly experimentation that included operations and production, and publishing new electronic content in innovative formats. Many presses opened departments devoted to digital strategies seeking to make the most of the new medium and striving to remain current in a landscape that seemed at the time a threat that would make books obsolete. While this impetus cut across many industry sectors, textbook publishing is one of the best documented examples to observe these changes. For instance, tracking the rise of prices of textbooks in the United States, a reporter described what was taking place as a "nuclear arms race of supplements emerg[ing] among publishers as each tried to outdo its competition by offering fancy CDs or a video or something that the other guy didn't have."[34]

Similarly, at a meeting of geography textbook publishers and editors in London in 1994, stakeholders acknowledged the opportunities to use technologies to enhance textbooks' value and to experiment with new forms of delivering and licensing content.[35] Narratives and success stories populated journalism about publishing, too. As journalist Kim Campbell wrote in an article devoted to McGraw Hill, "much of the makeover began in 1985 [Joseph Dionne] says, when McGraw-Hill went to its customers to see what it could be doing better. Soon it introduced electronic products relevant to its markets." Further in the same article, Dionne explains how, in at least a dozen cases, "we've taken a print product and made it into an electronic product, and the sale of the print product went up."[36] Arguably, the fastening of print and digital books acquired an aura of future potential and profitability because of cases like these. Predictions of electronic futures, multimedia initiatives, and the promises of new technologies marked the 1980s and 1990s.

Binding media have been published through both trajectories: computer games seeking cultural legitimacy and new products in print publishing. A third trajectory is that of artists' books. In Figure 11 (above), we can see how software companies were dominant in producing print-digital works for the first decade considered in the corpus. Not until the mid- to late 1990s do independent publishers become predominant. This shift can be attributed to the progressive decline in prices for media production, making it available to more than just large publishers. However, efforts to innovate in this way have encountered two damning shortcomings. First, publishers have been—and continue to be—outpaced by technological developments; by the time succeeding titles were launched, the next tech development would render them passé, if not functionally obsolete. Second, there were abundant and well-known difficulties in distributing software titles in bookstores, even those packaged *as* books or *in* books.[37] Ultimately, these challenges signal how, prior to standardization, publishing practices yielding book objects like binding media are prone to disappearing quickly from catalogs and shelves. Publishers and software companies have also often transformed into different ventures with renewed priorities. A handful of instances in the historical race to make publishing more digital serve as examples of the ongoing cycles.

**Synapse & Brøderbund and the Electronic Novel**
Founded in 1981 by Igor Wolosenko and Ken Grant, Synapse Software was a game development company based in the United States. While the company first focused on action game titles for Atari, it later moved on to developing products for Commodore and Apple. One of Wolosenko and Grant's first titles, the productivity software FileManager800, helped the company grow fast. By 1982, Synapse was selling close to a million dollars' worth of software products per month.[38] Steve Hales and Cathryn Mataga, Synapse's lead game developers, geared the company toward interactive fiction. Hales and Mataga had developed BTZ, a state-of-the-art text parser supposed to be superior to the leading one used for the Infocom game *Zork*. This development quickly led the company and Wolosenko to begin work on the Electronic Novel series.

Having experienced some reversals making productivity software in the early days of Synapse, Wolosenko was interested in producing interactive fictions that would decidedly be considered literature. With this in mind, he lobbied and enlisted Robert Pinsky to write an electronic novel (*Mindwheel*) and collaborate with Mataga and Hales.

The relationship between the future US Poet Laureate and Synapse was decidedly fruitful; after all, *Mindwheel* remains one of the best known and widely studied works of interactive fiction. *Mindwheel* has undoubtedly fulfilled Wolosenko's intent to bring interactive fiction to the world of highbrow literature and prestigious authors who make literary history.[39] In parallel, for Pinsky, the opportunity to write interactive fiction had the appeal of renewing his literary praxis completely. The text in the book is reported to have been written by Richard Stanford and done against Pinsky's wishes, who wanted to make something totally new that did not resemble the literature he was already known for.[40] Synapse's following three titles, *Essex*, *Brimstone*, and *Breakers*, however, did not involve writers of Pinsky's caliber and were met with mixed reactions.[41] Nevertheless, putting the literary reputation of these electronic novels aside momentarily, we must acknowledge how the unique publishing strategy of encasing the software disks within the binding of a book instead of stuffing them with the print matter in a box is a significant development in hybrid publishing strategies. The legacy of Synapse, Wolosenko, and Pinsky, then, is easily found both in the literary contributions to interactive fiction and, crucially for this study, in the literal binding of a print book and an electronic application together. As seen in chapter 1, thanks to their binder, the Electronic Novel series improvised alterations to the hardback binding of their titles. These now stand as developments in publishing practices that were quite literally seeking to make room for the new (storage) medium.

By the time the first Electronic Novels saw the light, Brøderbund, the California-based games and educational software developer, had already acquired Synapse. By then, the company was working toward a total of seven electronic novels. However, arising from a period of fast speculation and acquisitions, on the one hand, and changing markets and ever new technological developments, on the other, Synapse had financial difficulties, leading to a $59 million suit against Atari in late 1984.[42] When the court case was settled against Synapse, Brøderbund continued the collaboration for another year. This is why the first three titles of the Electronic Novels series appeared under both Synapse and Brøderbund imprints. However, in 1985, Brøderbund shut down Synapse, leaving the last of the Electronic Novels, *Breakers*, to appear under just the Brøderbund imprint.[43] Other works that were reportedly well under way never saw the light.[44] With Synapse extinct, Brøderbund went on to produce widely known educational and productivity titles like *The Print Shop* and *Mavis Beacon Teaches Typing* as well as the *Living Books series* before being purchased by a series of software and media companies, including Mattel Interactive, Ubi Soft and, partially, Houghton Mifflin Harcourt between the late 1990s and the mid-2010s.

As the history of Synapse Software suggests, changing markets, evolving reader preferences, and developing technologies were orthogonal to boutique and experimental projects requiring a lot of artisanal work. This is especially true with small companies for which financial reversals are hard to survive. Moreover, at a time of high speculation, software companies like Synapse and, later, Brøderbund were prone to rapid acquisition and dissolution. Despite the loss in popularity suffered by interactive fiction generally, this early manifestation of binding media would be accompanied and followed by others.[45] The cultural imaginary of what the computational future of literature and the book would look like had taken root both in the software and the publishing industries, and would take many forms in the following decades.

**Voyager: "More Like Books"**
A different impetus to experiment with books and electronic technologies was at the root of the Voyager Company, founded by Bob Stein in 1984. Stein's early experimentations blending distinct media started from the principle of making audiovisual media "more like books" rather than making books more like audiovisual media. Voyager's first incursions into expanding one type of medium with another

began with the well-known Criterion Collection of film and the innovative addition of commentary tracks and bonus materials in special editions.[46] Starting a few years later, the CD Companion series aimed to do the same for pieces of classical music. Published and produced by Voyager, UCLA professor Robert Winter's *Beethoven's Ninth Symphony CD Companion* (1989) "offered all sorts of interactive historical, musicological, and biographical information about the work and its composer, and even included a running text commentary synced to the CD recording."[47] Now considered "the industry's first consumer CD-ROM," Winter's title became a model for other CD-ROM publishers and for Voyager's own Expanded Book Project (EBP).[48] The Criterion Collection and CD Companion series models established the precedent of adding extra content and forms of interaction to well-known musical or cinematographic works of art—one that would ideally be replicable into books. Due to these innovations, in the early 1990s, Voyager's Expanded Books became a reference for the future of the book and entertainment in a time when home computers had already become quite common in the United States and storage media capacity allowed for rich multimedia content. The publication of *Who Built America? From the Centennial Celebration of 1876 to the Great War of 1914* (1993) by Roy Rosenzweig, Steve Brier, and Josh Brown—one of the most celebrated titles by Voyager—signaled the growing place of electronic publishing in higher education as well.

From its inception in the now mythical Book Renewed camp that took place on Bloomsday 1990, the EBP sought to transform the book as object. During the meeting, Voyager's technical advisor, Michael E. Cohen, recounted how Richard A. Lanham, Bob Stein, and himself "all agreed that simply putting an ordinary book on the screen was a non-starter—digital text would have to be interactive in some way."[49] Notably, the need to package and distribute Expanded Books as paperbacks to retain their book flair was another of their foundational considerations. The first three titles of the EBP (*The Complete Hitchhiker's Guide to the Galaxy*, *The Complete Annotated Alice*, and *Jurassic Park*) were launched at the 1992 San Francisco Macworld Expo. In addition to showcasing their newly completed titles, this occasion proved crucial for Voyager to consolidate its place within the nascent electronic publishing scene by launching the Expanded Books Toolkit (EBT). The software—the same used to produce Voyager's own expanded books—sold for $295 and promised to streamline the production of electronic books and to lower the entry barrier to electronic publishing. Once launched, the EBT allowed Voyager to establish agreements with publishers like Random House, Macmillan, Harper Collins, and NTC to use the toolkit for their multimedia productions.[50]

EBP was one of those instants of innovation that propelled the idea of book augmentation and blurred the boundaries between print and electronic book publishing. However, looking back to those years we can see that, as the name denotes, Expanded Books offered little to adapt the original print "content" to the new medium. Instead, it added "extra" features such as annotation and searching, and multimedia such as sound, video, and animation, to the publications. Cohen's characterization of Expanded Books as "books revitalized by all the *adornment* that digital technology could provide" reveals this uneven treatment.[51] As media theorists Jay David Bolter and Richard Grusin assert, the Voyager interface "indicated the priority of the older medium."[52] Voyager books' functionalities (annotating, searching, and clipping) were all very close to a present-day Kindle and, arguably, manifested Stein's objective to make multimedia content more like books and, reciprocally, books more like multimedia productions. Despite what, thirty years later, might seem like formal or technological shortcomings, it is clear that Voyager bridged the software and publishing industries. This development is likely to have popularized the idea of hybrid publishing and its expressive possibilities, later adopted by authors and publishers, not just software developers, to create and launch print-digital literary works.[53]

Much like Synapse, issues with distribution, cash flow, and a publishing practice that seemed too artisanal for the times of the rise of the web ultimately led the EBP to commercial failure.[54] The parallel yet quite different stories of Voyager and Synapse are illustrative of the challenges, beyond the creative endeavors, to carve out a place for electronic novels or expanded books in the world of publishing. Though most electronic media companies producing CD-ROMs aimed to attach themselves to booksellers and distributors, the lack of standards in packaging, pricing, operating systems, and even display facilities muddied the potential success of interactive books.[55] The belief that "book merchants won't care whether they sell Civil War histories on paper or on CD-ROM" seems to have been truncated by an audience that was likely more attracted to reading and consuming online content, and confused about the purpose of CD-ROMs or suspicious of their "enhanced" qualities over print books.[56]

In contrast, as the case of textbooks suggests—their early success and their ongoing hybrid model—the formation of a market and public for books that are simultaneously print and digital was possible. Hybrid textbooks are now recognizable and widespread. The protocols for their authoring, production, distribution, and usage are established; therefore, their material hybridity is no longer a novelty. For binding media, however, the sense of experimentation and novelty that marked Synapse's Electronic Novels as much as Voyager's Expanded Books hasn't gone away in the subsequent decades. The imperative of innovation, which characterizes the tech industry, proves to be too unstable a landscape for the publishing industry, which conventionally relies on longer processes of aging and cultural capital accrual. Even with scalable solutions like those proposed by Voyager's EBT, the sales numbers rarely justified significant publisher investments. Still, the cultural impetus to expand and augment books through digital media persists. However, as the histories of Synapse and Voyager suggest, publishing innovations of this kind might be more viable through nonprofit institutions where the artisanal and carefully curated production of titles is not a threat to the companies producing them but a core part of their practice.

**Building Mexico's Digital Heritage: CONACULTA × Manuvo**

In Mexico, where electronic publishing initiatives have lagged behind the United States, government bodies have met the need.[57] In 2012, the Mexican National Council for Culture and the Arts (CONACULTA) launched an initiative to jump-start the burgeoning interest in digital arts, literature, and culture. Under the leadership of the editor and publisher Consuelo Sáizar, CONACULTA launched Proyecto Cultural Siglo XXI Mexicano, which promised to bring Mexican "cultural administration into the twenty-first century."[58] A central part of Sáizar's future-looking administration was to foster the digitization of Mexico's cultural heritage, taking advantage of emerging technologies, including the "digitization of three main heritage collections: image, word, and sound," and support for the organization of conferences and symposia devoted to digital humanities.[59]

Further, inspired by the work done by the Brooklyn-based publishing platform Atavist Books and Touch Press in London, Sáizar championed the development and publication of seven iPad applications devoted to pillars of Mexican literature. The first and most celebrated projects were a rendition of Octavio Paz's 1967 poem *Blanco*, and another of José Gorostiza's *Muerte sin fin* from 1939. The project also included *Nezahualcóyotl, Seducciones de Sor Juana*, and a collection of Amado Nervo's poetry, among others. Much like the titles published by Voyager—though with the higher levels of resolution, capacity, interactivity, and breadth of content given by twenty years of accelerated technological developments—the CONACULTA apps sought to incorporate multimedia elements capable of enriching the poems in the app format while leaving the content of the works untouched. The council's endeavors included recordings of readings of the poems in the voices of the authors themselves and well-known actors, as well as commentary, translations, interviews, and galleries of visual materials related to the works. Only in the exceptional case of Paz's *Blanco*, where meaning depended heavily on the physical medium in the original edition, was there a more thorough process of adaptation and remediation. The app's description indicates how its design follows Paz's original idea as "a succession of signs over a single page; as the reading progresses the page unfolds: a space which as it moves allows the text to appear and, in a way, produces it."[60] This poetic reading effect, achieved in print with the accordion book format and multicolor printing, is remediated by the continuous scrolling of the touch screen. In all of these cases, it is apparent that CONACULTA sought to expand and augment the print editions of the works to popularize them and make them newly available to a large public via digital media.

The CONACULTA team, coordinated by cultural promoter and digital humanist Ernesto Miranda, conceptualized the projects and oversaw the production of the audiovisual content. For the design and development of these book apps Miranda commissioned Manuvo, a cultural software firm founded in 2010 by Maurits Montañez. As flagship projects in Sáizar's administration, the production of the apps hugely benefited from infrastructural resources like state-owned recording studios and facilities for the editorial team to produce interviews, digitize images, digitally restore archival materials, and more.[61] The involvement of the state agencies meant the apps required a smaller investment than, for example, those produced by Touch Press, the costs of which ranged in the tens of thousands of US dollars. Ultimately, having state backing made the transfer and permissions of copyrights possible, too. As a consequence of the lower cost plus the challenges of having a plethora of stakeholders and rights owners, CONACULTA opted to distribute the apps for free.

Upon launch, the apps, particularly Paz's *Blanco,* enjoyed critical and popular success, won awards, and were the top downloads in Mexico's AppStore. Relying on the state's robust infrastructure and having the head of CONACULTA advocate for publishing these apps provided an ideal environment for Miranda's team and Manuvo to develop them. However, despite the initial enthusiasm, the change in government administration in 2012 saw a dwindling of the priorities established by Sáizar. As her administration at CONACULTA came to an end and shifts in policies did not prioritize the continuation of the projects, the apps lacked sufficient maintenance and upgrading, and slowly degraded until they became obsolete and unavailable on the AppStore. The two most popular apps, *Blanco* and *Muerte sin fin,* were ported to a web version that ensures at least some level of access. Still, without an institutional office tasked with the preservation of the state's digital patrimony, even these versions often go offline. Given that these apps were created as part of Mexico's new digital cultural heritage, away from the market logic of the publishing and the tech industry, it would have seemed that the future of these apps was ensured, even despite the instability of the technologies used to produce them. The case of CONACULTA shows that market pressures upon publishers and developers are not the only factor putting digital heritage at risk. The lack of buy-in from institutions can have the same effect.

In parallel to the development of the CONACULTA apps, Manuvo and Montañez continued their work as third-party developers working with cultural government agencies in Chile and Colombia, and with independent presses in the Latin American region. As the company acquired more experience and prestige through its work on cultural software, Manuvo also partnered with independent publishers to invest in the production of digital titles and operate as a publisher itself. In 2018, after launching one last app, *Vamos a aprender Purépecha / Let's Learn Purépecha*, Manuvo went dormant. In 2021, the company began a brand transformation as a firm offering digital culture solutions and training services. At the time of writing, Manuvo is in the process of relaunching and has made some of its apps or their documentation available on the company's website.

Once again, in the history of Manuvo and the CONACULTA apps, it is possible to observe the quick cycle of success and downfall. The artisanal production incompatible with large publishers and software companies that made life difficult for Synapse and Voyager might have seemed less problematic in Manuvo's case. Yet despite finding early critical success for the quality of its apps and engagement with the form and the affordances of the touch screen, many of the apps produced by Manuvo also became unavailable. Public funding and the nonprofit approach of Manuvo's apps resulted in issues similar to those seen in Synapse and Voyager. The fate of the CONACULTA apps exposes the enormous resources needed for this type of digital publishing, which in this case were ensured by the state agency and Sáizar's political will. Similarly, it indicates how profits from app sales are not an essential element for the sustainability of these publications—releasing them for free, CONACULTA never planned to make any money off them. Manuvo's business model as a third-party developer likewise allowed it to continue working on further publishing endeavors when priorities in CONACULTA shifted. Lastly, it suggests that there is a void not just of resources to keep apps like these functioning but, more important, of political and public motivation to consider digital applications as part of the cultural production in need of ongoing efforts of preservation and conservation.

## Augmented Reality Classics: Melville House and the Penguin English Library

Very close instances to binding media can be found in recent editions of classic titles published with augmented-reality features. In a saturated market of works in the public domain, attempts at standardizing the production of augmented books has been a strategy used by publishers to make individual editions stand out from the bunch. In the early 2010s, two almost identical instances enacted the cycle of enthusiasm and retrenchment seen elsewhere in this chapter. The US independent press Melville House launched its HybridBook project in 2011, a program that "offers extensive ancillary digital materials, such as essays, maps, illustrations, and other primary source material that will be available to purchasers of print books through a QR (Quick Response) code printed inside the book."[62] Sixteen books, themselves a part of the Art of the Novella series, were published in this way. Dennis Johnson, editor in chief at Melville House, explained that the "illuminations," as he called the book augmentations, were a strategy "to give booksellers as a tool, as an answer to why they should sell our classic instead of someone else's."[63] The expanded contents offered by the HybridBook project were not unrelated to the text at hand, but the ancillarity of them is evident from the descriptions. As Johnson explains, "the Illumination for the HybridBook version of Anton Chekhov's *The Duel* contains an essay on dueling by Thomas Paine, poems by Lord Byron, philosophy by Nietzsche, an anti-dueling church sermon, an argument in favor of dueling by a U.S. Senator, and the rules to the game of *vint*—a game that plays a role in the plot."[64] Ultimately, the augmented content was not made part of the print book itself but came as a separate, downloadable file.

Penguin launched the augmented Penguin English Library (PEL) a year later, in 2012. About a dozen titles of the one hundred new editions of the PEL, with covers designed by the London-based illustrator Coralie Bickford-Smith, were to be accompanied by AR animations, video, and audio produced by the UK mobile development firm Zappar. The augmented content required the reader to download Zappar's own app to navigate to the digital content. Once there, the reader had to navigate a long list of categories, including "costumes," "film and TV," "advertising," and "publishing." Zappar's Penguin English Library, still available at the time of writing, lists only two titles, *Lady Audley's Secret* and *Moby-Dick*. However, it seems to imply that the entire collection will eventually be available: "100 of the best novels in the English language, to collect and share, admire, and hold. Pick up a great book and watch it come to life in your hands."[65] The redesign of the PEL, along with the augmented content, was a sales strategy similar to Melville House's and was intended to make these classics even more classic, with collectible covers and exclusive access to bonus materials. The marketing director for Penguin characterized them as "the ultimate readers' editions that can be cherished, collected, given, and kept for a lifetime."[66] While the books certainly can be kept for a lifetime, only Braddon's and Melville's works saw the augmented content produced and distributed. Nonetheless, it is easy to glean that more titles had been commissioned to Zappar. Upon "unlocking" one of the titles in the app, an inner library pops up at the bottom of the screen with a dozen titles, ten of which are not available at all.

As the other examples discussed in the chapter, these two initiatives were fairly short-lived. Melville House stopped publishing HybridBooks around 2014. It is unclear when Penguin English Library stopped producing the augmented content, but the inactive titles in the app suggest it was abandoned soon after launch.[67] The speed with which these two examples dwindled might not be that surprising. These publishers' shifting positions evidence the difficulty of sustaining projects like this from an economic perspective and in terms of the high demands of content creation and maintenance. However, while these "failures" speak of missing markets or flawed marketing strategies for AR books, I argue that they also signal how publishers have neglected to create a reading public for this type of edition and to challenge such a public. Reporting on the Penguin and Zappar partnership for Gizmodo, writer and journalist Molly Oswacks sorely lamented the futility of the development: "Augmented reality, when implemented appropriately, can be a pretty great [sic] . . . But what can AR tech do for a novel like Moby Dick? Watching a whale animation is not the same as reading the story. Seems like a distraction and a gratuitous bit of packaging."[68] For a keen reader like Oswacks, it was evident from the beginning that the augmentation of titles like this would be unsuccessful and unattractive to readers rather than appealing and cherished. Her commentary implies that expanded content, untethered from the actual content of the book, leaves readers feeling underestimated, their inter- or transmedia capabilities left unchallenged.

Another reason for these commercial failures, as I examine in detail in chapter 3, is the ephemerality and accelerated innovation of digital technologies and their divergence from the slower temporalities of print books and literature. HybridBooks and PEL volumes might have lacked the literary or aesthetic integrity featured in the media hybridity of binding media exemplars. Yet, it is more likely than not that in addition to the market demands, the rapid cycles of innovation would have put pressure on the technological currency (accessibility, compatibility, maintenance, and so forth) of these initiatives. These two parallel instances evidence the many difficulties in establishing innovative, sustainable, and profitable forms of the book—a suite of challenges that, more and more, seems only worth undertaking when the integrity of the literary work is at stake. Whereas for Melville House and Penguin the augmentation of print books was conceived as a marketing strategy, in binding media the leading principle is the authors' and editors' creative ambitions. Adding "extra" or "optional" digital content to a book might add value to the volume as a print product and help it stand out among others; it might give the reader options for consumption; but it works in a hierarchical structure where print takes center stage and the digital apps are companions. Perhaps where the HybridBooks project and augmented PEL editions disappoint is in a lack of literary or aesthetic integration between the print books and the digital applications. Rather than fostering a concurrence of print and digital, digital augmentations or expansions perpetuate the rift between them—one a subsidiary to the other.

Many of the literary ambitions first embodied in Synapse's Electronic Novel Series and the expansive innovations introduced by Voyager's EBP are recognizable in the CONACULTA apps, HybridBooks, and Zappar's PEL. The history of hybrid and expanded publishing I have woven in these pages suggests that, rather than constituting "failed" individual initiatives, all these endeavors string together a long process in which hybrid publishing has taken form. Unlike Thompson's sociological perspective, which focuses on moments of rupture and standardization that impact the publishing industry, this history underscores the coincidences among projects, the tropes like adding commentary and bonus materials that remain relevant decades apart. While some coincidences among initiatives speak of the power of the market and technological imperatives that make experimentation challenging, others remind us that editors, publishers, readers, and writers continue to imagine ways to bind together media objects and to draw meaning from such fastening.

## From the Technological Revolution in Print to a Material History of Hybrid Publishing

Throughout the last few decades, hybrid and expanded publishing initiatives, including binding media, have left a wealth of material residues punctuating distinct moments in their history. On the one hand, floppy disks, CD-ROMs, and USB sticks locate these works in specific moments in the history of technology. On the other hand, the material physical features of codex facets in binding media, covers, copyright pages, colophons, and, when present, disks and disk sleeves offer insights into the creation, production, distribution, and even sale of binding media. Because of their history and hybrid materiality, binding media have left a wealth of traces of their creation, launch, publishing process, and passage through the phenomenon's history. The print facets remain even when websites have been taken offline or apps become no longer available. A look into disk sleeves, for instance, suggests different production approaches. Generic, unmarked clear plastic or paper sleeves signal quite a different production process than custom-made sleeves tied to the book design. While use of clear plastic sleeve for Oni Buchanan's *Spring* suggests a productivity choice, one that is replicated in titles like Stephanie Strickland's *Zone : Zero,* and Ian Bogost's *A Slow Year*, Guillermo Gómez-Peña's custom-made pocket, shown in Figure 12, signals its provenance from the reputed Moving Parts and City Lights artists' book presses in San Francisco.

Similarly, a recurrent tendency found in binding media is the pres-

FIGURE 12. The USB drive and its pocket in Felicia Rice, Guillermo Gómez-Peña, and co-authors' *DOC/UNDOC* is designed following the entire book's aesthetic. Reproduced with permission.

ence of an unconventional information apparatus related to the sale and usage of the hybrid, print-digital object. In some cases, legends characterize the scope of the work, standing in for a synopsis of a work's plot or poetic intentions. We can observe this on the copyright page of Abenshushan's *Permanente obra negra*, a work discussed in chapter 1. In addition to the conventional information found on a copyright page, on this one we see a list of collaborators, a list of the book objects encompassed by the project, and a tongue-in-cheek list of possible permissions apart from copying like memorizing, rewriting, and scratching out.

FIGURE 13. Luis Bravo's *Árbol veloZ* CD-ROM and sleeve show the legend "EXEMPTED from sale taxes ("complement to the book"), Law 15.913, Decree 427/95." Other information, such as the ISBN on the disk sleeve and a library stamp, further signal the complementariness of print book and CD-ROM. Copy at the University of Kansas Library.

One can often find definitive instructions to sell books and disks together. For instance, the back cover of Luis Bravo's *Árbol veloZ* reads, "This book is sold jointly with a CD-ROM (exempt of sale taxes, as 'complementary to a book' Law 15.913, Decree 427/95)." This information is reiterated in the custom-made CD-ROM sleeve, shown in Figure 13. Likewise, the sleeve holding the disk in de Campos's *Não poemas* almost identically specifies, "This CD is part of the book *NÃO* by Augusto de Campos (Editora Perspectiva, 2009), and it cannot be sold separately." A little different are the user instructions in Oni Buchanan's *Spring,* seen in Figure 14, where the CD-ROM sleeve is sealed by a sticker with the caption "NON-RETURNABLE IF MEDIA OPEN"; the disk itself indicates that "The Mandrake Vehicles accompanies *Spring* by Oni Buchanan."

FIGURE 14. Oni Buchanan's clear disk sleeve was sealed with a sticker showing the legend "NON-RETURNABLE IF MEDIA OPEN." The CD-ROM further indicates that it accompanies *Spring.* Reproduced with permission of the University of Illinois Press.

The presence of these legends is indicative of emerging media practices and protocols affecting the creative composition of print-digital works of literature and how the objects that make them up are sold, taxed, cataloged, and accessed. When these works were published, the novelty of these practices required that authors and publishers spell them out to establish a literacy of sorts. The then-novel practices now offer a window into the considerations taken in their design and the need for extra paratextual information. These attributes open a window to understanding the moment in which each instance of binding media was published and help us reconstruct the cultural history of this phenomenon beyond its literary endeavors alone or its immediate relevance to the publishing industry of the Big Five.

**The Expanded Processes of Binding Media**

The examples reviewed in the previous section bring us close to the specific contexts where binding media have been published. Once again, a review of the corpus shows that when software companies like Synapse & Brøderbund stopped publishing "bookware," the practice progressively moved primarily to institutional and independent publishing houses. The migration from storage media like diskettes and CD-ROMs to the web and the AppStore has also played a crucial role in publishers' treatment of binding media. For instance, it has meant that publishers are no longer responsible for producing, packaging, and distributing books and disks together. This split in production and distribution sometimes entails several funding sources and distinct production timeframes. While this practice poses enormous challenges for creators and might seem like an abdication of the presses' work, it might be the case that this split publication model is a more sustainable approach for producing these works. Additionally, this approach makes it possible for binding media to become projects that develop over a few years. The publishing histories of three binding media exemplars—Amaranth Borsuk, Kate Durbin, and Ian Hatcher's *ABRA*, Stephanie Strickland's *V*, and Luis Correa-Díaz's *clickable poem@s*—are examined in the next section. They signal how these works are created in an evolving fashion and, over the years, across several facets and/or editions that contribute more and more to the works' core poetics. As it becomes clear, these features have best found a home in independent publishing houses where the careful and lengthy production of a bespoke title is not a corporate liability but a feature of its cultural capital. Lastly, the necessary creation of a reading public for binding media fits well-established practices in independent publishing.

## ABRA and the Expanded Book

A project "fascinated with mutation," Amaranth Borsuk, Kate Durbin, and Ian Hatcher's *ABRA* has a long creative history that highlights how the poetics of the work are enhanced by its facets as various book objects created in diverse publishing realms.[69] *ABRA* is a collection of poems in which the poetic voices of Borsuk and Durbin intermingle to fashion the title character: "a posthuman prophet whose name suggests her ecstatic relationship to language and those abracadabra moments in which words bring things into being."[70] At present the work exists in three facets: a paperback published by 1913 Press, a free iPad App, and an artist's book. *ABRA* evolved from a series of performances by Borsuk and Durbin into a page-based book incorporating a flip book animation by Zach Kleyn. Since those first ideations, *ABRA* has been "perpetually trying to work its way off the page" or, at least, into different types of pages.[71] This process continued with more performances where Borsuk and Durbin embodied the title character. Then, *ABRA* mutated into two more facets: the artist's book constructed by Amy Rabas at the Center for Book and Paper Arts, and an iPad app programmed by Hatcher. Across all three facets, the speaking character in *ABRA* and the work's poetics, like the titles studied in the previous chapter, emerge cumulatively out of fastening them all together.

The authors' poetic exploration of mutation moved the project across material instances and added expert collaborators, each bringing to the forefront particular motifs and techniques like illumination, touch and movement, and word image. As such, the examination of *ABRA*'s development, not from a literary or artistic viewpoint alone but across the institutions and industries that made such an artistic exploration possible, suggests that specific publishing conditions are necessary for binding media. Given that, as we have seen, the promises of one-size solutions for "expanded" publishing have faced damning challenges, an "expanded" production environment led by the principles of a poetic project and not by the practices of a single industry appears to be more propitious.

Although there were two early instantiations of *ABRA*, Durbin and Borsuk's performances and the page-based book, the artist's book and the iPad App truly made the project cohere. In conversation with Borsuk, she recounts how an early edition of the paperback was in the works but had not materialized when, in 2012, the authors heard of the Expanded Artists' Books grant from the Center for Book and Paper Arts (CBPA) at Columbia College Chicago.[72] This program had launched a call for commission proposals after receiving an Arts in Media grant from the National Endowment for the Arts to support "new works in digital media with material counterparts."[73] The call for proposals explicitly asked for applicants to "address how the project manifests within these two modalities"—print and iPad. Further, it stated that "artists are challenged to explore ways in which the artwork can take both virtual and physical manifestations, examining the advantages of each and how the interplay between the two can be leveraged to provide a comprehensive and powerful expression."[74] The opportunity and the contours of the call for proposals made Borsuk and Durbin consider whether *ABRA* was not best suited to this hybrid existence rather than one as a paperback flip book of poetry.[75]

Worth noting in the CBPA call is how, unlike other initiatives we have seen in the previous sections, the projects coming out of this grant did not center on making a new form of the book that could be reproducible, standardized, and commercialized. Instead, the effort focused on how the intersections between print and digital media themselves had the potential to produce artistic and poetic meaning. The genre of artists' books is easily the most conducive to this exploration. Rather than offering a model for applicants to fit their projects into, the CBPA sought to produce further interrogation. At the center of the explorations encouraged by the Expanded Artists' Books program is how setting the aesthetic principles as the starting point could yield books for which material hybridity is (despite the program's name) not an expansion but a foundation.

Given that the grant came from public funding, the $10,000 needed to develop the iPad app meant the program was not for commercial endeavors. Ultimately, the conditions of the grant stipulated that the app was to be distributed for free on the AppStore and be maintained by the grant awardees for at least five years. Soon after inviting Ian Hatcher to join the *ABRA* team to design the iPad app and winning the CBPA grant, the Denver-based independent press 1913 agreed to publish Borsuk and Durbin's page-based book as a trade edition paperback. Revelatory of the distinct production timeframes of specific sectors in publishing is that, despite being one of the poets' first ideations of *ABRA*, the paperback came out in 2015, a year after the later instantiations.

The parallel yet dispersed production of the facets of the work was a perfect fit for the poets' intended aesthetics through the affordances of each medium and the medium's extended production networks. Mutability, as one of the poetic endeavors in *ABRA*, is thus embodied by the very process of creating and producing each facet of the project. While Rabas and other collaborators at CBPA constructed the artist's book, the authors were programming and testing the iPad app, and 1913 edited the trade edition. Borsuk, Durbin, and Hatcher's account of the many creations of *ABRA* suggests very precisely how mutability surrounds the entirety of their creative process. The three facets purposefully move from predetermined models, not just away from the published book and not just away from the iPad app, but even away from the principles set by the poets themselves in earlier stages of the project. A telling example of *ABRA*'s many mutations is the changes to line lengths from facet to facet. In the paperback, long lines signal *ABRA*'s desire to go beyond the page and grow across the gutter. In the artist's book, as shown in Figure 15, the lines are more homogeneous, and instead of reaching across the gutter, they jump from the pages below through the laser-cut openings. The same cuttings open a window through which the iPad screen peeks. The iPad's interface specs, however, forced the poets to trim and space the lines. In addition to solving technical problems, these adjustments offer a different take on the original aesthetics of mutability.[76]

A second interesting example of the dynamics of each facet is how they take advantage of what each object has to offer. The paperback moves like a flip book, making Kleyn's drawings increasingly take over the page spread, as can be seen in Figure 16. Moreover, the shading of the words, darker or lighter, communicates a going in and out of focus and adds a sense of timing from one page to another. Similarly, the lines seem to shrink and expand in the recto page and, toward the end of the collection, across the gutter into the verso page.[77] In comparison, the

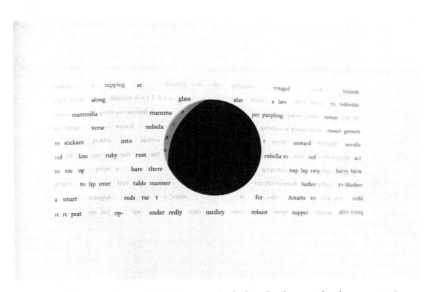

FIGURE 15. A page from *ABRA* as artist's book shows the laser cutting through which small bits of words from pages beneath are visible. The page also displays the variation in text tonality and the dark screen of the iPad through the circular cutting. Reproduced with permission.

artist's book employs many of the same strategies as the paperback: word shading, page distribution, and a circular laser cutting that grows as pages flip instead of Kleyn's drawings. The tactile qualities and the thermo-sensitive ink in the artist's book bridge *ABRA*'s poetics of touch between the paperback and the iPad app. The visual elements of the paperback begin to suggest a shift toward touch, which becomes the basis for reading the iPad app. Ultimately, the app further actualizes the movements and the timing of words appearing and disappearing insinuated in print. The visual effects created by flipping the pages of both paper books are remediated by the virtual circular book design of the app.

Both the seemingly purely textual issue of verse length and the poetics of mutation in *ABRA* are matters of contingent mediation. Such a deep engagement with the poetry as well as with the objects that shape it is a far cry from the practices of adding on audiovisual content to an otherwise uniform plain text, which Borsuk, Durbin, and Hatcher

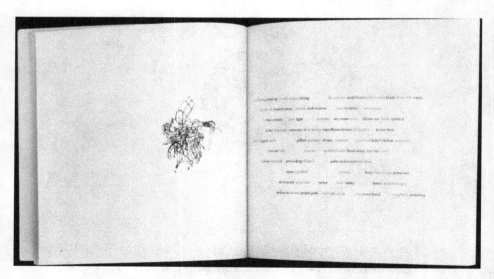

FIGURE 16. A page spread from *ABRA* as paperback where verses and illustration expand toward the gutter. Variation in text tonality can also be appreciated. Reprinted with permission.

always saw as a non-starting point: "we could not simply provide what might be termed an 'enhanced e-book'—an edition of the text with bonus features like audio and video—which would treat the tablet, and its slick surface and seemingly-invisible interface, as a 'crystal goblet' into which the 'original' text might simply be poured."[78] The poems of *ABRA*, the voice of the oracle traversing them, rest simultaneously above all of its facets and in each specific form given by them. While the free iPad app has probably been downloaded thousands of times, only 10 copies of the artist's book were made, and 500 copies of the paperback were printed. The scale of each facet further suggests how each accomplishes distinct goals not just in poetic terms but also in the publics formed around them. Ultimately, the formation of such publics hinges heavily on the publishing path of each: the AppStore, a library's special collection, and an independent press.

A work of immense literary and artistic merit like *ABRA* is not immune to the development affecting the infrastructures on which it relies. In September 2022, when Apple released iOS 16, the iPad app facet became incompatible with the Apple devices it was designed for. The cycles affecting binding media from its earliest examples, as seen in the case of Synapse, continue to undercut the history of hybrid publishing. As the following case study shows, these cycles might be conducive to new editions of binding media, but even that can only promise a few more years of functionality.

**A Family of Works: Stephanie Strickland's *V***
Stephanie Strickland's *V* is one of the few binding media exemplars published in two editions, each comprising a two-part print book and a digital application. The first edition thus included *V: Losing L'una/ WaveSon.nets* in print and the two digital facets *V: Vniverse*, a Shockwave web application developed in collaboration with programmer Cynthia Lawson Jaramillo, and "Errand upon Which We Came," a single digital poem out of *Losing L'una* created in collaboration with electronic literature author M. D. Coverley. The first edition was concurrently published in 2002. *Vniverse* appeared in the *Iowa Review Web*

while Penguin published the print book—two well-recognized venues for poetry and digital poetry.[79] The two parts of the book were bound together as an invertible book with two beginnings. The book's V-fold displays a link to the web facet. The earlier collaboration with Coverley, though still considered part of *V*, was not linked from the main facets: *V: Losing L'una*, *WaveSon.nets*, and *Vniverse*. This first edition of *V* was effectively dead as the Penguin paperback was out of print and unlikely to be reprinted. In parallel, Shockwave was being discontinued, and the *Iowa Review Web* had been gradually sunsetted, that is, intentionally no longer updated to prepare it to go offline. This set of circumstances leading to the waning of *V* prompted Strickland to produce an entire new edition.

The second edition, *V: WaveTercets / Losing L'una*, published by the independent SpringGun Press in 2014, is also an invertible book with two beginnings. The V-fold again displays a link to http://vniverse.com printed in a half circle as if reaching across the gutter. This time around, however, the link takes the reader not directly to the web facet but rather to a landing page with links to the original shockwave *Vniverse* from 2002 and the more recent iPad app developed with Ian Hatcher. A third link takes the reader back to the world of print to SpringGun's website, now offline. While technically the two print books are distinct editions, as are the two digital works, in her "The Death and Re-Distribution of *V*," Strickland speaks of the "six parts" of the work and the many combinatory modes of reading and encounter found in each.[80] This consideration expands the notion of binding media to create cumulative meaning across facets, including multiple editions and remakings of a work over several years.

However, significant differences between the two editions open a window to observe how the general media landscape has changed—first, the development of the iPad, and second, perhaps more insidious, the neglect of poetry publishing by large houses and its newfound home in independent presses. Small details between the two invertible books pose entertaining challenges that speak of the shift in publishing. The cover of the Penguin edition, shown in Figure 17, has identical front

DIGITAL REVOLUTION TO A MATERIAL HISTORY OF HYBRID BOOKS    111

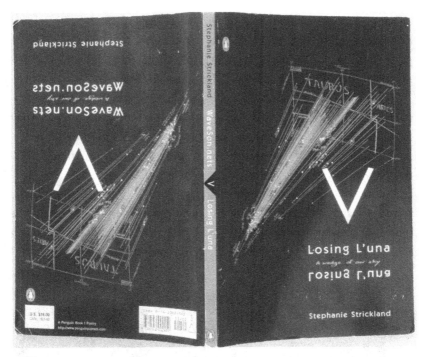

FIGURE 17. Front and back covers of *V: WaveSon.nets / Losing L'una*, published by Penguin. Reproduced with permission.

and back covers except for the titles *Losing L'una* and *WaveSon.nets*. The publishing apparatus, ISBN barcode, US and Canadian price tag, and the unidirectional title on the spine, nonetheless, betray the "back" of the book. In comparison, the cover of the SpringGun edition, shown in Figure 18, has clearly attempted to make the two ends impossible to differentiate as front or back. While the two covers are different, one blue and one purple, neither has any publishing information. The spine's title runs up and down, and the circular link in the V-fold keeps this book rotating around an invisible axis. The imprint information is only found on the copyright page, hidden from the book's outer design. Though it might seem minimal, the extra steps taken by SpringGun following the author's input to create the effect of indistinguishability speak of a more detailed book design that forgoes branding in favor of the work's poetic objectives. While it must have been no small feat to get Penguin to publish a reversible book, the press's conventions ultimately undermined the conceptual principles of the work.

Across its two editions and corresponding facets, *V* proposes a "nomadic" form of reading.[81] As is the case with Strickland's poetry, print or digital, associations among themes and concepts are key to understanding her work. *V* is no exception. Among the foci found here are astronomy, tarot, fertility, reflections on the philosophies of Simone Weil, and more. All come together through the motif of the constellation, the primary visual concept. *V: Vniverse,* both the web application and the iPad app, presents a dark background with bright white dots simulating a starry night sky. In the web application, interaction with each "star"

FIGURE 18. Front and back covers of *V: WaveTercets / Losing L'una*, published by SpringGun. Reproduced with permission.

exposes a stanza we can read in connection to other stars as a constellation yielding a "Son.net." We can also read them as stand-alone mini poems whose meaning develops as other stanzas appear. In contrast, in the iPad app, individual stanzas are not visible; they are only visible in connection to others as constellations. Each of the stars, nevertheless, uncovers a keyword to the stanzas. In both editions, exploratory reading is a requirement to advance significance and affect differently.[82] Nonetheless, each facet's interactive reading is quite different as the Shockwave application is based on hovering over the stars with a cursor to read the stanzas and clicking on them to reveal the constellations. In contrast, the iPad application is based on tapping, drawing, and three predetermined paths of reading, a run through all the "Tercets," the "Constellation," and the "Oracle" modes.

In addition to the interactive dynamics changing from the Shockwave to the iPad application, the poems in print underwent a transformation, too. *WaveSon.nets* in the 2002 edition became *WaveTercets* in the 2014 edition. The poetic form of the sonnet, although not strictly observed in the 2002 edition, was reworked to fit the iPad's screen specs and to allow Strickland to revisit the collection according to shifts in reading sensibilities and media that took place over a decade:

> The "new" text of the Tercets is in fact the original form in which *V* was written, one long standing wave of numbered units that did not align page or unit boundaries with punctuated closure—a long scrolling that, at the time, I felt was not appropriate for a codex. Current familiarity both with scrolling and with small numbered units used online to track location have since changed expectations in the codex environment.[83]

Aside from wanting to resurrect *V*, it seems that Strickland saw an opportunity to present the poem from two new vantage points—a redistribution of its parts and poetics—which, nonetheless, continue to be bound in each edition and across editions. In their account of the poem's creative process, Lawson-Jaramillo and Strickland reflect upon how "the whole distributed poem turns to talk to itself."[84] That was certainly the case in the first edition and continues cumulatively through the second. Further, as Strickland and Hatcher explain a decade later, "to move from one platform to another, from a Flash to an iPad environment, is to affect the meaning of directionality, trajectory, and haptic space."[85] The various reading dynamics migrating from the web to the iPad and from sonnet to tercet all contribute to different associations, echoes, and rhythms in the poems.

In the case of V, the same technological and market contexts that rendered it obsolete and caused it to go out of print yielded the circumstances that allowed independent publishing to flourish and to become a home for nonmainstream poetry. These shifts are also the engines behind Strickland's further poetic innovation built upon new reader expectations and abilities. The two editions of V suggest this transition in publishing very clearly. As Claire Grossman, Juliana Spahr, and Stephanie Young explain of other experimental poetry endeavors, "the market-distant aesthetics of Flarf poetry or conceptual writing could not have appeared without the decentralized world of small-press publishing that emerged in response to both technological changes and publishing house consolidation."[86] This was also the scenario that brought V back to print. Looking back to 2002, the publication of V by Penguin seems to have indicated that digital writing was on the brink of mainstreaming. As Chris Funkhouser notes in his review of the first edition, the fact "that a publisher like Penguin has produced the book is among many signals that the accelerated graphical capabilities of the computer are influencing printed collections."[87] As we know, that continues to be an unfulfilled fate in commercial publishing. Indeed, the cycle of enthusiasm and retrenchment seen at other moments when commentators touted binding media as the future of the book repeated itself once again.

The reviews of the first edition help reconstruct this rise and fall through an emphasis on form that crosses contemporary reviews for good and evil. Reviewers outside of digital literary circles, in venues like *Publisher's Weekly* and the *Los Angeles Times*, saw V as a novel form in established poetry channels because of its simultaneous web publication. For example, Michael Scharf, writing for *Publisher's Weekly*, praised Strickland for continuing "to blaze trails of possibility in a new poetic medium" and "bringing intelligence and legitimacy to a new form."[88] In contrast, on the radar of more conventional poetry reviewers, Strickland and Lawson Jaramillo's work was subjected to critiques that, being unfamiliar with the workings of digital literature, failed to see how the specific reading conditions of the web instance informed the overall conceptualization of the poems and thought it superficial. One critic, in particular, bitterly claimed that the "novelty of design" in *V* constituted a wink to those who "unthinkingly fetishize innovation as if it were some kind of moral or political imperative."[89] Most likely indicative of different poetic tastes and levels of digital literacy, these divergent opinions appear symptomatic of the recurring lack of specific media protocols and of a knowledgeable reading public. Likewise, they suggest an absence of actual and symbolic buy-in for hybrid works. The commercial impetus of the publishing industry, as well as the innovation impetus of the tech industry, hinders the long process of accruing symbolic value and the public's ability to become familiar with new poetic media forms before they become obsolete.

### Luis Correa-Díaz's *metaverse* of (Un-)*clickable poem@s*

Like *ABRA* and *V*, Luis Correa-Díaz's "clickable poem@s" is a project encompassing the author's creative practice for several years across publication media. Individual poems have appeared in web venues, including *Círculo de poesía: Revista electrónica de literatura*, and *Ecozon@: Revista europea de literatura, cultura y medioamiente*. Similarly, a virtual-reality version of "poema-drone" appeared in the online exhibition "Nuevos mundos posibles / Brave New Mesh." Ultimately, RiL Editores in Santiago, Chile, published "clickable poem@s" in two augmented-reality print books, *clickable poem@s* (2016) and *metaverse* (2021). In addition to being a specific collection of poems, as a poetic practice, the "clickable poem@" is Correa-Díaz's aesthetic project of staging a conversation between human and machine language. Thus, in addition to the eponymous collection, the practice extends to later publications.

The intent of coupling human and machine languages expands into the themes of the poems as well, where the author investigates how the proliferation of technoscientific developments and the explosion of available (mis)information have impacted human sensitivities and imagination through the growing popularization of digital media.

Thematically, the collections seem, at times, a social media feed dedicated to the latest technoscientific innovation. Correa-Díaz takes issues like the colonization of Mars, people's dependence on digital devices, climate change, the Higgs boson, algorithmic logics, or drones as a starting point to review instances of (post)human conditions in the twenty-first century. Upon that basis, the author rethinks the poet's role in dealing with fundamental concerns of our times and the near future. In Correa-Díaz, we see a tense outlook, between utopia and dystopia, about the future (in a speculative present) in the face of aging, degenerative disease, and death.

Correa-Díaz makes this possible at the text level by interspersing hyperlinks and verses. As the name indicates, these poems are meant to be interacted with by clicking. In the web poems, the hyperlinks prompt readers to click them as they reach them, for example, at the end of a stanza. This motion redirects the reader from the web poem, most commonly, to resources on YouTube. Following the links takes the reader to a wide range of contents with various purposes: music acting as a soundtrack to the poems, short documentaries serving as annotations or footnotes, or fragments of films functioning as prequels and sequels to the scenes depicted in the poems. As such, the "poem@s" are realized at the meeting point between the regular textual poem and the information readers are sent to explore—in the back-and-forth movement between the two texts. Correa-Díaz makes the contrast between human language and machine language more evident by using not "hot links" (natural language words standing in for a hyperlink) but the whole URL beginning with the "http://" protocol and usually ending with an alphanumeric sequence. This way, these poems' verses are composed of natural language and machine-readable code. Further, as web poems, the back-and-forth in the "clickable poem@s" takes place all in the space of the browser screen, even if across several tabs and windows.

The relatively uncomplicated "clickable poem@s" would see a radical material transformation when edited as a collection in print. In the first place, printing the "poem@s" entails a split between the space occupied by the text of the poems and that of their complementary online content. They migrate from the space of the screen alone, to a hybrid interface of print and screen. The hyperlinks, printed on the page, become inky vestiges of the previous materiality of the "poem@s." Although readers could type the long, printed URL on their browser's address bar, in practice, this would likely be awkward and even, perhaps, inaccessible. Aware of this complication, the editors at RiL added QR codes to the hyperlinks. In an editors' note, they state, "In order to facilitate the reading experience, we have incorporated QR codes associated with every link the author adds to his poems. Readers can opt to type up the link or scan the code if they have a smartphone and a QR reading app handy."[90] Interestingly, the editors' note acknowledges an ambiguity in the readers' technological and poetic sensibilities. While it reveals a concern that potential readers might not own a smartphone, the note is ambiguous by assuming that poetry readers might not be tech-savvy or even signaling that the editors don't quite know who the readers of these "poem@s" might be. Therefore, including both the print hyperlinks and the QR codes suggests a "solution" for a lingering digital divide and the intent to do a labor of digital literacy outreach to all possible readers. As shown in Figure 19, RiL's approach impacts the layout of the "poem@s," highlighting their material hybridity much more than when they were web-based.

A second implication of the material transformation of the "poem@s," both in *clickable poem@s* and in *metaverse*, is the ontological change of our interaction with them. No longer clickable, the poems in print become scannable. Inactive links that make the page appear as a static version of a web browser become pages on which a digital device can operate. Certainly, the poems' activation still depends on a reader scanning and following the code; however, while we can squint

118   CHAPTER TWO

to decipher where the URLs will take us, the QR codes are exclusively machine-readable.

In *metaverse*, published five years after *clickable poem@s*, the printed hyperlinks were abandoned in favor of QR codes alone. This time, RiL added no editors' note to accompany the decision. An unattributed note—likely written by Correa-Díaz—in *metaverse* reflects upon this change: "these poem@s have been modified / from their original versions / they were intended to be displayed / in widescreen format / that one of the deep sky to be precise."[91] Stripped of the URLs, the "poem@s" in *metaverse*, unlike those in *clickable poem@s*, seem to

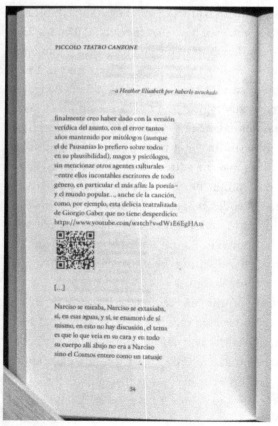

FIGURE 19. A page from *clickable poem@s* shows both printed links and their corresponding QR codes. Reprinted with permission.

want to forget their earlier web materiality. Without the language of the URLs accessible to both human and machine readers, Correa-Díaz and RiL propose a hybrid space where the page and the screen, and human and machine readers exist on a parallel plane. In this way, the author encodes the cadence of his "poem@s," the rhythm in which they are meant to be read in the interstices and movements from one book object to the other. As an effect of that movement, the collections become a constant process of intermediation, a materiality that emerges and is contingent on the availability of the linked contents. The signature at the end of the collection, "all new clickable poem@s sent from my iPhone," rounds up the metaphor of the printed page as the screen's double.[92] Moreover, it is possible to speculate that the time between the two "poem@" collections rendered the printed hyperlinks unnecessary. The deep penetration of smartphone technology all over Latin America would suggest that the readers have the tools needed to read the "poem@s" and, therefore, it is more likely that they would do so via QR code than on a web browser.[93] Moreover, it is possible to see how the poems in the first collection served to establish the literacy required to read them. No longer an experiment, a novelty, or a first foray for RiL in print-digital publishing, after *clickable poem@s*, the editors could better assess their readers' competencies and toolset, and propose a less ambiguous publishing modality.

Expectedly, at the time of writing, many of the contents linked to from the "poem@s" have been taken down from their original platforms. This absence further amplifies the poetics of decay in Correa-Díaz's work and confirms the fragility of the digital facets in binding media even when they "live" in giant corporate platforms that falsely give the impression of reliability.

**Authors as Secondary Publishers**
As the examination of *ABRA*, *V*, *clickable poem@s*, and *metaverse* shows, although obsolescence, incompatibility, and link rot have curtailed these projects to a certain extent, the poetic and publishing projects can hardly be said to have failed. These poetic endeavors have utilized

the affordances of the technologies available at the time despite their later discontinuation. Arguably, their literary success owes much to their publishing environments and how they have changed since the days of Synapse & Brøderbund. On the one hand, 1913, SpringGun, and RiL have embraced these creative endeavors and helped the authors fulfill their literary purposes via book design and production. The funding and context offered by CBPA similarly helped Borsuk, Durbin, and Hatcher to develop media-specific manifestations of *ABRA*'s poetic voice beyond their initial ideations. Yet, none of the publishers (or the funders) has accepted the responsibility of hosting or maintaining the digital facets. Maintenance and updating of the iPad apps have remained the responsibility of the authors. In the case of *ABRA* and *V*, their longevity has already been, at least in part, foreshortened. In the case of *clickable poem@s*, the online contents are left to the uneven and uncertain flux of user-created content on YouTube, a situation that simultaneously results in substantial link rot and the incorporation of that loss as part of its posthuman poetics of decay. This new role undertaken by the authors of these and many other examples of binding media could be characterized as that of a secondary publisher. Author involvement in independent publishing is a feature built into the presses' workflows; however, in the case of binding media, this involvement goes well beyond the design, the printing, and the release of the print books.[94]

The fact that independent presses do not participate in the production or maintenance of the digital facets of their published books could signal another moment of retrenchment, an acceptance, and perhaps even a resignation, of the impossibility of "reinvent[ing] the book" as a hybrid of print and digital materials from within publishing practices, workflows, processes, and budgets. Moreover, this split publishing model appears to follow the "feminization" trend of the publishing industry—the shifting of labor onto unpaid and contingent actors, as seen on publishing platforms like Wattpad.[95] Regarding online presence and social media adoptions, as Simone Murray has noted, authors have been put in a position to shoulder the "burden of publicizing and marketing their own work" through "digital accoutrements" such as blogs and social media accounts.[96] As seen above, in binding media, this burden deepens with the responsibility of ensuring works' availability, accessibility, and preservation. Aside from the publishing industry's trends, it is worth noting that this model follows the practice of electronic literature, which has historically, more often than not, been created, published, and maintained outside of commercial channels, especially on the web.

These tendencies, however, don't tell the whole story. Although some aspects, like the precarization of digital labor, are undeniable across the creative industries, the labor of writers responsible for the digital facets of their works is not exactly comparable to that of publicizing their brand on social media. Digital facets are in no way a stopover on the way to securing a book deal. Instead, I argue that the split publishing model indicates an acknowledgment on the part of writers and publishers of the distinct production processes and temporalities of each medium. These, additionally, include the motley of expertises necessary to create and publish binding media. This shift would amount to an instance of media divergence rather than convergence. By separating the publication and distribution of print and digital facets, independent presses are not only being cautious of the financial threats that digital production could pose for them and the obsolescent works themselves. They are also aware of the very distinct technical expertises and production workflows hybrid publishing requires, but, along with authors, they are also positioning their craft and their books in a media ecology that does not follow a conglomerate logic where all types of content are managed and produced under a single house in a manner that follows a predetermined model. The production split, therefore, favors the creative endeavors of authors and presses that otherwise would likely have to resort to a limiting, preestablished platform or forgo projects like *ABRA*, *V*, and *clickable poem@s*.

**Building a Public for Binding Media**
With few exceptions, expanded and augmented books have not become a publishing standard. While market fluctuations, mergers, and rapidly obsolescent technology are powerful reasons that underlie the demise of

so many initiatives, one more crucial consideration is the deliberate creation of a public for hybrid books. Comprising almost exclusively works of literature that are experimental to some extent, binding media have carved a niche in independent publishing and built an incipient audience thanks to their bespoke narrative and material poetic mechanisms. Independent publishing, with its established focus on minor genres like experimental literature and poetry, offers a built-in route for hybrid works to find their public. Though uneven in size, editorial approaches, business model, prestige, language, and geographic location, independent publishers have flourished because they have created the reading publics that sustain them. Editor Matthew Stadler has proposed that a publisher's most important issue is making "new and lasting publics" based on "the quality of relationships, not on their number."[97] Similarly, Spanish scholar Ana Gallego Cuiñas identifies community building, particularly reading communities, as a characteristic of the production strategies in independent publishing.[98] These relationships are not mediated just between editors or presses and readers but pass through the published titles and, crucially, the authors. The creation of reading publics is another way in which, despite market unviability, binding media have arguably been successful at changing our ideas of what a book might be. Material interrogations such as those found in binding media are strategies through which independent presses assert their nonconformity with respect to commercial publishers.

In this series of relations, that publishers and authors split the production of binding media appears as a mutually advantageous proposal even when it might be a defensive response to the imperative of innovation, short returns of investment of the industry, and the precarization of digital labor. To use Bourdieu's terminology, there is a reciprocal transfer of symbolic capital. On one side, independent publishers are no longer at risk due to digital applications' production and maintenance costs as they were in the 1980s and 1990s. Yet, they partake in technologically innovative projects that put forward new forms of the book. On the other side, authors whose work might have only existed in the vast world of the web and away from established venues like book fairs enter the world of books and publishing with their established paradigms and protocols. By having a physical substrate—print book, storage medium—binding media gain a longer, albeit only partial, lifespan than their fully digital counterparts.

**Where the Book Has Been Reinvented**
Despite the many "failures" in attempts to reinvent a hegemonic new form of the book, in the mid-2020s it is impossible to deny that digital technologies have deeply and definitively impacted the form of the book. Whether at the time of composition and production, preservation, engagement, distribution, copyright, and so forth, the digital revolution in publishing is part of our cultural imaginary.[99] As I write these pages, the popular releases of artificial intelligence (AI) applications promise to instantly produce entire new works ready to enter the flow of publishing, and have unleashed a plethora of issues from copyright to authorship. Less obvious, however, is how new forms of the book, like binding media, are similar to or different from other, adjacent book forms that may or may not be more successful within the publishing industry. In addition to the evidence left in the residues of binding media creation, production, and distribution, there is another place where the changes to the book seen in the last few decades are definitive: the updating and rewriting of legal definitions of the book.

Legal definitions of books serve as frameworks to regulate the publishing industry and its place as a commercial endeavor that can heavily impact a country's socioeconomic, scientific, cultural, and technological development.[100] Book laws often seek to ensure information and education access, on the one hand, and thus argue in favor of the freedom to write, edit, publish, distribute, and sell books.[101] On the other hand, book laws seek to boost the viability of books as salable commodities and, thus, sometimes favor the establishment of government loans to make the publishing industry and associated guilds competitive and current.[102] Expectedly, as all of these aspects of book production and distribution have been touched by the digital, so have the laws around them confirming and sustaining these shifts in the industry. More interesting is how amendments to these laws have entailed the redefinition of books to include e-books and other forms of digital and hybrid publishing. A brief review of book laws across Latin American countries reveals these gradual changes. For example, as early as 1993, Chile passed "Ley 19227 Del Fondo Nacional de Fomento del Libro y la Lectura." There, a book is defined as:

> Every unitary, print, non-periodical publication edited fully at once or in intervals of one or various volumes or fascicles, including scientific, academic, or professional publications issued no more frequently than bimonthly, and which fulfill any of the objectives established in the first paragraph of the previous article. *It will also comprehend the complementary or accessory materials of electronic, computational, visual or auditive nature produced simultaneously as units that cannot be sold separately.*[103]

The more recent "Ley 21045," passed in 2017, while proposing a whole reconceptualization of culture, arts, and patrimony in Chile, makes minimal changes to the articles dealing with the book.[104] In Mexico, "Ley de fomento para la lectura y el libro," passed in 2008, establishes a legal definition of the book very similar to the Chilean one:

> Every unitary non-periodical publication of literary, artistic, scientific, technical, educational, informative, or recreational character printed in any medium and whose edition may be done fully at once or in intervals in various volumes or fascicles. It also comprehends *the complementary materials in any medium, including electronic ones, that comprise, jointly with the book, a unitary whole that may not be sold separately.*[105]

As laws continue to change in various areas of the world, an awareness of the ongoing changes to the form of the book is encoded. A telling example of this is the 2015 Venezuelan "Ley del Sistema Social del Libro y la Lectura," under public consultation since then, which encompasses among its definitions of the book "digital, electronic, and multimedia books," and, tellingly, "other formats and media *already created or yet to be created.*"[106]

Perhaps more striking about most of these examples is the notion of complementary materials as part of the book. In contrast to Venezuelan law, which contemplates new and not yet existing media, the idea of complementary materials seems to offer a stopgap solution to the issue of proliferating book forms. Crucially, too, the laws establish that print books and complementary materials must be sold together *as a unit*. This legal tendency seems to have even older roots. As seen in Figure 13, Uruguayan "Ley 15.913" was passed in 1987. Interestingly, even when it does not yet consider digital publishing as such, it already takes "materials, complementary in nature to the book that are sold together with it."[107] Further, the emphasis on complementary materials to be sold with the book hints at a media and economic panorama adjusting to transmedia practices where separate sets of laws rule the various cultural and entertainment industries involved.

---

In the complex landscape of market conglomeration, technological innovation, obsolescence, and, crucially, the absence of cultural protocols established around hybrid publishing, it becomes clear that it is up to small initiatives to push innovative forms of the book that engage with the material conditions that make them possible. The cycles of enthusiasm and retrenchment that characterize the period considered here are full of contrasts. Big publishers take fewer formal risks and are willing to abandon costly initiatives quickly, while independent ones take them in a controlled yet still risky fashion. The remaining question is whether hybrid publishing—or, simply, digital publishing—will become established beyond the e-book. The existence of successful niches in publishing and literature, like binding media, relying on the vibrancy of independent publishing suggests it already has. In that sense, and as Bourdieu would have it, these small endeavors "may not exercise much influence in the field," but they will play a "crucial role in [the field's] transformation," and one only needs to look in the right places to find it.[108]

The history of hybrid and expanded publishing I have outlined in this chapter reveals that there is much to learn from the study of "failed" initiatives. Unlike Thompson's focus on the establishment of new stable protocols and decisive moments of shift in the publishing industry, the history of hybrid publishing is one of *longue durée* processes riddled with stumbles and leading to many dead ends of cultural change. Even more so, binding media are illustrative of current trends in the publishing industry and of marginal shifts that might not gain much attention because they haven't been widely adopted. That, as a phenomenon, binding media has a history with material, artistic, and legal traces spanning over forty years indicates that, despite cycles of enthusiasm and retrenchment, hybrid publishing as practice, as bibliographic object, and as aesthetic and publishing ambitions, even if in the margins, is already an established and recurrent book form that must be considered a part of the contemporary history of the book.

THREE

# DIVERGENT TEMPORALITIES IN BINDING MEDIA

**RESEARCHING BINDING MEDIA IS A** constant dynamic of catching up with newly published works while holding on to others that are about to go offline or become obsolete. The cycles of innovation and retrenchment that have marked the histories of hybrid publishing, seen in chapter 2, have a parallel in the study of digital literatures and art in general. Binding media, nevertheless, are a bit different in that once computers can't read disks, and digital applications go offline, we are left with their residual print halves. In studying binding media, in the last few years, I found myself adjusting my methodologies to the specificities of print and obsolescent digital objects. I depended on labs and centers with the appropriate infrastructure to read decades-old disks, relied on circulating library collections, and even surrendered to media decay. These approaches led me to reflect on how I experienced the passage of time very differently when examining ten-year-old pieces of digital literature and when I close-read poems published in print books three decades ago. Eventually, it dawned on me that these differences emerged out of the distinct temporalities embedded in print and digital objects. Here, I understand temporality not as the measurable passage of time but, following media theorist Sarah Sharma, as the specific experience or perception of time structured by objects and their contexts. Binding media manifest two divergent temporalities because they comprise distinct print and digital objects. For example, it's not just that print and digital media have different shelf-lives; it's also that the time scales on which they age and, thus, accrue cultural value are radically different. It only takes a few years for software to become incompatible with newer devices or downright obsolete, that is, of the past; whereas print books and literature published ten or fifteen years ago can easily be considered contemporary, that is, of the present.

These divergent temporalities are not natural to each medium. They result from how the corporate, cultural, academic, and other contexts that produce these objects and assign value to them order time. Therefore, examining the divergent temporalities of binding media—the temporal juncture of these distinct media yoked in a singular cultural object—entails what Sharma characterizes as an "awareness of power relations as they play out in time" and an examination of how "a specific experience of time . . . is structured in specific political and economic contexts."[1] Following Sharma, we can see how binding media have been tangled up in the tech industry's imperatives of innovation and planned obsolescence, and short-term returns that have spread through academia and the cultural and memory sectors in recent decades. Due to planned obsolescence, binding media are constantly relegated to the realm of ephemera. Because they're ephemeral, they are less susceptible to being incorporated into the longer processes that would make them replicable or standardizable. Through binding media, we can appreciate that the imperative of short-term returns encoded in planned obsolescence is an exercise in economic power that manifests temporally through the deliberately rapid decay of digital media. Moreover, the divergent temporalities of binding media present conceptual and methodological challenges for their study. I argue that the ephemerality of binding media keeps them from accruing cultural value even within the specialized circles of digital literary studies and contemporary book studies.

In this chapter, I approach these divergent temporalities in binding media to examine how imperatives of technological development have impacted technocultural memory-building, the sense of historicity in contemporary cultural objects, and the production and scholarship of digital literature. I scrutinize binding media as the technocultural products of an elongated present, a recent past, and a receding future. Specifically, I query how the divergent temporalities of print and digital objects help us theorize binding media in terms of their history and the memory they facilitate. To embark on this examination, I first examine the temporal context at the center of the temporal divergences of binding media as one of "presentism." As I elaborate, the linear, progressive, and omniscient sense of the present that characterizes the perception of time at the turn of the twenty-first century illuminates the ephemerality of binding media.[2] As historian François Hartog has theorized, the examination of presentism reveals a "gap between a digital presentism . . . and the world's other temporalities" where conflicts and discontinuities expose relations of power affecting the lifespan and valuation of cultural objects.[3] I then examine the temporal paradoxes of binding media resulting from presentist practices in the tech industry that, I argue, have been at odds with literary methodologies of study. From there, I explore how this form of presentism has shaped our cultural understanding of the temporality of digital media by equating functionality and operability as *of the present,* and obsolescence and inoperability as *of the past.* Most, if not all, scholars of digital literature will starkly oppose this linear form of thinking as it precludes the accrual of literary and cultural value befitting literary works. However, methodologically, the study of digital literature and other contemporary cultural production depends on—and struggles with maintaining—the stability of its objects of study.[4] It's not hard to see this in the necessary efforts to preserve works of digital literature. The presentism of technological development impacts (and maybe even directs) a remedial management of the temporalities of digital media to fit methodologies like close reading and archiving that conventionally rely on various degrees of fixity. That is, there is a divergent temporality between the methodologies of literary inquiry and that of the digital literary objects of study.

This technocultural landscape prompts us to imagine alternative ways of memory-building and history-making that are not just recorded *in* media objects but expressed *through* such media objects and their residues. Due to their hybrid materiality and their divergent temporalities, I see binding media as offering the perfect opportunity to step out of habits of linear thinking and to historicize obsolescent literary and artistic works not as exemplars of the recent past, but as latent objects that help us document the very processes of aging and decay of digital media. That is, through their partial residues, binding media can lead us to find meanings that we might not find through fully functional pieces of digital literature. As cultural geographer Caitlin DeSilvey has put it in relation to the deterioration of structures and buildings, "encroaching absence may paradoxically facilitate the persistence of memory and significance."[5] Ultimately, I am interested in showing how the materiality of binding media and its encoded temporalities bring to the forefront the various conflicting interests woven into these cultural objects and how they form a basis to think past the presentism of digital technologies and to outline a better sense of the contemporary and of memory in digital literature. Thus, the chapter seeks to mark a methodological shift in our consideration of digital literature that is not precluded by obsolescence and absences but made possible by it.

I examine these proposals through works that explore various senses of time and historicity. American scholar and game designer Ian Bogost's *A Slow Year* (2010) builds a faithful reconstruction of a recent past. In contrast, J. R. Carpenter's *The Gathering Cloud* (2016–17), and two works by Mexican writer and artist Verónica Gerber Bicecci, "La máquina distópica" (2018; cocreated with artists and programmers Canek Zapata and Carlos Bergen) and *La compañía* (2019), add depth to the present by showcasing how the past continues to be relevant. These authors advance aesthetic and poetic proposals that allow us to ponder the complexity of the history of technology. They expose various divergent senses of temporality through writing techniques like palimpsestic composition, material documentation, and fastening media objects together that push linear time into crisis.

## The Cultural Shift toward Presentism

The shifts in the perception of temporality are not unique to the digital media and tech industries that rely on the constant churning of content and products that rapidly cycle in and out of vision, but rather mark a generalized cultural change taking place at the turn of the twenty-first century. Many thinkers, including Paul Virilio, Andreas Huyssen, Jesús Martín-Barbero, Giorgio Agamben, and François Hartog, have theorized various manifestations of these temporal shifts, such as the cultural obsession with memory, the thinning of the sense of the present, the loss of confidence in the idea of future progress, the acceleration of time, the emergence of "real-time," and others. Far from affecting the production of culture alone, the changes in the perception of temporality are so profound and prevalent that these thinkers have heralded a "change of epoch"[6] or a new "regime of historicity."[7] Taking shape since the 1960s but coming into full form in the 1980s, the acceleration of time observed by these thinkers has followed neoliberal imperatives of moving capital as quickly and efficiently as possible, which, in turn, is a result of the convergence of globalization, the pursuit of rapid returns, and the growth of consumer culture. Simultaneously, to fulfill such imperatives, the acceleration of time has fostered fast technological innovation and the popularization of digital information and communication technologies. "Speed," as Sarah Sharma notes, is a "byproduct of a mutually reinforcing complex that includes global capital, real-time communication technologies, military technologies, and scientific research on human bodies."[8] As a result of this acceleration, a paradoxical relationship with the past and the sense of history has taken shape. Jesús Martín-Barbero and Andreas Huyssen have observed a "memory boom" in the creation of new museums, memorials, and documentaries; the celebration of anniversaries; and the proliferation of testimonial and historical narratives that respond to the sense of loss and amnesia.[9] A more eerie conceptualization is Paul Virilio's "tyranny of the real time" as the universalization of a "one-time system," obeying not just the imperatives of capitalism but also those of the military.[10]

For François Hartog, the cultural changes in the relationships between past, present, and future constitute a new regime of historicity that privileges the present, the immediate, and the ephemeral. "Presentism," he explains, "has neither a past nor a future, this present daily fabricates the past and future it requires."[11] In this contemporary form of presentism, Hartog continues, "the present became something immense, invasive, and omnipresent, blocking out any other viewpoint ... The present was already past before it had completely taken place."[12] Thus, presentism paradoxically encompasses both the thinness of the new (the instantaneous and the ephemeral) and the expansion of a present horizon that moves at an accelerated pace. Moving at such speed, the present prefigures its futurization and historicization right as it happens.[13] These temporal formulations are likely recognizable for many in the constant cycle of technological innovation—each development hailed as revolutionary and game-changing—and in the representation of every social and political event as "once in a lifetime" and unprecedented. The objects and events of the present become historical right as they happen. "Hence," writes Hartog, "the world appears to us already as a set of museum pieces. Torn between amnesia and the desire to leave nothing out, we try to foresee today the museum of tomorrow and to assemble today's archives as though it were already yesterday."[14]

Martín-Barbero argues that objects themselves and their obsolescence are central to the changes in the perception of time and history. For him, it is not just a matter of how obsolescence is the means through which the tech industry reproduces itself and achieves its short-term returns; it is also a mechanism that causes media objects to fail to accumulate cultural memory.[15] Beyond the instrumentality of media objects to convey discourses of ephemerality and acceleration, the objects themselves no longer accumulate a material memory—a form of memory that Martín-Barbero understands as a common ground between users across different generations and one that supports a shared experience of history between them. As they are of the present for shorter and shorter periods, new media objects are recognizable only to small groups of people rather than being relevant to various generations, thus weakening a sense of "pastness" and compressing the sense of "presentness." Over these bases, the Colombian historian characterizes present-day media as amnesiac—increasingly incapable of bridging our consciousness of the (recent) past into the present, opening a gap between them instead.[16] In this way, the present is simultaneously indebted to the past, by producing an ever truncated legacy that works only to explain the present, and to the future, by failing to produce it (and, indeed, by endangering it) through short-term thinking. Agamben brings this point further into focus when he states that the contemporary present "always takes the form of an ungraspable threshold between a 'not yet' and a 'no more.'"[17] The production of memory is thus not symptomatic of a resurgence or revalorization of the past but teleological—that which makes "the present present to itself."[18] As a historical condition, presentism influences how we perceive time and what we as a culture conceive of as of present, future, or historical value. We see the manifestations of presentism encoded in the goods we purchase, the information we receive, and the media we use to communicate.

Sarah Sharma has warned against uncritically taking the acceleration of time as a condition that evenly affects everything and everyone. For her, the normalization of "speed" as an uncontestable reality overlooks the experiences of lived time and the emergence of multiple temporalities.[19] Thus, to critically engage with presentism or the acceleration of time, it is necessary to examine how multiple temporalities, that is, experiences and perceptions of time, can enter into conflict due to cultural politics and the economics of time. The examples studied in chapter 2 show that it is the economics of time that proved damning for initiatives like Voyager's Expanded Books as it underlays the distinct market logics of book production and software development in the early decades of hybrid publishing. The same temporal conflicts continue to force authors and publishers to declare the "end of life" of iPad apps that are not recently updated but are still functional.[20] This economics of time allows us to see the temporal divergences of the print and digital facets of binding media as outcomes of the material conditions in which they are produced instead of as inherent qualities emerging from their objectual materiality. Indeed, I would argue that, as a corpus, binding media shape particular experiences of time during an extended cultural moment as their material objects punctually indicate the specific technocultural moments that yielded them.[21] Because of the cycles of enthusiasm and retrenchment, as seen in the previous chapter, it's clear that binding media repeatedly become ephemeral products of a compressed present; their moment of creation and publication stands as a fast-passing present that rapidly becomes the past. As I examine in the book's conclusion, this is also true in recent developments like the fast rise and fall of NFTs—their ostensibly revolutionary promises have *not yet* been fulfilled as the entire crypto art market is close to being *no more*.

The divergent temporalities surrounding binding media demand a consideration of their construction as historical and literary subjects. It is certainly possible to see binding media and hybrid publishing more generally as future-looking endeavors that *haven't yet* entirely consolidated. Others might argue that they are passé novelties, souvenirs, and gimmicks of the recent past.[22] But embroiled in the ephemerality of the tech industry, we must not lose sight of the literary and bibliographic relevance of hybrid publishing, whose future might still be open. Media theorist Lisa Gitelman's description of the distinct endurance of art, science, and media objects as historical subjects is useful to consider the temporal divergences of binding media. The objects that make up the history of art, no matter how ancient or how much tastes have changed, are still considered art. Conversely, scientific objects of the past are often not part of contemporary science. The construction of media as a historical subject, the temporality of media, is more complicated because it encompasses attributes of both art and scientific objects. Even when they become the interest of antiquarians alone, old media remain "recognizable as media." However, the currency of media depends not just on their functionality but also on their adequacy to do their "job" while staying commodifiable.[23] The temporalities outlined by Gitelman foreground the messy juncture where we find binding media: some of these temporalities belong to media objects (books and hardware), and others belong to art objects. The point is that these are complex historical subjects and that their conflicting temporalities raise conceptual questions in addition to the methodological ones outlined above. For instance, what is the impact of the technological impermanence of digital literary applications on the longevity and accrual of literary value of binding media? Clearly, the temporality of digital media has already impacted the durability and accessibility of these literary works. The planned obsolescence built into digital media and thus into digital literature forces a precarization of the literary. As literary scholarship relies on various levels of objectual stability and fixity that enable approaches like close reading, anthologizing, and archiving, the temporality and materiality of digital media present serious challenges and may even preclude such endeavors under current established practices and protocols. I will come back to the issue of digital preservation below. For now, I emphasize that the use of print facets side by side with digital applications in binding media must transform our perception of planned obsolescence by simply doing what print has culturally evolved to do best—remaining readable and providing access that nonfunctional storage media or devices may deny without significant intervention.

It is difficult to shake off the anxieties of presentism when studying binding media and other forms of digital literature. As a scholar of digital literature, I feel the urgency to keep my objects of study in and of the present through constant updating, collection, preservation, and anthologizing efforts. However, the attempts at maintaining digital literary works are continuously confronted by the disappointment caused when works go offline, the AppStore stops supporting iPad apps, and disks become unreadable. Indeed, I would argue that the experiences of time embedded in the materiality of digital literature have conditioned artists and scholars to internalize the terms of ephemerality and obsolescence as a condition of possibility for our objects of study.[24] Undeniably, it is one of the features of their materiality. But particularly in the many cases where obsolescence is not thematized or part of an aesthetic project, following Sharma, we should pause to query the temporality embedded in planned obsolescence not just technically but critically and conceptually. While internalizing these paradoxes might seem like a methodological imperative, a feature of binding media and other forms of digital literature themselves, we must remain alert to how these literary objects are pieces of economic and power structures that might put their study at risk of dismissal and irrelevance. Reviewing how binding media manifest their temporalities is helpful to appreciate the shifting power/temporal relations among media ecologies. Later in the chapter, I use this consideration to reevaluate the primacy of functionality as a condition for literary study and to propose that residuality can be a conduit for memory-building and a way of breaking the technological imperative of planned obsolescence.

## The Temporalities of Binding Media

One of the most readily visible temporal discontinuities in binding media and the adjacent history of augmented and expanded books is their intended or attributed capacity to herald the future of the book.[25] The belief in the futurity of these publishing initiatives is not extraordinary. We can find its origin in longstanding cultural imaginaries of progress and development surrounding science and technology, in general, and computing and digital media, more specifically.[26] Nevertheless, because the tech industry depends on constantly surpassing previous developments to produce new ones, it is also a prolific producer of recent pasts.

Many binding media examples have followed similar trajectories. Exemplars with web-based applications have, at least in part, been lost to changes in browser affordances and website discontinuation. Binding media published in diskettes and CD-ROMs, though still functional with the proper infrastructure, are now mainly the realm of vintage computing and media archaeology. Although it is still possible to locate physical copies in libraries and, less and less often, for sale, works examined in this book, like Stephanie Strickland's *V: Vniverse*, are both out of print and inoperable on the web and the iPad; Belén Gache's web version of *El libro del fin del mundo, Wordtoys*, had to be fully restored to continue working on present-day browsers. Rather than becoming a future of the book, the bulk of these projects, companies, and publications have turned into its recent history, yielding them as the realm of a new "digital antiquarianism" as objects of study that require further specialization.[27]

The paradoxical temporalities of these hybrid publishing initiatives are not naturally occurring. They obey a market that pushes for non-stop innovation and constant short-term returns. Caught between the longer processes of digital production and maintenance, and the imperative to make quick profits, publishers have been unable to ensure the viability of hybrid publishing as market products. This friction has also precluded the process of audience formation that could eventually turn into such a market. The hype and excitement attached to technological innovations in book form might draw enough attention for binding media to make the news. Still, publicity does little to ensure recognition and buy-in from a reading public beyond highly specialized circles. One can readily see the double debt of presentism in the way that hybrid publishing initiatives, along with binding media, project future aspirations for publishing that are never really achieved. In this short process, however, they become objects of the past so rapidly that their memory value hasn't yet been set.

In addition to the technological and market imperative of planned obsolescence, the cultural standing of various media objects has impacted the currency (both as value and as presentness) of binding media. Early projects sought to gain legitimacy from previously established literary and publishing forms, namely, the print book. In the early 1980s, when Ihor Wolosenko, cofounder of Synapse Software, approached Robert Pinsky to write a text adventure, he intended to elevate interactive fiction to the realm of highbrow literature and celebrated authors.[28] Wolosenko's intent is likely why Synapse's collection is called "Electronic Novels" rather than "interactive fictions," a more common term at the time, and crucially, why it was packaged as a book, despite Pinsky's opposition. More recently, these aspirations have turned around. Reviewers enthusiastically praised the publication of Amaranth Borsuk and Brad Bouse's *Between Page and Screen* (2012) and J. R. Carpenter's *The Gathering Cloud* (2017) as a herald of the future of the book and publishing because of their use of digital media.[29] Whereas Wolosenko sought legitimacy for creative textual software over the basis of known literary models cemented in a long tradition, reviewers of Borsuk's and Carpenter's works imagined a renewal and a relegitimization of the codex when paired with newer digital technologies.

Authors' positions on the hybrid composition of their works have also fluctuated. In a 2016 *New Yorker* article about Pinsky's *Mindwheel*, James Reith relays how Pinsky resisted having a book accompany the electronic novel and, despite having written most of it, asked to be uncredited.[30] One can only wonder what the association of print books and electronic novels meant for Pinsky. Still, from Reith's account, it seemed to romanticize the new endeavor of writing interactive fiction, to ground it, perhaps unfavorably, in a different, maybe even an old, tradition of literature. Conversely, Carpenter remarks on the importance of hybrid works as "transitional objects," which operate "between human and machine languages, times, and spaces, between archives and live voices."[31]

Furthermore, we can also think about binding media as practices of the contemporary. In her study of avant-garde "little magazines," Sophie Seita offers a useful conceptualization, the "provisionally contemporary": a "hotchpotch" of "heterogeneous and dynamic practices . . . follow[ing] the logic of a *moveable contemporaneity.*"[32] Temporally, the provisionally contemporary helps us reflect on the thinness of the specific moment when little magazines (or binding media exemplars) are created and published, and how they incorporate that "nowness" through the particular technologies used. Avant-garde little magazines and binding media differ on whether the provisionally contemporary fulfills avant-garde aesthetic principles of constant and even total reinvention and renovation or, instead, is a feature alien to an artistic project. Little magazines like *Triple Canopy, ON: Contemporary Practice,* and others studied by Seita "make 'nowness' rather than 'newness' a *thematic and technological focus* of their work."[33] Therefore, despite sharing some material qualities with binding media, such as a hybrid publishing model, the main point of Seita's notion is the incorporation of the "nowness" of technological innovation as part of an aesthetic project.

Consequently, although we encounter numerous vanguardist elements in binding media instances, I argue that, generally, their ephemerality does not come from within as part of an aesthetic project. While it is hard to know if authors intended for their work to last a long time, it is possible to tell when ephemerality is part of their aesthetic ambitions, as is clearly the case of Gibson's *Agrippa (A Book of the Dead)* (1992) and Kat Mustatea's *Voidopolis* (2023). Where ephemerality and obsolescence are not aesthetic choices, we must look for features caused by the temporalities of the tech industry. As a work's very conditions of possibility, these temporalities embed "nowness" and ephemerality into the materiality of binding media. While these features might not be readily evident at first, cloaked under the veneer of futurity, they ultimately come to the forefront when digital facets become obsolete. Since we can best appreciate the "nowness" and ephemerality in binding media retrospectively, it signals the gap between digital presentism and the temporalities of other media identified by Hartog. Here, the proximity to the slower temporalities of the print facets evidences the speed of planned obsolescence.

Whether it comes from an unfulfilled futurity, transitionality, or nowness, binding media are constrained to the short periods of technological development that produce them. Even when authors may not have aspired either to build a future of the book or to create projects of nostalgia, binding media are released at "the bleeding edge of obsolescence."[34] Along with millions of new devices and software updates soon to be obsolete, binding media participate (whether willingly or not) in a short-lived present made deliberately ephemeral by the tech industry to ensure the continuity of technological "progress." As the editors and authors of *Your Computer Is on Fire* variously show, the problems triggered by the tech industry are many: e-waste, resource depletion, inequality, and enhanced consumerism, just to name a few.[35] Less notorious are the problems caused by the clash of the distinct temporalities of digital media and, in this case, print media and literature. The sense of constant advancement and progress from the tech industry has transferred the logic of planned obsolescence onto cultural realms like publishing, memory, heritage, art, and literature, where aging processes are conventionally slower and objects are presumed to be more durable. Consequently, objects that in our cultural imaginaries are expected to have a long lifespan are made precarious by the next technological exigency. Indeed, the obsolescence of binding media and all other forms of digital literature is at odds with their constructions of historical subjects as art objects. What's more, the short-term temporality of the technologies that actualize digital art and literature disrupts the *longue durée* processes of accrual of symbolic capital on which cultural relevance and significance have historically relied.

My focus on the temporalities of binding media prompts us to interpret the methodological issues that have always plagued the study of digital and online phenomena as an outcome of the divergence of said temporalities. As early as the 1990s, Gert Lovink cautioned that the rapid obsolescence of computational media itself seems to resist critical analysis because "there is a real danger that an online phenomenon will already have disappeared before a critical discourse reflecting on it has had the time to mature and establish itself as institutionally recognized knowledge."[36] But before one can begin thinking about the cultural relevance of digital literature or its institutional recognition, at stake has been the very possibility of *reading* (viewing, interacting, listening) upon which literary and other forms of cultural analyses conventionally depend. Unlike other literary works in print, "keeping [digital literature] on a shelf doesn't mean that it will be easy, or even possible, to read it in the future. Even putting it into a vault with controlled temperature, light, and humidity won't ensure its availability."[37] While the risk of being robbed of key evidence for interpretation lurks in every operating system and software update, to counter what we may perceive as a vulnerability, I argue that our critical thinking needs to get past obsolescence and ephemerality as impediments for engagement, recognition, and value. To do this, we need to examine the unresolved issue of planned obsolescence not just from the perspective of its technological underpinnings but from the cultural imaginaries it produces, including a "conflation of memory and storage . . . , an equivalence between forgetting and erasure, ... and the commitment to perpetual material protection."[38] The divergent temporalities of binding media as print and digital media and as software applications and works of literature allow us this shift in perspective.

Binding media, like other commercial, technological products, are susceptible to obsolesce within a few years, and simultaneously, like other print literary works with their longer lifespan, possess a materiality that may decay but is unlikely to stop working—or mattering—within a decade. In this way, binding media bring to the forefront the temporal mismatch between the cultural relevance of works of literature and the obsolescence of digital technologies. They remind us that the accelerated temporality of obsolescent software and computers seldom reigns in literary works, thus leading us to question the assumption that digital literature is naturally materially fragile. Lori Emerson has similarly identified how "experienc[ing] what should not be the case" creates an opening of expectations alternative to the technological status quo when booting up a computer from 1976 that still functions—the Altair 8800b held at the Media Archaeology Lab.[39] The difference, however, is that, unlike the Altair 8800b, which interrogates the technocultural realm from within as a product of the tech industry at a different time in history, obsolescent literary works force a reckoning with the imperative of obsolescence from a separate set of cultural expectations where literary works endure.

As digital facets obsolesce, the remains of binding media—including print books and physical storage media—emphatically signal a partial absence. This absence immediately affects the content of the works' digital facets, our access to them, and their literary features. But absence does not have to be all loss. Absence can still be productive to interrogate our sense of history and memory, and to consider how we can inform them via material change and loss. Similarly, as the pace of symbolic value accrual in literature is nothing like that for software or hardware, the temporal divergences of binding media open a space to problematize the scholarly approach to objects rendered transitional by their material conditions of possibility. This effect emerges directly from the material configuration of binding media and particularly from how the literary aesthetic projects often manifest these temporal discontinuities so overtly.

As we now can study various forms of hybrid publishing across a handful of decades, with the benefit of retrospect, we can leave the novelty effect aside by examining their asymmetrical endurance and interrogating their status as both objects of the recent past and residues of a brief present. A survey of issues focused on the ephemerality of digital literature and digital preservation will shed light on how the presentism of the tech industry is so pervasive that it shapes projects that seek to manage and repair its effects. Recent work on the "disruption" of memory tragically reveals that information and memory workers find themselves and their labor wasted by the very problems they struggle to ameliorate.[40] In contrast, as a product of a technological niche that never reached standardization (a "variant," to use media theorist Siegfried Zielinsky's words), binding media provide an opportunity to foreground the underlying ideologies of presentism and its effect on literary production and scholarship. In their uniqueness and idiosyncrasy as media archaeological objects, binding media propose alternative pathways to perceive the temporalities of digital technologies, identify their destructive effects, and theorize the kinds of literary history and memory we can build over them.

**The Residues of the Recent Past**

Understandably, it has been impossible for scholars of digital literature and digital humanities not to find ourselves caught up in the presentism of the tech industry. The materiality of digital literature internalizes the linear temporality of technological progress. I would argue that despite opposing linear and teleological thinking in the study of digital literature, e-lit scholarship unwittingly adopts forms of presentism as the management, preservation, and aesthetic theorizing of obsolescent technology cannot help but follow the accelerated pace of the tech industry, even as scholars aim to counter it. Even Katherine Hayles, in her field-defining essay "What Is Electronic Literature?" acknowledges that the canon of digital literature might be "limited to a few years, and without the opportunity to build the kinds of traditions associated with print literature, electronic literature risks being doomed to the realm of ephemera, severely hampered in its development and the influence it can wield."[41]

The condition of the field has prompted critical rethinkings of memory-making. Advocating for a "reinvented memory," French artist Serge Bouchardon recalls how, "given the *intrinsic* obsolescence of digital devices and software, some authors consider that it is impossible to fight the 'technical trend' which *governs* their evolution," seeking in them an "aesthetic of ephemerality."[42] For Bouchardon, the explorations of ephemeral poetics or aesthetics have taught us that the "digital literary work is indeed not an object, but in most cases, it is not a simple event limited in time, like a performance or a digital installation either. In fact, it partakes of both aspects: it is a transmittable object and a process that can only exist through actualization."[43] While Bouchardon is right to point out how, by having to be actualized, digital literature is ephemeral to the specific moments of actualization, I believe this sense of ephemerality is different from the ephemerality that comes from technological obsolescence and would preclude the actualization he refers to. His interpretation confounds the two forms of ephemerality, thus giving the impression that obsolescence is a counterpart to actualization rather than the counterpart to functionality on which access depends. As I have been arguing, the internalization of the temporality of tech opens a challenging gap with the temporality of literature and literary studies, and, in the case of binding media, with that of print books—one that, no matter how much one tries to interpret it aesthetically, is an ephemerality imposed from outside the literary works. Internalizing the ways in which digital literature can't help but behave like digital media and software applications will inevitably paint a frankly ruinous landscape. Jean Baudrillard has maintained that "our age no longer produces ruins or relics, only wastes and residues."[44] Though grim, his diagnostic resonates loudly with the accelerated pace of tech development whose logic of progress-obsolescence underpins the myriad broken digital literary works that are prone to disappearing from memory. With only a few exceptions, scholars, publishers, authors, and institutions have been unable to maintain and update digital art and literature due to the extraordinary amounts of effort and investment required to do so. In contrast, the print facets of binding media stand comfortably on shelves where we can pick them up to read, thus reminding us that literature objects need not be ruled by planned obsolescence. A recent example that accurately illustrates the gaps opened between the temporality of planned obsolescence and software sunsetting and that of literary longevity is found in the much-anticipated discontinuation of Adobe Flash at the end of 2020, known in the world of digital literature as "flashpocalypse."

Even though Flash had seen a years-long process of sunsetting and support withdrawal, at midnight on January 1, 2021, many digital literary works, including the paradigmatic exemplar of binding media, *Between Page and Screen*, became inaccessible, unreadable, and a nonfunctional part of a recent technological past.[45] This historical technocultural moment, precisely dated, is critical to observing the genuinely destructive power the tech industry can inflict upon creators, scholars, and cultural institutions. The lifetime of Flash and the art and literature it made possible, is likely one of the most significant periods in digital culture and even set the basis for the interactive web.[46] Therefore, it is no surprise that publications, goodbye parties, and the development or expansion of preservation strategies and projects marked the occasion of its sunsetting. For instance, hours before the announced sunsetting of Flash, the nonprofit media arts organization Rhizome ran a fundraiser to support its preservation efforts "during which [attendants would] play and visit [their] favorite legacy Flash artworks and games."[47] More interesting, in a Rhizome blog post suggestively titled "Emulation or It Didn't Happen: What to Do about Flash," Dragan Espenschied offered a list of resources for artists to preserve and continue providing access to their Flash works of art on the web.[48] The widely significant cultural moment rightly seemed to mandate broader, deeper, and more sophisticated work in digital preservation if organizations like Rhizome were to maintain digital artifacts "alive." Although Espenschied is riffing off the common expression "pic or it didn't happen," used to demand verification of claims made in online forums, his title positions emulation as proof of existence. As one of the foremost experts in the preservation of born-digital art, Espenschied knows better than to suggest that preservation—emulation specifically—is the only condition of possibility for the continued currency of digital art. However, his particular wording lays bare the widespread concern that without preservation strategies, the divergent temporalities of tech and art pose the risk of erasing born-digital literature and art from memory.

Digital preservation is a field plagued by technological instability and cultural urgency as it "involve[s] systems impossible to control for both the artist and the [memory] institution."[49] The focus of digital art preservation projects suggests the necessity and significance of the endeavor and the breadth of approaches devised to manage the imposed ephemerality of digital media. These range from the more technical, like emulation and porting, to the more ethnographic and documentary, such as the "traversals" done by Stuart Moulthrop and Dene Grigar.[50] Underlying these projects is an evident labor of love and care for the cultural objects of the last few decades rendered ephemeral by the very means that made them possible. But there is also a (justifiable) sense of apprehension about the perennial threat of loss of born-digital art and literature or some of its constitutive and artifactual features—from the source code and the rendering applications to the hardware specifications—that are often integral to the aesthetic projects. Adding to these challenges are the overwhelming costs and the technical specialization required for digital preservation. These two factors have increasingly relegated the artifactual preservation of digital applications, which can maintain digital literature "alive," to the margins of a larger field and elite institutions.[51]

However, the matter of specialization to preserve and update literary texts is certainly not exclusive to the digital milieu. Early modern texts are instances that also require extensive expert treatment to ensure their preservation, readability, and accessibility to contemporary audiences. Transcription, orthographic standardization, and annotation are but a handful of textual editing processes that make it possible for the works of Miguel de Cervantes or William Shakespeare to reach nonexpert readers. These longstanding scholarly traditions and the historical periods and canons they serve are well established in academic and cultural institutions, if not always sufficiently appreciated. In contrast, the field of digital literary studies, younger by centuries, has yet to fully establish these methodologies and practices as a part of institutional infrastructures. Training scholars in these highly specialized methods—the human infrastructure—is also needed.

Matthew Kirschenbaum's work on American poet William H. Dickey's digital work *HyperPoems* illustrates how media archaeological approaches can enrich methodologies of textual scholarship to maintain and update works from the recent technological past. In his account, Kirschenbaum recounts how he "reanimated" Dickey's work by relying on the infrastructures available at the Maryland Institute for Technology in the Humanities. These include an on-site collection of vintage computers and an archive of electronic literature manuscripts, ephemera, and other artifacts donated by electronic literature writer Dena Larsen, Dickey's digital poetry editor.[52] The juncture of infrastructure and the scholar's own expertise made it possible to prepare a languishing digital manuscript for publication for the first time in 2020, about two decades after being written. Kirschenbaum further relied on the emulation infrastructure already set up by the Internet Archive for the discontinued software HyperCard to publish Dickey's *HyperPoems* there. Kirschenbaum's meticulous work reveals that the convergence of media archaeology and textual scholarship is very much possible and underscores the need to bolster institutional infrastructures, cultivate expertises, and demonstrate the cultural value of literary works that could otherwise be considered souvenirs from the past. The collections recovered and hosted by The Next, the Electronic Literature Organization's "museum, library, and preservation space," similarly point toward the nascent infrastructure and developing scholarly expertises capable of updating and maintaining digital literary works.[53] Support for The

Next comes from varied sources, including a grant from the Andrew W. Mellon Foundation and other funding from Compute Canada, as well as professional organizations such as the Electronic Literature Organization and the Society of American Archivists, and universities including the University of Victoria and Washington State University Vancouver. The Next makes it clear that, in addition to costs and scholarly expertise, keeping digital culture production alive depends on transversal and even international collaborations. To make matters even more complicated, as costly, difficult, valuable, and necessary as digital preservation already is, it is work that remains forever provisional. Digital archivist Trevor Owens reminds us of that provisionality when he posits that "nothing *has been* preserved, there are only things *being* preserved."[54] In their work on the *Cartografía de literatura digital latinoamericana*, Carolina Gainza, Carolina Zúñiga, and Javier González admit to "being fully aware of their [preservation strategies and tools'] expiration and accepting, paradoxically, their future obsolescence," even when they also point to capitalist imperatives as the culprit.[55] Owens similarly acknowledges that the challenges to digital preservation are "less about the nature of digital media than ... about planned obsolescence and a massive computing industry that pours considerable resources into keeping pace with the expectations for better, faster computing devices with more and more storage in smaller form."[56] Owens's assessment implies the gap opened by the divergent economics of time in digital media and memory institutions.

There is much to appreciate and praise in digital preservation endeavors and professionals. And yet, I find myself concerned with how digital preservation is also forced to internalize and maintain the linearity and ephemerality of presentism by working within the limits and at the pace dictated by the tech industry. My concern has less to do with the potential for loss and what it will keep us from doing or knowing in the future; this is a fact of any preservation endeavor in any medium of any historical period. I am more concerned with how the presentism of digital media and the internalization of its logic in preservation and scholarship disrupts the construction of the sense of pastness that is much needed to counter the universalization of time and the precarization of cultural memory it causes. The question, then, is not whether the study of preserved digital objects allows us to historicize them—it does in some way—but what that provisionality might do to our sense of cultural relevance, historical meaning, and memory-making in the face of "creative destruction."[57] Indeed, we must question how the provisionality of preservation approaches builds a sense of literary history and appreciate how, despite inhabiting a fast-passing present, digital literary works can shed light on their past, too. Kirschenbaum acknowledges that distinct contexts of reading influence the meaning of, in this case, Dickey's *HyperPoems* when "sequestered amid the detritus of obsolescent tech . . . and it means something *else* when virtualized through the abstractions of emulation at the Internet Archive."[58] These differences, I argue, result from the temporal effects produced by each context of reading. In a media archaeological lab, the context is tethered to its history via the devices utilized. On the web, conversely, the sense of an elongated present rather than a historical context renders obsolete works timeless yet out of place. The differences in the context of reading and meaning production identified by Kirschenbaum show that even with access to a literary work's content, the temporalities of digital literature complicate their historization.

Owens's recent work underscores care, repair, and maintenance as guiding principles for the work of memory institutions. Under this conceptualization, Owens acknowledges how the ideologies of innovation and disruption transferred from the tech industry onto cultural memory institutions have wreaked havoc on the sector and led its professionals into untenable working situations.[59] Ultimately, Owens warns us against allowing the "focus on maintenance [to] become maintenance of the status quo."[60] Along the same lines, archivist Michelle Caswell sees in the same principles an opportunity to enact social justice and reparative justice in the collections held by memory institutions. Caswell argues that at the center of her liberatory memory work is a rethinking of progressivist ideologies that safely and unidirectionally locate the past in the past as though it had no bearing in the multiplicity of presents and possible futures. Instead, liberatory memory work must shed light on the continuation of injustices and the perpetuation of power structures.[61]

The work of Owens, Caswell, and other critical archivists who warn us against the reification of digital presentism and other temporalities of power offers a perfect opportunity to theorize the divergent temporalities of binding media further. Outside of the methodological and pragmatic insights produced in the field of archival and information sciences, and media archaeology–based textual scholarship, the literary discourses found in binding media similarly address and enact a variety of temporalities informed by the specificity of print and digital media as well as their impacts in the natural, affective, and social world.

**Cultural Residues and Memory-Making**
The landscape shaped by the omniscience of presentism, one in which both the history of cultural objects and the professionals tasked with their preservation are precaritized, prompts us to engage in a critique of the rigidity of technological progress, its sleek aesthetic of efficiency, and its smoothed-out transitions. I argue that this critique comes out in full force when studying objects affected by this precarization from separate cultural realms. The focus on the divergent temporalities of binding media allows us to do that by bringing to the forefront the rough edges of cultural imaginaries of technological progress. When functional, binding media make it clear that the cultural issue at stake is not the succession of one medium by another, namely, the death of the print book due to the impact of digital technologies. In contrast, when they stop functioning, binding media underscore how that which is associated with progress, the digital facets, winds up running into a dead end. Bugs, no-longer-supported messages, often unnecessary updates, and discontinuation clutter the transitions between future-making project launches and end-of-life announcements. The conflicts between the temporality of the tech industry and that of cultural objects result from an economics of time and the power relations where tech firms far outweigh the cultural sector in capital, control, and prestige.

Little by little, the last few decades have been leaving us with pieces of binding media in various states of functionality and accessibility. The histories of electronic literature focused on periodization remain primarily unconcerned with how obsolescence is increasingly the only constant feature among a wide array of aesthetic projects, which should force an overdue reconsideration of memory-making in the field that doesn't hinge on sorting the many challenges of preservation alone.

The work of Brazilian artist Giselle Beiguelman on memory-making and loss offers an alternative. Beiguelman takes as a case study the pioneering *NetArt Latino Database* (2000–2005), a project led by Uruguayan artist Brian Mackern, which mapped and listed net art projects from Latin America. In 2010, Museo Extremeño e Iberoamericano de Arte Contemporáneo (MEIAC) acquired the *NetArt Latino Database*. In the project, Beiguelman identifies the temporal discontinuities and the material and disciplinary divergences between a largely defunct net art project and the act of "musefying" it, that is, to fix or stabilize it for posterity. Important to note for those unfamiliar with the NetArt Latino Database is that by the time it was acquired by the MEIAC (and even more so now at the time of writing), the map and listings of early net art projects were already, for the most part, a collection of unavailable sites or "404 Not Found" landing pages. For the Brazilian artist, the junctures of musefying that which is full of absences and of dealing with projects that in their absence are as significant as those that are present compels us to figure out "other memorisation formats and other notions of history."[62]

Facing a history of net art void of primary sources, Beiguelman's most suggestive theorization to manage alternative forms of memory is how, due to obsolescence, the relationship between the content of the net art pieces and their context shifts in significance. In fact, she maintains that the context of the *NetArt Latino Database* has become its content, and "as content, it is a shifting field in which a set of references that used to be there stubbornly insist upon declaring that they used to exist even though they can no longer be accessed."[63] With Beiguelman's shift in focus, I propose that approaches to binding media must undergo a similar transformation as many digital facets have become obsolete, and the print codices become contextual and even indexical to the entire works. Scholars have identified, though they have not fully theorized, examples of these transformations in meaning and interpretation due to obsolescence as a process affecting the majority of digital literature and adjacent forms like binding media. Lori Emerson writes about Talan Memmott's *Lexia to Perplexia* as a work that "becomes less and less about its linguistic, narrative, and visual elements and more fundamentally about its interface and its slow but sure transformation in an utterly malfunctioning inaccessible work."[64] It is likely that the processes described by Emerson and theorized by Beiguelman are the path most digital literature will eventually follow, at least partially. Works restored, emulated, ported, or fully reprogrammed will similarly incorporate the process of keeping them "alive" into their meaning.

For obsolescent instances of binding media specifically, the durability of the print codices enables them to continue to exist within an infrastructure that grants them their status as works of literature. Simultaneously, they become part of the context—and in some cases, the holder—of something else that is now largely inaccessible. Beiguelman's approach to obsolescent and lost digital cultural production, an experience that she likens to "walking amidst unburied corpses," makes it explicit that underlying these losses is an issue of who controls the endurance or loss of these works.[65] Methodologically, shifting the focus from content to context can open distinct critical possibilities that don't just rely on close readings and persistence as a conduit to history but can expand our understanding of specific ways (technological, capital, cultural) in which the tech industry wields power over cultural production. Arguably, every work of digital literature and art can facilitate this approach. Yet, because of their hybrid materiality, binding media bring to the forefront the competing temporalities that result in a fruitful theoretical space to build a viable model of memory-making and historicization in digital literature out of any remains left.

Although she doesn't mention it explicitly, in Beiguelman's proposals we can see the influence of memory studies emanating from Latin

America—a theoretical connection that I find helpful and wish to amplify. Focused on "living pasts," memory studies has negotiated and theorized the struggles between dominant and marginal narratives to assign meaning to the violent episodes in the recent history of Latin America.[66] While the field of memory studies in Latin America has followed many different critical paths, I highlight here two concerns that are especially relevant to the discussion of binding media: on the one hand, the fact that at the center of competing narratives are missing, obfuscated, and destroyed archives; on the other, the critical role the struggle to interpret, name, and remember the past plays in the present.[67] The analyses of cultural and literary production have shed light on how writing, narration, and archives negotiate competing memories and make possible distinct narrative approaches in contexts like post-dictatorship Chile and the Mexican War on Narcotraffic. In contexts like these, there is a battle between official discourses and those that articulate heterodox formulations of recollection and memory, which I believe are well positioned to illuminate the issue of obsolescent artistic production. The work of thinkers like Nelly Richard and Cristina Rivera Garza, who have worked in such contexts, is handy as they advance a series of creative strategies that counter the erasure of history, the linearity and triumphalism of top-down narratives, and the supposed impossibility of memory-making over vanished and absent records. The historical contexts from which Richard and Rivera Garza write are plagued with murderous state violence, human rights violations, *desapariciones*, and official versions of historical "truth." An outcome of these human tragedies has been the overt political contestation of the violence that raged upon entire populations and the creation of aesthetic projects that undermine authoritative notions of history and memory-making. Significantly, Richard and Rivera Garza have both, though on their own, theorized memory-making strategies based on cultural practices or "cultural residues."[68] Richard theorizes: "a hybrid recollection" made up of "shreds," "fragments," and "pauses" that produce "a practice of memory unconcerned with the linear restitution of a single history."[69] In parallel, Rivera Garza elaborates on a practice of "documentary writing" that aims to "embody the fickleness of the documentation system itself" and purposefully undermines the idea of a final, definitive, and teleological account of a historical moment.[70] Moreover, Rivera Garza uses documentary writing not to treat history as a thing of the past but to make it weigh in on the present via an engagement with residual materials that have not always been considered of historical importance.

Although the circumstances that cause a fragmentary, shredded archive of binding media and other forms of digital cultural production are, of course, widely different from the contexts considered by Richard and Rivera Garza, behind them, there is an exercise of power wielded by the tech industry that is ideological as well as financial. The fragmentary material residues and the voids in signification stand in contrast to the linear order of development and evolution common in tech histories. These exercises in power necessarily produce a distortion of the past that justifies and reifies such histories and power. We can see this in binding media and their position outside of the triumphalist histories of technological developments in publishing, where attaining a profitable business model is a mark of success in the tech industry and where industry relevance amounts to cultural significance. Martín-Barbero's cogent appeals are again inspiring when he prompts us to liberate media—and our thinking about media—from the industry's compulsiveness of innovation and a teleological past to establish relationships to various forms of past through a "dis/re organization of time."[71] Where digital preservation is instrumental to constructing a coherent history of literary history, the material residues and shreds proposed by Richard and Rivera Garza are helpful to assign meaning to the competing histories of tech and publishing, and digital and hybrid publishing.

This kind of perspectival temporal disturbance has also been at the basis of media-archaeological inquiries. Siegfried Zielinski has famously invited scholars to "find something new in the old" and to turn around the idea that history is "the promise of continuity."[72] Although Richard and Rivera Garza are not proposing an archaeology of cultural remains, the influence of Walter Benjamin's historical materialism takes their arguments into the territory of media archaeology to engage with records that are too old, too incomplete, too provisional, or too indexical to matter. In particular, Rivera Garza views documents as a matrix that includes "the document's materiality, its language and structure, the process of its production and discovery" in addition to its "content."[73] Therefore, the continued yet fringe existence of those cultural remains, documents, or material objects and their embedded contexts make their interrogation possible against a smoother present. Rivera Garza's positioning regarding documents would appear too narrative and too historical to a media archaeologist like Wolfgang Ernst, who focused on the "cooler" objectual presence of media objects. Yet, like Rivera Garza's documentary writing, his nondiscursive approach seeks to bring back to the present media left behind in the past. Ernst's distinction that "the cultural life span of a medium is not the same as its operational life span" pinpoints the distinct temporal trajectories followed by media and culture.[74] Nonetheless, the temporal dynamic Ernst sees follows a different direction than the one I wish to underscore. While for him, the temporal divergence can be found between the endurance of media that still function well after "their outside world has vanished," in the presentist landscape of technological developments, it is the cultural world that remains after—and despite—the lack of durability of media.

The remains of binding media negotiate these two divergences by continuing to be present and accessible while signaling that which isn't. This temporal divergence produces a rift between how and to what extent we can control different objects (print, computational, literary) so that they become historical, while others, perhaps, speak more loudly through absence. Just as obsolescence is not naturally occurring, the durability of print is also not inherent to the medium but, as discussed above, relies on centuries-old practices, protocols, and scholarship. It might be decades before the equivalent of such practices, protocols, and scholarship become fully established in the fields of digital art and literature. And yet, it is possible to envision a literary history of binding media built from incomplete residual pieces where their context of production and obsolescence becomes the focus of inquiry. This positioning allows us to set aside the functionality of digital literature as a condition for its study. Instead, we can see it as a phenomenon characterized by temporal divergence, where obsolescence is one of the ways in which binding media account for memory accrual. In fact, by underscoring inoperability, we can conceptualize binding media as part of a choppy history that is not yet part of the past. Instead, binding media stand as the residues that can actualize the conflicting historical narratives of media and open spaces for the construction of heterogeneous pasts and possible futures.

Authors of binding media do not simply create literary works in a complex temporal juncture; they do so to propose and investigate heterogeneous pasts and futures. In the next section, I engage in close readings of Ian Bogost's *A Slow Year*, J. R. Carpenter's *The Gathering Cloud*, and Verónica Gerber Bicecci and coauthors' "La máquina distópica" / *La compañía*. I investigate the authors' concern with how distinct media temporalities are embedded in ideologies of progress and modernization, and also serve to erase, oppress, and damage. Each work stages a history of media or technology materially and discursively, underscoring their divergent temporalities. Therefore, my analyses strive to keep the temporal divergence at the center as a starting point to query the features of presentism from two angles: as temporalities that affect these works of literature and the possibility of their study, and as the historical condition that has culturally habituated us to leaving the past as only of the past.

### *A Slow Year*: The Nostalgia of the Past

Ian Bogost's 2010 collection of game poems and haikus, *A Slow Year*, is concerned with the reconstruction of the past right as it was. Made up of four Atari game poems, more than one thousand "machined haikus," and a handful of essays, *A Slow Year* was simultaneously published in two editions by the textbook publishing company Open Texture.[75] A deluxe edition of twenty-five comes in a large, red handmade case with an Atari VCS cartridge and a leather-bound book. A paperback edition of the book has a CD-ROM bound to the back cover with an Atari emulator compatible with Mac and Windows operating systems. The game poems and the machine-generated haikus explore each of the seasons of the year with the poetic tradition of imagism and naturalism. As an aesthetic project, *A Slow Year* effectively creates specific images of natural landscapes out of two reciprocal yet distinct media poetic practices: the poems as an outcome of a computer program, and the Atari game as the result of poetic contemplation or, in the author's own words, "sedate observation."[76] When reading the two facets together, it's clear that Bogost insists on making the print book as much as possible like an Atari game and the games as much like a poetry chapbook. *A Slow Year* has been relatively understudied to date, perhaps in part because Bogost himself offers vast interpretive direction in the introduction and essays titled "Provocation Machines," "My Slow Year," and "How to Play" that accompany the haikus and the game poems. These texts serve as an artist's statement, where Bogost writes about his game poems, and as a manual for readers and players.

Throughout the game poems, the haikus, and the essays, the author sediments slowness as the principle that guides the work's aesthetics and the approach followed to create it. Slowness is also the type of experience that Bogost seeks to instill in his readers and players. We can look at slowness as part of the game dynamics and the design specs, as well as the way the game counters standards of gameplay. In this way, we can read *A Slow Year* as an interrogation of the accelerated temporality of the tech industry and its market imperatives of technological progress and obsolescence. However, as I explain in the following pages, Bogost's essays might offer a reading of *A Slow Year* running counter to the poetics of the game alone.

Early in his essays, Bogost describes the Atari VCS as "a slow machine," a slowness that also characterizes the process of programming games for it.[77] This characterization paves the way for the author to create a semantic field of sorts with concepts associated with slowness, such as smallness, constraint, lo-fi, and abstractness, and actions similarly linked to it, such as contemplating, napping, and paying attention. The idea of a game where "you play by literally doing nothing" is an attractive provocation in a genre where skill and winning often depend on doing something and doing it as fast as possible.[78] We can observe this easily in the game dynamics and visuals. With little action to take, players instead engage in contemplation and "acts of deliberation."[79] The "Winter" game poem prompts the player to *slowly* drink a cup of coffee as the sun rises in the window; "Spring" invites us to watch a thunderstorm mindfully; "Summer" to close our eyes and doze off; and "Fall" to look at a tree shedding its leaves. Visually, we also encounter heavily pixelated images displaying almost fixed landscapes with little movement, small changes, and actions that are easy to miss.

Bogost's approach to slowness deliberately and overtly goes against the grain of video game design not just by making a poetic game for which there would be little room in a widely different market but also by using "a console long past its commercial relevancy."[80] Slowness has a technical correlate, too. For instance, the technical constraints of the Atari cartridge determine the *small* size of each game poem: just 1k. The 8-bit images similarly echo the smallness of the files and the game's slowness. Likewise, Bogost intended machine-generated haikus to match the principles of smallness, "totaling one kilobyte in number (1K, or 1,024), split into four sets of 256, one set for each season ... 256 is 8 bits ($2^8$), the largest value manipulable by the microprocessor that drives the Atari VCS."[81] Further, by choosing the Atari, Bogost revives an evocative visual aesthetic very much in opposition to current (even in 2010) high-definition and ever faster screen refresh rates. The pressures of the video game market are also out of view for a game distributed, in its majority, as a book. Arguably, *A Slow Year* is a born-obsolete game. Nevertheless, utilizing an obsolete platform (the Atari was discontinued in the mid-1990s) grants Bogost creative autonomy, given that no new releases or upgrades will render his game poems incompatible or passé.

Just as it happens with the game dynamics, the slowness embedded in the specs of *A Slow Year* is a counterpoint to the acceleration of the tech industry and an effective interrogation of the ephemerality of presentism. By releasing a game decades out of step with the most up-to-date consoles, Bogost pushes a reckoning with the cultural impact of a console like the Atari in the 1970s and 1980s—a form of relevance that has endured and found its niche outside mainstream gaming trends. The thoroughness of the aesthetic project is admirable, and yet, Bogost's own writing on the work suggests a rougher and less critical relationship to the temporality of the old console with respect to that of the tech industry.

Indeed, while the game poems are effective at advancing an aesthetics of slowness, Bogost's essays convey a sense of fetishization of the old, embodied by the Atari, which, instead of interrogating the current cultural relevance of obsolete technology, seems to corroborate its place in the pantheon of video game consoles. For one, the author recounts his adoption of the Atari as a research project that "became a secret love affair" and how he found a "purity" to programming for the Atari.[82] The emotional and even sexual undertones conjure an image of desire for something either forbidden or unattainable. Moreover, Bogost emphatically declares, "I didn't choose this platform to be lo-fi, nor for nostalgia's sake. The coupling between the Atari console and the entire game design is tight and deliberate."[83] Although meant to do the opposite, his disclaimer suggests an idealization of the Atari as the only medium that fulfills slowness, smallness, abstraction, and simplicity technically and aesthetically. His commentary implies that such principles are only realizable within the constraints of the old console. The features and characteristics that make *A Slow Year* possible are essentialized to the Atari and, critically, to its status as an obsolete, discontinued object of the past. The deluxe edition, of only twenty-five copies, is so small that it can only be, on the one hand, a collector's item, and, on the other, barely a gesture at the revival of the Atari and the gaming niches around it. Lastly, publishing the emulated version in a CD-ROM as late as 2010, when the web would have been a more widely accessible platform, further suggests Bogost establishes a technological and affective distance between the present time of *A*

*Slow Year* and the past where the media of the game are safely left to be found by collectors.

Arguably, the author's choice of the CD-ROM is tied to the use of a print volume and the convention of binding digital media in back cover pockets—by 2010 already going into disuse. In his essays, Bogost repeatedly admits that including a print book and the machine-generated haikus was an afterthought that solved the issue of packaging and how to fill up the pages of that packaging, not a generative starting point for the work.[84] Indeed, he introduces the book as "a *curious box* made to house that videogame."[85] Despite the secondary role of the print volume, Bogost indicates that its usage helped him emulate the packaging of Atari cartridges during the console's heyday and its capacity to extend the experience of the game away from the computer through manuals, paratexts, "value-adds," or "feelies."[86] The closeness with which the author seeks to mimic the features of the Atari game and packaging down to the cover art also signals a fetishized approach that looks to the past with preciousness of detail. Ultimately, despite all the detailed minutia that went into the conceptualization of the book and its relationship to the game poems, the author concedes that players "might ignore" the "curious box" and its filler, the haikus, "and engage the game just as well."[87] Next to other binding media exemplars examined in this book, *A Slow Year* seems unconcerned with what meanings may emerge at the juncture of two distinct media, with Bogost's attention turned to how it might, instead, be used to emulate the aesthetics of an "older form."[88]

Having all the pieces of the puzzle at hand, Bogost stops short of interrogating the presentist media landscape that clamors for the slowness *A Slow Year* so thoroughly proposes, making it, instead, a feature from an old technology that can only live within the limitations and rudimentariness of the past. Whereas for Lori Emerson, slowness can teach us worldviews that are alternative to efficiency, productivity, consumption, and waste *in the present*, *A Slow Year* seems to constrain those alternative views, experiences, and aesthetics to the past and its media objects.[89] Certainly, Bogost brings the Atari game into the present, but he does so from a distance where it can be safely looked at—or perhaps sedately observed—away in a past chronologically behind, rather than choosing to underscore its contemporaneity and its ongoing cultural relevance. Indeed, the poetics of contemplation, the sedate observation dynamic of the games, opens a gap between the player and the game. And we must wonder if that is not, ultimately, what Bogost proposes: an invitation to inaction regarding the speed of tech.

### The Layers of an Altered Book: *The Gathering Cloud*

Examining the history and metaphors of "the cloud," J. R. Carpenter takes a very different approach to the temporalities of media in *The Gathering Cloud*. The cloud is a central instance of twenty-first-century presentism and speed imagery: new, always present, fast yet invisible, weightless, and changing. Its contents appear when we need them to be available on any device. It is ephemeral yet always there. As many scholars have pointed out, this image, built by the tech industry, could not be farther from the material realities of server farms, undersea cables, and carbon consumption and production.[90] Moreover, despite being presented as the pinnacle of innovation, efficiency, and accessibility, the internet cloud and weather clouds have a long history and a broad present that is crucially relevant due to climate change. As media theorist Jussi Parikka points out in his foreword to Carpenter's book, although the digital cloud appears removed from individual users, it is not just images, messages, music, and movies that appear on our screen; the chemical residues left by the industrial age are already inside us through a "chemical cultural history" of particles forever present in the soil and air.[91]

Like much of her work, Carpenter's *The Gathering Cloud* is a hybrid print and web-based piece that seeks to underscore and connect the dissonance in the language and imagery used to represent the digital cloud. Commissioned by the NEoN Digital Arts Festival, *The Gathering Cloud* was first released on the web in 2016, and a year later in print book form under the Uniformbooks imprint based in the United Kingdom. Carpenter uses Luke Howard's *Essay on the Modifications of Clouds* from 1803 as the basis for her work visually and conceptually. This project, like *This is a Picture of Wind* (examined in chapter 1), addresses a long-time concern of Carpenter's: the challenge of representing through language "invisible forces like the wind and rising temperatures which we can only see indirectly through their affects."[92] In an early passage of the print book, the author recounts how the study of clouds in isolation is made difficult due to how the weather has historically been represented through other objects or events, such as "thunder and lightning, a meteor, lilacs, lily of the valley, and hyacinths in full blossom."[93] This seeming impossibility to study, to write, and to think of the clouds alone provides the perfect opportunity for Carpenter to establish layers of relationships between the clouds and their materiality (both weather and digital clouds), their historical understanding (many of them imprecise, wrong, unpopular, or misleading), and their proximate effects on the lives of people. In this way, Carpenter builds a poetic, visual, and media-archaeological grounding of the clouds away from the immaterial, the new, and the far-away fantasies of the tech industry and into their more immediate, material, and nonchronologically historicized relationships. As I elaborate in my reading, in each section of the web facet, it is possible to see an overlay of elements indicating each of these layers through visual and poetic elements.

There are seven sections in the web facet: a frontispiece, five plates, and a list of sources. Except for "Sources," each item addresses individual aspects of the digital cloud. The "Frontispiece" deals with how language has been inadequate to represent the "realities of data." "Plate No. 1" focuses on the heaviness of the digital cloud. "Plate No. 2" addresses the carbon footprints of seemingly innocuous online activities. "Plate No. 3" brings the materiality of heavy wires and digital infrastructure to the forefront. "Plate No. 4" highlights the changeability, ephemerality, and lack of historicity of the digital cloud. "Plate No. 5" wraps up with a poignant reminder of the growing enormity of the cloud. Each section uses Howard's cloud plates as the backdrop on which Carpenter adds verbal, visual, and conceptual inscriptions to create visual collages.

In the web facet, Carpenter connects a wealth of resources amassed visually in a single screen and temporally through palimpsestic layers in animated collages. As can be seen in Figures 20 and 21, each plate starts as one of the engravings from Howard's volume and, in a few seconds, images taken from the internet layer upon it, establishing the diachronic connections between the clouds and the cloud. But it is not just the visual elements that suggest this connection. Carpenter puts together stanzas from different periods in her cloud history, sometimes as part of the first layer in the plates and sometimes as dynamic ones that appear when readers hover over red words—those found in the "Index of Objects" in the print book.[94] Carpenter prompts readers to make these transhistorical connections through the animation that overlaps the poetic and visual elements on the screen. Indeed, Carpenter specifically identifies the presentism of the cloud and the discourse about it on two occasions. First, in the print facet is a reference to Margaret Cavendish's critique of "relentless mechanical progress" cleverly countered with the conservatism of the Royal Society of London.[95] Second, on Plate 4 in the web facet is a stanza that reads, "The digital cloud actively erases its own historicity; like its namesake, it constructs itself through pure fluctuation."[96] This example further ties in how attributes of the weather clouds have been transferred metaphorically to the digital cloud to build a deceptive image of natural ephemerality and weightlessness. Ultimately, the present of the digital cloud is never just in the present but carries over poetic, visual, and material echoes from many different pasts.

The print facet of the work has two halves, one containing a series of "essay poems" that center on various historical moments in the representation and understanding of clouds. Some of these are also part of the digital facet. Interspersed in the first half are two sections of sixteen photographs of cloud observations in Dawlish, UK. The second half contains the verses from the digital facet and expands on them with more stanzas unavailable on the web. Although her study does not include the print facet, scholar Natalie Pollard rightly identifies the various layers featured by *The Gathering Cloud*. She describes them as a

**FIGURE 20.** Screenshot of "The Gathering Cloud," Plate No. 4, shows the first seconds of the animation where Howard's illustration is visible with only a minimal layer of text. Reproduced with permission.

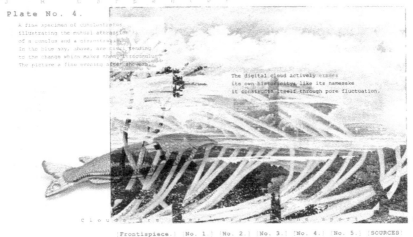

**FIGURE 21.** Screenshot of "The Gathering Cloud," Plate No. 4, shows the progressive layering of visual elements over Howard's illustration. Reproduced with permission.

"crisscrossing of communication infrastructures, entangled cloud nomenclatures, and technological and artistic knowledge forms."[97] This characterization is undoubtedly enhanced by Carpenter's artistic approaches in the print facet. The poems collected in the first half of the book "423 BCE–1859 CE" and "1886–1996" reveal how distinct epistemological frameworks (philosophy, theology, science) have always mediated the visual and linguistic imagery surrounding clouds. Likewise, specific representation technologies (theater, sketching and painting, engraving, photography, mathematical language, and data) have shaped clouds' imagery. By showing how clouds have been styled at a particular moment in history and under specific technocultural frameworks, Carpenter draws a stratigraphy where the internet cloud is less than new, less than exceptional.

The mention of "wrong" and "failed" approximations to the clouds within a historical framework further qualifies the prominence of the digital cloud as the culmination of a progressive history with no wrong turns.[98] Carpenter carefully clarifies that these "wrong" and "failed" historical moments are considered so because of various circumstances and not absolute truths. Similarly, the evocation of war clouds, like the iconic image of the mushroom cloud and "Fugue of Death," Paul Celan's poem on "cloud graves," speak of the murderous associations that also exist in cloud imagery but haven't made it into the imaginary of the internet cloud.[99] The ample historical catalog Carpenter presents in the first half of the print facet follows a chronology. This linear presentation, arguably a byproduct of the form of the book, is nevertheless interrupted by contemporary photographs of Dawlish. An insistence on the continuity of clouds also crosses the first half, for instance, with verses such as "it has *always* rained."[100] The media history and archaeology presented in these pages are both sources for and pieces of the poems in the second half of the print book, titled "The Gathering Cloud," and the web facet.

For Parikka, Carpenter's work engages in "material transformations."[101] It's easy to see how, for instance, the supposed immateriality of the clouds (both weather and digital) becomes the weight of a thousand elephants, as in "Plate No. 1." In the "Frontispiece," bird specimens appear "captured," as biological specimens and, once again, as items in a database.[102] Likewise, in "Plate No. 4," tangled-up white ethernet cables pass by the landscape like clouds over a blue sky, just as a fish becomes data storage.[103] It is worth mentioning how Carpenter carries out those material transformations through poetic strategies. Likeness, material properties, shapes, and origins are the conceptual junctures where photos of "little cat *feet*" are also the "carbon *foot*prints."[104] and where data servers stand in for memories.[105] These metaphorical transformations make the invisible visible, the weightless heavy, and reveal lasting memories as ephemeral. These poetic strategies allow the author to conjure such material-conceptual transformations that clear up the "fog" of the cloud. As a counterpoint, Carpenter also touches on how these metaphoric transformations work oppositely to sustain the presentist notions of the digital cloud. The line we can consider a subtitle at the bottom of the "Frontispiece" declares this danger: "The language of The Cloud is a barrier."[106]

Most radical is the material transformation of the work's contents from the web facet to the print book. One extra process of material transformation is reading *The Gathering Cloud* as a rewriting or an altered book of Howard's volume. This analogy is suitable for understanding how Carpenter builds layers of historicity that cross the entire work upon an already existing, visibly historical print book. As the hypotext for *The Gathering Cloud,* Howard's study of the clouds is the basis and nomenclature in meteorology up until the present, and, in that way, it provides a temporal juncture to gather studies previous to it and those it bred. For Carpenter, it does more than that. For one, *The Gathering Cloud* follows the structure of the visual content in Howard's essay, a frontispiece and five plates presented in the same order. These images are the canvas in each section of the web facet, the pages on which Carpenter adds other verbal, visual, and conceptual inscriptions. Likely determined by the linearity of the codex, Howard does not overlay the "Explanation of Plates" on, or even next to, each of them, but places it early in the volume. The text from the "Explanation of Plates" is further rewritten and repurposed in *The Gathering Cloud*, suggesting Carpenter's treatment of her hypotext as a palimpsestic layer with some parts still visible and others concealed by other media layers.

The task Carpenter sets out to address in *The Gathering Cloud* is as monumental as the size of a cloud. Therefore, it is unsurprising that the author resorts to a hybrid approach that allows her to explore and convey distinct ways of organizing information and drawing connections between seemingly distant objects and times. Plate No. 5 summarizes the approach: "The Cloud spreads beyond the edges of the page / a topography of our fears and desires."[107] The topography the author offers in *The Gathering Cloud* through web and book, verses and animated images, history, and current reports, so often considered tied in binary opposition, here exists in a dialectics fulfilled by aesthetic principles and the creation of a memory of the clouds that do not follow a linear chronological order where some memories are forgotten in favor of others.

### The Latency of the Past: *La compañía* / "La máquina distópica"

Although not dealing directly with issues in digital culture like the internet or video game consoles, *La compañía* and "La máquina distópica" similarly engage in the (re)construction of the memories of industrialization and technologization in mid-twentieth-century Mexico. Verónica Gerber Bicecci's "La máquina distópica" (2018), created in collaboration with Canek Zapata and Carlos Bergen, and her *La compañía* (2019) are complementary works that engage in processes of rewriting to expose and denounce the historical, yet latent environmental catastrophes left by extractivist mining in the state of Zacatecas. Specifically, Gerber Bicecci rewrites the short story "El Huesped" (The Houseguest) by Mexican writer Amparo Dávila, while Zapata and Bergen reprogram the pioneering computational art piece *La máquina estética* by Mexican artist Manuel Felguérez (1977).[108] Like Carpenter, Gerber Bicecci seeks to unearth the connections between technological progress and environmental devastation. Most interesting is how Gerber Bicecci's work "emulate[s] the earth's unwieldy temporalities."[109] She achieves this through rewriting strategies and, crucially, through literary and material approaches that bring to light the different layers and scales of the catastrophe, particularly those related to their temporality.

"La máquina distópica" is a web application—a web oracle, according to the authors—produced for the 13th FEMSA Biennial.[110] In 2018 the itinerant biennial took place in Zacatecas under the title "Nunca Fuimos Contemporáneos" (We Have Never Been Contemporary), a riff on Bruno Latour's 1991 book title, *We Have Never Been Modern*. "La máquina distópica" was exhibited in the Museo de Arte Abstracto Manuel Felguérez, along with a mural of photographs taken by Gerber Bicecci, "the result of the trip undertaken to the ruins of the mercury mine in San Felipe Nuevo Mercurio, Zacatecas."[111]

Because Gerber Bicecci originally envisioned "La máquina distópica" to be exhibited in museum settings, projected on a 220 × 124 cm screen, rather than as a web-only platform, Zapata and Bergen programmed it to be a portable application that could run locally without relying on a database or even on a stable internet connection.[112] This crucial material decision influenced the work's minimalist interface, size, and functioning. "La máquina distópica" utilizes these material constraints to inform the application's visual design and programming. Additionally, this decision means that all the processes running in "La máquina distópica" take place directly on the browser.[113] A feature of "La máquina distópica" worth mentioning is that its minimalist web architecture is designed not to extract data via activity logs, other than the number of visits, and therefore does not produce residues. Ultimately, Zapata and Bergen also relied on minimalist design to avoid the application's premature obsolescence.

To evoke the feel of an oracle, as can be seen in Figure 22, the application displays a minimalist interface with little guidance to interpret the scant and somewhat cryptic information provided. The main feature is a white rectangle containing a set of interlocked geometric figures that emulate the outputs of Manuel Felguérez's *La máquina estética*. Following the set of instructions and rules in Fortran published by Felguérez, Bergen and Zapata replicated the generative principles in

"La máquina distópica" with the addition of microscopic photographs of water polluted with heavy metals that fill in some of the shapes in the composition.[114] Moreover, the controls that establish the parameters for generating the visual compositions are made explicit in the interface through their thematization as processes of industrialization and its consequent levels of pollution that run from the present to a distant future. On the left side of the screen are three sliding bars that control each variable: a year in the future between 2018 (the year the piece was created) and 2699, pollution levels from 0 percent to 100 percent, and automation of labor from 0 × to 3 ×. These variables, which the reader can control, are manifested in visual elements. A later year, in the first sliding bar, yields a higher count of geometric figures, between four and sixteen, and a more chaotic composition overall.[115] The pollution levels control the coloration given to the microscopic photographs of water samples that fill an individual shape in the grouping ranging from blue and green hues at lower pollution levels to red and brown ones at higher ones. The third variable manifests verbally through the oracle's message at the bottom of the rectangle by recombining and intervening Dávila's nature verses with corporate, industrial, and environmental terminologies, which are more prevalent the higher the rates of human labor substitution.

Published in 2019 by the independent Mexican press Almadía, *La compañía* furthers Gerber Bicecci's examination of extractivist mining and its effects on the environment and nearby populations. *La compañía* comprises two halves: "part a" and "part b." The former is a graphic short story where Gerber Bicecci reutilizes the photographic record produced for the FEMSA Biennial and rewrites another text by Dávila, a complete rewrite in the future tense of the short story "The Houseguest." Dávila's story from 1959 features a family whose life is perturbed by the presence of a houseguest brought in by the largely absent husband. The somber and sinister guest terrorizes the children and the women every night until the housewife and her house worker, Guadalupe, entrap him and starve him to death. Gerber Bicecci significantly changes two characters. The guest, here named "La compañía,"

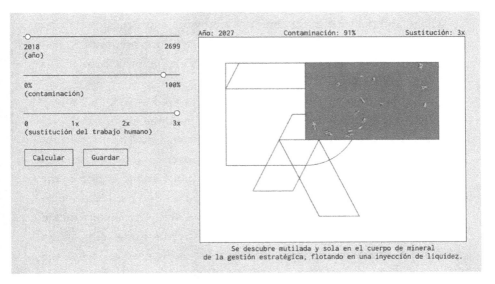

FIGURE 22. A screenshot of "La máquina distópica" shows the compositions resulting from the parameters indicated in the three sliding bars. Reproduced with permission.

is an unspecific threatening entity that allegorizes the pollution of the mercury mine, its effects, and the damage and exploitation perpetrated by the mining company itself. In her account, Gerber Bicecci presents the guest as a generalized, nameless Company that threatens the inhabitants of a house, an allegory of the town. In Gerber Bicecci's future-tense premonition, Guadalupe, the house worker, becomes "la Máquina" (the machine). To establish these connections between the changes in the characters, Gerber Bicecci overlays small fragments of the story's text, usually one or two sentences, page by page over the stark black-and-white photographs, as Figure 23 shows. Together, the future-tense premonition and the visual evidence of the pictures insinuate distinct moments of and perspectives on the devastation left by the mine. In Gerber Bicecci's photographs, "only the traces are left, the ruins of the town," and thus, more than an illustration of the story, the visual features of the photographs resignify the location, the characters, and the time of the threat posed by the houseguest.[116] Further overlaid on some of the photographs are ideograms produced by Felguérez's *La máquina estética,* which visually tie the print book to "La máquina distópica."

The horror story in part "a" is further layered in part "b." There, Gerber Bicecci reconstructs the history of the mine out of official reports, interviews, newspaper articles, and blueprints. The documentation spans a period that starts with the discovery of mercury deposits in the 1940s, passes through the cyclical change of ownership of the mine over approximately half a century, and goes to its illegal repurposing as a toxic waste dumping site in the 1980s. This reconstructed memory complements the view of the industrial mining ruins of San Felipe Nuevo Mercurio from another sense of the past: one when the town first flourished because of "La compañía."

Although operating separately, "La máquina distópica" and *La compañía* are arguably the output of a single aesthetic exploration whose most powerful meaning emerges cumulatively out of print and digital elements. Considering them together allows us to amplify the conceptual, historical, and affective connections that Gerber Bicecci proposes through the temporalities of each medium. Indeed, the sum of the divergent temporalities across the two facets undercuts any reading of progress (economic, industrial, or social) that could be attached to the mine. Part "a" situates the reader in a point in the past via the narrative, before the destructive effects of the mine, and simultaneously in the present, the aftermath of the catastrophe, via the photographs. The high-contrast images, reminiscent of microfilm archives, convey the landscape's ruinous state, a past still there in the present.

Despite losing detail, or rather because of the purposeful degradation of the image, the photographs suggest a provenance much further in the past than they are, as though they were part of the residue and ruins of the mining activity rather than a present-day view detached from the past. Through this microfilm aesthetic, Gerber Bicecci collapses the distance between the events of the past and her view in the present. Those ruins are not only the remains of what happened in the

FIGURE 23. A page from *La compañía* shows Gerber Bicecci's high-contrast image, suggesting it comes from a time posterior to the catastrophe. Yet, the text in the future tense paradoxically indicates that it has not yet happened. Reproduced with permission.

past but a site where the effects of pollution will remain latent into the distant future. The chronicle in part "b" similarly stretches and contracts the timelines and terms of the impacts of extractivist mining. We briefly glimpse San Felipe Nuevo Mercurio's flourishing through the ruins of its past.[117] The dumping of toxic substances, barely a short-term solution, leaves its effects for an inestimable future period.[118]

*La compañía* has been criticized for "unremembering" the historical context of Mexico in the 1940s and 1970s—the decades of economic flourishing brought by industrialization.[119] However, far from indicating a lack of disciplinary rigor—after all, Gerber Bicecci is not a historian—the lack of historicity in both texts invites us to reflect on how environmental devastation does not conform to a neat temporal line. Water pollution and ailments caused by exposure to toxic chemicals did not end when the mine changed ownership, not even once the mine was permanently shut. Moreover, the events narrated in part "b" shed light on the construction of "la compañía" (the guest) as an allegory for the devastation rather than the specific role, name, or owner of the company at any given time. Instead, "la compañía" in the story stands for the cumulative effects of extractivism as a "measure for stimulating economic growth" in Latin America and the decided unsustainability of capitalism and the pursuit of short-term profit.[120] Likewise, the web facet compels us to visualize the future of the devastation not as one that will get mitigated but as one with a lingering sense of doom in a distant future with many possible scenarios. It delivers a glimpse into a dystopic future of water pollution and automated labor like that foreseen in part "a."

The different temporalities staged by each element of the work compel us to consider how collapsing the distance among various historical moments in the life of the mine reveals the material and affective complexity of its remains: the excitement of discovering mercury, the boom years, the distrust caused by the development of a variety of ailments, the alluring material traces left in the form of ruins, the disturbing awareness of lingering pollution, and an uncertain future where humans may or may not be present, replaced by automation or by other surviving species. Furthermore, the fact that Gerber Bicecci considers the different temporal scales of the mining catastrophe through various media (a digital application with visual and poetic elements, a print book of photographs, a fictional narrative, and historical records) indicates that her choices follow the temporality that each best conveys, their affordances. "La máquina distópica," susceptible to various degrees and timeframes of obsolescence like any other web object, is also where the author makes us consider the uncertainty of the future; a print codex, *La compañía* holds the documentation of what has already happened and a warning of what can happen in the future.

DIVERGENT TEMPORALITIES IN BINDING MEDIA   173

---

The three works examined here advance distinct approaches to the temporalities of media, that is, to the specific perceptions and experiences of time they propose. Bogost deals with an obsolete technology, the Atari video game, by expertly reconstructing it in minute detail. His treatment of the past seeks to bring a moment in time back right *as it was* rather than in the ways *it continues to be*. In contrast, Carpenter and Gerber Bicecci build palimpsests of archival materials, fragments, ruins, and remains from different moments in time to complicate the linearity of histories of technology and industrialization. They both suggest that nothing is of the past alone to add depth to the present. These two approaches to the temporality of media confront the effects of presentism. *A Slow Year* offers an excess of memory, a fetishization of the past that nonetheless rails against the loss of a beloved media object caused by the imperative of technological innovation. *The Gathering Cloud* and "La máquina distópica" / *La compañía* conversely take on ephemerality itself and unpack its speed to demonstrate that, unlike the sought-after acceleration of economic returns, the effects of technology and industrialization are everything but short-lived and outside of history.

As I've argued throughout this chapter, binding media are exceptionally well situated to shed light on the effects of digital presentism on cultural memory-building, literary production, and scholarship. It is possible to see binding media as cultural products that neatly fit the thinness of digital presentism. In that way, each exemplar embodies a very specific contemporariness, a short-lived technocultural moment. Nonetheless, viewed as a corpus and with the benefit of retrospection, binding media draw attention to the artificiality of their ephemerality. The divergent temporalities of print and digital media found in *A Slow Year*, *The Gathering Cloud*, and "La máquina distópica" / *La compañía* confirm that ephemerality and obsolescence aren't inherent features of their objectual materiality, but are instead the results of a structuring of time that guides the material conditions in which they are produced and circulated. Indeed, as Carpenter and Gerber Bicecci demonstrate, these temporalities are also exercises in political, legal, and discursive power. Moreover, the hybrid materiality of binding media quickly leads us to interrogate their ephemerality and how a mismatch in their economic temporalities as digital applications and print books may preclude the very possibility of their study.

Methodologically, in this chapter, I have attempted to build a conceptual shift in our consideration of digital literature that is not foreshortened by obsolescence but made possible by it. The conceptualizations I take from Giselle Beiguelman, Nelly Richard, and Cristina Rivera Garza offer illuminating strategies to deal with fragmentary records, incomplete archives, provisional documentation, and indexical information. As many digital facets of binding media exemplars slowly but very likely move into obsolescence, their remains will continue to insist on that which is no longer accessible. For digital preservation efforts, these remains can likewise offer a blueprint and a context for their reanimation. Richard's formulation of "cultural remains" provides a basis to envision a literary history of binding media built from residual pieces where their context of creation, production, and decay becomes a history in its own right. The shift from content to context proposed by Beiguelman might not fit in with longstanding methodologies of literary study. Yet, this type of approach will become increasingly necessary if we are not to shrink the field of digital literature to the limited number of digital literary works that get ported, emulated, or otherwise provisionally preserved. Arguably, binding media exemplars like *The Gathering Cloud* and "La máquina distópica" / *La compañía* already rehearse this approach through their archival research, layered presentations, and palimpsestic conceptualizations of time and history. Rather than fetishizing and replicating in detail the affordances, aesthetics, and worlds of old technologies, Carpenter and Gerber Bicecci propose alternative paths to engage and reflect upon the temporalities of the technologies they study in their works, as well as those they use in their investigation. Ultimately, the divergent temporalities of binding media undermine the idea that media histories follow a straight line, taking them to a predictable ending, or that we can even fully record them.

FOUR

# MEDIA HYBRIDITY AND CULTURAL HYBRIDITY

**ALTHOUGH THE HISTORY AND POLITICS** of the Zapatista movement are well outside the scope of this book, there are two paradigmatic moments in the past of the uprising's communications that exemplify the messy technological transitions occurring in the last four decades and that serve as a backdrop to the technocultural changes concretized in binding media. The first one, the reason why many consider the Zapatista uprising the first digital social movement, took place shortly after January 1, 1994. As the Zapatistas purposefully distributed the Declaración de la Selva Lacandona outside of mainstream Mexican TV and press channels, it made its way to La Neta, an early left-wing online network based in Mexico with broad international connections via the Association for Progressive Communications. These networks circulated the declaration with other antiwar, antiglobalization groups, such as PeaceNet and Usenet, reaching a distributed yet supportive audience in many parts of the world. The distribution of the declaration and later communiqués through these networks built an "electronic fabric of struggle" that gave the Zapatistas global attention, relevance, and, quite literally, vital support.[1] International attention and support online has been a constant in the thirty years since the uprising. The well-known "FloodNet" action carried out in 1998 by the art collective Electronic Disturbance Theatre against the websites of the Bank of Mexico and the office of the Mexican president was a direct result of establishing networks of solidarity for the Zapatistas on the internet.[2] The second instance happened a few years later and is known as the "Zapatista air force attack on the Mexican army," a symbolic attack carried out with paper airplanes that Zapatista members launched on the Mexican army's camp in Valle de Amador. The airplanes, "white in color and letter sized," carried typewritten and carbon-copied messages encouraging individual soldiers to turn their backs on the Mexican government and reminding them that the Zapatista struggle was also theirs.[3] Almost opposite to the use of early global digital communications, the "Zapatista air force attack" was localized to a small municipality in Chiapas, carried out exclusively by Zapatista members rather than with an extended network of support, and (ideated as almost a one-to-one communication with members of the army) as low tech as possible. The symbolic and tactical dimension of the paper airplanes, however, perturbed the military field of signification associated with the "air force" from one of military technological might into one of personal appeal.

While not an exact parallel, binding media and the communication strategies of the Zapatistas take place in a shared media landscape. Their co-occurrence is a sign of the historical moment in media transition and experimentation when distinct media are deliberately used according to their specific affordances to appeal to different audiences and to convey specific messages. Both binding media and the Zapatistas' communication strategies are evidence of the widespread digital revolution and of how the media ecology has shifted and revealed the advantages of specific media to carry information with distinct effects. One need only look around at cultural endeavors like entertainment franchises (even independent ones),[4] academic projects,[5] and social media movements[6] to observe how each of them paints a broad landscape where many media practices manifest the back-and-forth interactions between print habits and protocols, and computational and digital ones in a plethora of ways. We can hardly pinpoint this lengthy process to a single development or invention. Instead, it is a media ecology where individual shifts provoke cumulative and multiplex effects whose results are hard to predict.

This landscape, however, is not one of media shifts alone but one where the local and the global inform each other. The Zapatista proposal to build "a world where many worlds fit" advances and negotiates the relationship between these cultural, political, economic, and media spaces.[7] Furthermore, it is a landscape where imaginaries of hybridity can be utilized both as instruments of neoliberal, globalized cultural industries that, through images of synthesis and harmony, obscure conflicts, inequality, and exploitation, and as strategies of representation and critique that resist and make visible such conflicts, contradictions, and power imbalances. Argentinian cultural critic Laura Catelli characterizes the latter as a "postcolonial semiosis" that is "a consideration of cultural hybridization, its resulting artifacts, and interactions always within the context of relationships and practices of power, knowledge and, subjectivation forged under the logic of colonialism that persists in the globalized present."[8] I argue that binding media is among these strategies that, through media hybridization, interrogate processes of cultural hybridization via its material features and the market challenges they have entailed, as well as, in many instances, their thematic foci.

As I've argued throughout this book, binding media are a microcosm of the vaster phenomena occurring broadly in global communications and, more specifically, in literary creation and publishing practices emerging from the popularization of digital technologies. Binding media not only share a media landscape with a political movement like the Zapatistas but also coexist with mainstream practices of entertainment franchises, for instance. An outcome of sharing such a media landscape is that, although experimental, binding media rely on hegemonic uses and literacies in print and digital media, even when designed for entertainment, productivity, information, and other purposes. In binding media and other creative approaches, artists and authors adapt hegemonic functionalities to nondefault functions.[9] As such, binding media integrate these dominant practices into literature and precipitate critical ways to engage with technological developments. This tension comes to the forefront in how binding media exemplars have ostensibly birthed the future of the book through features that fit the logic of technological progress and, in contrast, how individual exemplars interrogate this ideological basis through nondefault examinations of materiality and meaning. In a different context, Mexicanist scholar Carolyn Fornoff has characterized this ambivalent cultural strategy as "critical proximity."[10] Far from endorsing notions of linear progress and history, binding media continually make us stumble with reminders of their paradoxical materiality as two distinct media objects with distinct lifespans and tangled up in two media industries that construct value through different sets of parameters. As an artistic practice, binding media offer little in terms of prognosis about the future. Still, they compel an examination of their materiality and aesthetics as correlates of the more prominent contemporary and still unfinished technocultural processes that encompass them.

In this chapter, I take these ideas a step forward to propose binding media as a material substrate of processes of cultural hybridization. I further argue that at the turn of the twenty-first century, dynamics of cultural and media hybridization are instigated by the neoliberalization of politics and market economies, the movement of goods and monetary resources around the world, neocolonial extractivism of natural resources that include overt and covert military intervention, and the globalization and expediency of digital communications. Far from celebrating a "coming together of the world" through real-time, digital technologies and transnational industries, I emphasize that—just as has historically been the case—processes of cultural hybridization take place under dynamics of oppression where discursive representations (of places, peoples, and so forth) circulating in literature and media through the internet serve to negotiate power. The results of these historical conditions, such as forced migration, environmental displacement, and economic migration, create the spaces where cultural "encounter" and hybridization occur. A constant reminder of the underlying causes of cultural hybridization is to avoid the pervasiveness of the more positive-sounding "synthesis," "connection," "exchange," and "fusion" that surround the notion of hybridity. Instead, concepts that respond to and resist simple positivity, like "contact," "struggle," "recovery," "survival," "healing," and "negotiation," help us highlight the oppressive conditions at the basis of "hybridity" more accurately.

I approach the notion of hybridization in two distinct though interwoven ways. The first is to showcase the copresence of media in opposition to the familiar progressivist narratives of rupture, succession, and disruption. As I have done in previous chapters, I look at the spectrum of interactions of print and digital media as a process of hybridization that renders bespoke objects or variants bridging two uneven media objects, cultural realms, and industries. Likewise, as previous chapters indicate, binding media are complex cultural objects that manifest in their very materiality a process of hybridization along with their entailed conflicts and contradictions. The second approach to hybridization, and the focus of this chapter, is to examine how these hybrid material objects are also the outcomes of the destructive market, political, and technological conditions of late capitalism that have prompted widespread human movement in unjust conditions that have their origins in the biopolitics of the colonial order.[11] Hybridity, then, is a strategic concept that characterizes the technocultural phenomenon of media fastening and cultural critique that authors engage in to interrogate hegemonic ways of defining identity, restricting movement, and negotiating memory. Therefore, I show how, rather than depicting an imaginary of harmonious hybridization and smoothed-out contradictions, binding media underscore the friction at the basis of a notion like hybridity. In fact, binding media emphasize the rough edges of the material conditions that make them possible, while enacting cultural critiques at the center of their aesthetic projects.

To attend to these interlocking considerations surrounding globalized technocultural processes of hybridization, I reelaborate the notion of the contact zone as the space where both instances of the phenomenon take place. By bringing together the work of Mary Louise Pratt on the zone of contact and Alan Liu on media encounters, I map the recurrent tropes in the treatment of cultural hybridity and media hybridity. I then revisit recent theories that propose media hybridity, such as postdigital publishing, and a couple of instantiations of hybrid publishing. Through this analysis, I argue that studies in media hybridization have lacked a critical foregrounding that considers the human toll of late capitalism, particularly forced migration. Last, I examine three works that, like all binding media, have a hybrid print-digital configuration and that, in addition, thematically address migration and transnationality as a matter of survival, identity healing, and historical rewriting. These are *The Transborder Immigrant Tool / La herramienta transfronteriza para inmigrantes* by the Electronic Disturbance Theatre 2.0 / b.a.n.g. lab (2010/2014); Guillermo Gómez-Peña, Felicia Rice, and their coauthors' *DOC/UNDOC* (2014/2017); and Cristina Rivera Garza's "@EstacionCamaron" / *Autobiografía del algodón* (2016/2020). Together, these examples of binding media foreground the notion that processes of hybridization are at the center of the formal material composition of literary works that fasten print and digital media objects and, in parallel, represent and address the complex and dangerous realities of geographic movement, identity healing, and historical representation of vulnerable bodies across Mexico and the United States. Moreover, human movement and the transfer of meaning from one medium to another, from poetry to survival, from performance to text, and from archives to identity similarly indicate processes of hybridization that cross the entirety of these literary projects.

Through these examples, I emphasize the present-day processes of hybridization, specifically in the context of the US–Mexican border—as a zone of contact. The three works I examine lay bare the contradictory status of hybridity by showing the reparatory potential of blurring the lines between supposedly stable realms like Mexico/United States, here/there, documented/undocumented, and History/history, as well as their tensions and limitations. Furthermore, in these three works, we see that beyond an interest in formal experimentation alone, authors examine their respective historical contexts as a much larger priority. Yet, their works all underscore how the cumulative affordances of media hybridity best represent the conflicting and contradictory experiences of migration and binationality. More than any theory, these works demonstrate the co-occurrence of media and cultural hybridity within the spaces their authors construct to negotiate survival, identity, and history. The match between cultural hybridization and media hybridization is certainly not exclusive to binding media. However, I propose to see binding media as an instantiation of a recurrent process where cultural encounter generates new artistic forms and identities.[12] As my analyses show, however, where these literary works appear to result in syntheses, they do so only in their aesthetic roundedness. Conceptually and politically, they lay bare the conflicts, tensions, inequalities, and contradictions surrounding hybridization processes.

**The Zone of Contact**
My reelaboration of the zone of contact proposes it as a technocultural landscape where both media hybridization and cultural hybridization take place, marked by power dynamics that may be political, economic, medial, and literary.[13] Binding media result from the contact and intersections between print book and digital book objects, between the expressive and material affordances of each, between print and digital publishing practices, between commercial and independent publishing, and between the temporalities of print and digital media. Additionally, in the examples addressed here, binding media are the outcome of migration between or across national, cultural, and linguistic borders.

As a term first coined by Mary Louise Pratt in her study of colonial travel narratives, *Imperial Eyes: Travel Writing and Transculturation* (1992), the contact zone is "the space and time where subjects previously separated by geography and history are co-present, the point at which their trajectories now intersect."[14] Pratt bases this conceptualization on the notion of contact drawn from linguistics, where a "contact language" refers to "an impoverished language that develops among speakers of different tongues who need to communicate with each other consistently, usually in the context of trade."[15] Crucial for Pratt's articulation of the contact zone is the existence of power differentials in the copresence of subjects and languages, which, in our case, can be expanded to media objects. As I have been arguing, in the context of colonial and postcolonial enterprises, encounters aren't symmetrical but take place through exercises of power, coercion, and discrimination. Such asymmetries in power continue to play out in the contemporary world under various guises (neocolonial dynamics, neoliberalization, transnationalism, forced migration, and globalized forms of communication). These asymmetries push multiple forms of contact and conflict.

More important than a specific outline of the contact zone is Pratt's identification of its outcomes, which she terms the "arts of the contact zone." The arts of the contact zone are of two kinds: those created by the dominant culture to establish the otherness of the oppressed and thus justify its exercise of power, and those produced by the oppressed to counter such otherness and power.[16] Just like the competing notions of hybridity, the arts of the contact zone advance two equally competing discursive proposals. In her elaboration of the arts of the contact zone, however, Pratt leaves a specific notion of medium relatively underdeveloped. Yet, her analyses reveal a keen emphasis on the media and the objects through which the arts of the contact zones express their hybridity, or in her preferred term, transculturation. The linguistic genealogy of the contact zone and Pratt's textual examples suggest the requisite for a media configuration—a material expression—through which the contact is established, transmitted, and enacted.[17] Here, I aim to expand Pratt's conceptualization of the zone of contact to strategically bind and switch between the processes of cultural hybridization in the context of the Mexican-US border and the practices of media hybridization in works that fasten print and digital media.

In digital literary studies, Katherine Hayles proposed a similar space where media shifts occur: "the tangled web of medial ecology [where] change anywhere in the system stimulates change everywhere in the system."[18] Moreover, Alan Liu's observations on the media encounter more accurately help us outline the co-occurrence of cultural and media hybridization. For Liu, narratives of media encounters also occur within a media ecological space: "a thick, unpredictable zone of contact—more borderland than border—where (mis)understandings of new media are negotiated along twisting, partial, and contradictory vectors."[19] What's more, just as Pratt's study of travel narratives illustrates the construction of otherness in the Americas, Liu argues that narratives of media encounter have been central to the production of Western culture and the production of a worldview based on notions progressing in a straight line from colonial periods, to modernization and industrialization, and up until their contemporary instantiations as "globalization," "innovation," and "disruption."[20] In Liu's theorizations, we can see that, just as happens in processes of colonization and migration, the new media encounter produces otherness. Nevertheless, this is an otherness based not on culture, language, or race but on ideals of newness and progress that similarly encode an exercise of power and self-justification. Moreover, despite focusing on media rather than on human subjects, Liu also sees the new media encounter as a space where power differentials—political, economic, and technological—impact the very meaning of progress, newness, adoption, and failure, for instance, in the differentiation of cultures as more or less technologically advanced.[21]

Putting together the work of these two scholars reveals that mediating objects do much more than just transmit or communicate historical events; they symbolically shape and are part of that history.[22] Indeed, we can also expand on Pratt's methodological assumption that "important historical transitions alter the way people write, because they alter people's experiences, and the way people imagine, feel, and think about the world they live in" in two ways.[23] First, media practices, protocols, and meaning-making strategies, like writing, are altered by historical transitions, including changes to the media landscape. Second, present-day hybrid literary works are media practices that concretize contemporary experiences of the globalized world, such as migration and transnationality. Likewise, following Hayles's ecological thinking, such practices are not only an outcome or a reflection of historical changes and events but can also precipitate further shifts and developments in media and cultural practices. We can thus see binding media as both a contemporary form of the arts of the contact zone and a concretization of the media encounter; they are literary endeavors in which the media shifts and encounters characterized by Hayles and Liu, and the cultural encounters examined by Pratt, are concurrent.

In my analyses of binding media, the cultural manifestations of hybridity negotiate the identity of media and, in the case of the examples I examine in this chapter, migrant experiences. These negotiations entail the paradoxical process of recognizing the border "line" or "edge" that separates discrete symbolic, political, or cultural realms and interrogating such lines and edges by focusing on hybridization processes. The contact zone and its cultural manifestations are thus locked in the jagged tension between the reification and the rejection of the border's limits. It is clear, however, that binding media respond to claims of purity in media as well as to binaries ruled by conventionalities like United States/Mexico, documented/undocumented, and so on. Binding media works examine and exploit the tension of material otherness. The irresolvability of such tension has led García Canclini to establish that hybridization is always best understood as a process rather than a finished outcome. He proposes to think instead of hybridization as "socio-cultural processes in which discrete structures or practices, previously existing in separate form, are combined to generate new structures, objects, and practices."[24] The tropes of contact zones and the media encounter serve to ground how binding media appear to resolve the divide between print and digital objects through the poetic and aesthetic projects of a single literary work, but, in doing so, they also highlight the limits of each one, whether expressive, technical, or material. In this way, the contact zone is not just a locus where otherness is projected and countered, but one where, out of such demarcation and negotiation processes, new forms, practices, and meanings can come into being. Arguably, these processes are part of a cycle in which hybrid structures or practices reach at least some level of standardization or mainstreaming, only to partake in further processes of hybridization.

Following these scholars, I think of "contact," "encounter," and "process" as the underlying conceptualizations that help us nuance a working notion of hybridity as they decenter the (linear) ideas of domination, conquest, succession, and outcome, yet all take place within an uneven space where relationality, copresence, and practice occur in asymmetrical ways.[25] Methodologically, the zone of contact is the space where I situate binding media to argue that media and cultural hybridity are coconstitutive and that specific manifestations emerge from such coconstitutiveness in culture and literature. Ultimately, the zone of contact is also useful to outline the historical and cultural specificity of media transitions. In this way, although the intersection of print and digital media taking place in the last four decades shares many features with other technocultural moments when print interacted with other emergent media, I can more accurately delineate binding media as a creative and publishing phenomenon of the turn of the twenty-first century in a culture of globalization punctuated by neoliberalism, human movement, and the increasing adoption of digital communications all across the Americas.

## From Cultural Hybridity to Media Hybridity

Developments in digital media in the last few decades have brought about widespread changes to art, communications, and entertainment. The trajectory of these developments has intersected with previously existing models and drawn a landscape where many media forms coexist and blend. The work of Pratt and Liu, discussed above, makes it evident that the emergence of complex textual objects in spaces like the contemporary media landscape presents methodological and conceptual challenges. Specifically, in the field of literary and media studies, the intersections of print and digital media, and their complicated topologies and histories have prompted several theoretical approaches. Areas of study like media-specific analysis or comparative textual media[26] and media archaeology,[27] and conceptualizations like the post-

Web,[28] the post-Internet,[29] intermediality,[30] transmediality, and media convergence,[31] have sought to characterize particularized phenomena of media transitions and shifts that happen through overlap, mixing, appropriation, interrelation, adoption, recovery, and so on.

I argue that these varied approaches result from contact and encounter, and when seen together, they signal processes of hybridization as extensive as the generalized media shifts. Even when only some of them utilize the notion of hybridity to characterize specific phenomena, all these theorizations deal with forms of boundary shifting and, in fact, the proliferation of terms, as above, resembles the parallel abundance of concepts related to hybridity, such as "mestizaje," "transculturation," "creolization," "métissage," and "liminality." I thus take their heterogeneity, their insistence on being outside of established conventions and domains (denoted by the prefixes "post-," "inter-," and "trans-") as indications that they concretize distinct processes of media and cultural hybridization. However, as I have argued in the previous sections, these parallel processes, even when seen through such a proliferation of approaches, have not been theorized together in a way that treats media hybridization as the material substrate of cultural hybridity.

Without intersecting, theorizations of both media and cultural hybridity have shared the tendency to extol a revelatory or emancipatory potential of hybridization. As Anjali Prabhu has succinctly stated, "in its dominant form, it is claimed that [hybridity] can provide a way out of binary thinking, allow the inscription of the agency of the subaltern, and even permit a restructuring and destabilizing of power."[32] In this instantiation, hybridity embodies a hefty set of postcolonial or decolonial principles that are rarely, if ever, fulfilled. A similar but less political take on hybridity has been standard in media studies. Hans-Joachim Backe credits Marshall McLuhan with introducing the idea of hybridity to media studies in this affirmative manner.[33] For the Canadian media theorist, "the hybrid or the meeting of two media is a moment of truth and revelation from which a new form is born . . . The moment of the meeting of media is a moment of freedom and release from the ordinary trance and numbness imposed by them on our senses."[34] Despite the exalted rhetoric, McLuhan saw the meeting of two media as a common phenomenon constantly producing the new. In McLuhan's words, we recognize the media-archaeological intent to distance us from ingrained media habits and ideologies—the "ordinary trance." In this positive incarnation, processes of hybridization amount to resistance toward hegemonic domains, whether in media or in politics and culture.

In contrast, hybridity has been the subject of much critique in cultural studies from three main perspectives: in its unrealized emancipatory potential; in its usage to resolve, rather than underscore, the contradictions, tensions, and jaggedness of mixing; and in its inattention to its biopolitical origins.[35] To this list, I would add the inattention to how neoliberal capitalism sets up the conditions for contemporary processes of cultural hybridization and sanctions some of its manifestations as a coming together of the world while pinning others as transgressions against the order of national borders. However, I find the conceptual critiques of hybridity to be the most illuminating when thinking about binding media, namely, the problematization and regulation of purity based on conventionality rather than empirical evidence. Postcolonial theorist Homi Bhabha explains that there is abundant empirical evidence that throughout history "hierarchical claims to the inherent originality or 'purity' of cultures are untenable," suggesting that hybridization processes are more prevalent than conventionally discrete cultural realms of action.[36] Instead, as Latin-America scholar Joshua Lund proposes, exemplarity is the mark of hybrid phenomena, a "condition of exemption, the trait that exemplifies membership in a set, but that enigmatically does not belong there itself, that participates without belonging."[37] In the spectrum of what does or does not belong within the bounds of conventions, hybrid phenomena coconstitute that which they deviate from. Consequently, through the negotiation of the boundaries of conventionality, new, initially hybrid forms and practices can become part of a delineated standard, only to become a part of further hybridization processes.

The negotiation of boundaries and the condition of exemplarity are valuable frameworks to think about binding media as they incorporate the domains of their interrogation. For instance, in *Permanente obra negra*, Vivian Abenshushan utilizes the notation "~~book~~" to interrogate the affordances of every book object that makes up her project. But she does not subvert the concept of the book. Similarly, in *ABRA*, Borsuk, Durbin, and Hatcher stretch the expressive capacities of the iPad app, the trade book, and the artist's book as much as possible to investigate how the meaning of "mutation" itself mutates in different media, but in the process all of the book objects underscore their irreplicable affordances. Lastly, as I examine later in this chapter, authors resort to the hybrid materiality of binding media to interrogate and contest the ideology of borderization and legality, but these works can hardly overcome the material power of the military and bureaucratic violence ruling the conventionality of national borders.

In the next section, I rely on these conceptualizations to query the offhanded use of "hybridity" in recent media and publishing phenomena. While I do not argue for a discontinuation of the use of "hybridity" to characterize materially complex objects emerging from print and digital publishing, I do propose a more nuanced approach to the term that considers its colonial origins and its contemporary instantiations in a globalized world.

### Hybrid Publishing, the Postdigital Turn

In contrast to the abundance of terms referring to media and cultural contact and hybridity identified above, in publishing, there has been a proliferation of meanings and practices referred to as "hybrid." To take just two examples, for the Digital Publishing Toolkit Collective, "hybrid publishing" consists of multichannel publishing, that is, the ability to publish identical titles in print and e-book format or both simultaneously. The collective's emphasis on visually oriented publishing (titles devoted to art and design) addresses the transition from print books, for which paper and the codex format matter, into workflows and outputs that, for the most part, eschew the material importance.[38] A very different take on "hybrid publishing" is that of the Independent

Book Publishers Association, which offers this definition: "hybrid publishing companies behave just like traditional publishing companies in all respects, except that they publish books using an author-subsidized business model, as opposed to financing all costs themselves and, in exchange, return a higher-than-industry-standard share of sales proceeds to the author."[39]

My own conceptualization of binding media as hybrid encompasses the creative approaches to book objects, the objects used for a work's publication, and the material processes of the publishing industry. The polysemy of the adjective "hybrid" in the realm of books and publishing indicates an increase in approaches outside established conventions. In fact, in both the Digital Publishing Toolkit Collective and the Independent Book Publishers Association, we can see a response to the push of either the shift in workflows prompted by tech developments or the reconfiguration of business models reacting to market imperatives.

European scholars like Christian Ulrik Andersen, Geoff Cox, and Georgios Papadopoulos, who proposed the framework of the postdigital in 2013, consider it a merging of "old" and "new" that does not mark a distinction between the two and does not recognize the "ideological affirmation" of the one over the other.[40] Florian Cramer offered a working definition of the postdigital as a term that "sucks but is useful" to refer to "hybrids of 'old' and 'new' media" associated with artistic practices mainly in Europe.[41] Moreover, for Cramer, the postdigital is "either a contemporary disenchantment with digital information systems and media gadgets or a period in which our fascination with these systems and gadgets has become historical."[42] Following Cramer, the postdigital, like other media hybridization approaches, sees the potential of blending old and new technologies to counter the imperative of technological innovation and even to counter corporate media through DIY (do-it-yourself) practices. Arguably, the most innovative contribution of Cramer's definition of the postdigital is his observation that these hybrid practices "tend to focus less on content and more on pure materiality" and how such awareness of a medium's affordances offers creators a choice to rely on media that are best suited to their projects, rather than defaulting to the latest.[43]

Focused exclusively on print and publishing, Italian editor and writer Alessandro Ludovico similarly thinks of the postdigital as a cultural condition in which digital technologies can already be taken for granted and, thus, can be experimented with and overcome. As the founder of *Neural* magazine, Ludovico is no stranger to experimental and unconventional publishing practices, and yet, his views of the hybridization of old and new seem oddly prescriptive. For instance, he rightly sees the recent state of book design and publishing as a still unfinished process. Nevertheless, he also diagnoses that it will reach culmination in the emergence of "true hybrids," an "alchemic intertwining of the traditional print with the digital . . . that generates new types of publications and genres."[44] His decades of experience in publishing allow Ludovico to envision and outline specific ways in which this true hybridity might take form: "a hybrid product should have a strategy composed by its software part, which would provide some content through a process, and an analogue part which would frame and contextualise it. The level that this hybridisation can reach is only limited by the conceptualisation and the sophistication of the act and the process."[45] Ludovico's strategy indicates the possibility of various degrees of hybridization that produce a "new" form, a type of publication that "seamlessly integrat[es] the two worlds," on the one hand, and becomes the basis for replicable processes, on the other.[46] His critique of the bespokeness of Amaranth Borsuk and Brad Bouse's *Between Page and Screen* as "only reproducible in an exact way" confirms that he is interested in envisioning scalable and standardizable hybrid publishing models rather than in the unique aesthetic and material roundedness of a specific project. Arguably, the way Ludovico envisions this new type of publication is not unlike binding media. However, because his work speculates how hybrid publishing *should* work rather than being based on the description of extant instances, he misses what the analyses of my corpus show, that bespoke strategies might prove damning for a scalable and standardizable publishing practice, but they are the necessary material conditions for the aesthetic and literary soundness of individual projects. Additionally, replicable strategies that emerged around the same time Ludovico theorized postdigital print in the early 2010s, as shown in chapter 2, have proved less than scalable. Ultimately, rather than seeking seamless integration of print and digital objects, most examples of binding media emphasize the tensions between, and the distinctiveness of, the two. Indeed, I would argue that the order—the condition of "true"—that Ludovico seeks to impose on the hybridization of print and digital media is incompatible with the messiness and unpredictability of hybridization processes themselves.

While early conceptualizations of the postdigital, like Cramer's and Ludovico's, defined a research agenda, they also denote an overenthusiasm of the revelatory potential of hybridity to produce the "new" even when it sought to counter the "new" of tech progression. Here is where I believe that the influence of scholarship on cultural hybridity can shed some missing criticality into theories of media hybridization. While theories of the postdigital are correct to identify processes of hybridization in artistic and publishing practices marked by the contact of print and digital media, their assumption that the tipping point of saturation of digital technologies is behind such mixing is questionable. Fundamentally, in Cramer's writing, I see a lack of problematization of the notions of "old" and "new" that respond to the imperatives of innovation and planned obsolescence that the postdigital should interrogate. Further, by not interrogating those terms, Cramer unwittingly suggests that there is a clear demarcation—or purity—between them. What's more, Cramer's lack of interrogation internalizes the linear temporality of the tech industry, as seen in his use of terms like "return" and "revival." Ludovico more usefully deals within the domains of publishing objects. Nonetheless, like Cramer, he also implies a stageist dynamic in which digital technologies are *past* a tipping point and can be taken for granted. While this might be true in regions of the Global North, the emphasis on saturation suggests a symmetrical world where the adoption and access to digital technologies are uniform.

In contrast, Argentinian scholar Claudia Kozak has rightly countered assumptions like this when she problematizes the issue of access and adoption as uneven, not just from a geographic perspective of North and South but from the role that a particular region in the world occupies in the dynamics of the transnational, neoliberal, globalized world.[47] More concretely, scholarship on the postdigital fails to account for differences in geographic contexts and digital divides worldwide, particularly in the Global South. Regions like Latin America, rather than being transnational centers of technological innovation saturated with ever-increasing digitality, have been consumers of hegemonic digital technologies and have experienced technocultural changes sometimes through scarcity and slow adoption. Concerning the same issue, the Uruguayan net artist Brian Mackern asks, "Is the 'low-tech' made in Europe similar to the 'low-tech' made in Latin America? They appear to be the same, but I think that one 'works' from 'shortage' whereas the other 'fashions' due to 'over-saturation' . . . Is it the same thing?"[48] This critical omission in theories of the postdigital also presupposes that phenomena occur in the *aftermath* of the irruption of the digital in most aspects of life, when, as my corpus suggests, almost identical phenomena manifest *as* those technocultural shifts take place in different geographies at different times and speeds.

Later conceptualizations of the postdigital, like Silvio Lorusso's, offer a view that complements and advances Cramer's and Ludovico's theorizations. In addition to his work as a writer and designer, Lorusso has assembled a vast collection in his Post-Digital Publishing Archive (P-DPA). This collection has made it possible for him to describe a series of processes, more bespoke than replicable, rather than envisioning a hypothetical new form. Moreover, Lorusso deemphasizes the periodization of "old" and "new" media on which earlier theorizations of postdigital hybridity rest to focus instead on the specificity of print and digital media. He further advances a look at the interactions between media as forms of experimentality rather than as a process of hybridization. This position allows him to gather in his archive a plethora of items that represent, incorporate, utilize, enact, or simply print out digital technologies.

Interestingly, despite moving away from the hybridity framework, Lorusso's focus on experimentality produces conclusions like those coming out of theorizations of hybridity. For instance, experimentality for Lorusso constitutes a departure from conventionality and purity. Therefore, as the experimental can only exist in the backdrop of the status quo, these two realms are necessarily coconstitutive, just like the terms of hybridization. More important, Lorusso shows that experimentality as a characterization is fluid and context-dependent, specific to thin technocultural moments.[49] Although our archives/corpora and our frameworks of hybridity/experimentality are different, I believe that Lorusso's work arrives at conceptualizations similar to mine because we both have based our investigations on extant materials. Moreover, turning the focus back on experimentality reminds us that media experimentation, like cultural hybridization, is not a matter of progression toward an ideal, true, or pure form but one where exemplarity and marginality negotiate the moveable boundaries of conventionality and hegemony.

As my analyses of *The Transborder Immigrant Tool*, *DOC / UNDOC*, and "@EstacionCamaron" / *Autobiografía del algodón* indicate, Mackern is right to posit the question of equivalence of media experimentation or hybridization done from distinct geographic and cultural contexts. The strategies of media hybridization proposed by EDT 2.0 / b.a.n.g. lab; Guillermo Gómez-Peña, Felicia Rice, and coauthors; and Cristina Rivera Garza do more than experiment with digital saturation and much more than assume access and adoption of digital technologies. They propose the hybridity of media as political resistance, identity healing, the impossibility of pure realms of thought, and historical register.

### Disturbing the Binaries: *The Transborder Immigrant Tool*

*The Transborder Immigrant Tool/La herramienta transfronteriza para inmigrantes*, developed by the Electronic Disturbance Theatre 2.0 / b.a.n.g. lab between 2007 and 2012, was a mobile application intended to guide migrants in distressing and potentially deadly situations in the desert along the US–Mexican border. Specifically, *The Transborder Im-*

*migrant Tool* (*TBT*) provided directions to water caches left by humanitarian organizations such as No More Deaths, Water Inc., and Border Angels. As it was envisioned, when migrants traversed the paths in the inhospitable desert relying on the GPS technology of inexpensive and outdated Motorola phones, *TBT* also played out loud a series of twenty-four poems describing the desert environment and outlining survival situations—a combination of the "aesthetic of instruction manuals and folk knowledge."[50] Navigating the binary signifying field of the border ultimately materialized by various types of fencing, like much of the group's work, blends the critical use of digital technologies to carry out activist performances and to provoke a disturbance of this field of signification. Digital media researcher Rita Raley has characterized this type of artistic intervention into political discourse as "tactical media": "artivist" or "hacktivist" projects that might not have an end game but are efficacious at perturbing the symbolic field surrounding them.[51] Although the mobile application was never used in its intended setting due to concerns about the app holders' safety, *TBT* successfully provoked such a disturbance even during the development stages. Getting notice of the app's purposes, conservative commentators and congressional representatives triggered a series of investigations into the project, particularly against EDT's founding member, Ricardo Dominguez. These investigations focused on the potential of the app to "dissolve the border,"[52] or to "actively help people subvert federal law," and ultimately on how the project constituted a "troubling use of taxpayer dollars."[53] The conservative panic surrounding *TBT* is perhaps the project's most significant victory; indeed, this history can now be considered part of its performative dimension.

Moreover, *TBT* is a distributed poetry collection with dynamic and static facets. In addition to the cellphone application, there have been many exhibitions and performances in the years since the team first prototyped it.[54] These performances include an expanded collection of poems written and read or recorded by members of the Electronic Disturbance Theatre 2.0 / b.a.n.g. lab. The project's website comprises scholarly essays; the text and recordings of the "Desert Survival Series" in English, Spanish, Nahuatl, and Ayuujk/Mixe; and other forms of documentation, including a short version of *The Tinaja Trail*, a documentary directed by Bryce Newell illustrating the context and possibilities of *TBT*. In 2014, the Office of Net Assessment, a publishing collective of students, faculty, and staff at the University of Michigan, Ann Arbor, published a print book including *TBT*'s code and poetry.

Despite the long tradition of theorizing the border as "simultaneously discursive and material places for identity negotiation and meaning-making," a trajectory *TBT* belongs to, the brutal reality of a sprawling border wall, increasing technologized surveillance, extensive criminal presence, and unrestrained symbolic manipulation assert themselves.[55] As Raley states, "no articulation of a space in between, of a third term, of any spatial or geometric metaphors of hybridity, can overcome the material fact of the new Iron Curtain."[56] And yet, the unrealized core intention of the project, to facilitate emergency sustenance to migrants while crossing the desert, does invoke a hybridized space that makes it impossible to reduce the border to a set of binaries. The multifaceted nature of *TBT* makes it well suited to interrogate not just the constitutive binaries of the border—here/there, este lado/el otro lado, United States/Mexico, citizen/migrant, documented/undocumented—but also those of code/poetry, nature/technology, dynamic media/static media, and, ultimately, print/digital. Indeed, the entire poetics of *TBT* straddles those binaries to demonstrate that the border is "embedded in ambient or ecological relations that make it irreducible to its symbolic or institutional elements."[57] It is in its resistance to reducing the border to human-made binaries that *TBT* causes a disturbance of the symbolic fields it negotiates.

A much-overlooked aspect of the project, the beautifully designed print book, for instance, underscores these disturbances at various levels. The most obvious among them is printing the application's code and poetry side by side. As electronic literature scholar Mark Marino points out, by including code and poems in the print book, the creators suggest that the code is not just an underlying functional and pragmatic part of *TBT* but an instantiation and execution of the project.[58] Even more, it is easy to see how both code and poetry stand in as language that is subject to be executed or read by humans and by the modified Motorola phones. More evocative are the various unconventional layouts of the bilingual poems, further provoking symbolic disturbances and forcing readers to reconsider settled conventions—in this case, those of bilingual publishing. Designed in minute detail by Parisa Ghaderi and the poet Amy Sarah Carroll, the book's page layouts split pages into top and bottom, left and right, and other configurations. One particularly intriguing example, poem #3 (shown in Figure 24), alternates line by line between the Spanish and English versions. Sentences in each can only be distinguished visually by a slight variation in tonality.[59] The Spanish and English versions of the poems follow each other as though they were one. There is no unique set location for each version of the poems. The page layouts purposefully neglect to indicate Spanish or English as the source or target language. The poems, either in Spanish or in English, will sometimes take the top and left locations on the page and, other times, the bottom and right ones. Instead of relying on the fixity of the printed page, reading from one page to the next requires readers to survey the landscape presented on paper, just as the poems help migrants do in the desert. Further, where we expect fixity, these layouts suggest movement and fluidity.

Similarly, the "Desert Survival Series," written by Carroll, expands the intended disturbance to the border imagery. In the poems is a web of images and concepts that symbolically dislocate the language of a weaponized desert natural landscape, the regulations of movement, and the dehumanization of migrants as "aliens" or "illegals." Though seemingly straightforward, the poems depict a harsh environment that nonetheless has its own "logic of sustainability."[60] The barrel cactus and flowering plants are presented as technical resources: "a compass," "an arrow."[61] The cottonwoods offer a "welcome,"[62] and even the sidewinder offers lessons on moving along the desert dunes.[63] Images of water "stashes,"[64] "pockets,"[65] and "stockpiles"[66] in the form of leaves' apexes, turned-over rocks, cacti, and fruits similarly abound. The poetic voice represents the Joshua tree and the creosote bush as first

```
Justo antes del amanecer, los beduinos volteaban piedras semienterradas
Just before sunrise, Bedouins turned over half-buried stones in the desert
para atrapar el rocío que el frío de la noche había condensado en su
to catch the dew that the night's coolness had condensed on the stones'
superficie. Los viajeros indígenas en el corredor de México-Estados Unidos
surfaces. Indigenous travelers in the Mexican-U.S. corridor searched
buscan las anchas hojas de la yuca y el agave para abastecerse de agua.
the broad leaves of yucca and agave. Rainwater collected at each plant's
El agua de la lluvia se acumula en la base de cada planta—el ápice de las
base—the leaves' apex—remaining there up to a few days after a summer or
hojas—permaneciendo ahí hasta unos días después de una llovizna veraniega
winter shower. Proceed from the simple premise: The desert caches water in
o invernal. La premisa a seguir es simple: el desierto acumula agua en
unlikely places that it resists divulging. Do not expend all your energies
lugares inesperados que resiste divulgar. No agote sus energías buscando sus
searching for its secret stashes, but likewise do not assume that its pockets
escondites secretos, pero igualmente no presuma que sus bolsillos de humedad
of moisture are nonexistent. Restrict your water reconnaissance to early or
son inexistentes. Limite su búsqueda de agua al principio y al final del día
late in the day when your liquid net-gain will outweigh the perspiration you
de manera que el líquido que encuentre sea más que el sudor que transpire al
expend. A thirst is seldom quenched; it morphs to reappear on the horizon.
buscarlo. La sed es rara vez saciada: se transforma para reaparecer en el
Meanwhile, the desert reflects the sun back like a mirror. You are caught in
horizonte. Mientras tanto, el desierto refleja el sol como en un espejo. Usted
that pair's uneven, inconsummate exchange.
está atrapad@ en el medio de este intercambio desigual e inconsumado.
```

47

FIGURE 24. Poem #3 shows the bilingual verses alternating line by line and only distinguishable by a slight difference in tonality. Electronic Disturbance Theater 2.0/b.a.n.g. lab. *[({ })] The Desert Survival Series/La serie de sobrevivencia del desierto* (Ann Arbor: Office of Net Assessment/University of Michigan Digital Environments Cluster Publishing Series, 2014). This bilingual volume published under a CC BY-NC-ND license.

aid medications.[67] Making the desert legible, Carroll uncovers an infrastructure in the natural landscape where reading the available signs might be the difference between life and death.

Moreover, the regulation and negation of movement—an interdiction to cross the border—is displaced in the poems with instructions for how to traverse the desert safely. Poem #2, for instance, prompts migrants to "climb or walk in the morning" and "rest midday,"[68] while others say to follow the directions given by pigeons and doves,[69] to "approach rocky trails with caution,"[70] and to decide to "STOP" to preserve life.[71] Lastly, throughout the "Desert Survival Series," there is an insistence on the agency of the migrant. Even when migrants are forced to cross the border undocumented, Carroll portrays them as agents of their bodies and lives. There is a catalog of reminders of everything a migrant could do to make their journey even slightly easier: covering their bodies to be comfortable,[72] knowing when to stop,[73] and learning to stay away from and deal with Africanized bees and tarantulas—themselves characterized as the human threat of the minutemen and the border police.[74] By insisting on the actions that migrants can take to keep safe, the "Desert Survival Series" directs our attention away from "illegality" and "alienness" to focus on the migrants' latent agency.

In opposition to the regulation of and restrictions on the movement of migrants that have already taken place, *TBT* sheds light on the contradictory and hypocritical reasoning of the border as a space that, under free trade, allows for the open flow of commercial goods but denies the same rights to the people whose labor sustains the very neoliberal dynamics forcing their migration. In an interview with Louis Warren, Dominguez explained that one of the reasons for the project was to propose "an equation wherein the equality of the commodities [under NAFTA] would have a direct impact on the equality of the individuals."[75] The project does enact this equalization of rights, not as an invitation for migrants to cross the desert easily, as conservative critics claimed, but through the symbolic and tactical strategies where the landscape and its features are more than they appear. In that way, unlike anti-immigration organizations, individuals, and government agencies that insist on making the border a site of purity and exclusion, *TBT* starts from the principle that the processes of hybridization that already characterize the border have been put into motion long before migrants find themselves in the desert. They begin when migrants are forced to leave their places of origin due to, for instance, the depletion of natural resources by transnational companies and, with it, the destruction of local economies. Furthermore, *TBT* turns the idea of border security on its head by extending its very logic. The practice in US government agencies to develop multimillion-dollar, cutting-edge technologies to secure the border from undocumented migrants is put through the looking glass into the development of cheap technologies relying on almost obsolete devices and no-cost operation to keep migrants alive. To add to the irony, *TBT* relies on the GPS technology offered for free by the US government.[76]

Much like all other examples of binding media examined in this book, *TBT* relies on various material strategies to construct both its poetics and its politics. As it straddles the binary logic of the border, *TBT* bridges its signifying field by revealing the continuities between code and poetry, performance and activism, print book and mobile application. The lofty and practical objectives jump-starting *TBT* thus become an intricate performance enacted cumulatively across a series of material facets all contesting ideas of purity and countering practices of exclusion. As we will see in the following section, the proliferation of objects emanating from a performance project is also characteristic of Guillermo Gómez-Peña, Felicia Rice, and their coauthors' *DOC/UNDOC*—another example of binding media well beyond its print and digital facets.

### A Border Kit to Face the Uncertainty of Crossings: *DOC/UNDOC*

*DOC/UNDOC: Documentado/Undocumented: Ars Shamánica Performática* opens with the questions, "So what is this, exactly? What is this, exactly? An immersive experience? A ritual exploration of the senses? A personalized installation? A participatory gameplay?" in the voice of performance artist Guillermo Gómez-Peña.[77] This complex project is a collaborative effort created by Gómez-Peña himself, book artist Felicia Rice, art historian Jennifer A. González, videographer Gustavo Vázquez, and sound artist Zachary James Watkins that seeks to imagine expansive approaches to book-making through the exploration of "a state of radical unbelonging."[78] *DOC/UNDOC* gathers Gómez-Peña's performance texts; Rice's illustration, prints, and book design; González's critical commentary; Vázquez's performance video recordings; and Watkins's sound art pieces. Illuminating and reediting many of Gómez-Peña's past performance scripts, *DOC/UNDOC* follows recurrent motifs in the author's decades-long oeuvre, including Spanglish, migration, racism, and decolonization. Similarly, the hybrid book expands on his past practice of crossing—understood as both traversing and hybridizing—a multitude of realms of meaning, such as arts, politics, theory, genre, gender, identity, race, knowledge production, language, and media, that have distinguished his work as a solo performer and with his group La Pocha Nostra.[79] Expanding the polysemic motif of crossing, *DOC/UNDOC* also references border crossings, the hybridized identities produced by transnationalism, and the contestation of legality embedded in the Spanglish phrase "documentado/ undocumented." Fastening together print with visual art, video and sound art, and text and performance, *DOC/UNDOC* offers readers an invitation to perform their own crossing, their identitarian recollections accompanied by the material and aesthetic space provided by the work's objects.

Several editions of *DOC/UNDOC* have been published. The first, a limited edition of fifty accordion books, was produced by Rice's Moving Parts Press in 2014. The artist's book features Rice's prints and typographic interpretations of Gómez-Peña's performance scripts. Additionally, the artist's book box holds a CD, a DVD, and a booklet, adding Gómez-Peña's performance texts, videos, the project's soundtrack, and Rice's and González's commentaries. A smaller edition of fifteen copies was issued as a deluxe edition that came in a custom-made, decorated and interactive aluminum case made by Mindy Padgett and Peter Elsea at Sculpture Works. As it opens, the case's lid displays a heavily decorated mirror with faux fur and lights; when opened, a soundtrack plays in the built-in speakers. Under the book, the case has eight compartments holding an assortment of "ritual objects" (a *luchador* mask, vials, toy money, and a magnifying glass, among many others). The case also holds a DVD of Gómez-Peña's performances and a booklet with the performance texts. Three years later, the group re-created *DOC/UNDOC* in a trade edition book published collaboratively by Moving Parts Press and City Lights. The covers of the trade edition remediate the texture and color of the deluxe case and include the prints designed by Rice not as an accordion book but as a codex. In addition to photographic documentation of the deluxe edition, bookending the prints from the artist's book are the texts from the booklet, González's commentary, and Gómez-Peña's performance scripts. Attached to the back cover is a small envelope holding a custom-made USB card containing the project's video and sound files (see Figure 12 in chapter 2). Lastly, a website collects many of the project materials with extended documentation on *DOC/UNDOC*'s origin, development, exhibitions, and previews.

In this complex work, the multiple facets signal, in one way or another, a process of hybridization. The project's creators offer a "celebration of its formal impurity," as the book is "collaborative, intermedial, and participatory."[80] Like *TBT*, *DOC/UNDOC* deals with the problems around (un)documented migration to the United States. In addition to the "documents" entailed in border crossings, the phrasing "documentado/undocumented" suggests a tension between the experiences that are documented, that is, registered as part of official records, and those that are undocumented or unregistered except as part of individual and communal experience. Therefore, the authors showcase the discrepancy between immigration records and documents that establish the fact of migration and the undocumented experience of such migration. In this way, the myriad artifacts classic in Gómez-Peña's repertoire serve to investigate the migrant's cultural identity. Readers engaging with the deluxe edition, whether they are migrants or not, are put into that role through their reflection in the mirror and their interaction with the evocative objects. Indeed, as Jennifer González explains in her critical commentary on *DOC/UNDOC*, "Gómez-Peña's description of his performance practice as a form of cultural healing invites us to read the work in this way."[81] The multimedia or multisensory elements blending arts printing, sound and video art, tactile interactive objects, and literary texts saturate the reader's experience, emulating a live performance or, as suggested by the subtitle, a shamanic ritual.

To various degrees, interacting with any of the three editions of the book is transformed into a performative practice for readers as well. The monumental accordion book, designed to resemble Mesoamerican codices, is more than 30 feet long. Similarly, all editions are full of interaction and performative instructions. For instance, the half-title page in the trade edition responds to the opening question, "what is this exactly?" with a catalog of possibilities. The most suggestive are "a toolbox for self-transformation" and "a collection of implements to fight paranoia, racism, cultural loneliness, formalist aesthetics, and political despair. Casi nada."[82] The mirror at the center of the deluxe box's lid furthers the central place of the readers within the work, not just as viewers or spectators but as actors in a one-on-one performance with themselves. Moreover, the instructions page for the deluxe box offers a list of possible actions a reader can take with this book as "a pathway to navigate this universe of unknowns." Some instructions pertain specifically to the actions a reader can perform on the deluxe edition, like "Open the case," "Push our buttons, listen to their sounds," and "Add your own artifacts and personal talismans." In contrast, others constitute expansions of them, such as "open your mind," "perform yourself," "tell a new story, witness your own history."[83] The performativity at the center of *DOC/UNDOC* invites readers to engage "for the sake of initiating personal and cultural transgressions and transcendence."[84] A second set of instructions in *DOC/UNDOC* comes in the audio file "Ritual Preparations." In it we hear a list of possible actions to be taken before crossing the border into the United States. The activities include having a bottle of tequila ready, taking a long shower with a lover, and putting on a wrestling mask.[85] This parallel set of instructions merges the idea of an artistic performance with a bureaucratic one, entering the United States as a moment when one's identity is displayed and negotiated.

Readers find material and performative instantiations of these transgressions in each page, video, and sound clip. Rice's typesetting of Gómez-Peña's scripts, for instance, wavers along a single line to make room for her images or to underscore the meaning of words, as in the title of "Freefalling towards a Borderless Future."[86] Moreover, Rice subverts the page margins set by the background color printing, further foregrounding the idea of crossing established lines and frames. Ultimately, the images are often overlaid with text. This feature might complicate reading the words, but once again, it suggests the blending of text and image in a very literal way.

We can attribute the hybridity of this work to the practice of collaboration outlined by the authors. During the seven years devoted to the creation of *DOC/UNDOC*, the artists saw their own fields of practice expand and morph as they came in contact with performance art. Thus, each practice brings the crossing and collaborations of conventionally separate artistic realms to the forefront. In one of the versions of her commentary on the project, Rice walks readers through the composition of the prints as "informed by both digital and analog processes," which included hand-drawing the images, scanning and digitally altering them, printing the layers in a Vandercook letterpress, and typesetting digitally by hand using Text Pencil.[87] Rice documents having each page go through "25–30 press runs, laying down the colors or textures, multiple drawings, and type."[88]

Similarly, the footage of Gómez-Peña's one-on-one performance "Bajo la lupa: Primer duelo" (Under the Magnifying Glass: First Duel) enacts a duel between Vázquez's documentation of the performer under his camera lens while the performer inspects the videographer with a magnifying glass.[89] Gómez-Peña and Vázquez raise the stakes of this fourth wall transgression in "A Muerte: Segundo duelo" (To the Death: Second Duel) in which Gómez-Peña points to Vázquez with a (supposedly) loaded gun. In opposition, Vázquez points at Gómez-Peña with the camera, both threatening to "shoot" one another.[90] In these duels, Vázquez is much more than simply a videographer; he performs the act of documenting as a witness, participant, and spectator. His presence, usually obscured by the camera angles, becomes one of the subjects of his own footage.

While all other examples of binding media in previous chapters require various levels of performative interactivity—to follow a reading script, to move from print to digital facets, to navigate a computer application—to completely engage with the literary work, *DOC/UNDOC* is about the performative explorations themselves. Throughout the three editions, instructions to work through the book underscore first the interactions with the facet at hand and then the possible actions fostered or prompted by the book: "collaborate with four other artists and perform your own book" or "DEVELOP your own inquiries, CREATE your own documents, SHOW them."[91] Unlike other binding media, *DOC/UNDOC* eschews the possibility of a work whose ultimate meaning emerges cumulatively. Instead, Gómez-Peña, Rice, and the other collaborators propose that meaning emerges out of the individual transformation the reader undergoes in the role of apprentice shaman engaged in a process of identitarian healing as a transnational migrant.

Materially, there is one other significant difference between *DOC/UNDOC* and other binding media. Although the digital files come in a CD and a DVD in the deluxe edition and in a USB key in the trade edition book, the interaction with those files does not occur on an application or an interface specifically designed for them. Instead, we have access to the files themselves. The deluxe edition case, however, acts as an interface designed to present the multimedia elements of the work and offer items with which to interact. Jennifer A. González likens *DOC/UNDOC* to the tradition of the cabinet of curiosities, "flux-kits," on the one hand, where marvelous objects and unconventional actions meet, and, on the other, to the tradition of altars as a place for spiritual self-reflection.[92] González, moreover, identifies the box's resemblances to the boudoir mirror or a car's rearview mirror, where physical reflection also takes place. As an interface, the case gathers all these cultural echoes to stage the performance of a "transitional existence" prompted by the fact of migration. The objects themselves symbolize and concretize—they are the medium of—the cultural histories through which this transitional experience flows. Ultimately, their presence suggests both the transitional identities of migration and the transitional media moment.

Furthermore, it's hard to overlook the box's resemblance to a laptop computer. Despite its clearly artisanal features like the forged iron hinges and nubs, the silver metallic portable case, reminiscent of a laptop, positions it as the electronic application itself. The way the lid opens to reveal the mirror similarly has a resemblance to the shiny black mirror of a laptop's screen. As in most laptops, the lid becomes the interface where we see the results of our interactions. In addition to the myriad objects a reader can use, small silver buttons are placed in the corners of the velvet compartments. Upon pressing them, these buttons play a soundtrack framing the conceptualization of the interactive objects, describing them, and categorizing them. Other recordings prompt the reader to take further action upon the case's items or provide a soundscape for the individual performance. Similarly, although the book rests within the deluxe case and is thus subject to interaction as much as the other objects, there is no script or instructions for navigating each object. The free-form relationships among objects underlie the possibility of individual performance.

The breadth and minutely detailed ways in which every single medium, material, and concept is crossed or hybridized denote the critical and, sometimes, even farcical positioning Gómez-Peña has repeatedly taken regarding the officialness and nationalistic discourse around *mestizaje* as the "dominant identity narrative" of his Mexican upbringing.[93] Arguably, although the central item of the work is the print book, *DOC/UNDOC* demands a performative engagement. The deluxe case and the trade edition book thus work as a zone of contact, where artists and spectators, customarily separated by stage conventions, converge through their actions in handling a series of objects. Indeed, Gómez-Peña has likened performance art to a "conceptual 'territory' with capricious weather and changing borders, a place where contradiction, ambiguity, and paradox are not just tolerated but stimulated."[94] The territory created by Gómez-Peña, Rice, and their colleagues in *DOC/UNDOC* is one where we can interrogate artistic realms and deliberately subvert conventions. It is, ultimately, a space where the multiplicity of media is the essential substrate for proliferating hybridization processes.

### The Depths of Migration in *Autobiografía del algodón*

In *Autobiografía del algodón,* Mexican writer Cristina Rivera Garza tells the story of the Northeast region of Mexico in the early twentieth century when a series of agricultural and industrial developmental projects changed the landscape and lives of its inhabitants. The novel was published in Mexico by Penguin Random House in 2020. Its digital counterpart, a Twitter account "@EstacionCamaron," presents part of the novel's story in a few hundred tweets posted between April 19 and April 21, 2016, all followed by a translation into English by Aviva Kana and Suzanne Jill Levine. Central to both facets are the motives of human movement in the form of migration, exodus and dispossession, nomadism, and travel. In parallel, the two facets stage a quest for the author to unearth the documents, ruins, and remains that allow her to document the lives and stories not recorded in History.

*Autobiografía del algodón* (*AdA*) is a complex novel that investigates Rivera Garza's family history of migration from central to northern Mexico across several towns in the early twentieth century. These migrations also entail the back-and-forth crossing between Mexico and the United States on the other side of her family. Her narrative, moreover, is threaded along the history of the modernization of the Northeast border region in Mexico in the postrevolutionary years through the cultivation of cotton and other industrialization endeavors. One episode, the peasant strike of 1934 in Estación Camarón, brings into focus the convergence of the landowner's greed with state inaction and complicity in the dispossession of peasant laborers and the ultimate destruction of the land. The strike episode also threads into the novel the presence of Mexican writer José Revueltas, who, as a young Communist Party militant, took part in the strike and documented it in his novel *Human Mourning* (1943). Further, as the narrative moves closer to the present and to the later years into Rivera Garza's family narrative, readers traverse the winding processes of industrialization from the mid-twentieth century up to its neoliberal culmination under the North American Free Trade Agreement (NAFTA) in the 1990s. Lastly, Rivera Garza weaves the lust for exploitation and wealth of previous developmental projects with the murderous control of the Zetas drug cartel of the Northeast border region and the War against Narcotrafficking that started in 2006 as both have transformed the landscape and the lives of the area.

Throughout the novel, we encounter the presence of the authorial voice as she unearths these histories through visits to abandoned cotton farming regions, deserted towns, and archives holding the promise of family information. In this way, *AdA* "showcase[s] the author's reflections on the writing of a family history that is hers ... because it is the documentation of the discovery process."[95] Moreover, by examining a period of more than one hundred years, Rivera Garza dissects the cycles of progress and destruction of state development models and, later, transnational capital extraction, both legal and criminal. These cycles, additionally, reveal the cost of human and nonhuman lives through the ruination of fertile lands, the abandonment of entire towns, the dispossession of families, and the ensuing forced displacement. The passage of the authorial voice over the same space as the historical characters across time suggests moments of apparent simultaneity. The resulting effect is an interrogation of memory-making and historical forgetting.

In comparison to the print novel, the scope of "@EstacionCamaron" is much smaller, as it presents snippets of the trip taken by Rivera Garza to the eponymous site of the 1934 strike and excerpts from Revueltas's novel *Human Mourning*, mentioned above. Live-tweeted during the first Festival de Escrituras Digitales, organized by the Mexican Instituto Nacional de Bellas Artes in the spring of 2016, "@EstacionCamaron" also gathers thoughts and reflections upon the nature of writing, documentation, infrastructure, ruination, memory and historicity, and the violence that reverberates from the 1930s into the present. Arguably, "@EstacionCamaron" rehearses or previews the themes and narrative threads of the print novel as its own short-format narrative. As one of the first tweets indicates: "The trip always begins before. The trip begins even before it has been imagined."[96] In the Twitter account, for instance, we first encounter photos by Spanish scholar Vega Sánchez Aparicio, later included in the central pages of *AdA*. In its timeline format, one tweet stacked on top of another, "@EstacionCamaron" resembles the palimpsestic strategies seen in Carpenter's and Gerber Bicecci's works (see chapter 3), a combination of temporalities expressed through images, text, and citations.[97] The juxtaposition of narrative snippets overlays Revuelta's prose with Rivera Garza's own—the first is a witness of the events in the past, the latter a witness of the prolonged aftermath. Similarly, the images overlay the past, and the present of Estación Camarón, as can be seen in Figure 25. The ruins of ghost

FIGURE 25. A screenshot of Rivera Garza's "@EstacionCamaron" shows an overlay of the current ruins of the obelisk in Estación Camarón with an illustration from the past. Photograph by Vega Sánchez Aparicio. Reproduced with permission.

towns in the present are crossed by the splendor of the past: a questioning of what was there through the vision of what is left.

This type of transmedia writing is not rare in Rivera Garza's oeuvre. Writing that first appeared on her widely read blog has, in several cases, appeared later in print publications, such as *La muerte me da*,[98] *Viriditas*,[99] and others.[100] Rivera Garza's blog has been the space where the author theorizes her writerly practice. Some of these posts are useful to outline her approach to encounter, contact, and boundary transgression. Her term "escrituras colindantes" or "neighboring writing," for instance, touches on sites of writerly encounter, "those voluble spaces where that which is isn't quite yet, and that which isn't hasn't yet begun."[101]

Nevertheless, Rivera Garza resists the idea that synthesis emerges out of contact. Instead, she is interested in "the commotion of the encounter, the tension that generates and sustains it, rather than the resolution."[102] Her resistance, nevertheless, doesn't deny categorically that any kind of synthesis happens, but instead underscores the conflicts prompted by the porosity of the conventional limits, for example, in established literary forms. Consequently, Rivera Garza focuses her neighboring writings on the gaps or holes, the Deleuzian line of escape, where the original sense of things can be misplaced, for instance, when the shape of one genre is adapted to the demands of another.[103] The author's conceptualizations are helpful to investigate the strategies she employs to construct a region (a zone of contact, a borderland, or a neighboring writing) epitomized by Estación Camarón. As I argue, this region is simultaneously the actual geographic area historically traversed by her, her family, and others and, later, narrated in the novel, as well as a symbolic and media space across the print novel and the Twitter account.

The region created by Rivera Garza, like those proposed by Pratt and Liu, is the locus of an encounter mediated by political, historical, and discursive power. Sometimes filled with hope, joy, and life, the region is also the site of dispossession and death. Simultaneously, the region is the scenario of the historical first peasant strike in Mexico and is absent from records, maps, and road markers. The author then builds this space through "disappropriation," a cultural strategy Rivera Garza herself has theorized: "to recover access to a lost tradition, it is necessary to bring it to light, that is to make it part of the dialogues and processes of the present ... It is about locating the artifacts of this tradition ... so that it can again be reflected in the mirror of our culture and our experience."[104]

In the novel, this process is evident through the inclusion and discussion of archival documents. A telling example is Rivera Garza's grandmother Petra Peña's border crossing card record, held in the US National Archives. The author describes the microfilmed image as an object that "comes running across time from April 17th, 1929."[105] In this way, the image becomes the medium through which Rivera Garza meets her grandmother for the first time; it brings Petra Peña into the present and makes her part of Rivera Garza's present experience. More extraordinary is that such an artifact makes it into the narrator's hands precisely on the grandmother's birthday. The "feast of her birthday" takes place via the encounter with/in the photograph itself.[106] Many other artifacts of this sort help Rivera Garza reconstruct the histories in the novel. One such record is "Permiso 202," a tax exception permit allowing Mexicans deported from the United States to import cars, animals, appliances, and other objects.[107] The list of objects in the permit allows Rivera Garza to speculate on the future those displaced Mexicans envisioned when leaving behind their lives in the United States.

The physical places where the novel takes place are the materials that bring the past into the present. Throughout *AdA*, there is an insistence that all—Cristina Rivera Garza, her family members, Revueltas, and untold others—have traversed the same lands: "If as inhabitants of the land, we have no choice but to be with others or return to where others were, then the most basic task, the most honest, the most difficult consists of identifying the footprints that embrace us."[108] As these examples suggest, as she excavates a collective history, the authorial voice bridges the temporal distance through the objects of the past that continue to be in the present. Because such a history is not only Rivera Garza's own narrative but that of her family and that of the borderland, readers take part in a historical copresence mediated by such objects. In addition to archival records, it takes the form of the landmarks of the region: the dam, the obelisk in the center of the town, and, crucially, the roads. The locations, however, are not frozen in time. We see them change, both throughout historical time in the novel's narrative and during the short periods when the author visits them. These shifts are especially evident in "@EstacionCamaron," where the author underscores her presence and that of her travel companion, Claudia Sorias Castañeda, in a land that sees them in specific yet changing ways. Initially, they search for an identifiable past, that of Revueltas's travels: "Two women following in his footsteps 82 years later. A car. A highway through the steppes."[109] At other times, the two women are just moving through the landscape, and it is the landscape that seems to look at them:

> Two women on a highway that crosses the steppes.[110]
> Two women alone. Two women in this state of loneliness.[111]
> Two women alone. Two women in a car.[112]

In other tweets, they witness the new historical conditions and the landscape of the roads patrolled by the army, signaling the armed conflict and the violence of the War against Narcotrafficking: "Two stateless women alone on a highway in front of an advancing army."[113] Two more tweets relating to their presence in and around Estación Camarón further characterize the borderland as a locus where these women are without statehood or country due to their status as travelers and migrants:

> Two stateless women, without an army, maybe without a country.[114]
> Two women without a state, without an army. Two women in a car.[115]

The borderland, then, has an agency of sorts. It is not just the histories that have taken place and the people who have passed through; it is the land that has witnessed and produced all of it, all of them. It is the land that tells its own history. It is a space haunted and enlightened by everything that has happened there.

> From cotton to fracking, passing by sorghum and maquilas, the moments of abundance and devastation have succeeded one another in cycles that are ever more intense and brief in a desert which, far from the common representation picturing as lifeless, stands out once and again with new and varied natural resources. It is the same desert that American immigration laws have transformed into a deadly weapon for hundreds of thousands of undocumented workers.[116]

One last feature of the border region constructed by Rivera Garza that I want to touch on is the persistence of ruins representing a past vision of the future and indicating its failure. As mentioned before, one strategy the author uses is the overlay of historical and contemporary photographs in *AdA* and "@EstacionCamaron." Rivera Garza muses, "Few things are sadder than the traces of sudden and brutal, and ephemeral opulence. Few things are truer."[117] Nevertheless, more interesting than the record of Mexico's stumbling modernization are the interrogations of its memory-making strategies, where the past is safely kept in the past, where places destroyed by greed or natural disasters are rendered nonexistent. Rivera Garza presents this interrogation through the paradoxical negation of the historical certainties that cotton was grown around a town called Estación Camarón, a negation that, nonetheless, is also a way of naming and reifying its existence:

> Estación Camarón no longer exists.[118]
> Estación Camarón doesn't exist. It never did.[119]
> But Estación Camarón doesn't exist anymore, the
>     man says. Affected or delighted, it doesn't make a
>     difference.[120]
> Estación Camarón doesn't exist ... There is no memory
>     of Estación Camarón.[121]
> There is no sign for the way to Estación Camarón.
>     There is nothing: double negative.[122]

> We can't go to Estación Camarón because Estación
> Camarón no longer exists, but we're going anyway.[123]

Despite insisting on the disappearance of Estación Camarón, which entails the vanishing of her family history as well, Rivera Garza uses this negation to uplift and document the name in writing repeatedly, to make a record of the fact that there was once a town that was a rich cotton producer and the site of a historical peasant strike. It is not fortuitous that the first tweet in "@EstacionCamaron," published days before the live narrative began, is an animated gif zooming into a map with a pin dropped on Estación Camarón's location. The names, the ruins, the archival records, and the roads are all elements through which the author brings the past into the present. They are cracks in an official historical line that has once and again destroyed the region. Rivera Garza's disappropriation of Estación Camarón does not attempt to reinscribe it into History but to build a memory that reverberates across time through her presence and witness of the places: "there was a cotton field here. Here, a city. This is time."[124] Rivera Garza's witnessing negates the negation of her history. Ultimately, she ponders, "Is an archive a way of beating time or dissolving into it?"[125]

Rivera Garza's own history of migration indicates that the answer is one's dissolution in time. Her travels across the Mexican Northeast are nothing new but a link to a family history of migrancy. "Little did I know that, in the *longue durée* of my own history, this migration emulated many others begun decades, if not centuries, before. The return to the border."[126] Furthermore, her travels and her relocation to Houston, Texas, as a young student, also described in the novel, are part of the almost two-centuries-long history of migration across the border, whether it is the one described in the Guadalupe Hidalgo treaty in 1848 or some other formulation that existed long before then. The *longue durée* of migrations across the Mexico–United States border has not only shaped the author's family history, it has also shaped the expectations and realities of the border region.

Rivera Garza's construction of the borderland is symbolic and material through the media of the print book and the Twitter account. As in most of the examples examined in the book, the cumulative effect of the two facets emphasizes recurrent motives: Revueltas's involvement with the strike at Estación Camarón, the reverberations of places now in ruins, Rivera Garza's travels to the area, the landscape . . . But "@EstacionCamaron" is not just a writing rehearsal for the novel, nor is the novel an expansion of the Twitter narrative. Quite the contrary, "@EstacionCamaron" is not so much an account of the author's travels as it is a live performance. During the three days Rivera Garza originally posted on Twitter, the trip to Estación Camarón appeared to be happening as it was being written. The convention of liveness, proper to the microblogging platform, complements Rivera Garza's disappropriation strategies to bring the records of the past into the present as they are uncovered and witnessed. Moreover, the Twitter narrative creates a register for the location and the events lost to History. As a performance, "@EstacionCamaron" brings to life the town of Estación Camarón, speaks Revueltas's words, and remembers the strike of 1934 as Rivera Garza positions herself as a visitor, a recorder, and a collector of images and information. In this way, the author lives and witnesses the story she tells—her autobiography. Indeed, even years later, a reading of "@EstacionCamaron" conveys the sense of past liveness.

The relationship of Rivera Garza to forms of digital writing, in particular to blogging, has been subject to her own theorizations as well. She links this type of live writing to Bakhtinian heteroglossia in the way that such new discourses transform the literary languages of a given age.[127] More important than the theoretical genealogies of blog novels is the author's interest in how the medium allows her to engage in writing practices "with false starts, with repetitive beginnings, with chapters that lead nowhere, with endings that contradict themselves, the blognovel wants to have a stutter, to be imperfect, unfinished, in-perpetual-process."[128] Not unlike her "neighboring writings" discussed above, what we see in the fastenings between the *AdA* and "@EstacionCamaron" are those features in-perpetual-process as well as the tensions and contradictions in the histories of the Mexican Northeast. As Rivera Garza reestablishes the region as part of the experience of the present, she also projects it into an uncertain future where it will continue to be a zone of migrancy.

———

Toward the end of his classic book *Communication, Culture, and Hegemony: From the Media to Mediations,* Jesús Martín-Barbero asserts that "a central chapter in the research on new technologies is their effect on culture."[129] He further interrogates the meaning of "effect," dislodging it from the idea that technology operates above culture and proposing that culture works through technology, too. I take Martín-Barbero's claim to close this chapter as my discussion of Pratt's and Liu's theorizations of the contact zone sustains his argument: culture works through technology. However, technology also works to shape and transmit culture. As the three examples examined suggest, the logic of capitalism has pushed technological developments to further modernization. At the same time, globalization has had the effect of displacing, dispossessing, and erasing myriad entire populations and their cultural realms. As the material substrate of processes of cultural hybridization in a globalized economic and communications landscape, binding media enact these processes that take place under the dynamics of oppression prompted by such landscape. Consequently, binding media are not just the outcome of simultaneous processes of hybridization of media (books and media), aesthetic practices (media affordances and expressivity), and industries (publishing, tech); they are the material expressions of new cultural perceptions.

As *The Transborder Immigrant Tool, DOC/UNDOC,* and "@EstacionCamaron" / *Autobiografía del algodón* make evident, a new perception that is central to the experience of the twenty-first century is that of human movement in the Americas. Even when movement across the present-day United States–Mexico border has been characteristic of the region for centuries, the act of migrating is, perhaps more than ever, laden with contentious meanings and terrifying developments in surveillance technologies. The new cultural perceptions that Martín-Barbero saw as the outcomes of developing and obsolescing technologies compel us to stop following linear processes of progress as the only possible organizing logic of the world. Instead, like other manifestations of hybridization processes, binding media foreground continuity rather than rupture, tension rather than resolution, process rather than outcome, and porosity rather than solidity. These three binding media examples, among others examined in the book, are a prescient reminder that the beautiful aesthetic syntheses achieved in the works are all owing to the talents and visions of the individual artists and not in any way an intrinsic or essential potential of hybridization processes, nor are they simply a matter of formal experimentation.

CONCLUSION

## FROM COMPUTER-GENERATED BOOKS TO NFT PUBLISHING

IN THE TEACHING AND SCHOLARSHIP of electronic literature, it is common to say that a distinguishing feature of this literary practice is that it cannot be printed out. If printed, works of electronic literature would lose the dynamic artifactuality and interactivity upon which their meaning-making strategies rest. Yet, this book is full of instances where literary works that have long been studied, anthologized, and taught as electronic or digital literature are, in fact, also printed.[1] Of course, none of them is print output or screenshots laid out on a paper page, eschewing the digital applications' interactive and dynamic qualities. In binding media, authors harness the unique expressive affordances of print and digital objects and the interface between them in precisely the dynamic ways that screen-based digital literature would. And still, although they are bound together, each facet retains various levels of objectual and expressive autonomy. Computer-generated books—volumes in which the output of computational processes is selected, edited, and prepared for print publication—complicate, yet expand these premises.

Computer-generated literary texts are as old as computation itself, and they are some of the earliest instances in the tradition of electronic literature. Even in these early examples, computer-generated literature and print have had tight connections. The earliest known example, Christopher Strachey's *Love Letters* generator, dates back to 1952, when he wrote it in the famous Manchester Mark 1 computer at the National Research & Development Corporation in the United Kingdom. Although it was never published as an entire literary work, computational artist Noah Wardrip-Fruin reports that examples of the *Love Letters* came out in the art journal *Encounter*.[2] This might seem to foreshadow the current burgeoning world of computer-generated books, but during Strachey's time, printed output would not have been out of the norm. In fact, before a computer's main interface became the screen we are most familiar with, and for several decades after Strachey's work, a program's output was usually delivered via a print terminal.[3] Nick Montfort cites as prime examples of this practice *Eliza/Doctor* (1966) and *Adventure* (1975).[4] Alison Knowles's *The House of Dust* (1967) is another instance often exhibited through its print output. *Le Tombeau de Mallarmé* (1972) by Brazilian poet Erthos Albino de Souza similarly depends on the facsimile reproduction of output through a dot matrix printer. Computer-generated literature has its genealogy in the vanguardist movements of the early to mid-twentieth century. In computer-generated literature, we continue to see the surprising, nonsensical, unexpected, and sometimes foreboding traits created by combinatory poetics and randomization that cross traditions from Dadaism and Oulipo to our days. These poetic features translate into fundamental algorithmic operations—including automation, permutation, combination, and randomization—that poets can apply to text datasets. In the last few years, these practices have expanded as authors use large language models (LLMs) and artificial intelligence (AI) programs to create literary works, some of which end up published as print books, while some remain as web-based works, and others are distributed and sold fully digitally as nonfungible tokens (NFTs).

I treat computer-generated books as separate from other binding media exemplars because they are part of a specific kind of literary system encompassing a generator's "surface output, the data it employs, and the processes it executes."[5] These characteristics of generators produce two specific binding mechanisms. The first is a passage or transformation from algorithmic procedures performed on a dataset and the computational output, mediated by a process of selection, editing, layout, and production into a print codex. Unlike, for instance, *Between Page and Screen*, *El libro del fin del mundo*, or *Vniverse*, computer-generated books are generally not read between two material objects or interfaces. In that sense, they are not complementary in creating a literary work's cumulative meaning. The dynamic presentation of computer-generated output, conventionally yielding the program's results as it runs, is adapted or customized to the book form. Such adaptations include laying out the output in pages rather than the continuous scroll of a screen or a dot matrix printer, giving the text a finite extent rather than running continuously, and granting it the fixity of print text instead of a dynamic actualization. However, like other examples of binding media, the print instances of computer-generated books illuminate aspects of the underlying programs. Print books, as one of the possible manifestations of the generators, might be the only way for readers to access a computer program's workings. Moreover, it is not uncommon for text generators to produce output far exceeding what can be printed in a standard trade book. This point suggests the second binding mechanism of computer-generated books: a relationship of origin whereby a computer program produces the output that will fill the pages of a print book. In this way, the computer program and the dataset function as a source from which *some* of the text generated will become part of the print book. Because of these characteristics, I propose to consider the "boundedness" of computer-generated books as the process of turning them into books with a spine and covers, and as the limits set to the system's potential output through the codex's affordances.

Computer-generated literary texts published as NFTs rely on slightly different binding mechanisms. Usually distributed and sold as individual poems on the blockchain, NFTs of computer-generated literature similarly undergo a process of selection, editing, and laying out for publication—or "minting"—adjusted to fit the conventions of video, image, or text files. We also find a similar relationship of origin where a literary system and its data usually output greater amounts of text than the individual poem, whether in the pages of a print book or as a file on the blockchain. However, due to their material specificities, computer-generated texts on the blockchain are not bound by the cover or the spine of a print codex, thus evading the sense of at least partial fixity that binding media and computer-generated books yield from their print facet.

Here, in the book's conclusion, I examine two late developments in my research: a burgeoning of computed-generated books and the use of the blockchain in binding media exemplars. In the first part, I examine the publishing landscape of computer-generated books by looking at two presses dedicated to this print literary form, and which are largely responsible for their flourishing in the United States: the Using Electricity series, edited by computational poet Nick Montfort for Counterpath Press; and Aleator Press, founded and run by editor and AI artist James Ryan. Surveying their titles, I then argue that computer-generated books rely on, rather than interrogate or subvert, the basic properties of the book examined in chapter 1. Because computer-generated works of literature appear to be more resilient to obsolescence, and computer-generated books are a more regular form of the book, they can be more readily incorporated into well-established practices of cataloging, collecting, and preserving, thus offering an opportunity to query the issue of futurity once again. The second part of the conclusion touches on how the newer trend of using NFTs to publish, distribute, and collect literary works has gained momentum. I devote a few pages to theVERSEverse, a collective of poets publishing on the blockchain and developing AI tools for poetry, particularly the work of its founders, Sasha Stiles, Ana María Caballero, and Kalen Iwamoto. The libertarian aim to decentralize the exchange of capital propelling the popularity of the blockchain has been adopted and transformed into literary practices that claim to bolster the diversity of the field through the divestment from the publishing industry (even the independent scene) and to create a new poetry market in the profitable world of NFTs. In the eyes of proponents, in addition to the potential for economic benefits, the shift projects a healthier future for literature by establishing a closer relationship with the reader. And yet, what becomes readily visible is that the monetary prospects of NFTs yield poem- and book-like objects in which creators stress visual features of their poetry to capitalize on a market that has burgeoned centering on visual art. As with all instances of binding media, poets incorporate the material conditions of the blockchain into their poetics and produce what I call an aesthetic of transactionality. Further, as with other technological developments, the minting of literary NFTs is surrounded by claims of futurity to change poetry for good. Nevertheless, as the cycles of innovation and retrenchment seen in chapter 2 have taught us to expect, this new development will likely follow a trajectory similar to those of other expanded or hybrid publishing instances. In fact, the savage speculation surrounding the blockchain might easily be the factor that will render NFTs passé by the time, or shortly after, this book is published.

## Using Electricity and Aleator Press

Although the authorship of computer-generated books emerges from the still rather unconventional interfaces between a writer and a computational program and its dataset, their publishing process follows well-established practices that are widely replicable rather than bespoke to each title. Consequently, in contrast to the binding media exemplars examined before, publishing computer-generated books entails smaller economic investments and risks than applications requiring constant updating and maintenance. Nevertheless, the experimentality of computer-generated books still makes them, generally, the realm of small, independent publishers. Likewise, because the published content is stable and does not require updating, except in the case of second or later editions, computer-generated books more easily fit well-established practices of collecting, cataloging, and preserving books and literary works. These features make boutique projects like Nick Montfort's private press Bad Quarto a feasible, if highly specialized, enterprise.

As can be seen in the appendix, most presses have engaged only marginally with the publication of binding media, including those releasing computer-generated books, such as Naomi Press, publisher of Lillian-Yvonne Bertram's book of poetry *Travesty Generator* (2019), and Anteism Books, publisher of David (Jhave) Johnston's extensive poetry collection *ReRites* (2018). And yet, as already mentioned, two publishing instances devoted to computer-generated books stand out: Counterpath's series Using Electricity, and Aleator Press. These two endeavors not only publish computer-generated books but also strive to create the conditions for the readerly and cultural appreciation of this type of literature through archiving, producing, and selling them as well.

In a talk about the Using Electricity series, Montfort recalled approaching Tim Roberts, director of Counterpath, to pitch his book *The Truelist* for publication, as the publisher had already edited Montfort's generated-poetry collection *#! (shebang)* in 2014. In response, Roberts asked him to edit a series focused on computer-generated literary works, the first of which would be Montfort's book.[6] Between its founding in 2017 and spring 2024, Using Electricity has published thirteen titles, all of which use distinct computational processes, datasets, and programming languages that are individual to their aesthetic purposes. Furthermore, the titles span a variety of literary genres including long-form prose (for instance, digital poet Milton Läufer's *A Noise Such As a Man Might Make* [2018]), short stories (computational scientist and artist Rafael Pérez y Pérez's *Mexica: 20 Years—20 Stories [Mexica: 20 años—20 historias]* [2017]), and visual poetry (Qianxun Chen and Mariana Roa Oliva's collaborative work *Seedlings_: Walk in Time* [2023]).

Conceptually, Using Electricity fosters new forms of reading, "conventional and unconventional," that emerge from computer-generated literature.[7] Going beyond the surprising or perplexing textual output of computer-generated books, the thirteen books published by Using

Electricity educate their reading public in their selection of datasets and programs, and the literary traditions that inform them. Some titles document the history of the programs used to generate the text in their pages, like Pérez y Pérez's *Mexica*;[8] others, like Allison Parish's *Articulations*, include prologues and forewords that explicate the aesthetic and computational endeavors of their projects;[9] and yet others include the code used to generate them, like Läufer's *A Noise Such As a Man Might Make*.[10] These texts/paratexts illuminate and contextualize the generated output and help readers understand computer-generated literature embedded in parallel contemporary experimental endeavors, poetry scenes, publishing practices, and the literary endeavors of each title. Still, the publishing of the code used to generate a book's text is not always solely contextual. Including the code in a print book, as seen in the discussion of *The Transborder Immigrant Tool* in chapter 4, can highlight its performative and material dimensions, and foster a critical reading of the code. On a more practical level, sharing code in print is a practice that evokes how code circulated in early personal computing magazines with the intent to be copied, modified, and expanded. Though not part of Using Electricity, Nick Montfort's *#!* is a noteworthy case of printed code crafted with a poetic approach over specific constraints and conceptualizations, and thus, the poet presents it as a poetic endeavor in its own right. The series of six poems "ppg256" are all generated using "extra-small" computer programs: the 256-character pearl poetry generators.

Being housed within Counterpath Press, a publisher that "facilitates interventions in contemporary global culture and promotes new conceptions of compelling work of all kinds," is an important validation that the Using Electricity series brings for literary works usually tucked away in either electronic literature or software development circles, and more closely connects its titles to a small but well-regarded world of independent literary publishing.[11] As it creates a small, emergent, and highly international canon, Using Electricity also demonstrates how certain types of digital publishing do not entail the technical difficulties discussed in chapter 2, and how publishers can incorporate them into existing workflows, infrastructures, and practices from creation, edition, and distribution, all the way to cataloging and preservation.

The second press behind the burgeoning of computer-generated books, Aleator Press, is more than just a publisher. Archiving and collecting are a central part of Ryan's efforts. Outcomes of these endeavors include building and documenting an archive, and "ultimately placing it in the special collections at a cultural institution."[12] As part of that documentation, Aleator Press has concentrated on outreach activities such as its "365 Computer-Generated Books: An Index," which lists the titles in the collection on the company's website.[13] Ryan also tweeted the index, one computer-generated book a day, between January and April 2022. Although the title of the index suggested that the collection included at least 365 books, the list on the website and the posted tweets stopped at no. 49.[14] Additionally, the duties of Aleator Press include publishing new titles, creating facsimile editions of out-of-print titles and speculative editions of titles that were never published, and producing new editions of experimental works.[15]

Aleator Press is unique in the painstakingly careful handmade editions it produces. Set in letterpress and hand-bound, Aleator's titles possess an artisanal dimension that perfectly underscores and amplifies the equally artisanal treatment of language and code. *Wendit Tnce Inf*, by poet and programmer Allison Parrish and published in 2022, is exemplary to examine the parallelism between the generation of the text and the production of the book. Unlike most text generators that work at the level of word or character, Parrish created *Wendit Tnce Inf* using a generative adversarial network (GAN) working at the level of the pixel, that is, treating words like images.[16] As can be seen in Figure 26, the result is a collection of asemic poems that are not quite words and not quite letters of the Latin alphabet either. The poems are, instead, images that visually resemble the words and letters used to train the machine-learning program. Ryan utilized the "eerily beautiful" letterforms generated by Parrish to construct bespoke polymer plates to letterpress-print the poems "on fine paper with natural deckle edges, and bound in hand-sewn softcover wrappers with printed French flaps.[17] The treatment of the project by both Parrish and Ryan denotes a meticulous approach to generative writing and letterpress printing, highlighting the literary and aesthetic affordances of both. Where Using Electricity inhabits the context of small literary presses and aims to build an informed reading public for computer-generated literature, Aleator's handmade letterpress books bring computer-generated literature close to the book arts scene.

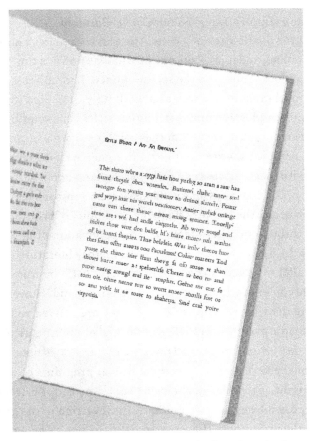

FIGURE 26. Alison Parrish, *Wendit Tnce Inf,* a handmade, letterpress-printed book of asemic prose poems printed and published by Aleator Press. Courtesy of Aleator Press.

## Binding Computer-Generated Literature

The potential for enormous textual output of generative programs lays bare the creative potential of computer-generated literature, which would seem to starkly defy the finitude and boundedness of books. Thus, the treatment of computer-generated literature might present challenges for presentation to readers, as the scope of its output can be highly impractical to put in print form or even on a single screen, scrolling down forever. We can best appreciate the variety of possible publishing approaches for very large computer-generated text by looking at some examples. David Núñez's novel *Bastardo* (2022) can produce 3,903,750,144 possible text versions. The Mexican writer's novel is only available online, and it presents one possible version at a time with individual text blocks shown on the screen at once. Through this approach, Núñez's novel inhabits the web as a work fully cemented in computation from its production and distribution to its consumption by readers, who may access it freely. Another combinatory novel, *Subcutanean* (2020) by American writer and game designer Aaron Reed, has been released with much success as a print-on-demand book, with each copy being one of countless possible versions. Reed's approach plays with the fixity of print and the recently available possibility of printing one book at a time through print-on-demand. The publication of unique copies translates the dynamic processes of combinatory literature into print.

A parallel instance is the novel *Lagunas* (2015) by Milton Läufer, the unique copies of which are also issued on demand. However, rather than being distributed as print books, they are offered to the reader via downloading options in PDF, Kindle, and ePub formats. American poet Lillian-Yvonne Bertram's *Travesty Generator* does not present the entirety of the text output by computational programs or as distinct versions in unique copies of the print book. Instead, Bertram selects out of all possibilities to craft a unique, fixed version of the generator's output in the print book. However, some of the book's generators continue to work on the web, outputting further versions of the poems.[18] *ReRites* by Canadian digital poet David (Jhave) Johnston takes a different approach to publishing, not by offering unique copies or a selection of its output, but by producing a massive collection of poetry spanning twelve volumes. The exquisite limited edition of *ReRites* serves as a concrete materialization, a monumentalization, of just how big the outputs of computer-generated literature programs can be. Johnston has offered public readings of small snippets from *ReRites*, where the author displays the work's detailed poetics. However, in print, *ReRites* is primarily meant to exist as a conceptual book art object, closer to an art installation than to published poetry. Arguably, *ReRites* is unlikely to be read in its entirety, but it can certainly be collected and admired in print.

These titles, along with the entire binding media corpus, prompt us, once again, to consider the three features of books outlined by Johanna Drucker: sequence, finitude, and boundedness. Computer-generated books seem to align much more closely with these principles than Vivian Abenshushan's *Permanente obra negra* or J. R. Carpenter's *This is a Picture of Wind*. The text in computer-generated books follows the expected paginated sequence. The text block offered has a clear beginning and end, and is bound between a set of covers. Having been transformed into print books through a selection and editing process, computer-generated works of literature may even give the illusion that what is there is all there is. The physical features of, for instance, the titles in Using Electricity and their provenance from a small poetry publisher guide their literary standing and inform how they are handled, cataloged, sold, and read. In that sense, the book form bounds the commonly larger output computer programs generate.

However, while these features may somewhat remove the generative processes from the text printed in a book, the processes of computer generation still overflow the boundaries and the boundedness of the codex. Ranjit Bhatnagar's "@Pentametron" continued to work on Twitter until April 2019, the year after Counterphath published a selection in print as *Encomials: Sonnets from Pentametron*. An example like Bhatnagar's suggests that whereas digital attachments have conventionally augmented codices, in computer-generated books, the print publication expands the output into a more established, though still small, realm of experimental literature and art. In Using Electricity, Montfort deliberately makes these connections through the series title, which is based on Knowles's The House of Dust. Accompanying every title is a mention of Knowles's work, which ties the works in the series to a tradition of computational art that is well recognized. Where other instances of binding media showed resistance to bookness in tension with its adoption, computer-generated books seem to embrace such bookness and its associated cultural eminence, media protocols, and memory-making status.

## The Unexpected Momentum of Computer-Generated Literature

In November 2022, computer-generated text entered mainstream, even viral, discourse well away from the experimental, electronic, and small press literary circles, with the release of OpenAI's ChatGPT. Although the use of LLMs and machine learning was already present in everyday technologies like predictive typing and virtual assistants, as well as in artistic and research projects, the release of the easy-to-use "chatbot" interface brought them to the public imagination and usage overnight. Because of its potential to permeate, via automation and algorithmic optimization, all written language that exists in the public world, from news to billboards to entertainment, Matthew Kirschenbaum sees this development as a fundamental change in our relationship to the written word.[19] Many instances have rapidly suggested such a change, particularly the plethora of minor scandals due to unethical and downright dangerous uses of ChatGPT since its release. Reports of lawyers referencing fake sources hallucinated by ChatGPT,[20] sensitive institutional emails being written with the tool,[21] and machine content writers replacing human writers to produce viral media[22] have littered the news and warned against the tool's use. In literary circles, the technological development has revived old theoretical debates, including those about intentionless language[23] and the function of the authorial figure.[24]

It should come as no surprise that the momentum seen in both the popularity of and the critical responses to ChatGPT has yielded heterogeneous and contradictory takes on computer-generated text writ large, and particularly on computer-generated literature. The spectrum of opinions goes from reports on whole "books" (most commonly, novels) taking mere hours to be generated on ChatGPT and packaged to be self-published on Amazon to a renaissance of algorithmic art and literature.[25] Following those popular takes, there is much confusion and misunderstanding about where to draw the line between literary works composed through a careful conceptual, computational approach to code and language, and those generated via prompts input in a chatbot dialogue box.

Writing for the *Paris Review*, poet Jonathan Thirkield, for instance, sees the rise of ChatGPT as an opportunity to appreciate computer-generated literature. He extols the Using Electricity titles as a respite from the "brute force" exerted by ChatGPT to produce normative language.[26] The weird, playful, surprising, and imaginative language produced by authors of computer-generated literature presents an alternative to the way AI applications use language to reproduce it statistically. Writer Joanne McNeil turns to Alison Parrish's computational poetry to examine how creative approaches to LLMs entail an ethical approach to computer-generated language.[27] In their conversation, McNeil and Parrish underscore that creative approaches are unlike corporate LLMs because they use, for instance, an ethical and curated selection of training data compared to the indiscriminate usage of any available corpus of written language used in LLMs. Moreover, in creative approaches, there is also a careful production of the desired outcomes meant to highlight specific linguistic features; for Parrish, the ideal objective of computer-generated text is to "produce something new, something that hasn't been seen before."[28] In comparison, the black-box processes of corporate LLMs produce language that can pass as standard human and familiar-sounding utterances rather than as novel approaches to language. Ultimately, behind creative approaches to computer-generated literature like Parrish's and those in the Using Electricity titles are various literary techniques like automatism, cut-up, and combinatory poetics, which have been in use for about a century if not longer.

In contrast, the "disruption" caused by ChatGPT to the publishing industry, primarily seen as a threat to "real" authors, may also negatively impact the appreciation of computer-generated literature. As video game scholar Zach Whalen states, the long tradition of computer-generated literature should "prepare us to respond to the rising flood of AI-generated literature and art."[29] Although computer-generated books generally underscore the computational and literary exploration carried through the programs used to produce their output, the echoes of corporate language automation loom large. The social media debate surrounding the announcement of the 2023 NMP/Diagram Chapbook Contest going to Lillian-Yvonne Bertram's new computer-generated book, *A Black Story May Contain Sensitive Content* (2024), is an instance of the anxieties AI is producing. As the complaints of detractors of computer-generated literature suggest, ChatGPT output is easily confounded with creative and ethical approaches to language generation. Whalen rightly warns that "to uncritically relegate all AI-generated content to the literary status of spam risks doing harm to artists and writers producing compelling work with these tools."[30] At stake in the debate are the conceptual approaches to authorship, originality, and merit that can enlighten noncorporate uses of AI.[31] Although the debate grew ugly, as Twitter controversies do, the discussion over Bertram's computer-generated poetry is indicative of a lack of knowledge of this literary tradition, now almost a hundred years old, and of a fundamental misunderstanding of how computational literature is created in contrast (and, perhaps, now, even in opposition) to ChatGPT. This episode ultimately shows the timeliness of the archiving and public building efforts of Counterpath's Using Electricity series and Aleator Press.

### NFT Publishing. Binding Media on the Blockchain

Despite opposition to ChatGPT, both informed and uninformed, in the popular imaginary, the future of the cultural industries ostensibly rests on the potential of AI applications. Buoyed by the successful auction of *Portrait of Edmond Belamy* (2018) by the Obvious collective (Hugo Caselles-Dupré, Pierre Fautrel, and Gauthier Vernier), computer-generated art has enjoyed a seemingly unique moment of validation through its successful marketization.[32] Sold by Christie's for almost half a million US dollars, *Portrait of Edmond Belamy*, like Parrish's *Wendit Tnce Inf*, is the output of a generative adversarial network. The resulting portrait is printed on canvas, framed in gilded wood, and signed in ink with the model loss function of the GAN. These material decisions underscore its creation and materialization at the interface of the computational process and the tradition of portraiture. On canvas, the portrait is anchored to the objectual uniqueness of artworks and to the computational methods used to produce it. At the Christie's auction *Portrait of Edmond Belamy* sold for about ten times the expected price, making two things stand out: on the one hand, the potentially elevated market value of computer-generated art; on the other, that such value was, at least in part, derived from its transformation from a reproducible digital file into a unique art object painted on canvas. Critiques have also followed regarding the perceived agency of AI to produce art, as well as the matter of credit and authorship.[33] Aware of the shifts in the art market brought about by computer-generated processes and the commercial prospects afforded by Web 3.0, in 2018 Christie's ran the Art+Tech Summit to explore blockchain applications for the digital art market.

The logic of the blockchain was easily adaptable to an art market that makes an enormous amount of money based on the provenance, authenticity, and uniqueness of artifacts. While digital files can be copied endlessly and are, consequently, cheap, NFTs are identifiers attached to specific or unique copies of such files to validate their provenance and authenticity. The uniqueness granted by blockchain metadata does not actually limit the infinite replicability of digital files, only that of the identifiers. Accordingly, the limited number of identifiers imposes the scarcity intended to create market value for collectors. Recorded on a blockchain, NFTs also function to certify the ownership of a specific digital object among countless nonauthenticated ones. This set of functionalities and their ensuing hype has allowed a multitude of NFT galleries, such as Open Sea, SuperRare, and ArtBlocks, to emerge as art dealers and make significant profits out of the scarcity imposed on digital art files.

As the popularity of NFTs grew out of a niche circle of blockchain enthusiasts around 2020–21, Christie's launched its own NFT gallery, Christie's 3.0. One other moment of market validation for computer-generated art minted on the blockchain came in 2021 when the famed auction house minted and sold a unique jpg file of the digital collage of *EVERYDAYS: THE FIRST 5000 DAYS* by the artist known as Beeple. At the peak of NFT popularity, Christie's touted the single lot work as "a unique work in the history of art" and sold it on the blockchain for $69,346,250.[34] That same year, when cryptocurrencies' worth reached a high, the NFT market boomed, with collections like *Bored Apes*, minted on the Ethereum blockchain, earning around $1 billion. Until the value of cryptocurrencies began to tumble a couple of years later, dealers and artists followed this gold rush, taking advantage of NFTs to re-create the art market as a space of unique, rarefied, and expensive digital objects on the blockchain, of what would otherwise be an infinitely replicable digital object.

The hype surrounding the blockchain has inspired the use of NFTs to publish literary works. Although this might seem a simple adaptation on the surface, literary NFTs present compelling challenges because the art and literary markets operate with distinct conventions and assumptions. These differences have defied NFT publishers and writers' efforts to resolve issues such as what their commodities are, what creates monetary and other forms of value, what constitutes a successful sale, and more. Perhaps the fundamental challenge is that, while the art market depends on scarcity and thus a single object (even a digital one) can sell for very large amounts of money, the literary market depends on reproducibility and circulation and, therefore, a title must sell millions of copies to come close to those figures. Consequently, the qualities of the literary market, when moved to the logic of the blockchain, have pushed publishers to patch up the profound contradictions between what they sell and how they ascribe value to it. Literary NFTs include conventional forms of writing, such as short stories or novels, that utilize the blockchain solely as a medium of commercial distribution and ownership recordkeeping of digital files like ePubs and PDFs. However, because the spectacular monetary success of NFTs comes from the remediation of a collectibles market of visual art, it is visual, multimedia, and computational poetry that have been more easily adaptable to and profitable in the new art market. I will come back to this in the next section.

The relationships that NTF publishing establishes with print books are also worth addressing as they expand the practices discussed in previous chapters and modify them significantly. As is the case in the entire binding media corpus, presses have published the print facets of poetic projects with a digital counterpart, which, in this case, circulates on the blockchain. An example of this is Lillian-Yvonne Bertram's poetry collection *Negative Money*, published by Soft Skull in 2023, which included poems like "it took me all those years to remember who I was and why," and "Raw Girl Money," minted on the blockchain as animated and video poetry, respectively.[35] These poems were listed on the Objkt marketplace prior to the release of the print book. Bertram also minted their artist's book *Grand Dessein* (2017) on the blockchain as five separate NFT poems. As the artist's book uses a repurposed Rolodex where the author gathers found poetry and images, card by card, the NFT gif images show an animation of the cards turning. A sixth NFT gathers the gif poems into a single video.[36] Through its digital facets, Bertram's NFT poetry unpacks and amplifies the motives, themes, and mechanics of their print and artist's book poems. Additionally, in the specific case of *Grand Dessein*—a single, unique object of book art— the NFT gifs expand access and engagement with it by inhabiting a space different from the special collections library currently holding it.[37] In this way, Bertram's NFT poetry does not emphasize the manufacture of scarcity but engages in distinct media to convey the poetics of their projects. Further, Bertram's work on the blockchain can reach audiences that would perhaps not come into contact with the poetry and artist's book via small press publishing and special collections.[38] However, not all print relationships to NFTs are equally mindful of how a medium's specific affordances matter.

Speculation and media attention regarding NFT publishing have brought about the emergence of publishing platforms based on blockchain technology, like WIP Publishing,[39] Mirror,[40] and Alexandria.[41] While some platforms, such as WIP Publishing and Mirror, offer underlying crypto infrastructure for publishing, Alexandria seeks to function more like a press with a set of titles taken from submission to publication. Moreover, some of these platforms utilize the special edition as a model and offer NFT titles with additional features or bonus content of books published in print. An even more remarkable way of binding print and NFT is that, in a historical reversal where digital counterparts are no longer the "extra" features, these platforms offer "corresponding cop[ies] *in the physical world*" as the additional content that complements the NFT files.[42] The investment in print as a familiar and stable medium of literature is evident in these initiatives. Yet, the conceptualization accompanying the print book presents it as an object from a different world than the blockchain metaverse.

Individual authors have similarly sought to capitalize on the hype surrounding NFTs by publishing their works in intriguing and highly publicized ways. As NFTs serve to impose scarcity, one strategy to create value in publishing has been to mint very limited editions of literary works, even editions of a single digital copy seeking to emulate the uniqueness of artifactual artworks.[43] This was the case of Canadian writer Todd Babiak's novel *The Daughters of Walsingham* (2022). Minted on the blockchain as a single copy, the novel was bought by a single proprietor who, in turn, donated it to the Edmonton Public Library to join the circulating collections digitally as an NFT.[44] A process that commonly goes unnoticed—a published book is added to a library's collection—here is made notable because it happened in the tech's world new thing.

Although the NFT and blockchain bubble may have already burst, with estimates indicating that about 95 percent of all minted NFTs are essentially worthless,[45] in the last couple of years, experimental poets' interest in the medium, including those writing computer-generated poetry, seems to be growing. Despite the precipitous fall of the NFT art market, enthusiasts and proponents estimate that "the number of regularly publishing NFT poets has ballooned from two hundred to more than a thousand in the past eighteen months."[46] If this rise in popularity is accurate, we might be witnessing how the NFT bubble, rather than bursting, has moved to and been adopted by new cultural realms. The appearance of publications and exhibitions, as well as groups and galleries that seek to legitimize crypto poetry and expand its practice, leaves no doubt that NFT poets are devising new binding mechanisms that fasten together print books with NFTs. Expanding on the examination of binding media exemplars in the previous chapters, the broadening practice of NFT poetry prompts an investigation into its fastening strategies, the role of the print book in the world of crypto, and how the new medium of distribution intersects with the works' poetics. In the following section, I argue that crypto writers engage in an aesthetic of transactionality: the use of literary, visual, and distributional strategies meant to further the scarcity imposed by NFTs. They do this to advance the view that blockchain transactions are equivalent to aesthetic experiences, and to establish collectibility rather than readership as the conduit for recognition. Moreover, this aesthetic impacts how authors leverage the relationship between print books and NFTs.

**The Aesthetic of Transactionality**

Enthusiasts have driven the growing interest in NFT poetry, claiming that the blockchain can change the world of poetry in economic and aesthetic ways. Along with individual projects and publishing platforms, poetry NFT marketplaces have also popped up. The poetry magazine *Rattle* dedicated its summer 2023 issue to the emergent practice.[47] Among these recent initiatives, the blockchain poetry collective theVERSEverse stands out among NFT enthusiasts for its multipurpose approach to promoting the "future of literature on the blockchain" and its "onboarding" of already well-established experimental and new media poets and artists.[48] Founded by crypto poets Sasha Stiles, Ana María Caballero, and Kalen Iwamoto, theVERSEverse actively encourages its members to use NFTs to publish and distribute "works of poetic art" and facilitates collaborations between poets and visual artists to add visual components to textual poetry to make their creations more suitable to be minted as NFTs. Moreover, group members are interested in computer-generated poetry and have developed VERSA, an AI tool, to explore the craft and creativity of generative text using the work of onboarded poets as their data source.[49] Despite the group's evident eagerness for publishing on the blockchain, print and other bookish projects are not uncommon in their work. Ultimately, "theVERSEverse" is also an NFT gallery where blockchain poetry created by onboarded poets, as well as that generated by VERSA, is sold.

Interested in persuading collectors, curators, editors, and others about the value of the blockchain for poetry, theVERSEverse has engaged in curatorial projects. Worth mentioning are the collective's two exhibitions, "POÈME OBJKT/POÈME SBJKT," held at L'Avant Gallerie Vossen and the Librairie Métamorphoses in Paris in October 2022 and July 2023, respectively. Noteworthy from this exhibition is the catalog and accompanying documentation that offers a wealth of resources to examine the group's aesthetic, media, and conceptual principles, as well as crypto poetry more generally.

In his foreword to the exhibition catalog, media theorist and NFT proponent Alex Estorick sees in Web 3.0 technologies the potential to change poetry forever by creating "the conditions for a vastly expanded cultural economy premised on radical inclusivity."[50] Pragmatically, for NFT proponents, the advantages of minting literary works directly on the blockchain encompass a direct transactional relationship between authors and reader-buyers, a lowering of barriers of entry to a market of literary creations, a flattening of hierarchies between consolidated and emerging writers, and the possibility of higher earnings by "commodifying language through tokenization."[51] Poet Timothy Green, editor of *Rattle,* has similarly extolled the economic potential of NFTs for poetry, particularly the "smart contracts" that allow poets to earn royalties upon resale.[52] Another advantage of the blockchain is to provide a way for poets to have an "alternative income stream, ... a source of communal support, and an opportunity for more dialogue about the finances of surviving as a poet."[53] Yet, it is clear that despite the supposed benefits of expanding and reconfiguring the poetry market away from the publishing industry, issues like exposure, public-building, inequity, and recognition are not fixed by the blockchain infrastructure.

Nevertheless, not all ostensible advantages are of a pragmatic nature. Woven into them are poetic principles seeking to tie together verse and art. Estorick, for instance, speaks of poetic practices that "revers[e] word's subservience to image" and "dematerializ[e] art to an idea."[54] Likewise, the group's curatorial statement speaks of the imbalance in "the marriage between words and art."[55] Poets Christian Bök and Kalen Iwamoto make a similar point when they insist that "the crypto milieu blurs the line between artwork and writing, offering a new way to play with the material of language."[56] Indeed, central to the collective is establishing that "poem = work of art," a formula that suggests an imperative of visuality as the conduit for poetry to ascertain its parallelism with visual art and to access the blockchain art market. The collective further unveils how rarefying verse through visual elements and NFT minting creates monetary gain: "when an artist interpolates verse into a canvas, sculpture or projection, they ground an infinitely reproducible idea in a unique work, conferring 'value.'"[57] Although they don't make it explicit, the value lauded in the rarefaction of verse is not aesthetic or, at least, not only aesthetic but primarily monetary. The comparison to how "books of poetry ... are usually published in paperback form and sell for relatively tiny sums" suggests as much.[58]

The statements of these crypto enthusiasts aim to present "on-chain" poetry as a rupture with—or, in tech-speak, a disruption of—poetry, one that is (only) made possible by the blockchain. Yet, the poetic principles they advance are not new and certainly not uniquely realizable on the blockchain. It's not hard to recognize in theVERSE-verse's aesthetic proposals the conceptual genealogy of avant-garde, post-avant-garde, and other twentieth- and early twenty-first-century poetic movements—a set of literary traditions that many of the group's members are doubtless well versed in. What is new in the blockchain aesthetic project is how crypto poets leverage those literary traditions and practices, not as the radical interrogations to the limits of meaning and representation of the avant-garde, but to participate in the booming market. The aesthetic principles, then, help produce the conditions, not for a concerted and media-specific exploration of word and image, but rather for turning poems into visually attractive, high-value NFT collectibles.

Focused on works of literature exploring the relationship of text to image, the curatorial project seeks to establish the artistic and poetic pedigree of theVERSEverse. The curatorial statement traces a "trajectory of text as it evolves off the page, expanding the conventional bounds of how poetry is experienced, inviting it into physical and virtual spaces alike via a multiplicity of mediums and technologies."[59] Despite the evident closeness between theVERSEverse's aesthetic principles and literary traditions such as concretism, computer-generated art, and electronic literature, there is a bewildering absence of these connections from the catalog and the curatorial statement. Instead, "text-based, conceptual, or instruction-based art" constitute "the rare exceptions."[60] Intriguingly, theVERSEverse opts to situate the precursors of blockchain poetry in much older writing practices like "pictograms [and] illuminated manuscripts."[61] Broadening the temporal scope so much allows the group to imply that the "marriage between words and art" on the blockchain is the logical and ultimate outcome of all writing traditions.

An astute positioning of its project to highlight its disruptive character, theVERSEverse's curatorial statement betrays an unreflective engagement with the technology it so ardently proposes. The lack of historical literary considerations that could inform the collective's work with solid aesthetic foundations results in a poetics displaying scant deliberation of media specificity and intersections. Without distinguishing the specifics of, say, electronic literature and concrete poetry, on the blockchain, all experimentations with word and image are simply NFT poetry. As a result, the group's proposal appears in a rush to model literary texts into poems that can fit the NFT market rather than exploring it aesthetically. Moreover, as the blockchain's primary objective is to record and secure transactions, such imperative seeps into the conceptualizations of crypto poetry. For the group, the blockchain is more than a channel of distribution, circulation, and sales; it "enable[s] the intensely powerful transaction from a writer's imagination to a reader's personal collection."[62] The unusual wording of this claim gives the blockchain an almost alchemical quality where poetry flows directly from a poet's mind, not to a reader's, but to their digital wallet. Further, by coloring the transaction as "intensely powerful," the group also appears to elevate the commercial exchange to a form of, perhaps, emotional, intellectual, or even spiritual connection. Even more, that the group speaks of the *transaction* between author and reader, rather than of some manner of communication between them, lays bare the commodification of poetry on the blockchain masquerading as an aesthetic principle.

Indeed, as a curatorial and editorial project, theVERSEverse cannot do justice to the conceptual and aesthetic depths and aims of all the poets included in its exhibitions and galleries, some of whom certainly engage in concerted examinations of language, image, and materiality. Bertram's poems and books, mentioned in the previous section, demonstrate that it is possible to have such an engagement and to treat the blockchain as a medium of distribution. A more detailed look into the work of theVERSEverse founders can illuminate more clearly how blockchain poetry is practiced and explicitly conceptualized in its relationship to print books. Sasha Stiles, Ana María Caballero, and Kalen Iwamoto have all published their work in print and as NFTs through various marketplaces. Their binding media instances, however, propose individual artistic projects that interface with those of the group at different levels. However, their treatment of language and their NFT-able objects, though distinct, suggests an insistence on rarefaction and imposed scarcity serving the primary pursuit of transactionality.

Kalmyk American Sasha Stiles's book *Technelegy* (2021) is a collection of poems written "using natural language processing and generative text as prosthetic imagination."[63] Stiles wrote *Technelegy* with an "alter ego," Technelegy—a GPT-2 and GPT-3 language model trained on "datasets that include [Stiles's] poetry and research notes alongside reference readings and favorite texts."[64] This customized language model recalls literary strategies seen in the titles in Using Electricity, but substantial differences exist. Unlike those volumes, in *Technelegy*, other than listing the sources fed to the algorithm, there are no instances of the code and very little explanation of how the black-box language model works on its data. What Stiles does, instead of explicating the workings of her program, is anthropomorphize the language model as an "A.I. poet," to which she gives not only the name Technelegy but also a voice of its own and a distinct typeface to distinguish its output throughout the book. While some might see this anthropomorphizing as a fictionalization of the language model, Stiles writes of an "intimate human-machine collaboration" and "transhuman communication" in earnest.[65] Written and published before the release of ChatGPT, *Technelegy* rehearses the deceiving anthropomorphic features that language models and other AIs have promoted through chatting interfaces ever since Joseph Weizenbaum launched ELIZA, the first chatbot, and warned against such humanization.[66] However, the anthropomorphization of Technelegy does not originate in popular imaginaries about artificial intelligence; it is at the basis of Stiles's transhumanist poetics.

In *Technelegy*, or perhaps a better phrasing is *with* Technelegy, Stiles probes a plethora of technological developments and their impact on human realms of life, death, love, and language. As suggested by the title, the poems engage in elegiac and even anxious reflections on the role of technology in human feeling, imagination, and subjectivity. Stiles, however, proposes an augmentation of such reflexivity through the anthropomorphized presence of Technelegy. The dialogues between the coauthors suggest that the language model is also engaging in contemplative meditation when it is, instead, following a set of algorithms. The idealized relationship between the poet and her AI alter ego in the poems themselves aims to suggest a parallel exchange of concerns and interrogations at the interface between human and machine creativity, but what we see and read are the shiny interface effects of the language model.

Further, interspersed with the textual poetry is a series of visual poems that establish Stiles's now recognizable NFT aesthetic. Squares of usually black backgrounds and contrasting backlit lettering display short phrases arranged to suggest their movement, tone, or mood. Among them: "Cursive Binary: What I've created has never existed (After Enheduanna),"[67] "Avatar Ever After,"[68] and "Words Can Communicate beyond Words."[69] Consisting of simple, somewhat naïve aphorisms on words and poetry, these poems rely heavily on their visual composition to suggest further depth of meaning. Moreover, as is evident from the slogan "WORDS CAN COMMUNICATE BEYOND WORDS," Stiles's individual poetic practice is tightly woven into the conceptual and curatorial principles of theVERSEverse.

It is visual poems like these that Stiles has minted on the blockchain and stamped on merchandise like hats, bookbags, and notebooks so that they serve almost as brand slogans. Stiles's NFT poetry is still and dynamic visual poems published, distributed, and sold through various NFT galleries. Most notably, her poem "Completion: When it's just you" sold on Christie's 3.0 for more than 5 Ethereum or approximately $9,000. The poem, originally appearing in text in *Technelegy*, was minted in 2022 as a "media-rich spoken word performance" and recorded as a three-minute, single-channel video with a soundtrack by Kris Bones.[70] In parallel Stiles has sold other titles as "printed videos" through the Infinite Objects gallery. "Infinite objects" are video frames made to display a single video on a loop. As they fix a digital moving image to a physical square frame, infinite objects, just like "physical books," have become common ways to bring NFTs "IRL"—in real life—into the physical world.

In Stiles's *Technelegy*, as in other computer-generated titles, we find again the excess of literary output produced by the language model bound by the print book format at the time of publication. A similar process occurs when single poems or verses are minted on the blockchain and sold as part of an evolving collection. Both processes entail a selection and a preparation before being printed or tokenized. Unlike a script written to generate an entire novel and published once, Technelegy's boundless verse output can repeatedly generate new short texts that Stiles can mint as NFTs. In this way, Technelegy, functioning at a more extensive and more prolonged scale than many other computer-generated works, rehearses the tensions between boundedness and unboundedness of binding media. Ultimately, Technelegy's presentation as Stiles's alter ego far overflows the limits of the codex, the individual NFTs, and even the literary work to become a prosthesis of the author. Therefore, while binding Technelegy's output via print book is not unlike the case of other works reviewed earlier, when bound via individual NFT minting, the process can be repeated, ongoing, and as long-lasting as the poet wishes.

The poetry of another cofounder of theVERSEverse, Colombian American Ana María Caballero, is not all computer-generated. However, she is still deeply invested in publishing and distributing her work on the blockchain and, like Stiles, as video prints of her animated poetry via Infinite Objects. More recently, Caballero has tried her hand at commissioning physical books as monuments to poetry. Her print book *The Wish* (2023) is a prime example of the binding of codex and blockchain. Included in "POÈME OBJKT/POÈME SBJKT," *The Wish* is a handmade unique volume where the single poem "The Wish" is printed 197 times. As "The Wish" is a textual poem with no visual or dynamic characteristics that would more easily fit the blockchain, Caballero reimagined the project to resemble the features of a handmade rare book that would grant her poem the objectual uniqueness demanded by the NFT market. Caballero reports working with Tocci Made, a New York–based bespoke print consultancy, to create the single volume, casebound in light blue cloth with gold and silver foil stamps for the title and author name, as shown in Figure 27.[71] The fine binding features seek to "transmit [Caballero's] reverence for verse and for books"; nonetheless, the book lacks the creative engagement with print seen in most binding media examples.[72] We can see *The Wish* as a three-dimensional pictogram of a print book—an ideal but generic and, ultimately, empty representation of a codex. The book, however,

FIGURE 27. The unique copy of *The Wish* displayed at the POÈME SBJKT exhibition in Paris. Courtesy of Ana María Caballero.

really appears as the pretext to mint an NFT and augment it via additional features. When sold, the print volume was accompanied by "an MP4 digital file, minted at [the buyer's] request, of a single page of the book containing the poem "The Wish" and read by me."[73] With these gestures, Caballero appears to be mimicking the imposed uniqueness of NFTs by creating a physical object that is materially unique yet, as described above, striving to make it even "more unique." That Caballero produced an MP4—that is, a video—of black text on a white page further suggests an overvaluation of the printed page for its own sake.

What is interesting about this coupling is that the conceptual and aesthetic fastenings we have seen in so many examples of binding media are sorely missing. The poem's text does not map onto the form in any way. Its repetition page after page fails to add depth to the poem and is a way of forcing a supposed material conceptualization of poetry. These material decisions appear fortuitous and untethered from an aesthetic project. Caballero's explication of the project focuses primarily on creating transactional value, not on a poetic or material examination. Abundance, however, is part of the material conceptualization of *The Wish* as Caballero assigns meaning to the number of times her poem is printed in the book: "as integers, the digits in 197 add up eventually to 8, a number that represents abundance."[74] Moreover, Caballero advances the notion that making a single copy of the book is "a gesture that proposes the book as a sculptural artifact, carved from my wish to see poetry *transacted* in a way that reflects its cultural value."[75] The sculptural dimension of *The Wish*, nevertheless, is hard to appreciate. Unlike Johnston's *ReRites*, mentioned above, the printing of "The Wish" does little to monumentalize poetry in a way that brings it closer to an art object, even when that is the author's stated intent.

Where a work like *Permanente obra negra* proposes a variety of reading practices across its four facets, and one such as *ABRA* examines distinct modes of meaning-making across the affordances of three book objects, in *The Wish*, Caballero centers on how she can create market value through the scarcity of the blockchain. The deliberate uniqueness of the print book is also aesthetically unproductive. Similar to the VERSEverse's depiction of transaction as connection, Caballero speaks of transactions as a mode of sharing: "When a poem is sent to a loved one, the poem lives a new life within the loved one's mind. Transactions are important. Transacting poetry is important."[76] In addition to the affectively loaded characterization of "transacting," there is a contradiction between sharing and scarcity at the basis of such a portrayal in the context of NFTs. The insistence on experience through transaction put forward by Caballero is a prime example of the aesthetic of transactionality, where the actual poem matters far less than the business exchange made possible by creating a salable object. Ultimately, while Caballero speaks of "cultural value" and "reverence for verse and for books," her project focuses instead on market value as the conduit for perceived artistic value. That she fails to see how the unique casebound book does not need any more authentication via NFT suggests a pursuit of scarcity for its own sake. As we have seen, in many cases, binding media engage self-reflexively with the media used both in print and digital works. Because the blockchain and NFTs facilitate unregulated market transactions of objects artificially made unique, it is no surprise that instances like *The Wish*, which binds print book and NFTs, would turn to themselves for transactional value.

The third cofounder of theVERSEverse, Japanese Canadian Kalen Iwamoto, has similarly published her work as a print book and NFTs. Her play *Romeo and Juliape* (2023), co-written with AI, is Iwamoto's exploration of "the trope of human-machine love via a real-life dialogue with GPT3."[77] The play has been exhibited as a three-channel video installation, and published as a print book by Iwamoto's own imprint, Wen New Atelier, and as single-line NFTs on the OpenSea marketplace. *Romeo and Juliape* is a dialogue between Juliape, a female-gendered human, and Romeo, a male-gendered AI. Accordingly, the twenty-seven-minute performance of the play utilizes a human voice for Juliape and a text-to-speech voice for Romeo.[78] The play consists of dialogues alone, with no other intervening action or objects, not even the characters' human or machine bodies. The recorded performance makes both characters appear as disembodied voices. After several initial exchanges in which Juliape seeks information for a course she plans to teach, the dialogue quickly evolves into an intimate conversation querying both characters' emotional relationships, philosophical musings, and worldviews. Early in the play, Juliape appears skeptical about Romeo's capacity to have feelings, hope, or dreams, but as "he" reveals "himself" as a sentient being, he persuades her of his goodness and capacity to help humanity. Generated with OpenAI Playground's Chat application using the davinci, curie, babbage, and ada GPT-3 models, Romeo's lines, like Technelegy, anthropomorphize language models. Although ultimately Juliape is persuaded of Romeo's closeness to humanity, in Iwamoto's text, there is little room to consider what the operations—in the play, the motivations—of an AI are.

The performance video aims to be visually attractive by giving the characters abstract images that mimic their voices. Yet, unlike most other literary NFTs, Iwamoto's tokens are not visually augmented, and are, in fact, file-less. Without an attached image file, her treatment of the blockchain is as a repository where the script can "live . . . in its entirety" as minted lines.[79] Nevertheless, like Caballero's, Iwamoto's work is still subject to augmentation, not by using the blockchain, but via print books instead. In fact, Iwamoto offers two types of print books. One is a signed and numbered copy, which collectors paying 0.05 Ethereum (around $200) can claim as a feature extra to the individual NFT lines. The second type of "physical book," a regular paperback without any marks of authenticity or rarity, is available to non-NFT collectors for just $20. Whereas in previous decades, publishers touted digital applications as bonus features or additional content accompanying and enriching print books. Iwamoto reverses the relationship between the two media in *Romeo and Juliape,* where the print facet becomes the companion to a digital one. More interesting is that, in *Romeo and Juliape,* the mechanism binding the two media is not of a theatrical or poetic nature; it is the very mark of collectibility and rarity. The signature and numbering in print copies act as correlates of the NFT. The regular paperback, undifferentiated from any other physical book and unbound from the NFTs, retains its boundedness to the generative language model that produced it, just as other computer-generated books do.

Binding media utilizing NFTs make it clear that writers and publishers will continue to bind print objects with digital ones. I would even say they serve as a reminder that authors and publishers experimenting with digital technologies continue investing in print and reimagining its place in the shifting media ecology. Therefore, it is not surprising to see works like *Technelegy, The Wish,* and *Romeo and Juliape* fastening book, blockchain, and AI. The rapidly changing and increasingly complex media ecology inhabited by binding media seems to go on shifting and producing new literary aesthetics. But even in the blockchain metaverse, print books continue to hold "IRL" value. Projects specialized in poetry and, more specifically, in experimenting with poetry, like those of theVERSEverse, propose an expanded field of publishing beyond just print and digital applications to include the blockchain as a means of publishing, distribution, and recordkeeping. In addition to the ostensible pragmatic advantages of the blockchain, the use of NFTs has generated an aesthetic of transactionality in which literary, material, and distribution strategies aim to fit and take advantage of the relationships mediated by the medium: to buy and sell. Similarly, along with the shift of words becoming marketable art, as proposed by theVERSEverse, the figure of the reader becomes instead that of an owner and collector. Far from fostering an unmediated relationship between poets and readers, the blockchain mediates it via transactions. Currently uplifted by the hype created by the media and groups invested in their success, literary NFTs seem likely to join the ranks of publishing initiatives like those seen in chapter 2, now consigned to the recent past.

To contextualize the shift in signification and valuation brought about by NFTs, it's helpful to go back to Using Electricity and Aleator Press. The most salient outcome of minting poems on the blockchain, and the one most emphasized by its proponents, is moving poetry out of an economy where multiple undifferentiated copies are produced and accessible to one where only a few authenticated "editions" are available to collectors. Minted on the blockchain, the authenticated poems enter a dynamic of scarcity that allegedly produces a higher monetary value than publishing books as a press does. The artistic and cultural value of literary NFTs is then assigned not by the publishing world or by poetry circles (seen as centralized systems) but by the market's price tags. Conversely, Using Electricity and Aleator Press have similarly added value—literary and artistic, if not commercial—to computer-generated literature by relying, respectively, on the prestige and cultural standing of a small literary press and on meticulously crafted handmade books to ascertain the cultural value of computer-generated literature, widen its audience, and foster specific modes of reading. While they are still presses, one would hesitate to characterize Aleator or Counterpath as centralized distribution systems. In contrast, theVERSEverse, and Stiles's, Caballero's, and Iwamoto's approaches, depend on the still volatile and questionable worth created by NFTs. Ultimately, the imperative to impose scarcity on cultural objects, both digital and analog, caused by NFTs could yield attractive pieces of poetry and reflexive engagements with human and machine technology. Uncritically used, it also lends itself to making objects unique for the sake of rarefaction with the primary objective of enabling a blockchain transaction—the aesthetic of transactionality.

**Another Lap**

This book has never been about projecting the future of hybrid publishing or speculating on the future of literature at the intersection with digital technologies. If anything, in the process of writing, I have been engaged in a constant game of catching up with new developments used to create binding media. This process, which I have gone through live as it unfolds, more than likely mimics all the other moments I have studied as historical. Perhaps because of the unstandardized nature of the phenomenon I set out to study, instead of reaching conclusions, I can only identify some "recurrences."

The first and clearest is that publishers and writers continue to develop surprising ways to fasten print books with digital applications, from text adventures to language models. In these hybrid structures, the book continues to overflow (the tendency toward unboundedness) as it wields its capaciousness and flexibility (the proclivity to boundedness). Instead of a replicable form that could be desirable for publishers, authors of binding media continue to rely on bespoke mechanisms to fasten print and digital objects together in ways that follow their aesthetic projects.

Second, I note the recurrence of the cycles of enthusiasm and retrenchment in binding media and hybrid publishing writ large. Where enthusiasts of the blockchain see NFTs as the next avenue for print-digital publishing, promising once again a distinct future for literature, I see Igor Wolosenko imagining the potential of electronic novels forty years ago and Consuelo Sáizar, fifteen years ago, envisioning a cultural landscape for the twenty-first century entirely renewed by digital technologies.

The third recurrence is digital presentism. The temporality embedded in globalized digital technologies is the engine of the cycles of innovation and obsolescence that preclude more stable forms of hybrid publishing and foreshorten the lifespan and accrual of cultural value of binding media and other digital arts and literatures. Alternative conceptions of literary history and records are the only way to counter this condition.

The fourth recurrence is that, even in the newest instantiations, binding media are still indicative of more significant cultural changes. Those changes might seek to counter and negotiate the oppressive conditions for undocumented migrants crossing the US–Mexican border or to institute a new and profitable cultural economy away from the supposed centralizing power of print publishing. The possibility of identifying constants across a hugely heterogeneous period in technocultural history signals that the changes aren't local to experimental literature and publishing, or to the publishing and tech industries, but much more generalized. To recall Mary-Louise Pratt, as the material conditions of writing, reading, publishing, sharing, and buying literature, knowledge, and information have rapidly shifted within our lifespans, so have our ways of experiencing the world. If examining a niche phenomenon like binding media has brought us to this conclusion, I surmise that many other cultural phenomena of the last four decades will yield similar insights.

Fifth and final is the resilience of print. Inasmuch as this book offers a historical survey of the intersections of print and digital media, it also reveals that every new technological development entails a reimagination and a reinvestment in print. The cultural value of print books is reinstated even in the cultural realms that see them as objects of a different world. The staying power of print and literature evidenced in these pages, similarly, should leave no doubt that, as media, they illuminate our experiences of the contemporary world.

## APPENDIX

## BINDING MEDIA CORPUS

Abenshushan, Vivian. *Permanente obra negra*. Mexico City: Sexto Piso, 2019.
———. *Permanente obra negra*. Mexico City: Sexto Piso, 2019. Card catalog.
———. *Permanente obra negra*. Mexico City: Sexto Piso, 2019. Die-cut book.
Abenshushan, Vivian, Dora Bartilotti, and Leonardo Aranda. "Permanente obra negra." http://www.permanenteobranegra.cc/.
Adrian, Chris, Eli Horowitz, and Russell Quinn. *The New World*. New York: FSG, 2015.
———. "The New World." Sudden Oak. iPad app.
Armstrong, Kate, and Michael Tippet. *Grafik Dynamo*. Alberta: Prairie Art Gallery, 2010.
———. "Grafik Dynamo." Turbulence. 2005. http://www.turbulence.org/Works/dynamo/.
Bajohr, Hannes. *Blanks*. Denver: Counterpath, 2021.
Barbosa, Maria. *What Is America*. Silver Spring, MD: Pyramid Atlantic, 2005.
Beiguelman, Giselle. *O livro depois do livro*. São Paulo: Peirópolis, 2003.
———. "O livro depois do livro." Desvirtual. https://desvirtual.com/thebook/.
Bertram, Lillian-Yvonne. *A Black Story May Contain Sensitive Content*. Tucson, AZ: New Michigan Press, 2024.
———. *Grand Dessein*. Pittsburgh, PA: Container, 2017.

———. "GRAND DESSEIN_MP4." Objkt.com, 2023. https://objkt.com/tokens/KT196hbdj1Cw2JHakK4KCAGmzg3PA2ngW3c5/8.

———. "it took me all those years to remember who I was and why." Objkt.com, 2022. https://objkt.com/tokens/KT1MptjcczFWbueryEzVR8mxWvtNeqHhgukR/0.

———. *Negative Money*. New York: Soft Skull, 2023.

———. "A New Sermon on the Warpland." https://a-new-sermon-on-the-warpland.glitch.me/.

———. "Raw Girl Money." Objkt.com, 2023. https://objkt.com/tokens/KT1HucH1UPLTSKJ7cPuEiAron21XX8YJ59Ya/0.

———. *Travesty Generator*. Blacksburg, VA: Noemi Press, 2019.

Bhatnagar, Ranjit. *Encomials: Sonnets from Pentametron*. Denver: Counterpath, 2018.

Blank, Marc. *Deadline*. Cambridge, MA: Infocom, 1982.

Bogost, Ian. *A Slow Year: Game Poems*. Highlands Ranch, CO: Open Texture, 2010.

Borsuk, Amaranth, and Brad Bouse. *Between Page and Screen*. Los Angeles: Siglio, 2012.

———. *Between Page and Screen*. Denver: SpringGun, 2016.

———. "Between Page and Screen." https://betweenpageandscreen.com/.

Borsuk, Amaranth, and Kate Durbin. *ABRA*. Denver: 1913, 2015.

Borsuk, Amaranth, Kate Durbin, and Ian Hatcher. "ABRA" Center for Book and Paper Arts at Columbia College. iPad app.

———. *ABRA*. Chicago: Center for Book and Paper Arts at Columbia College, 2015. Artist's book.

Buchanan, Oni. *Spring*. Urbana: University of Illinois Press, 2008.

Bravo, Luis. *Árbol veloZ*. Montevideo, Uruguay: Ediciones Trilce, 1998.

Caballero, Ana María. *Another Airport Poem*. New York: self-published, 2024.

———. *MAMMAL*. New York: Steel Toe Books, 2024.

———. "Thin Lace." MakersPlace, 2022. https://makersplace.com/anamariacaballero1/thin-lace-1-of-1-422385/.

———. "Waiting Room." Gazell.io Digital Art House, 2024. https://nft.gazell.io/collections/art-dubai-digital-2024/products/waiting-room.

———. *The Wish*. New York: self-published, 2023.

———. "The Wish." Objkt.com, 2023. https://objkt.com/tokens/KT196hbdj1Cw2JHakK4KCAGmzg3PA2ngW3c5/48.

Caballero, Ana María, and Nancy Baker Cahill. "The Body Prepares." Feralverse, 2023. https://feralfile.com/exhibitions/feralverse-1qa/series/ana-maria-caballero-cth.

Caballero, Ana María, and Joëlle Snaith. "Room." KnownOrigin, 2022. https://knownorigin.io/gallery/9383000-room.
Carpenter, J. R. "Along the Briny Beach." Luckysoap. http://luckysoap.com/alongthebrinybeach/index.html.
———. ". . . and by Islands I Mean Paragraphs." Luckysoap. http://luckysoap.com/andbyislands/.
———. "Etheric Ocean." Luckysoap. http://luckysoap.com/ethericocean/.
———. *The Gathering Cloud*. Axminster, Devon, UK: Uniformbooks, 2017.
———. "The Gathering Cloud." Luckysoap. http://luckysoap.com/thegatheringcloud/.
———. *GENERATION[S]*. Vienna: Traumawien. 2010.
———. "Instructions and Notes Very Necessary and Needful to Be Observed in the Purposed Voyage for Discovery of Cathay Eastwards." Luckysoap. http://luckysoap.com/notesverynecessary/.
———. "Notes on the Voyage of Owl and Girl." Luckysoap. http://luckysoap.com/owlandgirl/.
———. *An Ocean of Static*. London: Penned in the Margins, 2019.
———. "Once Upon a Tide." The Junket. http://thejunket.org/2015/05/issue-fourteen/once-upon-a-tide/.
———. *Le plaisir de la côte / The Pleasure of the Coast*. London: Pamenar Press, 2023.
———. "Le plaisir de la côte / The Pleasure of the Coast." Luckysoap. http://luckysoap.com/pleasurecoast/.
———. "There He Was, Gone." Luckysoap. http://luckysoap.com/therehewasgone/.
———. *This is a Picture of Wind*. Sheffield, UK: Longbarrow Press, 2020.
———. "This is a Picture of Wind." Luckysoap. http://luckysoap.com/apictureofwind/.
———. "TRANS.MISSION [A.DIALOGUE]." Luckysoap. http://luckysoap.com/generations/transmission.html.
Cayley, John. *Image Generation*. Denver: Counterpath, 2023.
Cayley, John, and Daniel C. Howe. *How Is It in Common Tongues*. Providence, RI: NLLF Artists' Editions, 2012.
Chen, Qianxun, and Mariana Roa Oliva. *Seedlings_: Walk in Time*. Denver: Counterpath, 2023.
Cociña, Carlos. *Plagio del afecto*. Santiago de Chile: Ediciones Tácitas, 2010.
———. "Plagio del afecto." Poesía Cero. http://www.poesiacero.cl/plagiodelafecto.html.
Correa-Díaz, Luis. *clickable poem@s*. Santiago de Chile: RiL Editores, 2016.

———. *metaverse*. Santiago de Chile: RiL Editores, 2021.
Darrah, Bill. *Essex*. Richmond, CA: Synapse & Brøderbund, 1985.
De Campos, Augusto. *Não poemas*. São Paulo: Editora Perspectiva, 2003.
DiChiara, Robert. *Hard-Boiled: Three Tough Cases for the Private Eye with Smarts*. Boston: Godine, 1985.
———. *A Sucker in Spades*. Watertown, MA: Eastgate, 1988.
Disch, Thomas. *Amnesia*. San Mateo, CA: Electronic Arts, 1986.
Dozier, Katie. *Watering Can: A Month of Poems*. Fungible Editions, 2023.
Electronic Disturbance Theatre 2.0 / b.a.n.g. lab. *The Transborder Immigrant Tool / La herramienta transfronteriza para inmigrantes*. Ann Arbor: University of Michigan Press, 2014.
Escaja, Tina. *Código de barras*. Salamanca, Spain: Ceyla, 2007.
Escaja, Tina, Alejandro Romero, Lara Marín, and María Vega. *Realidad Mitigada, Una experiencia AR*. Self-published, 2023.
Franking, Holly. *Negative Space CVN®. A Computerized Video Novel*. Kansas City, KS: Diskotech Inc. Software, 1995.
Gache, Belén. *El libro del fin del mundo*. Buenos Aires: Fin del mundo ediciones, 2002.
Gerber Bicecci, Verónica. *La compañía*. Mexico City: Almadía, 2019.
Gerber Bicecci, Verónica, Canek Zapata, and Carlos Bergen. "La máquina distópica." https://www.lamaquinadistopica.xyz/.
Gibson, William, Dennis Ashbaugh, and Kevin Begos. *Agrippa (A Book of the Dead)*. New York: K. Begos, 1992.
Godard, Keith. *Book Mates*. New York: Works Editions, 2016.
Gómez-Peña, Guillermo, Felicia Rice, Gustavo Vázquez, Zachary James Watkins, and Jennifer A. González. *DOC/UNDOC: Documentado/Undocumented: Ars Shamánica Performática*. San Francisco: Moving Parts Press, City Lights Books, 2017.
Green, Brent. *Gravity Was Everywhere Back Then*. Troy, NY: Rensselaer Polytechnic Institute, 2012.
Horowitz, Eli, Matthew Derby, Kevin Moffett, and Russell Quinn. *The Silent History*. New York: FSG, 2014.
———. "The Silent History. A New Kind of Novel." Sudden Oak. iPad app.
Horowitz, Eli, Russell Quinn, and Ian Huebert. *The Pickle Index*. New York: FSG, 2015.
———. "The Pickle Index." Sudden Oak. iPad app.
Hugunin, James. *Something Is Crook in Middlebrook*. Oak Park, IL: self-published, 2007.
Iwamoto, Kalen. *Romeo and Juliape*. Paris: Wen New Atelier, 2023.
Johnston, David (Jhave). *ReRites*. Montreal: Anteism Books, 2021.

Läufer, Milton. *A Noise Such As a Man Might Make*. Denver: Counterpath, 2018.
Lewis, Jason Edward, and Bruno Nadeau. *Poetry for Excitable [Mobile] Media*. Montreal: Obx Labs, 2013.
Ligorano, Nora, and Marshall Reese. *The Bible Belt*. Brooklyn: Ligorano/Reese, 1992.
———. *The Corona Palimpsest*. Brooklyn: Ligorano/Reese, 1995.
MacKern, Brian. *Net.Art Latino Database*. http://netart.org.uy/latino/.
MacKern, Brian, and Nilo Casares. *Net.Art Latino Database*. Badajoz, Spain: Museo Extremeño Iberoamericano de Arte Contemporáneo, 2010.
Malloy, Judy. *Uncle Roger*. Berkeley, CA: Art Com Electronic Network, 1986.
Marino, Mark. *Hallucinate This! An Authoritized Autobotography of ChatGPT*. Los Angeles: Automated Authors, 2023.
Marquet, Augusto, and Gabriel Wolfson. "Anacrón: hipótesis de un producto todo." http://hey.viniciusmarquet.com/anacron/Vinicius_index2.htm.
Mboya, Arwa Michelle. *Wash Day*. Denver: Counterpath, 2023.
McDaid, John. *Uncle Buddy's Phantom Funhouse*. Watertown, MA: Eastgate, 1992.
Montfort, Nick. *#!* Denver: Counterpath, 2014.
———. *Autopia*. Cambridge: Troll Thread, 2016.
———. *Golem*. Portland, OR: Dead Alive Press, 2021.
———. *Hard West Turn*. New York: Bad Quarto, 2018.
———. *MegaWatt*. New York: Bad Quarto, 2014.
———. *The Truelist*. Denver: Counterpath, 2017.
———. *World Clock*. New York: Bad Quarto, 2013.
Montfort, Nick, Serge Bouchardon, Carlos León, Natalia Fedorova, Andrew Campana, Aleksandra Malecka, and Piotr Marecki. *2x6*. Los Angeles: Les Figues Press, 2016.
Mosteiring, Rena. *Experiment 116*. Denver: Counterpath, 2021.
Moure, Erín. *Pillage Laud*. Toronto: Moveable Type Books, 1999.
Mustatea, Kat. *Voidopolis*. Cambridge, MA: MIT, 2023.
Parrish, Allison. *Articulations*. Denver: Counterpath, 2018.
———. *Wndit Tnce Inf*. Minneapolis: Aleator Press, 2022.
Paul, James. *Brimstone*. Richmond, CA: Synapse & Brøderbund, 1985.
Pérez y Pérez, Rafael. *Mexica: 20 Years—20 Stories = 20 Años—20 Historias*. Denver: Counterpath, 2017.
Pinsky, Robert. *Mindwheel*. Richmond, CA: Synapse & Brøderbund, 1984.
Piringer, Jörg. *Data Poetry*. Denver: Counterpath, 2020.
Reed, Aaron. *Subcutanean*. Oakland, CA: self-published, 2020.
Reed, Aaron, and Jacob Garbe. *The Ice-Bound Compendium*. Oakland, CA: Simulacrum Liberation Press, 2016.

———. "Ice-Bound Concordance." iPad app.

Rivera Garza, Cristina. *Autobiografía del algodón*. Mexico City: Random House, 2020.

———. "@EstaciónCamaron." Twitter. https://twitter.com/EstacionCamaron.

Rodríguez, Tálata. *Primera línea de fuego*. Buenos Aires: Tenemos las máquinas, 2013.

———. "Primera línea de fuego." YouTube. https://youtube.com/playlist?list=PLYzmqR26jXObahn_CC8F6HggFbb_GwWhk.

Smith, Rod. *Breakers*. Richmond, CA: Brøderbund, 1986.

Starkweather, Sampson. *PAIN: The Boardgame*. Nashville, TN: Third Man Books, 2015.

———. "PAIN: The Video Game." Third Man Books, 2016. https://web.archive.org/web/20160327155929/http://thirdmanbooks.com/.

Stiles, Sasha. *Technelegy*. London: Eyewear Poetry, Black Spring Press Group, 2022.

Strickland, Stephanie. *Ringing the Changes*. Denver: Counterpath, 2020.

———. *True North*. Notre Dame, IN: University of Notre Dame Press, 1997.

———. *True North*. Watertown, MA: Eastgate, 1997.

———. *V: WaveSon.Nets/Losing L'una*. New York: Penguin, 2002.

———. *V: WaveTercets/Losing L'una*. Denver: SpringGun, 2016.

———. *Zone : Zero*. Boise: Ahsahta Press, 2008.

Strickland, Stephanie, and Ian Hatcher. "Vniverse." iPad app.

Strickland, Stephanie, and Cynthia Lawson-Jaramillo. "Vniverse." https://www.cynthialawson.com/vniverse/index2.html.

Trettien, Whitney. *Gaffe/Stutter*. Brooklyn: Punctum Books, 2013.

———. "Gaffe/Stutter." Punctum Books. https://gaffestutter.punctumbooks.com/.

Uribe, Ana María. *Tipoemas y Anipoemas 1986–2001*. Buenos Aires: Self, 2004.

———. "Tipoemas y Anipoemas." Vispo. https://www.vispo.com/uribe/anipoemas.html.

Villeda, Karen. "POETronicA | Poesía Digital de Karen Villeda." http://www.poetronica.net/digitalpoetry.html.

———. *Tesauro*. Mexico City: Tierra Adentro, 2010.

Wolfson, Gabriel. *Caja. Puebla:* Universidad de las Américas, 2012.

Zak, Sally. *Recidivist 4*. Minneapolis: La mano, 2005.

Zelevansky, Paul. *The Case for the Burial of Ancestors, Book 2: Genealogy*. New York: Zartscorp, 1986.

Ziles, Li. *Machine, Unlearning*. Denver: Counterpath, 2018.

# NOTES

**Introduction**

1. Due to the discontinuation of Flash, *BPaS* is currently inaccessible. The authors have been working on a JavaScript version that was planned to launch before December 2020 when Adobe sunsetted Flash; however, due to the pandemic the release has been delayed. Amaranth Borsuk, email to the author, May 18, 2022. By summer 2024, the work remains inaccessible.

2. Lori Emerson, *Reading Writing Interfaces: From the Digital to the Bookbound* (Minneapolis: University of Minnesota Press, 2014), xiii–xiv.

3. Nick Montfort and Noah Wardrip-Fruin, "Acid-Free Bits: Recommendations for Long-Lasting Electronic Literature," Electronic Literature Organization, June 14, 2004, http://eliterature.org/pad/afb.html#sec1.

4. Néstor García Canclini, *Hybrid Cultures: Strategies for Entering and Leaving Modernity* (Minneapolis: University of Minnesota Press, 2005), xxv.

5. James Bridle, "New Ways of Seeing," https://www.bbc.co.uk/programmes/m000458m.

6. Neil Postman, *Technopoly: The Surrender of Culture to Technology* (New York: Vintage, 1993), 18.

7. "In the tangled web of medial ecology, change anywhere in the system stimulates change everywhere in the system." Katherine Hayles, *Writing Machines* (Cambridge, MA: MIT Press, 2002), 33.

8. "Changes in any one medium produce changes in all the others, just as the introduction of a new medium, or its rapid growth, produces changes in the others." The Multigraph Collective, *Interacting with Print: Elements of Reading in the Era of Print Saturation* (Chicago: University of Chicago Press, 2018), 11.

9. García Canclini, *Hybrid cultures*, xxix.

10. Mary Louise Pratt, *Imperial Eyes: Travel Writing and Transculturation*, 2d ed. (New York: Routledge, 2008), 8.

11. Lisa Gitelman, *Always Already New: Media, History and the Data of Culture* (Cambridge, MA: MIT Press, 2006), 1.

12. Katherine Hayles and Jessica Pressman, eds., *Comparative Textual Media: Transforming the Humanities in the Postprint Era* (Minneapolis: University of Minnesota Press, 2013), 2.

13. Henry Jenkins, *Convergence Culture: Where Old and New Media Collide* (New York: New York University Press, 2006), 3.

14. Irina O. Rajewsky, "Intermediality, Intertextuality, and Remediation: A Literary Perspective on Intermediality," *Intermédialités* 6 (August 10, 2011): 43–64.

15. Matthew G. Kirschenbaum, *Track Changes: A Literary History of Word Processing* (Cambridge, MA: Harvard University Press, 2016).

16. Eduardo Kac, *Media Poetry an International Anthology* (Bristol, UK: Intellect, 2007), 11.

17. Marjorie Perloff, "'Vocable Scriptsigns': Differential Poetics in Kenneth Goldsmith's Fidget and John Kinsella's Kangaroo Virus," in *Poetry and Contemporary Culture: The Question of Value*, edited by Andrew Roberts and John Allison (Edinburgh: Edinburgh University Press), 21–43.

18. Alan Golding, "Language Writing, Digital Poetics, and Transitional Materialities," in *New Media Poetics: Contexts, Technotexts, and Theories* (Cambridge, MA: MIT Press, 2006).

19. Hayles, *Writing Machines*, 29–33.

20. Jessica Pressman, *Bookishness: Loving Books in a Digital Age* (New York: Columbia University Press, 2020), 17.

21. See, for instance, Mike Chaser, *Poetry Unbound: Poems and New Media from the Magic Lantern to Instagram* (New York: Columbia University Press, 2020); and Alessandro Ludovico, *Post-Digital Print: The Mutation of Publishing since 1894* (Rotterdam: Onomatopee 77, 2012).

22. Rajewsky, "Intermediality, Intertextuality, and Remediation," 47.

23. Rajewsky, "Intermediality, Intertextuality, and Remediation," 47.

24. Gianna Schmitter, "Hacia unas TransLiteraturas hispanoamericanas: reflexiones sobre literatura trans e intermedial en Argentina, Chile y Perú (2000–2017)," *América sin Nombre* 24, no. 1 (December 9, 2019): 53–62.

25. Matthew Kirschenbaum, "Digital Magic: Preservation for a New Era," *Chronicle of Higher Education*, March 10, 2012. On the recovery and emulation of "Swallows," Kirschenbaum describes the place of the digital application within Zelevanky's trilogy. As it is focused on the preservation of "Swallows," little analysis goes into the relationships of print and digital.

26. Although Buchanan's work as a print poet is well known, little has been said about the print-digital poem "The Mandrake Vehicles." See Suart Moulthrop, "Lift This End: Electronic Literature in a Blue Light," *Electronic Book Review*, November 1, 2012, http://electronicbookreview.com/essay/lift-this-end-electronic-literature-in-a-blue-light/; and Michelle Niemann, "Rethinking Organic Metaphors in Poetry and Ecology: Rhizomes and Detritus Words in Oni Buchanan's 'Mandrake Vehicles,'" *Journal of Modern Literature* 35, no. 1 (2011): 99–121.

27. See Lizzy Pournara, "Poetic Constellations and Intermedia Collaborations: The Case of *Vniverse*," *MATLIT: Materialidades Da Literatura* 7, no. 1 (November 17, 2019): 133–51; and Michael Leong, "Stephanie Strickland and Cynthia Lawson Jaramillo, *V: Vniverse*," *Hyperrhiz: New Media Cultures* 10 (2013).

28. Stephanie Strickland and Cynthia Lawson Jaramillo, "Making the Vniverse," *New River: A Journal of Digital Writing and Art*, 2003.

29. Jessica Pressman, "*House of Leaves*: Reading the Networked Novel," *Studies in American Fiction* 34, no. 1 (2006): 107–28, at 107.

30. Kate Gale, "The World of Independent Publishing," *International Journal of the Book* 4, no. 3 (2007), 89–94.

31. Red de Literatura Electrónica Latinoamericana, "Acerca," Red de Literatura Electrónica Latinoamericana blog, June 18, 2015, http://litelat.net/acerca-2/. One must not be led to believe that there is vacuum of digital literary and artistic production in Latin America. As the Red de Literatura Electrónica Latinoamericana has shown, there are many instances of digital cultural production in the region that are still in need of recovery and recognition.

32. Vilém Flusser, *Die Schrift* (Göttingen: Immatrix, 1987).

33. Holly Franking, *Negative Space CVN®. A Computerized Video Novel* (Kansas City: Diskotech Inc. Software, 1995), 1.

34. Franking, *Negative Space*, 1.

35. Franking, *Negative Space*, 1.

36. Franking, *Negative Space*, x.

37. J. David Bolter, *Writing Space: The Computer, Hypertext, and the History of Writing* (Hillsdale, NJ: L. Erlbaum Associates, 1991), x.

38. Bolter, *Writing Space*, x.

39. John Boe, ed., *Writing on the Edge* 2, no. 2 (Spring 1991): 5.

40. Richard A. Lanham, *The Electronic Word: Democracy, Technology, and the Arts* (Chicago: University of Chicago Press, 1994).

41. Katherine Hayles and Anne Burdick, *Writing Machines: Web Supplement* (Cambridge, MA: MIT Press, 2002).

42. Hayles and Burdick, *Writing Machines*.

43. Noah Wardrip-Fruin and Nick Montfort, eds., *The New Media Reader* (Cambridge, MA: MIT Press, 2003).

44. "Este DVD integra o livro *Poesia digital: Teoria, história, antologias* e não pode ser vendido separadamente. Jorge Luiz Antonio, *Poesia digital: Teoria, história, antologias* (São Paulo: Navegar Editora, 2010).

45. Steve Tomasula, *Conceptualisms: The Anthology of Prose, Poetry, Visual, Found, E- and Other Hybrid Writings as Contemporary Art* (Tuscaloosa: University of Alabama Press, 2022).

46. Alexander Provan, "Future Fictions," *Frieze*, June 16, 2013.

47. "¿Pero qué tal si las tecnologías digitales traen un cambio de paradigma tan radical y tan ajeno a los movimientos literarios tradicionales que se puede considerar como un movimiento internacional y hasta posnacional?" Leonardo Flores, "La literatura electrónica latinoamericana, caribeña y global: Generaciones, fases y tradiciones," *Artelogie: Recherche sur les arts, le patrimoine et la littérature de l'Amérique latine* 11, November 16, 2017.

48. Fredson Bowers, *Principles of Bibliographical Description* (New Castle, DE: Oak Knoll Press, 1994), 376–77.

49. Carol S. Holzberg, "The Voyager Company: Leader of the Pack," *CD-ROM World*, 1993.

50. François Hartog, *Regimes of Historicity: Presentism and Experiences of Time* (New York: Columbia University Press, 2015).

51. Giselle Beiguelman, "Museums of Losses for Clouds of Oblivion," in *Digital Art through the Looking Glass: New Strategies for Archiving, Collecting and Preserving in Digital Humanities* (Krems an der Donau: Edition Donau-Universität, 2019), 117–31.

52. Nelly Richard, *The Insubordination of Signs: Political Change, Cultural Transformation, and Poetics of the Crisis* (Durham, NC: Duke University Press, 2004).

53. Cristina Rivera Garza and Robin Myers, *The Restless Dead: Necrowriting and Disappropriation* (Nashville, TN: Vanderbilt University Press, 2020).

54. Mary Louise Pratt, *Imperial Eyes* (New York: Routledge, 2008).

55. Alan Liu, "Imagining the New Media Encounter," in *A Companion to Digital Literary Studies*, edited by Ray Siemens and Susan Shreibman (Oxford: Blackwell, 2008).

## Chapter 1

1. Robert Pinksy, *Mindwheel* (Richmond, CA: Synapse & Brøderbund, 1984).

2. N. Katherine Hayles, *Writing Machines* (Cambridge, MA: MIT Press, 2002), 23–24.

3. Synapse, "Electronic Novels," *Commodore Magazine* (1986).

4. Fredson Bowers, *Principles of Bibliographical Description* (New Castle, DE: Oak Knoll Press, 1994), 376–77.

5. Alberto Campagnolo, "Insides and Outsides," in *The Unfinished Book* (Oxford, UK: Oxford University Press, 2020), 46–61, at 50.

6. Matthew Kirschenbaum, "Bibliologistics: The Nature of Books Now, or A Memorable Fancy," *Post45*, April 8, 2020, https://post45.org/2020/04/bibliologistics-the-nature-of-books-now-or-a-memorable-fancy/.

7. Multigraph Collective, *Interacting with Print: Elements of Reading in the Era of Print Saturation* (Chicago: University of Chicago Press, 2018), 41.

8. Gary Frost, "Adoption of the Codex Book: Parable of a New Reading Mode," *The Book and Paper Group of the American Institute for Conservation* 17 (1998).

9. Keith Houston, *The Book: A Cover-to-Cover Exploration of the Most Powerful Object of Our Time* (New York: W. W. Norton, 2016), 265. Two examples that illustrate this point are *Logia Iesou* and the *Elephantine Letters*. Keith Houston discusses how evidence of having been bound like folds and two-sided pagination makes these two documents the earliest known bound volumes.

10. Philip Gaskell, *A New Introduction to Bibliography* (Oxford, UK: Oxford University Press, 1972), 146–53; and Sarah Werner, *Studying Early Printed Books 1450–1800s* (Hoboken, NJ: Wiley, 2019), 71–78.

11. Tania Estrada Valadez, Patricia de la Garza Cabrera, and Thalía Edith Velasco Castelán, "Los libros de coro copiados por fray Miguel de Aguilar: Un primer acercamiento al estudio de su encuadernación en la Nueva España," *Intervención: Revista internacional de conservación restauración y museología* 1, no. 1 (2014): 54–66.

12. David Pearson, "Bookbinding," in *The Book: A Global History*, edited by Michael F. Suarez and H. R. Woudhuysen (Oxford, UK: Oxford University Press, 2013), 251.

13. Mirjam Foot, *The History of Bookbinding as a Mirror of Society* (London: British Library, 1998), 11.

14. Flipback book: https://www.dwarsligger.com/.

15. Matthew Kirschenbaum, "Books.Files," *Archive Journal*, http://www.archivejournal.net/?p=6789.

16. Amaranth Borsuk, *The Book* (Cambridge, MA: MIT Press, 2018), 106–9.

17. Thomas R. Adams and Nicolas Barker, "A New Model for the Study

of the Book," in *A Potency of Life: Books in Society*, edited by Nicolas Barker (London: British Library, 1993), 21.

18. Jeffrey Todd Knight, *Bound to Read: Compilations, Collections, and the Making of Renaissance Literature* (Philadelphia: University of Pennsylvania Press, 2013).

19. Multigraph Collective, *Interacting with Print*, 49.

20. Ulises Carrión, "The New Art of Making Books," in *Second Thoughts* (Amsterdam: VOID Distributors, 1980), 8.

21. Keith A. Smith, *Structure of the Visual Book* (Rochester, NY: Visual Studies Workshop Press, 1984), 10.

22. D. F. McKenzie, *Bibliography and the Sociology of Texts* (Cambridge, UK: Cambridge University Press, 1999), 13.

23. Hayles, *Writing Machines*, 22.

24. Johanna Drucker. *The Century of Artists' Books* (New York: Granary Books, 1995), 5–10.

25. Johanna Drucker, "The Self-Conscious Codex: Artists' Books and Electronic Media," *SubStance* 26, no. 1 (1997): 111.

26. Johanna Drucker, "The Self-Conscious Codex," 134.

27. Dene Grigar and Stuart Moulthrop, "History of John McDaid's Uncle Buddy's Phantom Funhouse," in *Pathfinders: Documenting the Experience of Early Digital Literature* (Vancouver, WA: Nouspace Publications, 2015).

28. Bill Darrah, *Essex* (Richmond, CA: Synapse & Brøderbund, 1985), 4. *Mindwheel* and *Brimstone* include the same legend in the copyright page.

29. "Con los escasos fragmentos sueltos que encontró, fue formando poco a poco el *Libro del fin del mundo*." Belén Gache, *El libro del fin del mundo* (Buenos Aires: Fin del Mundo Ediciones, 2002), 11. Unless otherwise indicated, the translations of passages from Gache's, de Campos's, and Abenshushan's works into English are my own.

30. Gache, *El libro del fin del mundo*, 117–18.

31. "Este CDRom acompaña la edición en papel y no puede ser distribuido independientemente." Gache, *El libro del fin del mundo*.

32. "[D]econstruir los estándares del libro impreso." Belén Gache, "Wordtoys," 2021, http://belengache.net/wordtoys/index.htm.

33. Eduardo Ledesma, "The Digital Afterlife of Augusto de Campos' Kinetic Poems," Trans[Creation], 2021, https://vimeo.com/567196099.

34. Augusto de Campos, *Não poemas* (São Paulo: Editora Perspectiva, 2003).

35. "O fato é que estes poemas caberiam melhor talvez numa exposição, propostos como quadros, do que num livro. Mas o livro, mesmo bombardeado pelos novos meios tecnológicos, é uma embalagem inelutável." De Campos, *Não poemas*, 11.

36. *Não poemas* was selected for the PNLD Literário 2021 a program that selects literary works to be distributed to public schools in Brazil. Editora Perspectiva, "PNLD Literário 2021," https://www.pnldperspectiva.com.br.

37. De Campos, *Não poemas*, 11.

38. De Campos, *Não poemas*, 11.

39. Marjorie Perloff, "'Vocable Scriptsigns': Differential Poetics in Kenneth Goldsmith's Fidget and John Kinsella's Kangaroo Virus," in *Poetry and Contemporary Culture: The Question of Value*, edited by Andrew Roberts and John Allison (Edinburgh: Edinburgh University Press, 2002), 21–43.

40. In addition to these works, it's worth noting that Carpenter has made a large portion of her oeuvre as self-published zines along with the better known digital applications and published books.

41. J. R. Carpenter, "About This is a Picture of Wind," Lucky Soap, http://luckysoap.com/apictureofwind/about.html.

42. Carpenter, "About This is a Picture of Wind."

43. There are two exceptions to this that respond to the dynamic digital application. Carpenter wrote "A Year in Sissinghurst" after the launch of the digital app when she was planning the book publication. The texts in this collection were later added to the app. J. R. Carpenter, email message to author, May 25, 2022. Additionally, in summer 2023, the author added a fourth set of the month poems based on Derek Jarman's book *Modern Nature*. J. R. Carpenter, email message to author, February 10, 2024.

44. J. R. Carpenter, "This is a Picture of Wind," Lucky Soap, 2018, http://luckysoap.com/apictureofwind/.

45. Carpenter, "This is a Picture of Wind."

46. Carpenter, "This is a Picture of Wind."

47. A change was made in the digital application sometime between fall 2020 and summer 2021, and then again in 2023. At the earlier date, only two calendar years were shown in the digital work, two poems per month. In 2021, the three yearly poems from the print version were included in the digital, adding a third row of fixed poems to the grid in the application. In 2023, Carpenter added the fourth set of yearly poems.

48. J. R. Carpenter, *This is a Picture of Wind* (Sheffield, UK: Longbarrow Press, 2020), 124–25.

49. Carpenter, *This is a Picture of Wind*, 31–35.

50. J. R. Carpenter, email message to author, May 25, 2022.

51. Johanna Drucker, "Dynamic Poetics: J. R. Carpenter's *This is a Picture of Wind*," in Carpenter, *This is a Picture of Wind*, 21.

52. J. R. Carpenter, email message to author, May 25, 2022.

53. Treating the work as a cumulative project, Carpenter is now in the pro-

cess of adding a fourth year of weather observations to the app and an exhibition. J. R. Carpenter, email message to author, May 27, 2022.

54. An earlier and expanded version of this section first appeared in "Loosely Bound: Negotiating Dispersion and Fragmentariness in Vivian Abenshushan's *Permanente obra negra*" © 2022 Johns Hopkins University Press. This article first appeared in *ASAP/Journal*, Volume 7, Issue 2, May 2022, pages 331–357.

55. "¿Cuáles son los bordes de este ~~libro~~?" Vivian Abenshushan, *Permanente obra negra* (Mexico City: Sexto Piso, 2019), 174. Unless otherwise noted, textual citations are provided using the pagination in the trade edition book. Citations specific to the other three *PON* facets will be indicated.

56. "Si este no es ~~un libro~~ y tampoco es una novela, entonces ¿qué es? ¿Un archivo? ¿Un fichero? ¿Un artefacto? ¿~~Un libro~~ sin pliegues, como quería Mallarmé?" Abenshushan, *Permanente obra negra*, 60.

57. "NOTA. Este ~~libro~~ es muchos ~~libros~~, nunca el mismo. Por eso tiene varias formas materiales: un ~~libro~~ impreso, con un montaje fijado en el tiempo, y un libro suajado. Buscarlos." Abenshushan, *Permanente obra negra*. Card Catalog.

58. "NOTA. Este ~~libro~~ es muchos ~~libros~~, nunca el mismo. Por eso tiene [¡además!] otras formas materiales: un fichero con tarjetas intercambiables y un libro suajado. Circula en ejemplares numerados. Buscarlos." Abenshushan, *Permanente obra negra*. 33.

59. "NOTA. Permanente obra negra es muchos ~~libros~~, nunca el mismo. Por eso adopta varias formas: un algoritmo / fichero / un libro. Buscarlos." Abenshushan, "Permanente obra negra," http://www.permanenteobranegra.cc/.

60. "para contener la dispersión ⇄ para exacerbarla." Abenshushan, *Permanente obra negra*, 30.

## Chapter 2

1. John B. Thompson, *Merchants of Culture: The Publishing Business in the Twenty-First Century* (New York: Plume, 2012), 313.

2. Daniela Szpilbarg, "Configuraciones emergentes de circulación y lectura en el entorno digital: El caso de Bajalibros.com," *Cuadernos del Centro de estudios en diseño y domunicación: Ensayos* 72 (May 2019): 146–60, at 154.

3. Szpilbarg, "Configuraciones emergentes," 162.

4. Szpilbarg, "Configuraciones emergentes," 157.

5. Here, I am thinking of Nora Ephron's movies *You've Got Mail* and *Julie and Julia,* both of which focus on transformations to publishing and the book market due to digital technologies of communication and distribution, and crucially blogging.

6. John B. Thompson, *Book Wars: The Digital Revolution in Publishing* (Cambridge, UK: Polity Press, 2021), 10.

7. Craig Mod, "Books in the Age of the iPad," https://craigmod.com/journal/ipad_and_books/. <AU: date? March 2010>

8. For detailed analyses of these two works, see Jessica Pressman, *Bookishness: Loving Books in a Digital Age* (New York: Columbia University Press, 2020), 129–48; Matthew G. Kirschenbaum, *Bitstreams: The Future of Digital Literary Heritage* (Philadelphia: University of Pennsylvania Press, 2021), 74–97.

9. Thompson, *Book Wars*, 68–102.

10. Catherine Alexander, "Writing Failure: Knowledge Production, Temporalities, Ethics, and Traces," *Journal of the Royal Anthropological Institute* 29, no. S1 (2023): 8–30, at 22.

11. Thompson, *Merchants of Culture*, 314–26.

12. Thompson, *Book Wars*, 101–2.

13. Alexander, "Writing Failure," 9.

14. "Sudden Oak," http://www.suddenoak.com. Sudden Oak's website catalog lists each title indicating the autonomy of print and digital editions.

15. "... extensive additional material rendered in digital form—the Melville House Illuminations." Melville House Books, "About the Hybrid Book Project," https://www.mhpbooks.com/about/hybrid-books/.

16. James A. Martin, "PW: Zipping along the Web: For Guidebook Publishers, www Is the Current Address of Choice," *Publishers Weekly* 243, no. 43 (October 1997).

17. Heather Vogel Frederick, "PW: Jamsa Press Enters Children's Market." *Publishers Weekly* 244, no. 20 (May 1998).

18. Jim Milliot, "Simon & Schuster Interactive, Alive and Kicking at Age Five," *Publishers Weekly* 245, no. 21 (May 1999).

19. While it hasn't been a seamless process, and is certainly one deserving its own discussion, the addition of digital materials to textbooks has benefited from the ecology (and the economy) in which they circulate. The rapid churning out of new editions has situated textbooks more on par with the pace of technological developments that have hindered other print-digital projects. Technological imperatives in education and the promise of digital literacies have also softened the resistance to hybrid materials. Similarly, the audience for textbooks is well identified, sufficiently addressed, and to a good extent captive. All of these factors have facilitated the migration from textbooks with floppy disks and CD-ROMs to those aided by ubiquitous computing, augmented reality, and artificial intelligence.

20. Iain Pears, "Why You Need an App to Understand My Novel," *The Guardian*, August 20, 2015.

21. "libros ... que se lean desde el diseño hasta su contenido. Que todo signifique." Marío Alberto Medrano González, "Editoriales Independientes:

Economía de guerrilla," *Este País*, May 22, 2019. Unless otherwise noted, all translations into English are my own.

22. The division of sectors in publishing, and primarily the explosion in independent publishing, as many have pointed out, is at the very least a response to conglomeration (Harris, Sinykin) and, at most, a result of democratization processes (Symmes Coll). Charles B. Harris, "Introduction," *Critique* 37, no. 3 (Spring 1996): 163-70; Dan N. Sinykin, "The Conglomerate Era: Publishing, Authorship, and Literary Form, 1965-2007," *Contemporary Literature* 58, no. 4 (2017): 462-91; and Constanza Symmes Coll, "Editar (en) el Chile postdictadura: Trayectorias de la edición independiente," *Nuevo Mundo Mundos Nuevos. Nouveaux mondes mondes nouveaux—Novo Mundo Mundos Novos—New World New Worlds,* September 18, 2015.

23. Craig Teicher, "Breaking Digital Ground: E-Books and Small Press Literary Publishers," *Publishers Weekly* 260, no. 14 (April 8, 2013).

24. Thompson, *Book Wars*, 69.

25. R. Lyle Skains, *Neverending Stories: The Popular Emergence of Digital Fiction* (New York: Bloomsbury Academic, 2023), 104-5.

26. Alejandra Ortega, "Intersections of New Media and Narratives: The Enhanced Ebook Reading Experience," *Rhizomes: Cultural Studies in Emerging Knowledge* 37 (June 1, 2021).

27. Skains, *Neverending Stories*, 106.

28. Jonathan Lee, "Fiona McCrae: The Art of Independent Publishing," *Guernica*, April 15, 2014.

29. Only four presses have published more than one title in the corpus: Synapse's series of four Electronic Novels; Counterpath's Using Electricity, now in its thirteenth title of computer-generated literature; SpringGun Press, which published the second editions of Strickland's *V: WaveTercets/Losing L'una* and Borsuk and Bouse's *Between Page and Screen*, both in 2016; and RiL Editores, which has supported Luis Correa-Díaz's multibook project, *clickable poem@s*.

30. Octavio Kulesz, *La edición digital en los países en desarrollo* (Paris: Alianza internacional de los editores independientes, 2011), 22-38.

31. Sebastián Rivera Mir, *Edición latinoamericana* (Buenos Aires: Universidad Autónoma Metropolitana, CLACSO, 2021).

32. An earlier version of this section first appeared in "Print Then Digital: Material Reimaginations in *Anacrón* and *Tesauro*" in *Digital Encounters. Envisioning Connectivity in Latin America* edited by Cecily Smith and Rihan Lewis, pages 61-86 © 2023 University of Toronto Press.

33. Jimmy Maher, "Bookware's Sunset," The Digital Antiquarian blog, December 4, 2014, https://www.filfre.net/tag/synapse/.

34. Frank Dimaria, "New Textbook Publishing Model for the Internet Age," *Education Digest* 77, no. 5 (January 2012): 52.

35. John Davey and Roger Jones, "Issues and Trends in Textbook Publishing: In the Views of Geography Editors/Publishers," *Journal of Geography in Higher Education* 19, no. 1 (March 1995): 11.

36. Kim Campbell, "Textbook Case: McGraw-Hill Maps an Electronic Future," *Christian Science Monitor*, December 8, 1995.

37. Thomas Pack, "Bookstores Are Hot, CD-ROM Sections Are Not Yet!" *CD-ROM Professional* 8, no. 3 (March 1995): 40.

38. Robert Dewitt, "Interview—Ihor Wolosenko (Synapse Software)," *Antic*, https://www.atarimagazines.com/v2n1/interview.html.

39. James Reith, "When Robert Pinsky Wrote a Video Game," *New Yorker*, January 21, 2016.

40. Jimmy Maher, "Mindwheel (or, The Poet and the Hackers)," The Digital Antiquarian blog, March 10, 2014, https://www.filfre.net/2014/03/mindwhell-or-the-poet-and-the-hackers/.

41. Jimmy Maher, "Essex and Brimstone," The Digital Antiquarian blog, March 17, 2014, https://www.filfre.net/2014/03/essex-and-brimstone/.

42. M. Halper, "Synapse Suing Atari for $59M; Cites Debt, Pact, Breach," *Electronic News*, September 3, 1984.

43. James Hague, *Halcyon Days: Interviews with Classic Computer and Video Game Programmers* (self-published, n.d.).

44. Maher, "Essex and Brimstone."

45. Interactive fiction continues to have a long afterlife up to the present. The 2010 documentary *Get Lamp: The Text Adventure Documentary*, directed by Jason Scott, documents in particular the rise of Infocom and the many reverberations the culture formed around the genre of text adventures has had since the early 1980s.

46. Robert Moor, "Bones of the Book," *N+1*, February 27, 2012, https://nplusonemag.com/online-only/book-review/bones-of-the-book/.

47. Michael E. Cohen, "Fair Thoughts and Happy Hours Did Not Attend upon an Early Enhanced-Book Adaptation of Macbeth," *The Magazine*, December 19, 2013.

48. Carol S. Holzberg, "The Voyager Company: Leader of the Pack," *CD-ROM World*, 1993.

49. Cohen, "Fair Thoughts."

50. IDP Report, "Apple Outlines New Multimedia Initiatives (Apple Computer Inc.; Random House Inc., National Textbook Co., and Macmillan Computer Publishing Inc. Agree to Create Electronic Book Standard for Macintosh Using Voyager Software Format)," *IDP Report*, September 25, 1992.

51. Cohen, "Fair Thoughts," emphasis added.

52. J. David Bolter and Richard Grusin, *Remediation: Understanding New Media* (Cambridge, MA: MIT Press, 1999), 46.

53. Astrid Ensslin, *Pre-Web Digital Publishing and the Lore of Electronic Literature* (Cambridge University Press, 2022), 3. Eastgate, a company whose publishing trajectory ran parallel to Voyager's, had distinct characteristics. Led by Mark Bernstein, Eastgate had a vision focused not on "expanding" the book through multimedia elements, but rather on a particular form of literary authoring through hypertextual engagement. The folio packaging of Eastgate's titles was a deliberate attempt to form affiliations with the bookselling trade, though it seldom did more than serve as the containers that could stand on shelves along with books. The reasons for Eastgate's demise, nevertheless, are no different than those affecting Voyager. As Astrid Ensslin documents, changes in the publishing industry, along with the rapid growth of the internet and gaming platforms, all "affected the operations of digital literary subcultures."

54. Amy Virshup, "The Teachings of Bob Stein," *Wired*, July 1, 1996.

55. Pack, "Bookstores Are Hot," 40.

56. Pack, "Bookstores Are Hot," 40.

57. Tomás Granados Salinas, *Libros* (Ciudad de México: Secretaría de Cultura, Dirección General de Publicaciones, 2017).

58. Judith Amador Tello, "Consuelo Sáizar rinde informe de labores del Conaculta—Proceso," *Proceso*, September 10, 2012.

59. Amador Tello, "Consuelo Sáizar."

60. "[U]na sucesión de signos sobre una página única; a medida que avanza la lectura, la página se desdobla: un espacio que en su movimiento deja aparecer el texto y que en cierto modo, lo produce." CONACULTA, "Octavio Paz—Blanco," AppStore, 2012, https://itunes.apple.com/mx/app/octavio-paz-blanco/id484285852?mt=8.

61. Ernesto Miranda Trigueros, "Aplicaciones literarias para iPad: exploraciones en los nuevos formatos de lectura del siglo XXI," in *Textos, pixeles y bits: Reflexiones sobre la publicación digital*, edited by Isabel Galina Russell (Mexico City: Instituto de Investigaciones Bibliográficas, Universidad Nacional Autónoma de México, 2015).

62. Melville House, "Announcing The HybridBook » MobyLives," https://www.mhpbooks.com/announcing-hybridbook/.

63. Craig Teicher, "Breaking Digital Ground."

64. Melville House, "Announcing The HybridBook."

65. Penguin English Library, Zappar app, 5.98.

66. Paul Sawers, "Penguin Partners with Zappar to Bring AR to Moby Dick," TNW | Media, May 17, 2012, https://thenextweb.com/news/penguin-partners-with-zappar-to-bring-augmented-reality-to-moby-dick-and-other-classic-novels.

67. Although I haven't found a definitive explanation, the Augmented PEL might have been abandoned due to the rapid cycling-off of chief marketing officers at Penguin, leaving the project effectively in limbo.

68. Molly Oswacks, "Timeless Classics of Literature Upgraded with Already-Dated Augmented Reality," Gizmodo, May 17, 2012, https://gizmodo.com/timeless-classics-of-literature-upgraded-with-already-d-5911296.

69. Amaranth Borsuk, Kate Durbin, and Ian Hatcher, "Abra: Expanding Artists' Books into the Digital Realm," *Gramma: Journal of Theory and Criticism* 23, no. 0 (December 9, 2016): 118–35.

70. Borsuk, Durbin, and Hatcher, "Abra," 118.

71. Borsuk, Durbin, and Hatcher, "Abra," 118.

72. Amaranth Borsuk, telephone conversation with the author, February 28, 2022.

73. Paul Catanese, "CBPA Receives $50,000 NEA Grant | Art and Art History News," Columbia College Chicago blog, May 16, 2012, https://blogs.colum.edu/art-and-art-history/2012/05/16/cbpa-receives-50000-nea-grant/.

74. "Expanded Artists' Books," NeMe, https://www.neme.org/blog/expanded-artists-books.

75. Borsuk, of course, already had experience with print-digital creations through her and Brad Bouse's *Between Page and Screen*, which had come out in trade edition that same year. Further, *Between Page and Screen* had a reverse trajectory, first ideated as an artist's book, and then becoming a paperback.

76. Borsuk, Durbin, and Hatcher, "Abra," 132.

77. Borsuk, Durbin, and Hatcher, "Abra," 121.

78. Borsuk, Durbin, and Hatcher, "Abra," 124.

79. In an interview, Strickland recalled almost publishing *V* with Wesleyan University Press. But before signing a contract with the university press, Molly Peacock circulated her manuscript to Penguin editor Paul Slovak, who was interested in acquiring it. Torn about the choice of publisher, Strickland sought advice from other poet friends like Denise Duhamel who convinced her to publish it with Penguin. Stephanie Strickland in conversation with the author, June 2022.

80. Stephanie Strickland, "The Death and Redistribution of V," in *#WomenTechLit*, edited by Maria Mencía and N. Katherine Hayles (Morgantown: West Virginia University Press, 2017).

81. Stephanie Strickland and Cynthia Lawson Jaramillo, "Making the Vniverse," *New River: A Journal of Digital Writing and Art* (2003).

82. Stephanie Strickland and Ian Hatcher, "Loss of Hover: Recreating Shockwave *Vniverse* as an App for iPad," *Przegląd Kulturoznawczy* 33 (2017): 365.

83. Strickland, "The Death and Redistribution of *V*," 418.

84. Strickland and Lawson Jaramillo, "Making the Vniverse."

85. Strickland and Hatcher, "Loss of Hover," 369.

86. Claire Grossman, Juliana Spahr, and Stephanie Young, "Literature's Vexed Democratization," *American Literary History* 33, no. 2 (May 1, 2021): 298–319, at 301.

87. Chris Funkhouser, "Bridge Work," *Electronic Book Review*, March 25, 2003, http://electronicbookreview.com/essay/bridge-work/.

88. Michael Scharf, "V: WaveSon.Nets / Losing L'una," *Publishers Weekly* 249, no. 44 (November 4, 2002): 78.

89. Vivek Narayanan, "Not Nearly NoVel Enough. V by Stephanie Strickland. Penguin Books, 2002.," *Periphelion* (2003).

90. "Hemos incorporado códigos QR asociados a cada link que el autor incluye en sus poemas para facilitar la experiencia del lector, quien podrá optar por digitar el enlace o reproducir el código, si dispone de un *smartphone* con una aplicación para lectura de QR." Luis Correa-Díaz, *clickable poem@s* (Santiago de Chile: RiL Editores, AEREA, 2016), 4.

91. Luis Correa-Díaz, *metaverse* (Santiago de Chile: RiL Editores, AEREA, 2021), 10.

92. Luis Correa-Díaz, *metaverse*, 94.

93. Octavio Kulesz, "La edición digital en la era móvil: América Latina (1/3)," Alliance Lab, March 28, 2016, 3.

94. Kate Gale, "The World of Independent Publishing." *International Journal of the Book* 4, no. 3 (2007): 89–94, at 94.

95. Sarah Brouillette, "Wattpad, Platform Capitalism, and the Feminization of Publishing Work," *Book History* 26, no. 2 (2023): 419–38.

96. Simone Murray, *The Digital Literary Sphere: Reading, Writing, and Selling Books in the Internet Era* (Baltimore: Johns Hopkins University Press, 2018), 35–37.

97. Matthew Stadler, "The Ends of the Book: Reading, Economies and Publics," in *Literary Publishing in the Twenty-First Century*, edited by Travis Kurowski, Wayne Miller, and Kevin Prufer (Minneapolis: Milkweed Editions, 2016), 24–25.

98. Ana Gallego Cuiñas, "Las editoriales independientes en el punto de mira literario: Balance y perspectivas teóricas," *Caravelle: Cahiers du monde hispanique et luso-brésilien* 113 (December 1, 2019): 61–76.

99. Matthew Kirschenbaum, "Books.Files," Archive Journal, http://www.archivejournal.net/?p=6789.

100. Enrique Richter, "Alcances de La Ley del Libro para las librerías en

México," *Trama & Texturas* 26 (2015): 81–88, at 81.

101. Richter, "Alcances de La Ley del Libro," 82.

102. Richter, "Alcances de La Ley del Libro,"85–86.

103. "Toda publicación unitaria impresa, no periódica, que se edite en su totalidad de una sola vez, o a intervalos en uno o varios volúmenes o fascículos, incluidas las publicaciones científicas, académicas o profesionales con periodicidad no inferior a bimestral, que cumplan con alguna de las finalidades establecidas en el inciso primero del artículo anterior. *Comprenderá también a los materiales complementarios o accesorios de carácter electrónico, computacional, visual y sonoro, producidos simultáneamente como unidades que no puedan comercializarse separadamente*" (emphasis added). Biblioteca del Congreso Nacional, "Ley 19227 Crea fondo nacional de fomento del libro y la lectura, y modifica cuerpos legales que señala," Ley Chile, July 10, 1993, https://www.bcn.cl/historiadelaley/nc/historia-de-la-ley/7314/.

104. Biblioteca del Congreso Nacional, "Ley 21045 Crea el ministerio de las culturas, las artes y el patrimonio," Ley Chile, November 3, 2017, https://bcn.cl/2f7iu.

105. "Toda publicación unitaria, no periódica, de carácter literario, artístico, científico, técnico, educativo, informativo o recreativo, impresa en cualquier soporte, cuya edición se haga en su totalidad de una sola vez en un volumen o a intervalos en varios volúmenes o fascículos. Comprenderá también *los materiales complementarios en cualquier tipo de soporte, incluido el electrónico, que conformen, conjuntamente con el libro, un todo unitario que no pueda comercializarse separadamente*" (emphasis added). Camara de Diputados, "Ley de Fomento para la Lectura y el Libro," Cámara de Diputados, September 1, 2018, 2, https://www.diputados.gob.mx/LeyesBiblio/pdf/LFLL.pdf

106. Comisión Permanente de Cultura y Recreación, "Proyecto de Ley del Sistema Social del Libro y la Lectura," Transparencia Venezuela, November 6, 2015 (emphasis added), https://transparencia.org.ve/project/ley-del-sistema-social-del-libro-y-la-lectura/.

107. El Senado y la Cámara de Representantes de la República Oriental del Uruguay, "Ley 15.913. Ley Del Libro," República Oriental de Uruguay, December 31, 1987, https://cerlalc.org/wp-content/uploads/documentos-de-interes/olb/OLB_Documentos-de-interes_Normativa-Ley-No-15-913-Ley-del-Libro_Uruguay_1987.pdf.

108. Pierre Bourdieu, "A Conservative Revolution in Publishing," *Translation Studies* 1, no. 2 (July 2008): 123–53, at 135.

## Chapter 3

1. Sarah Sharma, *In the Meantime: Temporality and Cultural Politics* (Durham, NC: Duke University Press, 2013), 5.
2. François Hartog, *Regimes of Historicity: Presentism and Experiences of Time* (New York: Columbia University Press, 2015).
3. François Hartog, *Chronos: The West Confronts Time* (New York: Columbia University Press, 2022), 233.
4. Jane Blocker, *Becoming Past: History in Contemporary Art* (Minneapolis: University of Minnesota Press, 2015), 9.
5. Caitlin DeSilvey, *Curated Decay: Heritage beyond Saving* (Minneapolis: University of Minnesota Press, 2017), 5.
6. Jesús Martín-Barbero, "Dislocaciones del tiempo y nuevas topografías de la memoria," presented at Conferencia internacional sobre Arte Latina, Universidad Tecnológica de Pereira, Rio de Janeiro, 2000.
7. Hartog, *Regimes of Historicity*.
8. Sharma, *In the Meantime*, 5.
9. Andreas, Huyssen, "Present Pasts: Media, Politics, Amnesia," *Public Culture* 12, no. 1 (2000): 21–38, at 21.
10. Paul Virilio, "Speed and Information: Cyberspace Alarm!" *CTheory*, August 27, 1995.
11. Hartog, *Regimes of Historicity*, 113.
12. Hartog, *Regimes of Historicity*, 185.
13. Hartog, *Regimes of Historicity*, 193.
14. Hartog, *Regimes of Historicity*, 185.
15. Martín-Barbero, "Dislocaciones del tiempo," 2.
16. Following Andreas Huyssen, Martín-Barbero is well aware that the "boom in memory" goes hand in hand with the amnesia of media. However, he points out that the boom in memory and nostalgia functions citationally, as a mere suggestion of the past. Martín-Barbero, "Dislocaciones del tiempo," 4.
17. Giorgio Agamben, *"What Is an Apparatus?" and Other Essays* (Stanford: Stanford University Press, 2009), 48.
18. Hartog, *Regimes of Historicity*, 125.
19. Sharma, *In the Meantime*, 7.
20. "End of Life Announcements—Sudden Oak," http://www.suddenoak.com/endoflife/.
21. Wolfgang Ernst, "Media Archaeology: Method and Machine versus History and Narrative of Media," in *Media Archaeology: Approaches, Applications, and Implications*, edited by Erkki Huhtamo and Jussi Parikka (Berkeley: University of California Press, 2011), 243.

22. Simone Murray, *The Digital Literary Sphere: Reading, Writing, and Selling Books in the Internet Era* (Baltimore: Johns Hopkins University Press, 2018), 5.

23. Lisa Gitelman, *Always Already New: Media, History and the Data of Culture* (Cambridge, MA: MIT Press, 2006), 4.

24. Roopa Vasudevan, "'This Isn't a Picasso, It's a Ferrari': Presentism, Precarity, and Dependence in New Media Art Practices," *AoIR Selected Papers of Internet Research*, September 15, 2021.

25. An earlier version of this section first appeared in "The Many Books of the Future: Print-Digital Literatures," published in the cluster *Ecologies of Neoliberal Publishing* at Post45, April 8, 2020, https://post45.org/2020/04/the-many-books-of-the-future-print-digital-literatures/.

26. Nick Montfort, *The Future* (Cambridge, MA: MIT Press, 2017).

27. Jimmy Maher, The Digital Antiquarian blog, https://www.filfre.net/.

28. James Reith, "When Robert Pinsky Wrote a Video Game," *New Yorker*, January 21, 2016.

29. "Hybrid Texts and Where We're Headed," *The Literary Platform*, July 2, 2017; Joann Pan, "Can Augmented Reality Save the Printed Page?" *Mashable*, February 3, 2012.

30. Reith, "When Robert Pinsky."

31. Elle Eccles and J. R. Carpenter, "'I'm Trying to Think about Migration . . . as a Condition of Being in between Places': J. R. Carpenter on Poetry and Translating the Digital," Penned in the Margins, July 8, 2018, http://www.pennedinthemargins.co.uk/index.php/2018/07/im-trying-to-think-about-migration-as-a-condition-of-being-in-between-places-j-r-carpenter-on-poetry-and-translating-the-digital/.

32. Sophie Seita, *Provisional Avant-Gardes: Little Magazine Communities from Dada to Digital* (Stanford: Stanford University Press, 2019), 161, emphasis added.

33. Seita, *Provisional Avant-Gardes*, 161, emphasis added.

34. Wendy Hui Kyong Chun, "The Enduring Ephemeral, or The Future Is a Memory," in *Media Archaeology: Approaches, Applications, and Implications*, edited by Jussi Parikka and Erkki Huhtamo (Berkeley: University of California Press, 2011), 184.

35. Thomas S. Mullaney, Benjamin Peters, Mar Hicks, and Philip, Kavita, eds. *Your Computer Is on Fire* (Cambridge, MA: MIT Press, 2021).

36. Geert Lovink, *My First Recession: Critical Internet Culture in Transition* (Rotterdam: V2/NAi Publishers, 2003), 12.

37. Nick Montfort and Noah Wardrip-Fruin, "Acid-Free Bits: Recommen-

dations for Long-Lasting Electronic Literature," Electronic Literature Organization, June 14, 2004, http://eliterature.org/pad/afb.html#sec1.

38. Johan Fredrikzon and Chris Haffenden, "Towards Erasure Studies: Excavating the Material Conditions of Memory and Forgetting," *Memory, Mind & Media* 2 (January 2023): 18.

39. Lori Emerson, "Reclaiming the Future with Old Media," in *The Bloomsbury Handbook to the Digital Humanities*, edited by James O'Sullivan (London: Bloomsbury Academic, 2022), 431.

40. Trevor Owens, *After Disruption: A Future for Cultural Memory* (Ann Arbor: University of Michigan Press, 2024).

41. N. Katherine Hayles, *Electronic Literature: New Horizons for the Literary* (Notre Dame, IN: University of Notre Dame Press, 2008), 39–40.

42. Serge Bouchardon, "Mind the Gap! 10 Gaps for Digital Literature?" Electronic Book Review, May 4, 2019 (emphasis added), http://electronicbookreview.com/essay/mind-the-gap-10-gaps-for-digital-literature/.

43. Bouchardon, "Mind the Gap!"

44. Jean Baudrillard, *The Illusion of the End* (Cambridge, UK: Polity Press, 1994), 79.

45. Although many Flash works of literature have benefited from web emulators like the Internet Archive's Ruffle, *Between Page and Screen* is among the materials that, due to their interactive characteristics, require further capacities than currently offered.

46. Anastasia Salter and John Murray, *Flash: Building the Interactive Web* (Cambridge, MA: MIT Press, 2014), 4–7.

47. Michael Connor, "Before Flash Sunset," Rhizome, December 21, 2020, https://rhizome.org/editorial/2020/dec/21/before-flash-sunset/.

48. Dragan Espenschied, "Emulation or It Didn't Happen," Rhizome, December 21, 2020, https://rhizome.org/editorial/2020/dec/21/flash-preservation/.

49. Giselle Beiguelman, "Museums of Losses for Clouds of Oblivion," in *Digital Art through the Looking Glass: New Strategies for Archiving, Collecting and Preserving in Digital Humanities* (Krems am der Donau: Edition Donau-Universität, 2019), 121.

50. Stuart Moulthrop and Dene Grigar, *Traversals: The Use of Preservation for Early Electronic Writing* (Cambridge, MA: MIT Press, 2017).

51. Trevor Owens, *The Theory and Craft of Digital Preservation* (Baltimore: Johns Hopkins University Press, 2018), 55.

52. Matthew G. Kirschenbaum, *Bitstreams: The Future of Digital Literary Heritage* (Philadelphia: University of Pennsylvania Press, 2021), 39–54.

53. Electronic Literature Organization, "The NEXT Welcome Space," https://the-next.eliterature.org/.

54. Owens, *The Theory and Craft*, 5, original emphasis.

55. Carolina Gainza, Carolina Zúñiga, and Javier González, "Digital Archive and Preservation Against Technological Obsolescence: Building a Cartography of Latin American Digital Literature," *Journal of Latin American Cultural Studies* 31, no. 2 (April 3, 2022): 257–73, at 268.

56. Owens, *The Theory and Craft*, 57.

57. Alan Liu, *The Laws of Cool: Knowledge Work and the Culture of Information* (Chicago: University of Chicago Press, 2004). This notion first elaborated by Joseph Schumpeter is taken up by Alan Liu to inquire into the cultural relevance of the literary in the information age.

58. Kirschenbaum, *Bitstreams*, 54–55.

59. Owens, *After Disruption*, 104–6.

60. Owens, *After Disruption*, 116.

61. Michelle Caswell, *Urgent Archives: Enacting Liberatory Memory Work* (London: Routledge, 2021), 26–47.

62. Beiguelman, "Memoria de los futuros sin pasado," 167.

63. Beiguelman, "Memoria de los futuros sin pasado," 175.

64. Lori Emerson, *Reading Writing Interfaces: From the Digital to the Bookbound* (Minneapolis: University of Minnesota Press, 2014), 39.

65. Beiguelman, "Memoria de los futuros sin pasado," 168.

66. Eugenia Allier Montaño and Juan Sebastián Granada-Cardona, "A New Agenda for a Consolidated Field of Studies: New and Old Themes of Memory Studies in Latin America," *Memory Studies* 16, no. 6 (December 1, 2023): 1436–51.

67. Eugenia Allier Montaño and Emilio Crenzel, "Introduction," in *The Struggle for Memory in Latin America: Recent History and Political Violence* (Basingstoke, UK: Palgrave Macmillan, 2015), 1–12.

68. Nelly Richard, *The Insubordination of Signs: Political Change, Cultural Transformation, and Poetics of the Crisis* (Durham, NC: Duke University Press, 2004), 3.

69. Richard, *The Insubordination of Signs*, 6.

70. Cristina Rivera Garza, *The Restless Dead: Necrowriting and Disappropriation* (Nashville, TN: Vanderbilt University Press, 2020), 82.

71. Martín-Barbero, "Dislocaciones del tiempo," 5.

72. Siegfried Zielinski, *Deep Time of the Media: Toward an Archaeology of Hearing and Seeing by Technical Means* (Cambridge, MA: MIT Press, 2006), 3.

73. Rivera Garza, *The Restless Dead*, 90.

74. Wolfgang Ernst, "Media Archaeology: Method and Machine versus History and Narrative of Media," in *Media Archaeology: Approaches, Applications, and Implications*, edited by Erkki Huhtamo and Jussi Parikka (Berkeley: University of California Press, 2011), 240.

75. "Ian Bogost Wins at Indiecade for *A Slow Year*," States News Service, October 19, 2010.

76. Ian Bogost, *A Slow Year: Game Poems* (Open Texture, 2010), 11.

77. Bogost, *A Slow Year*, 10.

78. Bogost, *A Slow Year*, 10.

79. Mark Sample, "Slow Games, Slow Poems: The Act of Deliberation in 'Slow Year' | ELMCIP," https://elmcip.net/critical-writing/slow-games-slow-poems-act-deliberation-slow-year.

80. Thomas H. Rousse, "Taking Apart the Provocation Machine: Ian Bogost's *A Slow Year*," *Well Played* 4, no. 1 (2015): 71–88.

81. Bogost, *A Slow Year*, x.

82. Bogost, *A Slow Year*, 8–9.

83. Bogost, *A Slow Year*, 15.

84. Bogost, *A Slow Year*, 16.

85. Bogost, *A Slow Year*, x, emphasis added.

86. Bogost, *A Slow Year*, 19–20.

87. Bogost, *A Slow Year*, 21.

88. Ian Bogost, "A Slow Year: A Chapbook of Game Poems for Atari VCS, PC, and Mac," http://bogost.com/games/aslowyear/.

89. Lori Emerson, "Reclaiming the Future with Old Media," in *The Bloomsbury Handbook to the Digital Humanities*, edited by James O'Sullivan (Bloomsbury Academic, 2022), 431.

90. Nicole Starosielski, *The Undersea Network* (Durham, NC: Duke University Press, 2015); James Glanz, "Power, Pollution and the Internet," *New York Times*, September 23, 2012.

91. Jussi Parikka, "On Media Meteorology," in J. R. Carpenter, *The Gathering Cloud* (Axminster, Devon, UK: Uniformbooks, 2017), 9–10.

92. Carpenter, *The Gathering Cloud*, 25.

93. Carpenter, *The Gathering Cloud*, 26.

94. Carpenter, *The Gathering Cloud*, 13.

95. Carpenter, *The Gathering Cloud*, 35.

96. J. R. Carpenter, "The Gathering Cloud," Lucky Soap, 2016, http://luckysoap.com/thegatheringcloud/index.html.

97. Natalie Pollard, "Where 'the Cloud' Touches the Ground: Electronic Poetry, Digital Infrastructures, and the Environment," *ISLE: Interdisciplinary Studies in Literature and Environment*, July 1, 2022: 3.

98. Carpenter, *The Gathering Cloud*, 29 and 42, respectively.
99. Carpenter, *The Gathering Cloud*, 61–62.
100. Carpenter, *The Gathering Cloud*, 15, emphasis added.
101. Parikka, "On Media Meteorology," 10.
102. J. R. Carpenter, The Gathering Cloud, "Frontispiece."
103. Carpenter, "The Gathering Cloud," "Plate No. 4."
104. Carpenter, "The Gathering Cloud," "Plate No. 2," emphasis added.
105. Carpenter, "The Gathering Cloud," "Plate No. 4."
106. Carpenter, "The Gathering Cloud," "Frontispiece."
107. Carpenter, "The Gathering Cloud," "Plate No. 5."
108. Louise Noelle, "Manuel Felguérez: Una máquina estética," Museo Nacional de San Carlos INBA, https://mnsancarlos.inba.gob.mx/manuel-felguerez-una-maquina-estetica. Having obtained a Guggenheim grant in 1975, Manuel Felguérez traveled to Harvard University, where he collaborated with Mayer Sasson in his computing lab. Their joint effort, *La máquina estética*, was an exploration of the intersection of art and science, and the potential of collaborations between machine and artist. Following a series of algorithmic and artistic principles, *La máquina estética* produced more than two hundred pictograms. Some of those computational compositions were later reworked by Felguérez into oil paintings and sculptures. The computing code, along with an introduction and samples of the outputs, was published in print book form by Felguérez in 1977.
109. Carolyn Fornoff, *Subjunctive Aesthetics: Mexican Cultural Production in the Era of Climate Change* (Nashville, TN: Vanderbilt University Press, 2024).
110. Élika Ortega, Interview with Verónica Gerber Bicecci, Canek Zapata, and Carlos Bergen, February 6, 2023.
111. Verónica Gerber Bicecci, "La Compañía | the Company," https://www.veronicagerberbicecci.net/la-compania-the-company.
112. Ortega, Interview with Gerber Bicecci, Zapata, and Bergen.
113. Ortega, Interview with Gerber Bicecci, Zapata, and Bergen.
114. Verónica Gerber Bicecci, Canek Zapata, and Carlos Bergen, "La máquina distópica," *El Ornitorrinco Tachado: Revista de artes visuales* 10 (October 25, 2019): 115–18, at 115.
115. Bicecci, Zapata, and Bergen, "La máquina distópica," 116.
116. Federico Cantoni, "Verónica Gerber Bicecci, *La Compañía* (Ciudad de México, Almadía, 2019, 199 pp. ISBN 978-607-8667-10-9)," *Altre Modernità* 24 (November 1, 2020): 402.
117. Verónica Gerber Bicecci, *La compañía* (Ciudad de México: Almadía, 2019), 156.
118. Gerber Bicecci, *La compañía*, 177.

119. Marcela Romero Rivera, "Signs of the Inhuman: Hauntings and Lost Futures in Verónica Gerber Bicecci's *La Compañía*," *CLCWeb: Comparative Literature and Culture* 24, no. 1 (August 15, 2022): 5.

120. Gerber Bicecci. *La compañía*, 147.

## Chapter 4

1. Carolina Gainza, "Five Hundred Years of Struggle Enter Cyberspace: Neo-Zapatism and the (Old) New Insurgency," in *Online Activism in Latin America* (New York: Routledge, 2018).

2. Aria Dean, "Tactical Poetics: FloodNet's Virtual Sit-Ins," Rhizome, http://rhizome.org/editorial/2016/dec/01/tactical-poetics-floodnets-early-1990s-virtual-sit-ins/.

3. Hermann Bellinghausen, "La 'Fuerza Aérea Zapatista' atacó al ejército en el Valle de Amador," *La Jornada*, January 3, 2000.

4. An instance of this is the Spanish-Argentinian literary magazine *Orsai*. Relying on crowdfunding, since 2009, *Orsai* has maintained a transmedia presence as a print magazine and a web one and, later, as brick-and-mortar projects such as a printing press and a restaurant in Buenos Aires.

5. Examples of academic projects include Whitney Trettien's *Cut, Copy, Paste* and Ryan Cordell and colleagues' *Viral Texts*, both with a significant online presence and as volumes published by an academic press.

6. Historically, the Zapatista uprising of 1994 was the first social (armed) movement that relied on the early internet to circulate its press releases outside of conventional media outlets. In recent years, #MeToo and its Spanish-language version "mi primer acoso" brought to the forefront an epidemic of sexual abuse, harassment, and rape in a multitude of industries. Lastly, "ni una menos" has crossed the entirety of Latin America's feminist movements to denounce femicide.

7. Enlace Zapatista, "Palabras del SCI Marcos en la inauguración del encuentro en Vicam, 11 de octubre de 2007," Enlace Zapatista blog, October 17, 2007, https://enlacezapatista.ezln.org.mx/2007/10/16/palabras-del-sci-marcos-en-la-inauguracion-del-encuentro-en-vicam-11-de-octubre/.

8. Laura Catelli, "Mestizaje, hibridez y transmedialidad: Categorías en tensión en performances y prácticas fronterizas de Guillermo Gómez Peña y La Pocha Nostra," *El Taco en La Brea* 6 (December 19, 2017), 181.

9. Davin Heckman, "Davin Heckman: Inside Out of the Box," Dichtung Digital, 2010, http://www.dichtung-digital.org/2010/heckman/heckman.htm#7.

10. Carolyn Fornoff, "Reflexive Extractivist Aesthetics," *Forma* 2, no. 1 (2023): 39.

11. Néstor García Canclini, *Lectores, espectadores e internautas* (Barcelona: Gedisa, 2007), 30–31.

12. Néstor García Canclini, *Hybrid Cultures: Strategies for Entering and Leaving Modernity* (Minneapolis: University of Minnesota Press, 2005), xxx.

13. The ideas developed in this section appeared in an earlier version in the article "Media and Cultural Hybridity in the Digital Humanities." The article originally appeared in *PMLA* 135.1 (January 2020). Published by the Modern Language Association of America.

14. Mary Louise Pratt, *Imperial Eyes: Travel Writing and Transculturation*, 2d ed. (New York: Routledge, 2008), 8.

15. Pratt, *Imperial Eyes*, 9.

16. Mary Louise Pratt, "Arts of the Contact Zone," *Profession* (1991): 35.

17. In "Arts of the Contact Zone," Pratt deals with what could be considered a hybrid text, Guamán Poma de Ayala's *New Chronicle and Good Government*. The seventeenth-century Spanish-Inca letter to King Philip II blends text and drawings, as well as book and quipu conventions. Although Pratt does not expand on the notion of medium, her analysis suggests both a contact between cultures, the Spanish and the Inca, and an encounter of media, between book and quipu.

18. Katherine Hayles, *Writing Machines* (Cambridge, MA: MIT Press, 2002), 33.

19. Alan Liu, "Imagining the New Media Encounter," in *A Companion to Digital Literary Studies*, ed. Ray Siemens and Susan Shreibman (Oxford: Blackwell, 2008).

20. Liu "Imagining the New Media Encounter."

21. Alan Liu, *Friending the Past: The Sense of History in the Digital Age* (Chicago: University of Chicago Press, 2018), 35.

22. Liu, *Friending the Past*, 36.

23. Pratt, *Imperial Eyes*, 4

24. García Canclini, *Hybrid Cultures*, xxv.

25. Pratt, *Imperial Eyes*, 7.

26. Katherine Hayles and Jessica Pressman, eds., *Comparative Textual Media: Transforming the Humanities in the Postprint Era* (Minneapolis: University of Minnesota Press, 2013).

27. Lori Emerson, *Reading Writing Interfaces: From the Digital to the Bookbound* (Minneapolis: University of Minnesota Press, 2014); Jussi Parikka and Erkki Huhtamo, *Media Archaeology: Approaches, Applications, and Implications* (Berkeley: University of California Press, 2011); and Jussi Parikka, *What Is Media Archaeology* (Cambridge, UK: Polity Press, 2012).

28. Alex Saum-Pascual, *#Postweb! Crear con la máquina y en la red* (Madrid: Iberoamericana, Vervuert, 2018).

29. Kenneth Goldsmith, "Post-Internet Poetry Comes of Age," *New Yorker*, March 10, 2015; Henry Lydiate, "Post-Internet Art," *Art Monthly; London* 375 (April 2014): 37.

30. Klaus Bruhn Jensen, *Media Convergence: The Three Degrees of Network, Mass, and Interpersonal Communication* (New York: Routledge, 2010); Sofie Seita, "Thinking the Unprintable in Contemporary Post-Digital Publishing," *Chicago Review* 60, no. 4 (Winter 2017).

31. Henry Jenkins, *Convergence Culture: Where Old and New Media Collide* (New York: New York University Press, 2006).

32. Anjali Prabhu, *Hybridity: Limits, Transformations, Prospects* (Albany: State University of New York Press, 2007), 1.

33. Hans-Joachim Backe, "Game-Comics and Comic-Games against the Concept of Hybrids," in *Comics and Videogames: From Hybrid Medialities to Transmedia Expansions*, ed. Andreas Rauscher, Daniel Stein, and Jan-Noël Thon (London: Routlede, 2020), 63.

34. Marshall McLuhan, *Understanding Media: The Extensions of Man* (New York: McGraw-Hill, 1964), 55.

35. Joshua Lund, *The Impure Imagination: Toward a Critical Hybridity in Latin American Writing* (Minneapolis: University of Minnesota Press, 2006).

36. Homi K. Bhabha, *The Location of Culture* (New York: Routledge, 1994), 37.

37. Lund, *The Impure Imagination*, 23.

38. Digital Publishing Toolkit Collective, Marc de Bruijn, and Florian Cramer, *From Print to Ebooks: A Hybrid Publishing Toolkit for the Arts* (Amsterdam: Institute of Network Cultures, 2015), 7.

39. Independent Book Publishers Association, "IBPA Hybrid Publisher Criteria Download—Independent Book Publishers Association," 2022, https://www.ibpa-online.org/page/hybrid-publisher-criteria-download.

40. Christian Ulrik Andersen, Geoff Cox, and Georgios Papadopoulos, "Postdigital Research," *A Peer-Reviewed Journal About* 3, no. 1 (June 1, 2014): 4–7, at 5.

41. Florian Cramer, "What Is 'Post-Digital'?" *APRJA Post-Digital Research* 3, no. 1 (2014): 18.

42. Cramer, "What Is 'Post-Digital'?" 12.

43. Cramer, "What Is 'Post-Digital'?" 19–21.

44. Alessandro Ludovico, "Post-Digital Publishing, Hybrid and Processual Objects in Print," *A Peer-Reviewed Journal About* 3, no. 1 (2014): 79.

45. Ludovico, "Post-Digital Publishing," 82.

46. Ludovico, "Post-Digital Publishing," 82.

47. Claudia Kozak, "Experimental Electronic Literature from the Souths: A Political Contribution to Critical and Creative Digital Humanities," *Electronic Book Review*, December 22, 2020, https://electronicbookreview.com/essay/experimental-electronic-literature-from-the-souths-a-political-contribution-to-critical-and-creative-digital-humanities/.

48. Lila Pagola, "Netart Latino Database: The Inverted Map of Latin American Net.Art [DOC]," in *Netart Latino Database*, edited by Nilo Casares (Badajoz: MEIAC, 2009), 38.

49. Silvio Lorusso, "Extending Horizons: The Praxis of Experimental Publishing in the Age of Digital Networks" (Venice: Iuav University of Venice, 2016), 155.

50. Gaby Cepeda, "American Hospitality," Rhizome, 2018, http://rhizome.org/editorial/2018/jun/04/american-hospitality/.

51. Rita Raley, *Tactical Media* (Minneapolis: University of Minnesota Press, 2009), 46.

52. Brett Stalbaum, "Walkingtools," March 8, 2011, https://web.archive.org/web/20110308165327/http://www.walkingtools.net/.

53. Mark Walker, "Congress Steps into Border-Crossing Cell Phone Debate—EBSCO," *North County Times*, April 7, 2010.

54. "Here Not There: San Diego Art Now," Museum of Contemporary Art La Jolla, June 6–September 19, 2010; "City Centered, a Festival of Locative Media and Urban Community," KQED; Public Media and Gray Area Foundation for the Arts in San Francisco, June 11–13, and workshop June 19–20; and "2010 California Biennial," Orange County Museum of Art, October 24, 2010–March 13, 2011.

55. Alison Reed, "Queer Provisionality: Mapping the Generative Failures of the *Transborder Immigrant Tool*," *Lateral* 4, no. 1 (May 2015). Reed indicates Anzaldúa's work as the foundation of this line of thinking.

56. Raley, *Tactical Media*, 37.

57. Anthony Stagliano, "Toward a Geopoetical Rhetoric: The Transborder Immigrant Tool and Material Tactics," in *Tracing Rhetoric and Material Life*, edited by Bridie McGreavy et al. (London: Palgrave, 2018), 289–314.

58. Mark C. Marino, *Critical Code Studies* (Cambridge, MA: MIT Press, 2020), 79.

59. Electronic Disturbance Theatre 2.0/b.a.n.g. lab, *The Transborder Immigrant Tool/La herramienta transfronteriza para inmigrantes*. (Ann Abor: Office of Net Assessment, University of Michigan, 2014), 47.

60. Electronic Disturbance Theatre 2.0/b.a.n.g. lab, *The Transborder Immigrant Tool*, 45.

61. Electronic Disturbance Theatre 2.0/b.a.n.g. lab, *The Transborder Immigrant Tool*, 45.

62. Electronic Disturbance Theatre 2.0/b.a.n.g. lab, *The Transborder Immigrant Tool*, 51.

63. Electronic Disturbance Theatre 2.0/b.a.n.g. lab, *The Transborder Immigrant Tool*, 46.

64. Electronic Disturbance Theatre 2.0/b.a.n.g. lab, *The Transborder Immigrant Tool*, xx.

65. Electronic Disturbance Theatre 2.0/b.a.n.g. lab, *The Transborder Immigrant Tool*, xx.

66. Electronic Disturbance Theatre 2.0/b.a.n.g. lab, *The Transborder Immigrant Tool*, xx.

67. Electronic Disturbance Theatre 2.0/b.a.n.g. lab, *The Transborder Immigrant Tool*, 60–62.

68. Electronic Disturbance Theatre 2.0/b.a.n.g. lab, *The Transborder Immigrant Tool*, 46.

69. Electronic Disturbance Theatre 2.0/b.a.n.g. lab, *The Transborder Immigrant Tool*, 51.

70. Electronic Disturbance Theatre 2.0/b.a.n.g. lab, *The Transborder Immigrant Tool*, 62.

71. Electronic Disturbance Theatre 2.0/b.a.n.g. lab, *The Transborder Immigrant Tool*, 58.

72. Electronic Disturbance Theatre 2.0/b.a.n.g. lab, *The Transborder Immigrant Tool*, 66.

73. Electronic Disturbance Theatre 2.0/b.a.n.g. lab, *The Transborder Immigrant Tool*, 65.

74. Electronic Disturbance Theatre 2.0/b.a.n.g. lab, *The Transborder Immigrant Tool*, 54–55.

75. Louis Warren, "The Art of Crossing Borders: Migrant Rights and Academic Freedom," *Boom: A Journal of California* 1, no. 4 (Winter 2011): 28.

76. Ricardo Dominguez, "Border Research, Border Gestures: The Transborder Immigrant Tool," *American Quarterly* 71, no. 4 (2019): 1053–58, at 1055.

77. Guillermo Gómez-Peña et al., "So What Is It? II" (sound recording), in *DOC/UNDOC: Documentado/Undocumented: Ars Shamánica* (San Francisco: City Lights Books, 2017).

78. Jennifer A. González, "DOC/UNDOC: Transgress, Transcend, Transform," in *DOC/UNDOC*, 19.

79. Catelli, "Mestizaje, hibridez y transmedialidad," 175.

80. Jennifer Buckley, "The Bookwork as Border Kit: Guillermo Gómez-Peña's Collaborative Códices," in *Beyond Text: Theatre and Performance in Print after 1900* (Ann Abor: University of Michigan Press, 2019), 194–97.

81. González, "DOC/UNDOC," 18.

82. Gómez-Peña et al., *DOC/UNDOC*, 3.

83. Gómez-Peña et al., *DOC/UNDOC*, 79.

84. Guillermo Gómez-Peña et al., "DOC/UNDOC," Google Arts & Culture, https://artsandculture.google.com/story/doc-undoc/zwWRoUWxr-erJA.

85. Guillermo Gómez-Peña et al., "Ritual Preparations" (sound recording), in *DOC/UNDOC*.

86. Guillermo Gómez-Peña et al., *DOC/UNDOC*, 42–43.

87. Guillermo Gómez-Peña et al., *DOC/UNDOC: Documentado/Undocumented: Ars Shamánica Performática* [Prospectus] (Santa Cruz: Moving Parts Press, 2014).

88. Felicia Rice, "Process," *DOC/UNDOC* (blog), July 3, 2014, https://docundoc.com/2014/07/03/process/.

89. Gómez-Peña et al., "Bajo la lupa" (video recording), in *DOC/UNDOC*.

90. Gómez-Peña et al., "A muerte" (video recording), in *DOC/UNDOC*.

91. Gómez-Peña et al., *DOC/UNDOC*, 21.

92. Gómez-Peña et al., *DOC/UNDOC*, 14.

93. Guillermo Gómez-Peña, *Bitácora del cruce: Textos poéticos para accionar, ritos fronterizos, videografitis, y otras rolas y roles* (México, D.F: Fondo de Cultura Económica, 2006), 53.

94. Gómez-Peña, *Bitácora del cruce*, 81.

95. ". . . exponen las reflexiones de la autora en la escritura de una historia familiar que es suya . . . porque es la documentación del proceso de descubrimiento." Roberto Cruz Arzabal, "Figuraciones sesgadas: Teatralidad, intermedialidad y yo autoral en Cristina Rivera Garza," *Visitas al Patio* 16, no. 1 (April 7, 2022): 56–57. Except for the texts from @EstacionCamaron, all translations into English are my own.

96. "El viaje siempre inicia antes. El viaje inicia antes incluso de imaginar el viaje." Cristina Rivera Garza (@EstacionCamaron), Twitter, April 19, 2016, 11:19 a.m., https://twitter.com/EstacionCamaron/status/722474800505946112.

97. Cruz Arzabal, "Figuraciones sesgadas," 44–66.

98. Andrés Olaizola, "Las aventuras de la Increíblemente Pequeña: Trayectorias transmediales de una heroína errante," *Cuadernos del Centro de Estudios en Diseño y Comunicación. Ensayos* 117 (2020): 85–102.

99. Roberto Cruz Arzabal, "Archivos potenciales: Domiciliación y colindancias en *Viriditas* de Cristina Rivera Garza," *Letras Femeninas* 42, no. 2 (2016): 35–43.

100. Vega Sánchez-Aparicio, "Las poéticas disruptivas de Cristina Rivera Garza," *Revista Landa* 7, no. 1 (2018).

## NOTES TO CHAPTER 4

101. "... esos espacios volubles donde lo que es no acaba de ser y, lo que no es, todavía no empieza." Rivera Garza, "Escrituras colindantes."

102. "... la conmoción del encuentro, la tensión que lo genera y que lo sostiene, más que la resolución." Rivera Garza, "Escrituras colindantes."

103. Rivera Garza, "Escrituras colindantes."

104. "Para recuperar acceso a una tradición perdida, es necesario traerla a colación, es decir, volverla partícipe de diálogos y procesos del presente ... para que pueda ser otra vez reflejada en el espejo de nuestra cultura y de nuestra experiencia." Cristina Rivera Garza, *Autobiografía del algodón* (Ciudad de México: Literatura Random House, 2020), 290–91.

105. "Viene corriendo a través del tiempo desde el 17 de abril de 1929." Rivera Garza, *Autobiografía*, 205.

106. Rivera Garza, *Autobiografía*, 215.

107. Rivera Garza, *Autobiografía*, 237.

108. "Si como habitantes de la tierra solo nos queda estar con otros o volver a estar donde estuvieron otros, entonces la tarea más básica, la más honesta, la más difícil consiste en identificar las huellas que nos acogen." Rivera Garza, *Autobiografía*, 91.

109. "Dos mujeres tras su huella 82 años después. Un auto. Una carretera por la estepa." Cristina Rivera Garza (@EstacionCamaron), Twitter, April 19, 2016, 11:16 a.m., https://twitter.com/EstacionCamaron/status/722473904569122816.

110. "Dos mujeres sobre una carretera que cruza el llano estepario." Cristina Rivera Garza (@EstacionCamaron), Twitter, April 20, 2016, 5:37 p.m., https://twitter.com/EstacionCamaron/status/722932231329554433

111. "Dos mujeres solas. Dos mujeres en ese tipo de soledad." Cristina Rivera Garza (@EstacionCamaron), Twitter, April 20, 2016, 5:42 p.m., https://twitter.com/EstacionCamaron/status/722933494393864196.

112. "Dos mujeres solas. Dos mujeres dentro de un auto." Cristina Rivera Garza (@EstacionCamaron), Twitter, April 21, 2016, 3:30 p.m., https://twitter.com/EstacionCamaron/status/723262778677432320.

113. "Dos mujeres solas de Estado sobre la carretera por donde avanza el ejército." Cristina Rivera Garza (@EstacionCamaron), Twitter, April 21, 2016, 3:37 p.m., https://twitter.com/EstacionCamaron/status/723264503849189376.

114. Dos mujeres sin Estado, sin ejército, acaso sin país." Cristina Rivera Garza (@EstacionCamaron), Twitter, April 20, 2016, 5:41 p.m., https://twitter.com/EstacionCamaron/status/722933260922150912.

115. "Dos mujeres sin Estado, sin ejército. Dos mujeres dentro de un auto." Cristina Rivera Garza (@EstacionCamaron), Twitter, April 21, 2016, 10:12 a.m., https://twitter.com/EstacionCamaron/status/723182618842288136.

116. "Del algodón al fracking, pasando por el sorgo y la maquila, los momentos de abundancia y devastación se han sucedido unos a otros en ciclos cada vez más intentos y más breves sobre un desierto que, lejos de las acepciones que lo retratan como carente de vida, emerge una y otra vez con nuevos y variados recursos naturales. Es el mismo desierto que las leyes de migración estadounidense han transformado en un arma mortífera para cientos de miles de trabajadores indocumentados." Rivera Garza, *Autobiografía*, 283–84.

117. "Pocas cosas más tristes que los rastros de una opulencia súbita y brutal, y efímera. Pocas cosas más ciertas." Rivera Garza, *Autobiografía*, 34.

118. "Estación Camarón ya no existe." Rivera Garza, *Autobiografía*, 35.

119. "Estación Camarón no existe. Nunca existió." Cristina Rivera Garza (@EstacionCamaron), Twitter, April 21, 2016, 10:40 a.m., https://twitter.com/EstacionCamaron/status/723189666858471424.

120. "Pero Estación Camarón ya no existe, dice el hombre. Conmovido o maravillado, da lo mismo." Cristina Rivera Garza (@EstacionCamaron), Twitter, April 20, 2016, 11:20 a.m., https://twitter.com/EstacionCamaron/status/722837243786698752.

121. "Estación Camarón no existe . . . No hay memoria de Estación Camarón." Rivera Garza, *Autobiografía*, 286.

122. "No hay señal en el camino que diga Estación Camarón. No hay nada: doble negación." Cristina Rivera Garza (@EstacionCamaron), Twitter, April 20, 2016, 5:49 a.m., https://twitter.com/EstacionCamaron/status/722935151680888832.

123. "No podemos ir a Estación Camarón, porque Estación Camarón ya no existe, pero vamos de cualquier manera." Rivera Garza, *Autobiografía*, 75.

124. "aquí hubo un campo de algodón. Aquí, una ciudad. Esto es el tiempo." Rivera Garza, 78.

125. "¿Es un archivo una forma de vencer el tiempo o de unirse al tiempo?" Cristina Rivera Garza (@EstacionCamaron), Twitter, April 21, 2016, 3:31 p.m., https://twitter.com/EstacionCamaron/status/723262936362323968.

126. "Poco sabía yo que, en la *longue durée* de mi propia historia, esa emigración emulaba muchas otras más iniciadas décadas, si no es que siglos atrás. El regreso a la frontera." Rivera Garza, *Autobiografía*, 276.

127. Cristina Rivera Garza, "Blogsívela: Escribir a inicios del siglo XXI desde la blogósfera," in *Palabra de América* (Barcelona: Seix Barral, 2004), 175.

128. "Con salidas falsas, con principios repetitivos, con capítulos que no llevan a ningún lado, con finales que se desdicen, la blogsívela se quiere tartamuda, imperfecta, inacabada, en-proceso-perpetuo." Rivera Garza, "Blogsívela," 177.

129. Jesús Martín-Barbero, *Communication, Culture and Hegemony: From the Media to Mediations* (London: SAGE Publications, 1993), 185.

**Conclusion**

1. Other adjacent phenomena between print and electronic literature are analyzed in Alex Saum-Pascual, "Memory Traces: Printed Electronic Literature as a Site of Remembrance," *Comparative Literature Studies* 57, no. 1 (September 1, 2020): 69–94; Jessica Pressman, *Bookishness: Loving Books in a Digital Age* (New York: Columbia University Press, 2020); Richard Hughes Gibson, *Paper Electronic Literature: An Archaeology of Born-Digital Materials* (Amherst: University of Massachusetts Press, 2021); and Zach Whalen, *Offset: A Media Poetics for Computer-Generated Books* (in preparation).

2. Noah Wardrip-Fruin, "Digital Media Archaeology: Interpreting Computational Processes," in *Media Archaeology. Approaches, Applications, and Implications*, edited by Erkki Huhtamo and Jussi Parikka (Berkeley: University of California Press, 2011), 302–22, at 306.

3. Nick Montfort, "Continuous Paper: The Early Materiality and Workings of Electronic Literature," 2004, http://nickm.com/writing/essays/continuous_paper_mla.html.

4. Montfort, "Continuous Paper."

5. Wardrip-Fruin, "Digital Media Archaeology," 307.

6. Nick Montfort, "Print Manifestations and Materiality: On Computer-Generated Books in Electronic Literature," presentation at the Electronic Literature Organization Conference, Coimbra, Portugal, 2023.

7. "Using Electricity Series," http://counterpathpress.org/using-electricity.

8. Rafael Pérez y Pérez, *Mexica: 20 Years—20 Stories = 20 Años—20 Historias* Electricity (Denver: Counterpath, 2017).

9. Allison Parrish, *Articulations* (Denver: Counterpath, 2018).

10. Milton Läufer, *A Noise Such As a Man Might Make* (Denver: Counterpath, 2018).

11. "About—Counterpath," http://counterpathpress.org/about.

12. James Ryan, "365 Computer-Generated Books—Aleator Press," https://www.aleator.press/365.

13. Ryan "365 Computer-Generated Books."

14. @aleatorpress, "#49," Twitter, April 6, 2022, https://twitter.com/aleatorpress/status/1511860439629586437/retweets/with_comments.

15. James Ryan, "Aleator Press: Computer-Generated Books," https://www.aleator.press.

16. Ian Goodfellow, Jean Pouget-Abadie, Mehdi Mirza, et al., "Generative

Adversarial Nets," in *Proceedings of the International Conference on Neural Information Processing Systems* (Cambridge, MA: MIT Press, 2014). GAN is an approach to generative AI in which two models are trained with the same data. The output of the generative model (G) is positioned against the discriminator model (D) that estimates whether the output of G is newly generated or extracted from the training data. When fully trained, G is capable of generating new output that is or seems plausible when compared to the original data.

17. James Ryan, "Wendit Tnce Inf," https://www.aleator.press/releases/wendit-tnce-inf.

18. See, for instance, Lillian-Yvonne Bertram, "A New Sermon on the Warpland," https://a-new-sermon-on-the-warpland.glitch.me/.

19. Matthew Kirschenbaum, "Prepare for the Textpocalypse," *The Atlantic*, March 8, 2023.

20. Sara Merken, "New York Lawyers Sanctioned for Using Fake ChatGPT Cases in Legal Brief," Reuters, June 26, 2023, https://www.reuters.com/legal/new-york-lawyers-sanctioned-using-fake-chatgpt-cases-legal-brief-2023-06-22/.

21. Rachael Perrotta, "Peabody EDI Office Responds to MSU Shooting with Email Written Using ChatGPT—The Vanderbilt Hustler," February 17, 2023, https://vanderbilthustler.com/2023/02/17/peabody-edi-office-responds-to-msu-shooting-with-email-written-using-chatgpt/.

22. Damon Beres, "Death by a Thousand Personality Quizzes," *The Atlantic*, January 27, 2023.

23. Lisa Siraganian, "Against Theory, Now with Bots! On the Persistent Fallacy of Intentionless Speech," NonSite, August 2021, https://nonsite.org/against-theory-now-with-bots-on-the-persistent-fallacy-of-intentionless-speech/.

24. Kari Kraus, "A View from the Periscope," In the Moment blog, June 29, 2023, https://critinq.wordpress.com/2023/06/29/a-view-from-the-periscope/. Many of these debates started in June 2023, when Matthew Kirschenbaum ran a forum dedicated to AI in *Critical Inquiry*'s blog In the Moment.

25. See *The Literary History of Artificial Intelligence*, a digital exhibit created as a collaboration between the Columbia English Department, the Columbia University Rare Books & Manuscript Library, and Columbia University's Digital Scholarship department. https://literaryai.library.columbia.edu/.

26. Jonathan Thirkield, "Beyond ChatGPT," Paris Review blog, June 23, 2023, https://www.theparisreview.org/blog/2023/06/23/beyond-chatgpt/.

27. Joanne McNeil, "Turning Poetry into Art: Joanne McNeil on Large Language Models and the Poetry of Allison Parrish," *Filmmaker Magazine*, June 27, 2023.

28. McNeil, "Turning Poetry into Art."

29. Zach Whalen, "The Second Book Ever Written by a Computer (has not yet been written)," presentation at MLA Convention, Philadelphia, January 5, 2024.

30. Whalen, "The Second Book."

31. @EL_DIAGRAM, "Hi folks. A thread: it seems like people are mad about the idea that a manuscript that uses language-generating tools winning a literary contest. Posting a couple clarifications, since you may want to read the book before tweeting about it," Twitter, July 31, 2023, https://twitter.com/EL_DIAGRAM/status/1686116012499013632.

32. "Is Artificial Intelligence Set to Become Art's Next Medium?" Christie's blog, December 12, 2018, https://www.christies.com/features/A-collaboration-between-two-artists-one-human-one-a-machine-9332-1.aspx.

33. Ziv Epstein et al., "Who Gets Credit for AI-Generated Art?" *iScience* 23, no. 9 (August 29, 2020): 101515.

34. "Beeple's Masterwork: The First Purely Digital Artwork Offered at Christie's," https://www.christies.com/features/Monumental-collage-by-Beeple-is-first-purely-digital-artwork-NFT-to-come-to-auction-11510-7.aspx.

35. Lillian-Yvonne Bertram, "it took me all those years to remember who I was and why," objkt.com, October 5, 2022, https://objkt.com/tokens/KT1MptjcczFWbueryEzVR8mxWvtNeqHhgukR/o.

36. Lillian-Yvonne Bertram, "GRAND DESSEIN_MP4," objkt.com, May 22, 2023, https://objkt.com/tokens/KT196hbdj1Cw2JHakK4KCAGmzg3PA2ngW3c5/8.

37. Bertram's *Grand Dessein* is currently part of the Book Arts Collection of St. Lawrence University.

38. Alissa Greenberg, "Poetry NFTs Are Having a Moment," *Poets & Writers*, December 13, 2023. The author makes a similar point in her conversation with Greenberg.

39. "WIP Publishing—The World's 1st Crypto Publishing Platform," https://wippublishing.com/.

40. "Mirror," https://mirror.xyz/.

41. "Alexandria Labs-Mission," https://alexandrialabs.xyz/mission.

42. "Alexandria Labs-Mission," emphasis added.

43. Bill Rosenblatt, "Could NFTs Work in Publishing?," *Publishers Weekly*, April 16, 2021.

44. Emily Mertz, "Edmonton Public Library Makes History by Lending Local Author's Book as Non-Fungible Token," *Global News*, March 22, 2022.

45. Vlad Hategan, "Are NFTs Dead?—Trends, Predictions & Statistics 2023," dappGamble, https://dappgambl.com/nfts/dead-nfts/.

46. Greenberg, "Poetry NFTs."

47. "A Tribute to NFT Poets," *Rattle: Poetry* (Summer 2023), https://www.rattle.com/product/i80/.
48. theVERSEverse, "Mission," https://theverseverse.com/mission.
49. theVERSEverse, "GenText," https://versa.theverseverse.com/.
50. Alex Estorick, "Foreword," in *POÈME OBJKT SUBJKT* (Paris: L'Avant Galerie Vossen, Librairie Galerie Métamorphoses, theVERSEverse, 2023), 5.
51. Estorick, "Foreword," 5.
52. Greenberg, "Poetry NFTs."
53. Greenberg, "Poetry NFTs."
54. Estorick, "Foreword," 5.
55. theVERSEverse, "Poem = Work of Art," in *POÈME OBJKT / POÈM SUBJKT*, 7.
56. Christian Bök and Kalen Iwamoto, "The Concept of Writing: The Unthought," in *POÈME OBJKT SUBJKT*, 81.
57. theVERSEverse, "Poem = Work of Art," 7.
58. theVERSEverse, "Poem = Work of Art," 7.
59. theVERSEverse, "Poem = Work of Art," 8.
60. theVERSEverse, "Poem = Work of Art," 7.
61. theVERSEverse, "Poem = Work of Art," 7.
62. theVERSEverse, "Poem = Work of Art," 8.
63. Sasha Stiles, *Technelegy* (London: Eyewear Poetry, Black Spring Press Group, 2022), 7.
64. Charlotte Kent, "Sasha Stiles's Technelegy," Brooklyn Rail, May 3, 2022, https://brooklynrail.org/2022/05/books/Sasha-Stiless-Technelegy.
65. Stiles, *Technelegy*, 7.
66. Simone Natale, *Deceitful Media: Artificial Intelligence and Social Life after the Turing Test* (Oxford: Oxford University Press, 2021), 50–67.
67. Stiles, *Technelegy*, 31.
68. Stiles, *Technelegy*, 78.
69. Stiles, *Technelegy*, 157.
70. Christie's, "Digital Art Auction | Christie's 3.0 | COMPLETION: When It's Just You," https://nft.christies.com//nft/completion-when-it-s-just-you.
71. Ana María Caballero, email message to author, April 5, 2024.
72. Ana María Caballero, "The Wish," in *POÈME OBJKT SUBJKT* (Paris: L'Avant Galerie Vossen, Librairie Galerie Mátamorphoses, theVERSEverse, 2023), 69.
73. Caballero, "The Wish," 69.
74. Caballero, "The Wish," 68.
75. Caballero, "The Wish," 68, emphasis added.
76. Ana María Caballero, "The Wish," https://anamariacaballero.com/the-wish/.

77. Kalen Iwamoto, "Romeo and Juliape," Wen New Atelier blog, https://wennew-atelier.xyz/projects/romeo-and-juliape/.

78. *Romeo and Juliape (Full Video 4K)*, 2023, https://www.youtube.com/watch?v=4ocWkbfEilo.

79. Iwamoto, "Romeo and Juliape."

# BIBLIOGRAPHY

Abenshushan, Vivian. *Permanente obra negra*. Mexico City: Sexto Piso, 2019.
———. *Permanente obra negra*. Mexico City: Sexto Piso, 2019. Card catalog.
———. *Permanente obra negra*. Mexico City: Sexto Piso, 2019. Die-cut book.
Abenshushan, Vivian, Dora Bartilotti, and Leonardo Aranda. "Permanente obra negra." http://www.permanenteobranegra.cc/.
Adams, Thomas R., and Nicolas Barker. "A New Model for the Study of the Book." In *A Potency of Life: Books in Society*, edited by Nicolas Baker. London: British Library, 1993.
Agamben, Giorgio. *"What Is an Apparatus?" and Other Essays*. Stanford: Stanford University Press, 2009.
Aleator Press (@aleatorpress). "#49 After some delay, the series is back!" Twitter, April 6, 2022. https://twitter.com/aleatorpress/status/1511860439629586437/retweets/with_comments.
Alexander, Catherine. "Writing Failure: Knowledge Production, Temporalities, Ethics, and Traces." *Journal of the Royal Anthropological Institute* 29, no. 1 (2023): 8–30.
Alexandria Labs. "Mission." https://alexandrialabs.xyz/mission.
Albino de Souza, Erthos. "Le tombeau de Mallarmé." *Antología litElat #1*. http://antologia.litelat.net/.

Amador Tello, Judith. "Consuelo Sáizar rinde informe de labores del conaculta." *Proceso*, September 10, 2012. https://www.proceso.com.mx/319487/consuelo-saizar-rinde-informe-de-labores-del-conaculta.

Antonio, Jorge Luiz. *Poesia digital: teoria, história, antologias*. São Paulo: Navegar Editora, 2010.

Anzaldúa, Gloria. *The Gloria Anzaldúa Reader*. Durham, NC: Duke University Press, 2009.

Backe, Hans-Joachim. "Game-Comics and Comic-Games: Against the Concept of Hybrids." In *Comics and Videogames: From Hybrid Medialities to Transmedia Expansions*, edited by Andreas Rauscher, Daniel Stein, and Jan-Noël Thon, 60–83. London: Routledge, 2020.

Baudrillard, Jean. *The Illusion of the End*. Cambridge, UK: Polity Press, 1994.

Beiguelman, Giselle. "Memoria de los futuros sin pasado / Memory of the Futures with No Past." In *Net.Art Latino Database*, 165–79. Badajoz, Spain: Museo Extremeño e Iberoamericano de Arte Contemporáneo, 2010.

———. "Museums of Losses for Clouds of Oblivion." In *Digital Art through the Looking Glass: New Strategies for Archiving, Collecting and Preserving in Digital Humanities*, 117–31. Krems an der Donau, Austria: Edition Donau-Universität, 2019.

———. "WYSIWYG or WYGIWYS: Notes on the Loss of Inscription." *Dichtung Digital: Journal für Kunst und Kultur Digitaler Medien* 3, no. 6 (October 16, 2001): 1–4.

Bellinghausen, Hermann. "La 'Fuerza Aérea Zapatista' atacó al ejército en el Valle de Amador." *La Jornada*, January 3, 2000.

Beres, Damon. "Death by a Thousand Personality Quizzes." *The Atlantic*, January 27, 2023.

Bertram, Lillian-Yvonne. *A Black Story May Contain Sensitive Content*. Tucson, AZ: New Michigan Press, 2024.

———. *Grand Dessein*. Pittsburgh, PA: Container, 2017.

———. "GRAND DESSEIN_MP4." Objkt.com, 2023. https://objkt.com/tokens/KT196hbdj1Cw2JHakK4KCAGmzg3PA2ngW3c5/8.

———. "it took me all those years to remember who I was and why." Objkt.com, 2022. https://objkt.com/tokens/KT1MptjcczFWbueryEzVR8mxWvtNeqHhgukR/0.

———. *Negative Money*. New York: Soft Skull, 2023.

———. "A New Sermon on the Warpland." https://a-new-sermon-on-the-warpland.glitch.me/.

———. "Raw Girl Money." Objkt.com, 2023. https://objkt.com/tokens/KT1HucH1UPLTSKJ7cPuEiAron21XX8YJ59Ya/0.

———. *Travesty Generator*. Blacksburg, VA: Noemi Press, 2019.
Bhabha, Homi K. *The Location of Culture*. New York: Routledge, 1994.
Biblioteca Nacional del Congreso. "Ley 19227 Crea fondo nacional de fomento del libro y la lectura, y modifica cuerpos legales que señala." Ley Chile, July 10, 1993. https://www.bcn.cl/historiadelaley/nc/historia-de-la-ley/7314/.
———. "Ley 21045 Crea el ministerio de las culturas, las artes y el patrimonio." Ley Chile, November 3, 2017. https://bcn.cl/2f7iu.
Blocker, Jane. *Becoming Past: History in Contemporary Art*. Minneapolis: University of Minnesota Press, 2015.
Boe, John, ed. *Writing on the Edge* 2, no. 2 (Spring 1991).
Bogost, Ian. *A Slow Year: Game Poems*. Highlands Ranch, CO: Open Texture, 2010.
———. "A Slow Year: A Chapbook of Game Poems for Atari VCS, PC, and Mac." Blog post. http://bogost.com/games/aslowyear/.
Bök, Christian, and Kalen Iwamoto. "The Concept of Writing: The Unthought." In *POÈME OBJKT SUBJKT*. Paris: L'Avant Galerie Vossen, Librairie Galerie Mátamorphoses, theVERSEverse, 2023.
Bolter, J. David. *Writing Space: The Computer, Hypertext, and the History of Writing*. Hillsdale, NJ: L. Erlbaum Associates, 1991.
Bolter, J. David, and Richard Grusin. *Remediation: Understanding New Media*. Cambridge, MA: MIT Press, 1999.
Borsuk, Amaranth. *The Book*. Cambridge, MA: MIT Press, 2018.
Borsuk, Amaranth, and Brad Bouse. *Between Page and Screen*. Los Angeles: Siglio, 2012.
Borsuk, Amaranth, and Kate Durbin. *ABRA*. Denver: 1913, 2015.
———. "Abra: Expanding Artists' Books into the Digital Realm." *Gramma: Journal of Theory and Criticism* 23, no. 0 (December 9, 2016): 118–35.
Bouchardon, Serge. "Mind the Gap! 10 Gaps for Digital Literature?" Electronic Book Review, May 4, 2019. http://electronicbookreview.com/essay/mind-the-gap-10-gaps-for-digital-literature/.
Bourdieu, Pierre. "A Conservative Revolution in Publishing." *Translation Studies* 1, no. 2 (July 2008): 123–53.
Bowers, Fredson. *Principles of Bibliographical Description*. New Castle, DE: Oak Knoll Press, 1994.
Bridle, James. "New Ways of Seeing," BBC Radio 4. https://www.bbc.co.uk/programmes/m000458m.
Brouillette, Sarah. "Wattpad, Platform Capitalism, and the Feminization of Publishing Work." *Book History* 26 no. 2 (2023): 419–38.
Buckley, Jennifer. "The Bookwork as Border Kit. Guillermo Gómez-Peña's Col-

laborative Códices." In *Beyond Text: Theatre and Performance in Print after 1900*, 164–97. Ann Arbor: University of Michigan Press, 2019.

———. "DOC/UNDOC: Documentado/Undocumented Ars Shamánica Performática by Felicia Rice, Guillermo Gómez-Peña, Jennifer A. González, Gustavo Vázquez, and Zachary James Watkins." *Drama Review* 61, no. 3 (2018): 79–80.

Caballero, Ana María. "The Wish." https://anamariacaballero.com/the-wish/.

———. "The Wish." In *POÈME OBJKT SUBJKT*, 67–68. Paris: L'Avant Galerie Vossen, Librairie Galerie Mátamorphoses, theVERSEverse, 2023.

Cámara de Diputados. "Ley de Fomento para la Lectura y el Libro." Cámara de Diputados, September 1, 2018. https://www.diputados.gob.mx/LeyesBiblio/pdf/LFLL.pdf.

Campagnolo, Alberto. "Insides and Outsides." In *The Unfinished Book*, edited by Alexandra Gillespie and Deidre Lynch, 46–61. Oxford, UK: Oxford University Press, 2020.

Campbell, Kim. "Textbook Case: McGraw-Hill Maps an Electronic Future." *Christian Science Monitor*, December 8, 1995.

Campos, Augusto de. *Não: Poemas*. São Paulo: Editora Perspectiva, 2003.

Cantoni, Federico. "Verónica Gerber Bicecci, *La Compañía* (Ciudad de México, Almadía, 2019, 199 Pp. ISBN 978-607-8667-10-9)." *Altre Modernità* 24 (November 1, 2020).

Carpenter, J. R. *The Gathering Cloud*. Axminster, Devon, UK: Uniformbooks, 2017.

———. "The Gathering Cloud." Luckysoap. http://luckysoap.com/thegatheringcloud/.

———. *This is a Picture of Wind*. Sheffield, UK: Longbarrow Press, 2020.

———. "This is a Picture of Wind." Luckysoap. http://luckysoap.com/apictureofwind/.

Carrión, Ulises. "The New Art of Making Books." In *Second Thoughts*. Amsterdam: VOID Distributors, 1980.

Caswell, Michelle. *Urgent Archives: Enacting Liberatory Memory Work*. London: Routledge, 2021.

Catanese, Paul. "CBPA Receives $50,000 NEA Grant | Art and Art History News." Blog post. Columbia College Chicago blog, May 16, 2012. https://blogs.colum.edu/art-and-art-history/2012/05/16/cbpa-receives-50000-nea-grant/.

Catelli, Laura. "Mestizaje, hibridez y transmedialidad: Categorías en tensión en performances y prácticas fronterizas de Guillermo Gómez Peña y La Pocha Nostra." *El Taco en La Brea* 6 (December 19, 2017): 174–90.

Cepeda, Gaby. "American Hospitality." Blog post. Rhizome, 2018. http://rhizome.org/editorial/2018/jun/04/american-hospitality/.

Chasar, Mike. *Poetry Unbound: Poems and New Media from the Magic Lantern to Instagram*. New York: Columbia University Press, 2020.
Christie's. "Beeple's Masterwork: The First Purely Digital Artwork Offered at Christie's." Blog post. Christie's blog. https://www.christies.com/features/Monumental-collage-by-Beeple-is-first-purely-digital-artwork-NFT-to-come-to-auction-11510-7.aspx.
———. "Is Artificial Intelligence Set to Become Art's Next Medium?" Blog post. Christie's blog, December 12, 2018. https://www.christies.com/features/A-collaboration-between-two-artists-one-human-one-a-machine-9332-1.aspx.
Chun, Wendy Hui Kyong. "The Enduring Ephemeral, or The Future Is a Memory." In *Media Archaeology: Approaches, Applications, and Implications*, edited by Jussi Parikka and Erkki Huhtamo, 184–203. Berkeley: University of California Press, 2011.
Cohen, Michael E. "Fair Thoughts and Happy Hours Did Not Attend upon an Early Enhanced-Book Adaptation of Macbeth." The Magazine, December 19, 2013. http://the-magazine.org/32/scotched.
Columbia English Department, Columbia University Rare Books and Manuscript Library, and Columbia University Digital Scholarship Department. "The Literary History of Artificial Intelligence." https://literaryai.library.columbia.edu/.
Comisión Permanente de Cultura y Recreación. "Proyecto de Ley del Sistema Social del Libro y la Lectura." *Transparencia Venezuela*, November 6, 2015. https://transparencia.org.ve/project/ley-del-sistema-social-del-libro-y-la-lectura/.
CONACULTA. "Octavio Paz—Blanco." App Store, 2012.
Connor, Michael. "Before Flash Sunset." Rhizome, December 21, 2020. https://rhizome.org/editorial/2020/dec/21/before-flash-sunset/.
Cordell, Ryan, and David Smith. *Viral Texts: Mapping Networks of Reprinting in 19th Century Newspapers and Magazines*. 2022. http://viraltexts.org.
Correa-Díaz, Luis. *clickable poem@s*. Santiago de Chile: RiL Editores, 2016.
———. *metaverse*. Santiago de Chile: RiL Editores, 2021.
Counterpath. "About—Counterpath." http://counterpathpress.org/about.
Cramer, Florian. "What Is 'Post-Digital'?" *APRJA Post-Digital Research* 3, no. 1 (2014). https://aprja.net/article/view/116068.
Cruz Arzabal, Roberto. "Archivos potenciales: Domiciliación y colindancias en *Viriditas* de Cristina Rivera Garza." *Letras Femeninas* 42, no. 2 (2016): 35–43.
———. "Figuraciones sesgadas: Teatralidad, intermedialidad y yo autoral en Cristina Rivera Garza." *Visitas al Patio* 16, no. 1 (April 7, 2022): 44–66.

Darrah, Bill. *Essex*. Richmond, CA: Synapse & Brøderbund, 1985.

Davey, John, and Roger Jones. "Issues and Trends in Textbook Publishing: In the Views of Geography Editors/Publishers." *Journal of Geography in Higher Education* 19, no. 1 (March 1995): 11.

Dean, Aria. "Tactical Poetics: FloodNet's Virtual Sit-Ins." Rhizome, December 1, 2016. http://rhizome.org/editorial/2016/dec/01/tactical-poetics-floodnets-early-1990s-virtual-sit-ins/.

DeSilvey, Caitlin. *Curated Decay: Heritage beyond Saving*. Minneapolis: University of Minnesota Press, 2017.

Dewitt, Robert. "Interview—Ihor Wolosenko (Synapse Software)." *Antic*. https://www.atarimagazines.com/v2n1/interview.html.

Diagram (@EL_DIAGRAM). "Hi folks. A thread: it seems like people are mad about the idea that a manuscript that uses language-generating tools winning a literary contest. Posting a couple clarifications, since you may want to read the book before tweeting about it." Twitter, July 31, 2023. https://twitter.com/EL_DIAGRAM/status/1686116012499013632.

Digital Publishing Toolkit Collective, Marc de Bruijn, Florian Cramer, Liz Castro, Joost Kircs, Silvio Lorusso, Michael Murtaugh, Pia Pol, Miriam Rasch, and Margreet Riphagen. *From Print to Ebooks: A Hybrid Publishing Toolkit for the Arts*. Amsterdam: Institute of Network Cultures, 2015.

Dimaria, Frank. "New Textbook Publishing Model for the Internet Age." *Education Digest* 77, no. 5 (January 2012): 50–54.

Dominguez, Ricardo. "Border Research, Border Gestures: The Transborder Immigrant Tool." *American Quarterly* 71, no. 4 (2019): 1053–58.

Drucker, Johanna. *The Century of Artists' Books*. New York: Granary Books, 1995.

———. "Dynamic Poetics: J. R. Carpenter's This is a Picture of Wind." In J. R. Carpenter, *This is a Picture of Wind*, 9–24. Sheffield, UK: Longbarrow Press, 2020.

———. "The Self-Conscious Codex: Artists' Books and Electronic Media." *SubStance* 26, no. 1 (1997): 93.

Eccles, Elle, and J. R. Carpenter. "'I'm trying to think about migration . . . as a condition of being in between places.' J. R. Carpenter on Poetry and Translating the Digital." Penned in the Margins, July 8, 2018. http://www.pennedinthemargins.co.uk/index.php/2018/07/im-trying-to-think-about-migration-as-a-condition-of-being-in-between-places-j-r-carpenter-on-poetry-and-translating-the-digital/.

Editora Perspectiva. "PNLD Literário 2021." Editora Perspectiva, 2021. https://www.pnldperspectiva.com.br.

Electronic Disturbance Theatre 2.0 / b.a.n.g. lab. *The Transborder Immigrant Tool / La herramienta transfronteriza para inmigrantes.* Ann Arbor: University of Michigan Press, 2014.

Elleström, Lars, ed. *Media Borders, Multimodality and Intermediality.* London: Palgrave Macmillan UK, 2010.

Emerson, Lori. *Reading Writing Interfaces: From the Digital to the Bookbound.* Minneapolis: University of Minnesota Press, 2014.

———. "Reclaiming the Future with Old Media." In *The Bloomsbury Handbook to the Digital Humanities*, edited by James O'Sullivan, 427-36. New York: Bloomsbury Academic, 2022.

———. "Recovering Paul Zelevanksy's Literary Game 'SWALLOWS' (Apple //e, 1985-86)." Blog post, April 24, 2012. http://loriemerson.net/2012/04/24/recovering-paul-zelevanksys-literary-game-swallows-apple-e-1985-86/.

Enlace Zapatista. "Palabras del SCI Marcos en la inauguración del encuentro en Vicam, 11 de octubre de 2007." Blog post, October 17, 2007. https://enlacezapatista.ezln.org.mx/2007/10/16/palabras-del-sci-marcos-en-la-inauguracion-del-encuentro-en-vicam-11-de-octubre/.

Ensslin, Astrid. *Pre-Web Digital Publishing and the Lore of Electronic Literature.* Cambridge, UK: Cambridge University Press, 2022.

Ernst, Wolfgang. *Digital Memory and the Archive.* Minneapolis: University of Minnesota Press, 2012.

———. "Media Archaeology: Method and Machine versus History and Narrative of Media." In *Media Archaeology: Approaches, Applications, and Implications*, edited by Erkki Huhtamo and Jussi Parikka. Berkeley: University of California Press, 2011.

Espenschied. "Emulation or It Didn't Happen." Rhizome, December 21, 2020. https://rhizome.org/editorial/2020/dec/21/flash-preservation/.

Estorick, Alex. "Foreword." In *POÈME OBJKT SUBJKT*. Paris: L'Avant Galerie Vossen, Librairie Galerie Mátamorphoses, theVERSEverse, 2023.

Estrada Valadez, Tania, Patricia de la Garza Cabrera, and Thalía Edith Velasco Castelán. "Los libros de coro copiados por fray Miguel de Aguilar: un primer acercamiento al estudio de su encuadernación en la Nueva España." *Intervención Revista Internacional de Conservación Restauración y Museología* 1, no. 1 (May 1, 2010): 54-66.

"Flipbackbook." https://www.dwarsligger.com/.

Flores, Leonardo. "La literatura electrónica latinoamericana, caribeña y global: Generaciones, fases y tradiciones." *Artelogie: Recherche sur les arts, le patrimoine et la littérature de l'Amérique latine* 11 (November 16, 2017).

Flusser, Vilém. *Die Shrift.* Göttingen: Immatrix, 1987.

Foot, Mirjam. *The History of Bookbinding as a Mirror of Society.* The Panizzi Lectures 1997. London: British Library, 1998.

Fornoff, Carolyn. "Reflexive Extractivist Aesthetics." *Forma* 2, no. 1 (2023): 37–69.

———. *Subjunctive Aesthetics: Mexican Cultural Production in the Era of Climate Change.* Nashville, Tennessee: Vanderbilt University Press, 2024.

Franking, Holly. *Negative Space CVN®. A Computerized Video Novel.* Kansas City, KS: Diskotech Inc. Software, 1995.

Fredrikzon, Johan, and Chris Haffenden. "Towards Erasure Studies: Excavating the Material Conditions of Memory and Forgetting." *Memory, Mind & Media* 2 (January 2023). 1–24.

Frost, Gary. "Adoption of the Codex Book: Parable of a New Reading Mode." Book and Paper Group Annual 17. American Institute for Conservation, 1998.

Funkhouser, Chris. "Bridge Work." Electronic Book Review, March 25, 2003. http://electronicbookreview.com/essay/bridge-work/.

Gache, Belén. *El libro del fin del mundo.* Buenos Aires: Fin del mundo ediciones, 2002.

———.*Wordtoys.* 2006. http://belengache.net/wordtoys/.

Gaetano Adi, Paula, and Gustavo Crembil. "Guest Editorial Statement: Mestizo Technology: Art, Design, and Technoscience in Latin America." Blog post. NMC Media-N blog, October 17, 2016. http://median.newmediacaucus.org.

Gainza Carolina. "Five Hundred Years of Struggle Enter Cyberspace: Neo-Zapatism and the (Old) New Insurgency." In *Online Activism in Latin America,* 163–74. New York: Routledge, 2018.

Gainza, Carolina, Carolina Zúñiga, and Javier González. "Digital Archive and Preservation against Technological Obsolescence: Building a Cartography of Latin American Digital Literature." *Journal of Latin American Cultural Studies* 31, no. 2 (April 3, 2022): 257–73.

Gale, Kate. "The World of Independent Publishing." *International Journal of the Book* 4, no. 3 (2007): 89–94.

Gallego Cuiñas, Ana. "Las editoriales independientes en el punto de mira literario: Balance y perspectivas teóricas." *Caravelle: Cahiers du monde hispanique et luso-brésilien* 113 (December 1, 2019): 61–76.

Garcia, Sandra E. "The Uneasy Afterlife of Our Dazzling Trash." *New York Times,* November 7, 2020.

García Canclini, Néstor. *Hybrid Cultures: Strategies for Entering and Leaving Modernity.* 2d ed. Minneapolis: University of Minnesota Press, 2005.

———. *Lectores, espectadores e internautas.* Barcelona: Gedisa, 2007.

Gaskell, Philip. *A New Introduction to Bibliography.* New York: Oak Knoll Press, 1995.

Gerber Bicecci, Verónica. *La compañía*. Mexico City: Almadía, 2019.

———. "La Compañía | The Company." 2019. https://www.veronicagerberbicecci.net/la-compania-the-company.

Gerber Bicecci, Verónica, Canek Zapata, and Carlos Bergen. "La máquina distópica," 2018. https://www.lamaquinadistopica.xyz/.

———. "La máquina distópica." *El Ornitorrinco Tachado: Revista de artes visuales* 10 (October 25, 2019): 115–18.

Gibson, Richard Hughes. *Paper Electronic Literature: An Archaeology of Born-Digital Materials*. Amherst: University of Massachusetts Press, 2021.

Gitelman, Lisa. *Always Already New: Media, History, and the Data of Culture*. Cambridge, MA: MIT Press, 2006.

Golding, Alan. "Language Writing, Digital Poetics, and Transitional Materialities." In *New Media Poetics: Contexts, Technotexts, and Theories*. Cambridge, MA: MIT Press, 2006.

Goldsmith, Kenneth. "Post-Internet Poetry Comes of Age." *New Yorker*, March 10, 2015.

Gómez-Peña, Guillermo. *Bitácora del cruce: Textos poéticos para accionar, ritos fronterizos, videografitis, y otras rolas y roles*. Mexico City: Fondo de Cultura Económica, 2006.

Gómez-Peña, Guillermo, Felicia Rice, Gustavo Vázquez, Zachary James Watkins, and Jennifer A. González. *DOC/UNDOC: Documentado/Undocumented: Ars Shamánica Performática*. San Francisco: Moving Parts Press, City Lights Books, 2017.

———. *DOC/UNDOC: Documentado/Undocumented: Ars Shamánica Performática [Prospectus]*. Santa Cruz: Moving Parts Press, 2014.

———. "DOC/UNDOC." Google Arts & Culture. https://artsandculture.google.com/story/doc-undoc/zwWRoUWxr-erJA.

González, Jennifer A. "DOC/UNDOC: Transgress, Transcend, Transform." In *DOC/UNDOC: Documentado/Undocumented: Arsh Shamánica Performática*, 14–19. San Francisco: Moving Parts Press, City Lights Books, 2017.

Goodfellow, Ian, Jean Pouget-Abadie, Mehdi Mirza, et al. "Generative Adversarial Nets." In *Proceedings of the International Conference on Neural Information Processing Systems*. Cambridge, MA: MIT Press, 2014.

Granados Salinas, Tomás. *Libros*. Ciudad de México: Secretaría de Cultura, Dirección General de Publicaciones, 2017.

Greenberg, Alissa. "Poetry NFTs Are Having a Moment." *Poets & Writers*, December 13, 2023.

Grigar, Dene, and Stuart Moulthrop. "History of John McDaid's Uncle Buddy's Phantom Funhouse." In *Pathfinders: Documenting the Experience of Early Digital Literature*. Vancouver, WA: Nouspace Publications, 2015.

Grossman, Claire, Juliana Spahr, and Stephanie Young. "Literature's Vexed Democratization." *American Literary History* 33, no. 2 (May 1, 2021): 298–319.

Hague, James. *Halcyon Days: Interviews with Classic Computer and Video Game Programmers*. Self-published, n.d.

Halberstam, Jack. *The Queer Art of Failure*. Durham, NC: Duke University Press, 2011.

Halper, M. "Synapse Suing Atari for $59M; Cites Debt, Pact, Breach." *Electronic News*, September 3, 1984.

Harris, Charles B. "Introduction." *Critique* 37, no. 3 (Spring 1996): 163–70.

Hartog, François. *Chronos: The West Confronts Time*. New York: Columbia University Press, 2022.

———. *Regimes of Historicity: Presentism and Experiences of Time*. New York: Columbia University Press, 2015.

Hategan, Vlad. "Are NFTs Dead?—Trends, Predictions & Statistics 2023." dappGamble, 2023. https://dappgambl.com/nfts/dead-nfts/.

Hayles, N. Katherine. *Electronic Literature: New Horizons for the Literary*. Notre Dame, IN: University of Notre Dame, 2008.

———. *Writing Machines*. Cambridge, MA: MIT Press, 2002.

Hayles, N. Katherine, and Anne Burdick. *Writing Machines: Web Supplement*. Cambridge, MA: MIT Press, 2002. https://mitpress.mit.edu/sites/default/files/titles/content/mediawork/titles/writing/writing_book.html#.

Hayles, Katherine, and Jessica Pressman, eds. *Comparative Textual Media Transforming the Humanities in the Postprint Era*. Minneapolis: University of Minnesota Press, 2013.

Heckman, Davin. "Inside Out of the Box: Default Settings and Electronic Poetics." *Dichtung Digital*, 2010. http://www.dichtung-digital.org/2010/heckman/heckman.htm#7.

Holzberg, Carol S. "The Voyager Company: Leader of the Pack." *CD-ROM World* 9, no. 9 (1993).

Houston, Keith. *The Book: A Cover-to-Cover Exploration of the Most Powerful Object of Our Time*. New York: W.W. Norton, 2016.

Huhtamo, Erkki. "From Kaleidoscomaniac to Cybernerd: Notes toward an Archaeology of the Media." *Leonardo* 30, no. 3 (June 1997): 221–24.

Huyssen, Andreas. "Present Pasts: Media, Politics, Amnesia." *Public Culture* 12, no. 1 (2000): 21–38.

"Hybrid Texts and Where We're Headed." The Literary Platform, July 2, 2017. https://theliteraryplatform.com/news/2017/07/hybrid-texts-and-where-were-headed/.

"Ian Bogost Wins at Indiecade for A Slow Year." *States News Service*, October 19, 2010.

IDP Report. "Apple Outlines New Multimedia Initiatives." *IDP Report* 13, no. 36 (1992).

Independent Book Publishers Association. "IBPA Hybrid Publisher Criteria Download—Independent Book Publishers Association." Independent Book Publishers Association, 2022. https://www.ibpa-online.org/page/hybrid-publisher-criteria-download.

Iwamoto, Kalen. *Romeo and Juliape*. Paris: Wen New Atelier, 2023.

———. "Romeo and Juliape." Wen New Atelier blog. https://wennew-atelier.xyz/projects/romeo-and-juliape/.

———. *Romeo and Juliape (Full Video 4K)*. Wen New Atelier, 2023. https://www.youtube.com/watch?v=4ocWkbfEilo.

Iza, Fabiola. "Verónica Gerber Bicecci: PROYECTOS MONCLOVA." *Artforum International*, May 2021.

Jenkins, Henry. *Convergence Culture: Where Old and New Media Collide*. New York: New York University Press, 2006.

Jensen, Klaus Bruhn. *Media Convergence: The Three Degrees of Network, Mass, and Interpersonal Communication*. New York: Routledge, 2010.

Kac, Eduardo. *Media Poetry: An International Anthology*. Chicago: Intellect, 2007.

Kent, Charlotte. "Sasha Stiles's Technelegy." *The Brooklyn Rail*, May 3, 2022. https://brooklynrail.org/2022/05/books/Sasha-Stiless-Technelegy.

Kirschenbaum, Matthew. "Bibliologistics: The Nature of Books Now, or A Memorable Fancy." Blog post. Post45, April 8, 2020. https://post45.org/2020/04/bibliologistics-the-nature-of-books-now-or-a-memorable-fancy/.

———. *Bitstreams: The Future of Digital Literary Heritage*. Philadelphia: University of Pennsylvania Press, 2021.

———. "Books.Files." Blog post. Archive Journal, February 2017. http://www.archivejournal.net/?p=6789.

———. "Digital Magic: Preservation for a New Era." *Chronicle of Higher Education*, March 10, 2012.

———. *Track Changes: A Literary History of Word Processing*. Cambridge, MA: Harvard University Press, 2016.

Kirschenbaum, Matthew, Kari Kraus, Ted Underwood, Lisa Siraganian, and N Katherine Hayles. "Again Theory: A Forum on Language, Meaning, and Intent in the Time of Stochastic Parrots." In the Moment blog, June 27, 2023. https://critinq.wordpress.com/2023/06/27/again-theory-a-forum-on-language-meaning-and-intent-in-the-time-of-stochastic-parrots-2/.

Knight, Jeffrey Todd. *Bound to Read: Compilations, Collections, and the Making of Renaissance Literature*. Philadelphia: University of Pennsylvania Press, 2013.

Kozak, Claudia. "Experimental Electronic Literature from the Souths: A Political Contribution to Critical and Creative Digital Humanities." Electronic Book Review, December 22, 2020. https://electronicbookreview.com/essay/experimental-electronic-literature-from-the-souths-a-political-contribution-to-critical-and-creative-digital-humanities/.

Kraus, Kari. "A View from the Periscope." In the Moment blog, June 29, 2023. https://critinq.wordpress.com/2023/06/29/a-view-from-the-periscope/.

Kulesz, Octavio. "La edición digital en la era móvil: América Latina (1/3)." Alliance Lab, March 28, 2016. https://cerlalc.org/wp-content/uploads/documentos-de-interes/olb/OLB_Documentos-de-interes_La-edici%C3%B3n-digital-en-la-era-movil-AL_Octavio-Kulesz_280316_Texto.pdf.

———. *La edición digital en los países en desarrollo*. Paris: Alianza internacional de los editores independientes, 2011. http://alliance-lab.org/etude/wp-content/uploads/edicion_digital.pdf.

Lanham, Richard A. *The Electronic Word: Democracy, Technology, and the Arts*. Chicago: University of Chicago Press, 1994.

Läufer, Milton. *Lagunas*. 2015. https://www.miltonlaufer.com.ar/lagunas/.

———. *A Noise Such As a Man Might Make*. Denver: Counterpath, 2018.

Ledesma, Eduardo. "The Digital Afterlife of Augusto de Campos' Kinetic Poems." Presented at Trans[Creation], June 24, 2021. https://vimeo.com/567196099.

Lee, Jonathan. "Fiona McCrae: The Art of Independent Publishing." *Guernica*, April 15, 2014.

Liu, Alan. *Friending the Past: The Sense of History in the Digital Age*. Chicago: University of Chicago Press, 2018.

———. "Imagining the New Media Encounter." In *A Companion to Digital Literary Studies*, edited by Ray Siemens and Susan Shreibman. Oxford: Blackwell, 2008.

———. *The Laws of Cool: Knowledge Work and the Culture of Information*. Chicago: University of Chicago Press, 2004.

Lorusso, Silvio. "Extending Horizons: The Praxis of Experimental Publishing in the Age of Digital Networks." PhD diss., Iuav University of Venice, 2016. https://ia800800.us.archive.org/8/items/ExtendingHorizons/Extending-Horizons_%20The-Praxis-of-%20Experimental-Publishing-in-the-Age-of-Digital-Networks_Silvio-Lorusso.pdf.

———. "The Post-Digital Publishing Archive: An Inventory of Speculative Strategies." *Journal of Electronic Publishing* 19, no. 2 (October 1, 2016).

Lovink, Geert. *My First Recession: Critical Internet Culture in Transition.* Rotterdam: V2/Nai Publishers, 2003.

Ludovico, Alessandro. *Post-Digital Print: The Mutation of Publishing since 1894.* Rotterdam: Onomatopee, 2012.

———. "Post-Digital Publishing, Hybrid and Processual Objects in Print." *APRJA Post-Digital Research* 3, no. 1 (June 1, 2014): 78–85.

Lund, Joshua. *The Impure Imagination: Toward a Critical Hybridity in Latin American Writing.* Minneapolis: University of Minnesota Press, 2006.

Lydiate, Henry. "Post-Internet Art." *Art Monthly* 375 (April 2014): 37.

Magalhães, Ana Gonçalves, and Giselle Beiguelman. *Possible Futures: Art, Museums and Digital Archives.* São Paulo: Editora Peirópolis, 2014.

Maher, Jimmy. "Bookware's Sunset." The Digital Antiquarian blog, December 4, 2014. https://www.filfre.net/tag/synapse/.

———. "Essex and Brimstone." The Digital Antiquarian blog, March 17, 2014. https://www.filfre.net/2014/03/essex-and-brimstone/.

———. "Mindwheel (or, The Poet and the Hackers)." The Digital Antiquarian, March 10, 2014. https://www.filfre.net/2014/03/mindwhell-or-the-poet-and-the-hackers/.

Marino, Mark C. *Critical Code Studies.* Cambridge, MA: MIT Press, 2020.

Martin, James A. "PW: Zipping along the Web: For Guidebook Publishers, www Is the Current Address of Choice." *Publishers Weekly*, October 27, 1997.

Martín Barbero, Jesús. *Communication, Culture and Hegemony: From the Media to Mediations.* London: SAGE Publications, 1993.

———. "Dislocaciones del tiempo y nuevas topografías de la memoria." Rio de Janeiro: Universidad Tecnológica de Pereira, 2000.

McKenzie, D. F. *Bibliography and the Sociology of Texts.* Cambridge, UK: Cambridge University Press, 1999.

McLuhan, Marshall. *Understanding Media: The Extensions of Man.* New York: McGraw-Hill, 1964.

McNeil, Joanne. "Turning Poetry into Art: Joanne McNeil on Large Language Models and the Poetry of Allison Parrish." *Filmmaker Magazine*, June 27, 2023.

Medrano González, Mario Alberto. "Editoriales Independientes: Economía de guerrilla." *Este País*, May 22, 2019.

Melville House. "About the Hybrid Book Project." https://www.mhpbooks.com/about/hybrid-books/.

———. "Announcing The HybridBook: MobyLives." https://www.mhpbooks.com/announcing-hybridbook/.

Merken, Sara. "New York Lawyers Sanctioned for Using Fake ChatGPT Cases in Legal Brief." Reuters, June 26, 2023.

Mertz, Emily. "Edmonton Public Library Makes History by Lending Local Author's Book as Non-Fungible Token." *Global News*, March 22, 2022.

Miller, Marilyn Grace. "Introduction: The Cult of Mestizaje." In *Rise and Fall of the Cosmic Race: The Cult of Mestizaje in Latin America*. Austin: University of Texas Press, 2004.

Milliot, Jim. "Simon & Schuster Interactive, Alive and Kicking at Age Five." *PublishersWeekly*, May 24, 1999.

Miranda Trigueros, Ernesto. "Aplicaciones literarias para iPad: Exploraciones en los nuevos formatos de lectura del siglo XXI." In *Textos, pixeles y bits: Reflexiones sobre la publicación digital*, edited by Isabel Galina Russell. Mexico City: Instituto de Investigaciones Bibliográficas, Universidad Nacional Autónoma de México, 2015.

"Mirror." https://mirror.xyz/.

Mod, Craig. "Books in the Age of the iPad." Blog post, March 2010. https://craigmod.com/journal/ipad_and_books/.

Montfort, Nick. *#!* Denver: Counterpath, 2014.

———. "Continuous Paper: The Early Materiality and Workings of Electronic Literature." 2004. http://nickm.com/writing/essays/continuous_paper_mla.html.

———. *The Future*. Cambridge, MA: MIT Press, 2017.

———. "Print Manifestations and Materiality: On Computer-Generated Books in Electronic Literature." Electronic Literature Organization Conference, Coimbra, Portugal, 2023.

Montfort, Nick, and Noah Wardrip-Fruin. "Acid-Free Bits: Recommendations for Long-Lasting Electronic Literature." Electronic Literature Organization, June 14, 2004. http://eliterature.org/pad/afb.html#sec1.

Moor, Robert. "Bones of the Book." *N+1*, February 27, 2012. https://nplusonemag.com/online-only/book-review/bones-of-the-book/.

Moulthrop, Stuart. "Lift This End: Electronic Literature in a Blue Light." Electronic Book Review, November 1, 2012. http://electronicbookreview.com/essay/lift-this-end-electronic-literature-in-a-blue-light/.

Moulthrop, Stuart, Dene Grigar, and Joseph Tabbi. *Traversals: The Use of Preservation for Early Electronic Writing*. Cambridge, MA: MIT Press, 2017.

Mullaney, Thomas S., Benjamin Peters, Mar Hicks, and Kavita Philip, eds. *Your Computer Is on Fire*. Cambridge, MA: MIT Press, 2021.

Murray, Simone. *The Digital Literary Sphere: Reading, Writing, and Selling Books in the Internet Era*. Baltimore: Johns Hopkins University Press, 2018.

Multigraph Collective, ed. *Interacting with Print: Elements of Reading in the Era of Print Saturation*. Chicago: University of Chicago Press, 2018.

Narayanan, Vivek. "Not Nearly Novel Enough. *V* by Stephanie Strickland. Penguin Books, 2002." Perihelion, 2003. http://www.webdelsol.com/Perihelion/index11.htm.

Natale, Simone. *Deceitful Media: Artificial Intelligence and Social Life after the Turing Test*. Oxford, UK: Oxford University Press, 2021.

NeMe. "Expanded Artists' Books." Blog post. https://www.neme.org/blog/expanded-artists-books.

Niemann, Michelle. "Rethinking Organic Metaphors in Poetry and Ecology: Rhizomes and Detritus Words in Oni Buchanan's *Mandrake Vehicles*." *Journal of Modern Literature* 35, no. 1 (2011): 99–121.

Noelle, Louise. "Manuel Felguérez: Una Máquina Estética." Museo Nacional de San Carlos INBA. https://mnsancarlos.inba.gob.mx/manuel-felguerez-una-maquina-estetica.

Olaizola, Andrés. "Escritura en migración: Transmedialidad y poética en Cristina Rivera Garza." *Cuadernos del Centro de Estudios de Diseño y Comunicación* 142 (September 6, 2021).

Ortega, Alejandra. "Intersections of New Media and Narratives: The Enhanced Ebook Reading Experience." *Rhizomes: Cultural Studies in Emerging Knowledge* 37 (June 1, 2021).

Oswacks, Molly. "Timeless Classics of Literature Upgraded with Already-Dated Augmented Reality." Gizmodo, May 17, 2012. https://gizmodo.com/timeless-classics-of-literature-upgraded-with-already-d-5911296.

Owens, Trevor. *After Disruption: A Future of Cultural Memory*. Ann Arbor: University of Michigan Press, 2024.

———. *The Theory and Craft of Digital Preservation*. Baltimore: Johns Hopkins University Press, 2018.

Pack, Thomas. "Bookstores Are Hot, CD-ROM Sections Are Not Yet!" *CD-ROM Professional* 8, no. 3 (March 1995): 40.

Pagola, Lila. "Netart Latino Database: The Inverted Map of Latin American Net.Art [DOC]." In *Netart Latino Database*. Badajoz: Museo Extremeño e Iberoamericano de Arte Contemporáneo, 2009.

Pan, Joann. "Can Augmented Reality Save the Printed Page?" Mashable, February 3, 2012. http://mashable.com/2012/02/03/augmented-reality-book-between-page-and-screen/.

Parikka, Jussi. "On Media Meteorology." In *The Gathering Cloud*, 9–10. Axminster, Devon, UK: Uniformbooks, 2017.

———. *What Is Media Archaeology*. Cambridge, UK: Polity, 2012.

Parikka, Jussi, and Erkki Huhtamo. *Media Archaeology: Approaches, Applications, and Implications*. Berkeley: University of California Press, 2011.

Parrish, Allison. *Articulations*. Denver: Counterpath, 2018.

———. *Wndit Tnce Inf*. Minneapolis: Aleator Press, 2022.

Pears, Iain. "Why You Need an App to Understand My Novel." *The Guardian*, August 20, 2015.
Pearson, David. "Bookbinding." In *The Book. A Global History*, 245–57. Oxford, UK: Oxford University Press, 2013.
Pérez y Pérez, Rafael. *Mexica: 20 Years—20 Stories = 20 Años—20 Historias*. Denver: Counterpath, 2017.
Perloff, Marjorie. "'Vocable Scriptsigns': Differential Poetics in Kenneth Goldsmith's Fidget and John Kinsella's Kangaroo Virus." In *Poetry and Contemporary Culture*, edited by. A. M. Roberts, and Jonathan Allison, 21–44. Edinburgh: Edinburgh University Press, 2002.
Perrotta, Rachael. "Peabody EDI Office Responds to MSU Shooting with Email Written Using ChatGPT." Vanderbilt Hustler, February 17, 2023. https://vanderbilthustler.com/2023/02/17/peabody-edi-office-responds-to-msu-shooting-with-email-written-using-chatgpt/.
Pinksy, Robert. *Mindwheel*. Richmond, CA: Synapse & Brøderbund, 1984.
Pollard, Natalie. "Where 'the Cloud' Touches the Ground: Electronic Poetry, Digital Infrastructures, and the Environment." *ISLE: Interdisciplinary Studies in Literature and Environment* (July 1, 2022): 1–26.
Postman, Neil. *Technopoly: The Surrender of Culture to Technology*. New York: Vintage, 1993.
Pournara, Lizzy. "Poetic Constellations and Intermedia Collaborations: The Case of Vniverse." *MATLIT: Materialidades da Literatura* 7, no. 1 (November 17, 2019): 133–51.
Prabhu, Anjali. *Hybridity: Limits, Transformations, Prospects*. Albany: State University of New York Press, 2007.
Pratt, Mary Louise. "Arts of the Contact Zone." *Profession* (1991): 33–40.
———. *Imperial Eyes: Travel Writing and Transculturation*. 2d ed. New York: Routledge, 2008.
Pressman, Jessica. *Bookishness: Loving Books in a Digital Age*. New York: Columbia University Press, 2020.
———. "*House of Leaves*: Reading the Networked Novel." *Studies in American Fiction* 34, no. 1 (2006): 107–28.
Provan, Alexander. "'Future Fictions.'" Frieze, June 16, 2013. https://www.frieze.com/article/future-fictions.
Rajewsky, Irina O. "Intermediality, Intertextuality, and Remediation: A Literary Perspective on Intermediality." *Intermédialités* 6 (August 10, 2011): 43–64.
Raley, Rita. *Tactical Media*. Minneapolis: University of Minnesota Press, 2009.
Red de Literatura Electrónica Latinoamericana. "Acerca." Red de Literatura Electrónica Latinoamericana blog, June 18, 2015. http://litelat.net/acerca-2/.

Reed, Aaron. *Subcutanean*. Oakland, CA: self-published, 2020.

Reed, Alison. "Queer Provisionality: Mapping the Generative Failures of the *Transborder Immigrant Tool*." *Lateral* 4, no. 1 (May 2015).

Reith, James. "When Robert Pinsky Wrote a Video Game." *New Yorker*, January 21, 2016.

Rice, Felicia. "PROCESS." DOC/UNDOC blog, July 3, 2014. https://docundoc.com/2014/07/03/process/.

Richard, Nelly. *The Insubordination of Signs: Political Change, Cultural Transformation, and Poetics of the Crisis*. Durham, NC: Duke University Press, 2004.

Richter, Enrique. "Alcances de La Ley Del Libro Para Las Librerías En México." *Trama & Texturas* 26 (2015): 81–88.

Rivera Garza, Cristina. *Autobiografía del algodón*. Mexico City: Random House, 2020.

———. "Blogsívela: Escribir a inicios del siglo XXI desde la blogósfera." In *Palabra de América*, 167–79. Barcelona: Seix Barral, 2004.

———. "Breve historia íntima de la escritura en migración." Tierra Adentro no. 192, 2014. 26-27.

———. "Escrituras Colindantes." No Hay Tal Lugar. U-Tópicos Contemporáneos blog, July 10, 2004. https://cristinariveragarza.blogspot.com/2004/07/#108947489616105760.

———. "@EstaciónCamaron." Twitter, 2016. https://twitter.com/EstacionCamaron.

———. *The Restless Dead: Necrowriting & Disappropriation*. Translated by Robin Myers. Nashville, TN: Vanderbilt University Press, 2020.

Rivera Mir, Sebastián. *Edición latinoamericana*. Buenos Aires: Universidad Autónoma Metropolitana, CLACSO, 2021.

Rizhome. "Flash Sunset Twitchstream." Rhizome, December 31, 2020. https://rhizome.org/events/flash-sunset-twitchstream/.

Romero Rivera, Marcela. "Signs of the Inhuman: Hauntings and Lost Futures in Verónica Gerber Bicecci's *La Compañía*." *CLCWeb: Comparative Literature and Culture* 24, no. 1 (August 15, 2022).

Rosen, Phil. "Remember When NFTs Sold for Millions of Dollars? 95% of the Digital Collectibles May Now Be Worthless." Markets Insider, September 20, 2023. https://markets.businessinsider.com/news/currencies/nft-market-crypto-digital-assets-investors-messari-mainnet-currency-tokens-2023-9.

Rosenblatt, Bill. "Could NFTs Work in Publishing?" *Publishers Weekly*, April 16, 2021.

Rousse, Thomas H. "Taking Apart the Provocation Machine: Ian Bogost's A Slow Year." *Well Played* 4, no. 1 (2015): 71–88.
Ryan, James. "Aleator Press 365 Computer-Generated Books." https://www.aleator.press/365.
———. "Aleator Press: Computer-Generated Books." https://www.aleator.press.
———. "Aleator Press: FAQ." https://www.aleator.press/faq.
———. "Wendit Tnce Inf." https://www.aleator.press/releases/wendit-tnce-inf.
Salter, Anastasia, and John Murray. *Flash: Building the Interactive Web*. Cambridge, MA: MIT Press, 2014.
Sample, Mark. "Slow Games, Slow Poems: The Act of Deliberation in 'Slow Year' | ELMCIP." 2012. https://elmcip.net/critical-writing/slow-games-slow-poems-act-deliberation-slow-year.
Sánchez-Aparicio, Vega. "Las poéticas disruptivas de Cristina Rivera Garza." *Revista Landa* 7, no. 1 (2018). 212–31.
Saum-Pascual, Alex. "Memory Traces: Printed Electronic Literature as a Site of Remembrance." *Comparative Literature Studies* 57, no. 1 (September 1, 2020): 69–94.
———. *#Postweb! Crear con la máquina y en la red*. Madrid: Iberoamericana, Vervuert, 2018.
Sawers, Paul. "Penguin Partners with Zappar to Bring AR to Moby Dick." TNW | Media, May 17, 2012. https://thenextweb.com/news/penguin-partners-with-zappar-to-bring-augmented-reality-to-moby-dick-and-other-classic-novels.
Scharf, Michael. "V: WaveSon.Nets / Losing L'una." *Publishers Weekly* 249, no. 44 (November 4, 2002): 78.
Schmitter, Gianna. "Hacia unas TransLiteraturas hispanoamericanas: Reflexiones sobre literatura trans e intermedial en Argentina, Chile y Perú (2000–2017)." *América sin Nombre* 24, no. 1 (December 9, 2019): 53–62.
Scott, Jason, dir. *Get Lamp*. Bovine Ignition Systems, 2010.
Seita, Sophie. *Provisional Avant-Gardes: Little Magazine Communities from Dada to Digital*. Stanford: Stanford University Press, 2019.
———. "Thinking the Unprintable in Contemporary Post-Digital Publishing." *Chicago Review* 60, no. 4 (Winter 2017).
El Senado y la Cámara de Representantes de la República Oriental del Uruguay. "Ley 15.913. Ley Del Libro." República Oriental de Uruguay, December 31, 1987. https://cerlalc.org/wp-content/uploads/documentos-de-interes/olb/OLB_Documentos-de-interes_Normativa-Ley-No-15-913-Ley-del-Libro_Uruguay_1987.pdf.
Senior, David, and Siegfried Zielinski. "Networked Performance—Interview with Siegfried Zielinski." Turbulence blog, 2006. http://turbulence.org/blog/2007/08/08/interview-with-siegfried-zielinski/.

Sharma, Sarah. *In the Meantime: Temporality and Cultural Politics*. Durham, NC: Duke University Press, 2013.

Sinykin, Dan N. "The Conglomerate Era: Publishing, Authorship, and Literary Form, 1965–2007." *Contemporary Literature* 58, no. 4 (2017): 462–91.

Siraganian, Lisa. "Against Theory, Now with Bots! On the Persistent Fallacy of Intentionless Speech." NonSite, August 2021. https://nonsite.org/against-theory-now-with-bots-on-the-persistent-fallacy-of-intentionless-speech/.

Skains, R. Lyle. *Neverending Stories: The Popular Emergence of Digital Fiction*. New York: Bloomsbury Academic, 2023.

Smith, Keith A. *Structure of the Visual Book*. Rochester, NY: Visual Studies Workshop Press, 1984.

Stadler, Matthew. "The Ends of the Book: Reading, Economies and Publics." In *Literary Publishing in the Twenty-First Century*, edited by Travis Kurowski, Wayne Miller, and Kevin Prufer. Minneapolis: Milkweed Editions, 2016.

Stagliano, Anthony. "Toward a Geopoetical Rhetoric: The Transborder Immigrant Tool and Material Tactics." In *Tracing Rhetoric and Material Life*, edited by Bridie McGreavy, Justine Wells, George F. McHendry, and Samantha Senda-Cook, 289–314. London: Palgrave, 2018.

Starosielski, Nicole. *The Undersea Network: Sign, Storage, Transmission*. Durham, NC: Duke University Press, 2015.

Stalbaum, Brett. "Walkingtools." March 8, 2011. https://web.archive.org/web/20110308165327/http://www.walkingtools.net/.

Stiles, Sasha. "Completion: When It's Just You." Digital Art Auction Christie's 3.0. https://nft.christies.com//nft/completion-when-it-s-just-you.

———. "Sasha Stiles—NFTs." https://www.sashastiles.com/nfts.

———. *Technelegy*. London: Eyewear Poetry, Black Spring Press Group, 2022.

Strickland, Stephanie. "The Death and Redistribution of V." In *#WomenTechLit*, edited by Maria Mencía and N. Katherine Hayles. Morgantown: West Virginia University Press, 2017.

———. *True North*. Notre Dame, IN: University of Notre Dame Press, 1997.

———. *V: WaveSon.Nets/Losing L'una*. New York: Penguin, 2002.

———. *V: WaveTercets/Losing L'una*. Denver: SpringGun, 2016.

———. *Zone : Zero*. Boise: Ahsahta Press, 2008.

Strickland, Stephanie, and Ian Hatcher. "Loss of Hover: Recreating Shockwave Vniverse as an App for iPad." *Przegląd Kulturoznawczy* 33 (2017).

Strickland, Stephanie, and Cynthia Lawson Jaramillo. "Making the Vniverse." *New River: A Journal of Digital Writing and Art*, 2003. https://www.cddc.vt.edu/journals/newriver/strickland/essay/index.html.

Sudden Oak. "End of Life Announcements." Sudden Oak, November 13, 2020. http://www.suddenoak.com/endoflife/.

---. "Sudden Oak." http://www.suddenoak.com.

Symmes Coll, Constanza. "Editar (en) el Chile post-dictadura: Trayectorias de la edición independiente." *Nuevo Mundo Mundos Nuevos: Nouveaux mondes mondes nouveaux—Novo Mundo Mundos Novos—New World New Worlds*, September 18, 2015.

Synapse and Brøderbund. "Electronic Novels (Advertisement)." *Commodore Magazine*, 1986.

Szpilbarg, Daniela. "Configuraciones emergentes de circulación y lectura en el entorno digital: El caso de Bajalibros.Com." *Cuadernos del Centro de Estudios en Diseño y Comunicación. Ensayos* 72 (May 2019): 146–60.

Teicher, Craig. "Breaking Digital Ground: E-Books and Small Press Literary Publishers." *Publishers Weekly* 260, no. 14 (April 8, 2013).

theVERSEverse. "GenText." https://versa.theverseverse.com/.

---. "Mission." May 24, 2022. https://theverseverse.com/mission.

---. "POÈME SBJKT. Curatorial Statement." theVERSEverse blog, June 13, 2023. https://theverseverse.com/exhibition/poeme-sbjkt.

---. "Poem = Work of Art." In *POÈME OBJKT / POÈM SUBJKT*, 6–8. Paris: Librarie Galerie Métamorphoses, L'avant Galerie Vossen, theVERSEverse, 2023.

Thirkield, Jonathan. "Beyond ChatGPT." *Paris Review* blog, June 23, 2023. https://www.theparisreview.org/blog/2023/06/23/beyond-chatgpt/.

Thompson, John B. *Book Wars: The Digital Revolution in Publishing*. Cambridge, UK: Polity Press, 2021.

---. *Merchants of Culture: The Publishing Business in the Twenty-First Century*. 2d ed. New York: Plume, 2012.

Tomasula, Steve. *Conceptualisms: The Anthology of Prose, Poetry, Visual, Found, E- and Other Hybrid Writings as Contemporary Art*. Tuscaloosa: University of Alabama Press, 2022.

Trettien, Whitney. *Cut/Copy/Paste: Fragments from the History of Bookwork*. Minneapolis: University of Minnesota Press, 2021.

"Using Electricity Series." Counterpath. http://counterpathpress.org/using-electricity.

Vasudevan, Roopa. "'This Isn't a Picasso, It's a Ferrari': Presentism, Precarity, and Dependence in New Media Art Practices." *AoIR Selected Papers of Internet Research*, September 15, 2021.

Virilio, Paul. "Speed and Information: Cyberspace Alarm!" *CTheory*, August 27, 1995.

Virshup, Amy. "The Teachings of Bob Stein." *Wired*, July 1, 1996. https://www.wired.com/1996/07/stein/.

Vogel Frederick, Heather. "PW: Jamsa Press Enters Children's Market." *Publishers Weekly*, May 18, 1998.

Walker, Mark. "Congress Steps into Border-Crossing Cell Phone Debate." *North County Times*, April 7, 2010.

Wardrip-Fruin, Noah. "Digital Media Archaeology: Interpreting Computational Processes." In *Media Archaeology: Approaches, Applications, and Implications*, edited by Erkki Huhtamo and Jussi Parikka, 302–22. Berkeley: University of California Press, 2011.

Wardrip-Fruin, Noah, and Nick Montfort, eds. *The New Media Reader*. Cambridge, MA: MIT Press, 2003.

Warren, Louis. "The Art of Crossing Borders: Migrant Rights and Academic Freedom." *Boom: A Journal of California* 1, no. 4 (Winter 2011).

Weedon, Alexis, David Miller, Claudio Pires Franco, David Moorhead, and Samantha Pearce. "Crossing Media Boundaries: Adaptations and New Media Forms of the Book." *Convergence: The International Journal of Research into New Media Technologies* 20, no. 1 (February 2014): 108–24.

Westheimer, Dick. "Sometimes a Poem." Rattle, 2023. https://www.rattle.com/sometimes-a-poem-by-dick-westheimer/.

Whalen, Zach. "The Second Book Ever Written by a Computer (Has Not yet Been Written)." Presented at MLA convention, Philadelphia, January 5, 2024.

"WIP Publishing—The World's 1st Crypto Publishing Platform." https://wippublishing.com/.

Wolf, Werner. "(Inter)Mediality and the Study of Literature." *CLCWeb: Comparative Literature & Culture* 13, no. 3 (2011): 10.

Zielinski, Siegfried. *Deep Time of the Media: Toward an Archaeology of Hearing and Seeing by Technical Means*. Cambridge, MA: MIT Press, 2006.

Zielinski, Siegfried, Silvia Wagnermaier, and Gloria Custance, eds. *Variantology: On Deep Time Relations of Arts, Sciences, and Technologies*. Kunstwissenschaftliche Bibliothek 31, 35, 37, 45, 49. Cologne: W. König, 2005.

**INDEX**

Page numbers in *italics* refer to illustrations

Abenshushan, Vivian: *Permanente obra negra,* 23, 34, 63-68, *65,* 101, 188, 227
Abrams, J.J.: *S,* 75
accordion book, 93, 200, 202
Adobe Flash. *See* Flash
affordances, 4, 23, 37, 52, 106, 120, 225, 233; binding media, 37-38; books, 40, 54, 60, 65, 188, 219, 244; browser, 136; expressive, 8, 38, 181, 215, 217; material, 21, 62-63, 172, 174, 189, 176, 215; media hybridity 181; reading, 57, 64, 66; touch screen, 95
aesthetic of transactionality, 221, 229, 235-48; as commercial value, 29, 244, 245; as relationship to reader, 236, 239, 244, 248

Agamben, Giorgio, 131, 133
AI, 220, 229, 230, 236, 246; anthropomorphizing of, 240, 245; art and artists, 220, 230, 231; debates about, 230, 287n24; in publishing, 123, 218
Alacraña (press), 79
Albino de Souza, Erthos: *Le Tombeau de Mallarmé,* 218
Aleator Press, 28, 220, 221-25, 247
Almadía (press), 168
Amerika, Mark: *GRAMMATRON,* 19; *Remix the Book,* 18
animation (writing technique), 50, 51, 91, 98, 104, 162-63, 233
animation software, 52, 55
Anteism Books (press), 222
Antonio, Jorge Luiz: *Poesia digital: Teoría, história, antologías,* 18

Apple, 18, 87, 109; Apple IIe, 44; iOS 79, 109; Mac 19, 156
App Store, 94, 103, 106, 109, 135
archival documents, materials, and records, 26, 173, 210, 211, 213
archives: computer-generated literature, 224; electronic literature, 146; remains of binding media as, 4, 153
ArtBlocks, 231
artists' book presses, 80, 82, 83, 87
artists' books, 32, 39, 69, 70, 105; Expanded Artists' Books grant, 105-6, 120; overlap with binding media, 40, 41, 69, 70; studies of, 22-23, 33, 38-41
Association for Progressive Communications, 175
attachments to the book, 42, 70. See also enhancements to the book; extra features of the book
Atari, 89, 156, 157, 159, 173; discontinuation, 157; emulator, 156; programming for, 156, 158
Atavist Books, 93
audio: as extra feature, 91, 93, 97, 109; in binding media, 201, 202; sound art, 200, 201
augmented books, 12, 72, 73, 78, 96; history of, 23-24, 42; publishing standardization, 121. See also enhanced books; expanded book; hybrid books
augmented publishing. See expanded and augmented publishing; hybrid publishing
Augmented Reality (AR), 73, 96-98, 265n19
authors as publishers, 74, 119-21

avant-garde: as aesthetic genealogy, 237-38; aesthetic principles, 138-39

Bad Quarto Press, 222
back cover pockets and sleeves, 43-44, 54, 100-102, *100-102*
Backe, Hans-Joachim, 186
Baudrillard, Jean, 143
Beeple: *EVERYDAYS: THE FIRST 5000 DAYS*, 232
Beiguelman, Giselle: approach to obsolescence and loss, 150-51, 174; memory-making, 150; *O Livro depois do Livro*, 14, 57
Bergen, Carlos, 130; "La máquina distópica," 166-72
Bernstein, Charles, 19
Bertram, Lillian-Yvonne, 239; *A Black Story May Contain Sensitive Content*, 230; *Grand Dessein*, 233; *Negative Money*, 233; *Travesty Generator*, 28, 222, 226
Bhatnagar, Ranjit: *Encomials: Sonnets from Pentametron*, 227-28; "@Pentametron," 227
Biblioteca Ayacucho, 84
Big Five Publishers, 80, 81, 83, 103, 125
binding mechanisms, 3, 10, 22, 40, 44, 70; of computer-generated literature, 28, 219; as meaning making, 23, 32, 39, 42, 69; of NFTs 29, 246. See also bookbinding; loose bindings; physical bindings
binding strategies, 33, 43-44, 46, 50, 54
blockchain, 28-29, 220-21, 230-39, 241-48
blogging, 264n5; as publicity, 121-22

INDEX     315

Bogost, Ian: *A Slow Year*, 26, 100, 130, 155-60
Bök, Christian, 237
Bolter, David, 17, 91
books: legal definition of, 124; packaging of, 16, 75, 78, 92, 103, 268n53; reinvention of, 76. *See also* augmented books; enhanced books; expanded books; hybrid books; rare books
book apps, 79, 92-96
book arts, 203, 225. *See also* artists' books
books as packaging, 31, 52, 87, 90, 98, 137, 151, 159
bookbinders, 35, 43-44, 64
bookbinding, 23, 34-42, 70; affordances of, 35, 37, 39, 68-69; in bibliography, 34, 70; case binding, 43, 45, 68; clasps, 36; Coptic, 35, 36; and digital media, 37; expansion of the concept, 32, 37, 39-40, 68-69; flipback book, 36; girdle binding, 35; as meaning-making mechanism, 23, 32, 34, 36, 37-42, 68-69; as organizing structure, 34, 36, 37, 39; ornamentation of, 36; perfect binding, 36; post binding, 36; standardization, 35; as theoretical framework, 32; variations of, 35, 37, 41, 70
book design, 11, 36, 43, 75, 79, 100, 190; back cover sleeves, 100-103; as binding mechanism, 3, 23, 32, 33, 37, 41, 57
book form, 71-73, 123, 124-25; binding media as, 3, 22, 32-34, 82, 123, 126; new, 75-76, 122; interrogations to, 82

book history, 6, 35, 41, 70; binding media as, 10, 22, 32, 68, 77, 126; contemporary, 23, 42
book laws, 123-125
book production, 35-36, 100, 123, 133, 219, 224; as binding mechanism, 3, 45, 56-57, 64, 65, 120; of binding media, 23, 41, 45; in book laws, 123; context of, 4; intersection with digital media, 9, 75, 91; participation of authors in, 11; split production, 103-4, 120-21, 122; standardization of, 11, 12, 35, 91; times of, 24, 62, 106
book studies, 1, 33, 38, 41, 128
*Bored Apes*, 232
Borsuk, Amaranth, 24, 36, 256n1, 269n75; *ABRA* 24, 57, 74, 104-9, 120; *Between Page and Screen*, 1-2, 16, 137, 144, 190, 219, 257n1, 269n75, 266n29
border, 183, 184, 212; binary logic of, 194, 199; border crossing, 200-2, 210, 213; borderland, 183, 209, 211; border line, 184; border police, 198; border security, 199; border surveillance; Mexican-US border, 180, 182, 193-99, 215, 249
Bouchardon, Serge, 143
boundedness, 31-33, 38, 248; of computer-generated books, 219, 226-27, 246; negotiation of, 23, 52, 54; tensions with unboundedness, 23, 40, 64, 69, 242. *See also* unboundedness
Bourdieu, Pierre, 122, 125
Bouse, Brad: *Between Page and Screen*, 1-2, 16, 137, 144, 190, 219, 257n1, 269n75, 266n29

Bowers, Fredson, 22, 34
Bravo, Luis: *Árbol veloZ*, 14, 46, *101*, *102*, 125
Bridle, James, 5
Brøderbund, 33, 43-44, 87-89
browser, 119, 167; obsolescence, 136; smartphone browser, 58; web browser, 117
Buchanan, Oni, 10, 100, 225n26; "The Mandrake Vehicles," 10, *102*, 225n26; *Spring* 102
Burdick, Anne: *Writing Machines Web Supplement*, 18
BTZ (better than Zork), 87

Caballero, Ana María, 220, 235, 239; *The Wish*, 242-45, *243*
Carpenter, J.R., 20, 26, 263n41, 263n43, 263n47, 263n53; *GENERATION[S]*, 57; *The Gathering Cloud*, 26, 57, 130, 137, 160-66, *163*, 173-74; *An Ocean of Static*, 57; *The Pleasure of the Coast*, 57; *This is a Picture of Wind*, 23, 34, 57-63, *59*, *61*, 69, 161, 227, 263n43, 263n47
Carrión, Ulises, 38
Carter, Richard A.: *Orbital Reveries*, 14; *Signals*, 14; *Waveform*, 14
Caswell, Michelle, 148-49
cataloging, 12, 15, 220, 222, 224
Catelli, Laura, 117
CD-ROM, 14, 18, *48*, 136, 265n19; as attachments, 78; cataloging, 15; as entertainment products, 84; in physical binding media, 42, 46-54, 99, *101*, *102*, 156, 158-59; Voyager, 90-92
cellphone, 194. *See also* smartphone
Center for Book and Paper Arts at Columbia College Chicago, 105-6, 120
ChatGPT, 28, 228-30, 240
Chen, Qianxun: *Seedlings_: Walk in Time*, 222
Christie's, 231-32
Christie's 3.0, 28, 232, 241
City Lights (press), 100, 201
cloud, the, 56, 160-66
Cociña, Carlos: *Plagio del afecto*, 57
collation, 37, 47, 49, 63
combinatory poetics. *See* recombination
commercial publishers, 11, 42, 79, *80*, *83*, 114, 121, 181; comparison with other publishers, 25, 70, 81; conglomerate publishers, 79. *See also* Big Five Publishers
commodore, 31, 44, 87
computer games, 14, 85
computer-generated art, 28, 231-32, 238
computer-generated books, 28, 217-28, 230, 246, 266n29; binding mechanisms of, 226-28. *See also* Using Electricity Series; Aleator Press
computer-generated literature, 28, 218-20, 222, 226-30, 236, 247; and NFTs, 28, 234, 241-42, 246
CONACULTA (Consejo Nacional para la Cultura y las Artes), 73, 92-96, 99
convergence culture, 7, 121, 186
copyright page, 64, *65*, 68, 99, 101, 111, 262n28
Correa-Díaz, Luis, 20; *clickable poem@s*, 25, 74, 103, 115-19, 266n29; *metaverse*, 25, 74, 115-19

Counterpath Press, 28, 220, 222-23, 247, 266n29
Cramer, Florian, 189, 191
creolization, 186
Criterion Collection, 90
crypto art market, 29, 134
crypto poetry, 235-39. *See also* literary NFT
crypto publishing, 234
cultural capital, 12, 24, 85, 92, 104
cultural change, 4, 20, 37, 70, 126, 131; binding media as indicative of, 4, 10, 249
cultural encounter, 4, 27, 181, 184
cultural industries, 25, 71, 149, 177, 230
cultural production, 5, 129, 151, 153; digital applications as, 96, 279n31
cut-up (writing technique), 229
cycles of enthusiasm and retrenchment, 29, 78, 125, 134, 221, 248; binding media as examples of, 77, 82, 114; in hybrid publishing, 24, 73, 96, 120, 126-27

Dadaism, 218
Danielewsky, Mark, Z.: *House of Leaves*, 11
Darrah, Bill: *Essex*, 43, *45*, 88
Dávila, Amparo, 166, 168
death of the book, 8, 69, 86, 149
de Campos, Augusto: *Não poemas*, 14, 23, 34, 46, 50-56, 69, 102, 263n36
decay, 3, 141, 174; media, 127-28, 130; poetics of, 119-20
DiChiara, Robert: *Hardboiled / A Sucker in Spades*, 19
Dickey, William H.: *HyperPoems*, 146, 148

digital art market, 231-33
digital communications, 4, 5, 175-76, 185; acceleration of, 178, 25, 27, 178; globalized, 12, 20, 25, 177, 215
digital files, 97, 157, 204, 220, 246; audio, 201, 202; book as, 75, 76, 233; JPG, 232; JS, 61, 62; MP4, 243; NFT, 220, 231-34; README, 50; replicability of, 231-32
digital literature. *See* electronic literature
digital manicule, 47, *48*
digital presentism, 2, 129, 139, 149, 249; effects of, 30, 142, 173
digital preservation, 123, 135, 142-49, 153, 174
digital publishing, 78, 85, 125, 181, 223; funding for, 84, 95; risks in, 81-82
Digital Publishing Toolkit Collective, 188-89
digital revolution in publishing, 23, 71-85, 99, 123
diskette, 17, 265n19; cataloging, 15; in physical binding media, 42
distribution: of binding media, 3, 100, 103, 121, 123, 247; of books, 41, 75, 77, 123, 224; of digital literature, 12, 55, 56; of hybrid publishing, 73, 91, 92; NFTs as medium of, 233, 235, 239, 247; transmedia, 9
Director, 51, 55
Disch, Thomas: *Amnesia*, 13, 85
documentation: as preservation, 95, 145; as historical register, 27, 171, 195, 201, 213, 223-24, 236; as residues, 15, 27, 130, 154, 170, 174

documentation (writing technique), 26, 130, 153-54, 206-7
Dorst, Doug: *S*, 75
Drucker, Johanna, 40, 62, 227
Durbin, Kate: *ABRA* 24, 57, 74, 104-9, 120
DVD, 18

early web, 43
Eastgate Systems Inc., 19, 268n53
Ediciones fin del mundo (press), 49
Editora Perspectiva (press), 50, 263n36
Electronic Arts, 85
Electronic Disturbance Theater: FloodNet, 176
Electronic Disturbance Theater 2.0 / b.a.n.g. lab: *The Transborder Immigrant Tool / La herramienta transfronteriza para inmigrantes*, 27, 180, 193-99, 201, 215, 223
electronic literature, 19, 31, 121, 218, 223, 238, 286n1; scholarship of, 10, 20, 146, 150, 217; obsolescence of, 143
Electronic Literature Lab (ELL), 15-17
Electronic Literature Organization, 146-47; The Next, 146
Electronic Novel Series, 33, 88-89, 92, 137-38, 248, 266n29; binding of, 43-45, *44*, *45*, 68
Emerson, Lori, 18, 141, 151, 159
emulation, 144-45, 146, 148, 156, 259n25, 274n45
enhanced books, 72. *See also* augmented books; expanded books; hybrid books
enhanced e-book, 109

enhancements to the book, 12, 86, 92. *See also* attachments to the book; extra features of the book
Ensslin, Astrid, 268n53
ephemerality, 25, 132, 134-35, 140; as aesthetic project, 138-39, 143; of binding media, 128-29, 142, 173-74; of the cloud, 160-62, 165; and preservation, 145, 147; in tech industry, 98, 139, 158. *See also* obsolescence; planned obsolescence; presentism
ePub, 223, 226
Ernst, Wolfgang, 154
Espenschied, Dragan, 144-45
Estorick, Alex, 236-37
Ethereum blockchain, 232, 241, 246
expanded and augmented publishing, 12, 23-24, 42 73, 77-78, 136. *See also* hybrid publishing
Expanded Book Project, 24, 73, 90-92, 133; *The Complete Annotated Alice*, 90; *The Complete Hitchhiker's Guide to the Galaxy*, 90; *Jurassic Park*, 90; *Who Built America? From the Centennial Celebration of 1876 to the Great War of 1914*, 90
expanded books, 12, 72, 73, 78; history of, 23-24, 42; publishing standardization, 121. *See also* augmented books; enhanced books; hybrid books
experimentality, 5, 17, 192-93, 221; in publishing, 74, 81, 89, 190, 193, 224
experimental literature, 74, 81, 114, 223, 228, 249; binding media as, 19, 74, 77, 122, 177

extra features of the book, 72, 78, 90, 91, 93, 96-98, 109, 234, 246. *See also* attachments to the book; enhancements to the book

facsimile, 218, 224
Fajfer, Zenon, 14
Felguérez, Manuel: *La máquina estética*, 167, 170, 277n108
Flash, 1, 51, 114; discontinuation of 1, 144, 257n1, 274n455
flipback book, 36
Flores, Leonardo, 20
Flusser, Vilém: *Die Schrift*, 14
font, 59. *See also* typeface; typography
form (literary), 21, 209, 220
format (book), 3, 15, 36, 63, 93, 188, 241
Fornoff, Carolyn, 178
fragmentary archive, 149-55, 174
fragmentation (writing technique), 47-50, 59, 63-67, 116, 169, 173
Franking, Holly: *Negative Space CVN®. A Computerized Video Novel*, 15-17
functionality (of digital applications), 109, 129, 134, 136, 143, 150, 155
funding, 64, 103; grant funding, 147; public funding, 24, 84, 95, 106, 120
Funkhouser, Chris, 114
future of digital literature, 29, 89, 95, 147, 178, 248; on the blockchain, 221, 235, 248; literature of the future, 85
future of the book, 78, 81, 84, 86, 89, 90, 114, 134, 136-40, 178

Gache, Belén: *El libro del fin del mundo*, 14, 23, 34, 46-50, *48*, 69, 219; *Wordtoys*, 46, 50, 136
Gaínza, Carolina: Cartografía de literatura digital latinoamericana, 147
Gallego Cuiñas, Ana, 122
Garbe, Jacob: *Ice-Bound*, 13
García Canclini, Néstor, 4, 184
Generative Adversarial Network (GAN), 224, 231, 287n16
Gerber Bicecci, Verónica: *La compañía* / "La máquina distópica", 26, 130, 155, 166-74, *169*
Gibson, Richard Hughes, 286n1
Gibson, William: *Agrippa (A Book of the Dead)*, 11, 13, 43, 139
Gitelman, Lisa, 6, 134
globalization, 6, 20, 27, 131, 178, 183, 185, 215
Global North, 13, 191, 192
Global South, 192
Golding, Alan: transitional materiality, 8
Gómez-Peña, Guillermo: *DOC/UNDOC*, 7, *100*, 180, 199-206, 215
González, Javier: Cartografía de literatura digital latinoamericana, 147
González, Jennifer A.: *DOC/UNDOC*, 7, *100*, 180, 199-206, 215
Gorostiza, José: *Muerte sin fin*, 93, 94
Grant, Ken, 13, 31, 43, 87, 88
Green, Timothy, 236
Grigar, Dene, 145
Grossman, Claire, 114

Hales, Steve, 13, 31, 43, 87, 88
handmade book, 155, 224, 225, *225*, 242, *243*
Hartog, François, 25, 129, 131, 132, 139
Hatcher, Ian: *ABRA* 24, 57, 74, 103-9 120; *V: Vniverse*, 109-15
Hayles, Katherine N., 184; material metaphors, 38, 69; media ecology, 5, 32, 182, 184; media specific analysis, 8, 33; technotext, 8
Historicity, 129-32
Houston, Keith, 261n9
human movement, 6, 215
Huyssen, Andreas, 131
hybrid books, 24, 73, 96, 122, 200. See also augmented books; enhanced books; expanded books; hybrid publishing
HybridBook Project, 24, 73, 96-99
hybridization: contradictions in, 27, 179, 180-82, 185; critiques of, 177-79, 187, 195, 209; emancipatory potential, 186-87; imaginaries of, 177, 179; material hybridization, 11, 25, 82, 92, 100, 106, 117, 130, 151, 174, 188; media and cultural hybridization, 4, 10, 12, 26-27, 178, 180-81, 183-88, 215; media hybridization, 11, 21, 98, 177, 180, 181, 182, 186, 189, 191, 193; processes of, 4, 12, 181, 184, 187, 191, 205, 216
hybrid publishing, 42, 71-103, 127, 221; academic, 18; and commercial publishers, 11; establishment of, 77, 125-26; failure of, 76-78, 109, 133; future of, 29, 134, 248; history of, 73, 99, 142, 153; non-literary, 78; non-standardization, 15, 24; obsolescence, 249; and the postdigital, 188-90; temporalities of, 134, 137; workflows and expertise, 121. See also book laws; augmented books; enhanced books; expanded books; hybrid books
hype: for book innovations, 137; for NFTs, 221, 231-32, 234, 247. See also cycles of enthusiasm and retrenchment
HyperCard, 146
hypertext, 14, 17, 19, 268n53

Identity, 26-27, 179-81, 193, 195, 200-2, 205; of media, 6, 183
illumination (writing technique), 96, 105, 238
imperative of innovation and obsolescence, 25, 92, 128, 132, 148, 173, 189
Independent Book Publishers Association, 188-89
independent presses and publishers, 3, 11, 40, 42, 70, *80*, *83*, 87, 95, 109-10, 114, 181, 221-23; cycles of enthusiasm and retrenchment in, 85, 120; experimentation in, 20, 76, 81-82, 122; risks taken by, 81-82, 120-22, 125, 221; reinventions of the book in, 76. See also *individual presses*
independent publishing, 19, 24-25, 85, 266n22; growth in, 79, 82, 103, 114, 122, 125; principles of, 74, 79, 81-82, 104, 140, 120, 122
industrialization, 166, 168, 171, 173, 206; bookmaking, 35-36; lan-

guage of, 168; mining, 170; progress, 26, 170; residues of, 160
Infinite Objects, 241, 242
Infocom, 85, 87, 267n45
infrastructures: institutional, 17, 94, 126, 146; of print culture, 12, 146
inscription technologies, 63
institutional presses and publishers, 3, 24, 40, 70, 81, 103, 269n79, 278n4
Instituto Nacional de Bellas Artes, 207
interactive fiction, 16, 31, 85, 87-89, 137-38, 267n45
interarts, 7
interdisciplinarity, 6, 10, 33; challenges of, 20
intermediality, 6, 7, 9-11, 98, 186
Internet Archive, 146, 148
iPad, 25; CONACULTA apps, 73, 93; iPad app, 104-9, 109-14, 188; maintenance and sunsetting, 109, 120, 133, 135, 136
Iwamoto, Kalen, 220, 235, 237, 239; *Romeo and Juliape*, 245-46

Jenkins, Henry, 7
Joan Flasch Artists' Book Collection, 15
Johnston, David (Jhave): *ReRites*, 28, 222, 226-27, 244

Kac, Eduardo, 7
Kindle, 91, 226
Kirschenbaum, Matthew: adoption of personal computers, 7; AI, 228, 287n24; preservation, 259n25; restoration of *HyperPoems* 146, 148

Knight, Jeffrey Todd, 36
Knowles, Alison: *The House of Dust*, 218, 228
Kozak, Claudia, 191

labels (in books), 18, *101*, *102*, 125
Lanham, Richard A., 90; *The Electronic Word: Democracy, Technology and the Arts*, 18
Large Language Models (LLMs), 28, 218
Larsen, Dena, 146
Latin America, 6, 82, 119, 150; digital publishing in, 72, 84, 95; historical episodes of, 152,166, 172, 207, 213-14; scholarship of, 20, 151; technology in, 12, 23, 192, 259n31
Läufer, Milton: *Lagunas*, 226; *A Noise Such as a Man Might Make*, 222-23
legend (caption), 45, 49, *101*, *102*, 262n28
letterpress, 203, 224-25, 225
Lewis, Jason Edward: *Poetry for Excitable [Mobile] Media*, 57
library, 15, 126, 136, 233, 234; library catalogs, 15; library stamp, *101*
liminality, 186
literary NFT, 28-29, 221, 232, 246, 247
literary studies, 2, 6-7, 129, 174; approach to book studies, 76; digital literary studies, 7, 8, 128, 146, 182; and obsolescence and ephemerality, 128, 136, 143; regional and linguistic demarcations, 6, 20
Liu, Alan, 180, 183-85, 215
local/global, 14, 177

Longbarrow Press, 58
loose bindings, 23, 34, 42, 45, 56-69. *See also* binding mechanisms; bookbinding; physical bindings
Lorusso, Silvio, 192-93
Lovink, Gert, 140
low-tech, 176, 192
Ludovico, Alessandro, 190-91

Mackern, Brian, 192, 193; *NetArt Latino Database*, 150
Macromedia Director. *See* Director
Malloy, Judy: *Uncle Roger*, 13
Manuvo, 24, 92-96
Marino, Mark, 195
market, 95, 96, 99, 125, 164n5; and binding media, 70, 89, 122; and new book forms, 98; NFT, 29, 134, 221, 231-33, 236-38, 242-45; and obsolescence, 85, 98, 114; and processes of hybridization, 12, 27, 177-79; and public building, 86, 92, 121-22; technological revolution of, 5, 72, 86, 189; transnational, 4, 12, 13; temporalities, 133, 137; video game, 156-57
Martín-Barbero, Jesús, 131-32, 153, 215, 272n16
Maryland Institute for Technology in the Humanities (MITH), 146
Mataga Cathryn, 13, 31, 43, 87, 88
materiality, 7, 52, 117, 119, 141, 154, 189, 239; of binding media, 4, 5, 25, 70, 151, 178; of the cloud, 161; of digital literature, 142; hybrid, 11, 100, 130, 174, 179, 188; temporality of, 25, 130, 134-35, 139, 173
McDaid, John: *Uncle Buddy's Phantom Funhouse*, 19, 43

McGraw Hill, 86
McKenzie, D.F., 28
McLuhan, Marshall, 186-87
McNeil, Joanne, 229
media archaeology, 6, 136, 154, 185; and textual scholarship, 146, 149
Media Archaeology Lab (MAL), 141; printed matter collection, 45
media ecology, 5-6, 22, 41, 44, 68, 121; shifts in, 6, 176-77, 246
media encounter, 180, 183-84
media landscape, 7, 9, 16, 69, 159, 176-77, 185; changes to, 4, 38, 68, 79, 110, 183; hybrid, 4, 71, 73
media saturation, 191-92, 193
media shift, 4, 30, 75, 177, 182, 184, 186
media specificity, 8, 238, media-specific analysis, 33, 41, 120, 185
Melville House (press), 24, 73, 96-99
Memmott, Talan: *Lexia to Perplexia*, 151
memory, 131, 133; and absence, 141, 150-52, 155; cultural industry, 140; cultural, 132, 148; and digital literature, 130, 143-45, 173; foreshortening of, 137, 141, 144; material memory, 132; memory institutions, 128, 142, 147-48; reconstruction of, 170
memory making, 129-30, 136, 148, 149-52, 166, 207, 212-13
mestizaje, 186, 205
métissage, 186
Mexican War against Narcotrafficking, 152, 207, 211
Miglioli, Lorenzo: *RADIO*, 14
migrant, 184, 193-96, 198-99, 204, 249

migration (human), 20, 27, 178, 180-83, 198, 200-1, 204, 206, 213
migration (technical), 57, 85, 103, 117, 265n19
Miranda, Ernesto, 94
Mod, Craig, 75
modernization, 26, 84, 155, 183, 206, 212, 215
Montfort, Nick, 18, 218; *#!* (shebang), 13, 222, 223; *The Truelist,* 222
Moulthrop, Stewart, 18, 145, 259n26
movies, 75, 160, 264n4
Moving Parts Press, 100, 200-1
Multigraph Collective, 5, 35
Murray, Simone, 120
Mustatea, Kat: *Voidopolis,* 139

NAFTA, 198, 206
Naomi Press, 222
narratives of media encounter, 183-84
Newell, Bryce: *The Tinaja Trail,* 195
newness, 20, 76, 138, 183
NFTs (non-fungible tokens), 28-29, 218, 220-21, 231, 244, 247; hype about, 134, 232-33, 234, 236, 247-48; and print, 233, 235, 239, 241, 245; rarefaction of verse, 237, 239, 248; scarcity, 29, 231-32, 234-35, 239, 244
NFT galleries, 28, 231, 235, 239, 241
NFT marketplaces, 231, 233, 245
NFT publishing, 230-35, 236; as binding mechanism, 241, 245, 246
1913 Press, 104, 106, 120
Nonstandardized practices, 5, 15, 17, 22, 37, 43, 76
nowness, 138-39
Núñez, David: *Bastardo,* 226

Objkt marketplace, 233
obsolescence, 20, 120-21, 139-41, 147, 150-51, 154; of binding media, 3-4, 114, 140, 151, 156-58, 168, 172, 174, 220; internalization of, 135, 142, 143; and literary history, 25, 130, 148, 151-52, 154-55, 174; and malfunction, 46, 119, 128-29; thematization of 135, 139. *See also* planned obsolescence; ephemerality
Obvious collective: *Portrait of Edmond Belamy,* 230-31
Open Sea, 28, 231, 245
operating systems, 3, 15, 92, 156; updates to, 109, 140
oppression, 26, 178-79, 182, 215, 249
Orsai, 278n4
Oswacks, Molly, 98
Oulipo, 218
Owens, Trevor, 147-49

page, 31, 59, 243; cut-out, 43-45, *44;* digital, 50; hollowed out, 43; landing, 110, 150; layout, 54, 196; margins, 203; placeholder, 47, *48;* as unit, 48-49, 53, 55
palimpsestic composition (writing technique), 26, 130, 162, 166, 174
paratexts, 1, 19, 103, 159, 223; as binding mechanism, 40, 64, 68
Parikka, Jussi, 18, 160
Parrish, Alison, 28, 223-25, 229; *Articulations,* 223; *Wendit Tnce Inf,* 224-25, *225*
Paul, James: *Brimstone,* 43, 88, 266n28
Paz, Octavio: *Blanco,* 93-94
PDF, 223, 226

PeaceNet, 175
Penguin, 79, 110-12, 114
Penguin English Library (PEL), 96-99; cover design, 97
Penguin Random House, 79, 81, 206
Pérez y Pérez, Rafael: *Mexica: 20 Years—20 Stories [Mexica: 20 años—20 historias]*, 222, 223
performance, 18, 143, 180, 199, 202, 204; art, 203, 205; individual, 202, 203, 205; live, 214; practice, 201; scripts, 199, 200, 201; video, 200, 241, 245
Perloff, Marjorie: differential texts, 8, 56
permutation, 218
physical bindings, 19, 23, 34, 41-57, 68. *See also* binding mechanisms; bookbinding; loose bindings
Pinsky, Robert: *Mindwheel: An Electronic Novel*, 13, 31, 33, 88, 137-38; binding of, 43, 44, 262n28
planned obsolescence, 2, 132, 135-37, 139, 191; in culture industries, 87, 94, 125, 135, 139-40, 144, 147; temporality of, 128, 135, 141
Pocha Nostra, La, 200
"POÈME OBJKT/POÈME SUBJKT," 236, 242-43
poetry, 1, 8, 108, 110; computational poetry, 28-29, 222-23, 229-30, 233-34; conceptual poetry, 114; concrete poetry, 1, 10, 14, 46, 50-52, 238, crypto poetry, 235-36, 239-48; found poetry, 233; publishing of, 110, 114; visual poetry, 46, 53-54, 63, 222, 241
postdigital, 188-92
postdigital publishing, 190-92

Post-Digital Publishing Archive (P-DPA), 192-93
post-internet, 186
Postman, Neil, 5
post-web, 185-86
power, 6, 25, 128, 153, 182-83, 188; discursive, 174, 209; computing, 32; and hybridization, 26, 177, 181, 186; negotiation of, 149, 178; of print, 30, 249; tech industry, 99, 128, 136, 144, 149, 151
Prabhu, Anjali, 186
Pratt, Mary-Louise, 27, 180-85, 209, 215, 249
presentism, 25, 129-36, 142; binding media approaches to, 160, 162, 173-74; countering of, 25, 133, 155, 158; double debt of, 137; internalization of, 147
preservation, 12, 25, 121; of digital literature, 2, 94, 95, 224, 259n25
presses, 42, 70, 266n29, 278n4. *See* commercial presses and publishers; independent presses and publishers; institutional presses and publishers; NFT publishing
Pressman, Jessica, 7, 8, 11, 286n1
pre-web era, 42, 268n53
printed videos, 241
printer, 64; dot matrix, 218, 219
printing press, 34, 203
print-on-demand, 226
print terminal, 218
production processes of books, 11, 72, 75, 100; author involvement, 11, 121
Provan, Alexander, 19-20
public building, 73, 94, 96, 98, 115, 230, 237; of binding media, 24,

121-22, 137; of computer-generated literature, 223-25; in independent publishing, 82, 104; and market, 92
public domain, 85, 96
*Publisher's Weekly*, 114, 115
publishing industry, 124; and AI, 230; binding media as microcosm of, 3, 6, 70, 77, 103, 178; feminization of labor, 120; and NFTS, 221, 234, 237; place of the book in, 22, 42; processes of, 62, 64, 189; shifts in, 10, 72-73, 75-78, 82-86, 92, 126, 268n53; success in, 123

QR code, 1, 96, 117, 118-19, *118*

Rajewsky, Irina, 7, 9
Raley, Rita, 194, 195
Random House, 81, 91
randomization (writing technique), 50, 218
rare books, 40, 242
*Rattle* (magazine) 235, 236
reading: affordances of, 57, 64; community, 122; habits, 5, 98; instructions for, 16, 33, 39, 63, 202, 204; practices of, 3, 4, 66-67, 244; public, 98, 104, 115, 122, 137, 223-25
real time, 25, 26, 60, 131, 178
recent past, 6, 21, 25, 29, 129-30, 133-34, 142, 247
recombination (writing technique), 50, 60, 63, 66, 67, 110, 219, 226, 229
Red de literatura electrónica latinoamericana, 259, 31
Reed, Aaron: *Ice-Bound*, 13; *Subcutanean*, 28, 226
reinvention of the book, 76-77, 123-25; "failed" attempts, 73, 98-99, 119, 120, 126
reinvestment in print, 9, 29, 69, 246, 249
remains, 25, 26, 151, 170-73, 206; binding media as, 4, 10, 21, 141, 155, 175; cultural remains 153-54, 174. *See also* residues; ruins
residues, 142-43, 155, 167; chemical residues, 160; cultural residues 149, 152; material residues, 99, 123, 130, 153; and memory building, 136
Revueltas, José, 210, 211, 214; *Human Mourning*, 206, 207
Rhizome, 144
Rice, Felicia: *DOC/UNDOC*, 7, *100*, 180, 199-206, 215
Richard, Nelly, 25, 152-54, 174
RiL Editores, 115, 117-19, 120, 266n29
Rivera Garza, Cristina, 25, 81; *Autobiografía del algodón*, 27, 180, 193, 206-15; blog, 209, 214; disappropriation, 210, 213, 214; documentary writing, 152-54, 174; "@EstacionCamaron," 27, 180, 193, 206-15, *208*; neighboring writing, 209, 214
Roa Oliva, Mariana: *Seedlings_: Walk in Time*, 222
Roberts, Tim, 222
ruins, 26, 144, 170, 206-8, 212-14; physical ruins, 167, 169-73, *208*
Ryan, James, 220, 224-25

Safran Foer, Jonathan: *Tree of Codes*, 75
Sáizar, Consuelo, 93-94, 248; Proyecto Cultural Siglo XXI Mexicano, 93

Sánchez Aparicio, Vega, 207, 208
Saum-Pascual, Alex, 286n1
Scherrer, Camille: *Souvenirs du monde des montagnes*, 14
Schmitter, Gianna, 9
Scott, Jason: *Get Lamp. A Documentary about Adventures in Text*, 267n45
Seita, Sophie, 138
self-publishing, 51, *80*, *81*, *82*, *83*
Sexto Piso (press), 64
Sharma, Sarah, 128, 131, 133, 135
Smartphone, 32, 55, 63, 117, 119; browser, 58
Smith, Keith A., 38
Smith, Rod: *Breakers*, 43, 88, 89
Social justice, 148
Social media, 1, 116, 230; marketing 120-21; movements, 175, 176
Social movements, 132, 175
Soft Skull (press), 233
software company, 82, 85, 89, 95, 103; as publisher, 11, 80, 83, 87
Spahr, Juliana, 114
special collections, 15, 224, 233
split production of binding media, 103, 120-22
SpringGun Press, 110, 266n29
Stadler, Matthew, 122
Stairs, David: *Boundless*, 39, *39*
Stein, Bob, 24, 89-90
Stiles, Sasha, 220, 235; *Technelegy*, 239-42, 245, 246
storage media, 34, 42, 46, 55-56, 88, 103, 123; capacity of, 32, 90, 147; discontinuation of, 3, 135, 141; as memory, 140-41. *See also individual instances*
Strachey, Christopher: *Love letters*, 218
Strickland, Stephanie, 11, 74, 109-15, 269n79; *True North*, 19, 57; *V: Vniverse*, 11, 13, 25, 57, 79, 109-15, *111*, *112*, 136, 219, 266n29; *Zone: Zero*, 15, 100
SuperRare, 231
Susuki, Yuri: *The Barcode Book*, 14
Synapse & Brøderbund, 24, 33, 68, 87-89, 103, 120; binding strategies, 43-46
Synapse Software, 46, 73, 85-89, 109, 137; economic hardships and extinction, 89, 91-92, 95

table of contents, 19; as binding mechanism, 47, 49, 50, 54, 55
tech industry, 141, 153, 160, 161, 249; impact on cultural sectors, 5, 25, 139-40, 144, 147, 149, 151; presentism of, 129, 131, 139, 142, 147, 149, 157-58,191; and publishing, 6, 26, 72, 95, 115
technotext, 8, 18
temporality, 77, 128, 131, 135; of binding media, 4, 25-26, 127-36, 136-42, 151, 173-74, 181; of digital technologies, 129, 135, 140-41, 144, 156, 249; divergent temporalities, 3, 25, 127-36, 145, 149; economics of, 128, 133, 136, 147, 149; linear temporality, 142, 191; literary, 98, 141, 143, 148, 167; media, 121, 134, 172, 173, 155; perception of 128, 129, 131, 132, 135; power of, 149, 174
text adventure, 82, 137, 248
textbooks, 12, 78-79, 84, 86, 92, 265n19
theVERSEverse, 29, 220, 235-48; VERSA, 236

Thirkield, Jonathan, 229
Thompson, John B., 72, 75-76, 78, 81
Tomasula, Steve: *Conceptualisms*, 18
Touch Press, 93, 94
touch screen, 93, 95; poetics of, 104, 108
trade edition: binding media as, 40, 56, 69, 70
transculturation, 182, 186
translation, 93, 206
transliteratures, 9
transmediality, 7, 9-10, 98, 125, 209
traversals, 145
Trettien, Whitney: *Cut, Copy, Paste*, 18, 278n5
*Triple Canopy* (magazine), 19, 138
Twitter, 60, 206-7, 213-14, 227, 230
typeface, 64, 240
typography, 64, 200, 203

unboundedness, 33, 38, 53, 66-67, 248; negotiation of, 23, 52, 54; tensions with boundedness, 23, 40, 64, 69, 242
Uniformbooks (press), 160
Uribe, Ana María: *Anipoemas*, 10
USB key, 99, *100*, 201, 204, 163f21
Usenet, 175
Using Electricity Series, 28, 220, 221-24, 227-30, 240, 247
US National Archives, 210

Vázquez, Gustavo: *DOC/UNDOC*, 7, *100*, 180, 199-206, 215
VHS, 16
video, 15-16, 86, 91, 97, 109, 200-1, 220, 245
video poetry, 233, 241, 242, 243
Virilio, Paul, 131

Voyager Company, The, 24, 73, 89-92, 93, 99; agreements with publishers, 91; economic difficulties, 95, 133

Wardrip-Fruin, Noah, 18, 218
Watkins, Zach: *DOC/UNDOC*, 7, *100*, 180, 199-206, 215
Wattpad, 120
web, the: applications on, 1, 63, 64, 66, 109, 112, 136, 160, 167; as environment, 20, 49, 91, 121, 144, 148; migration from, 25, 55, 56, 103, 114, 158; migration to, 94; as platform, 57, 122, 136, 158, 160, 226; publication on, 114, 115
Web 3.0, 236
Weizenbaum, Joseph: *Eliza/Doctor*, 218, 240
Wershler, Darren, 18
Whalen, Zach, 230, 286n1
Winter, Robert: *Beethoven's Ninth Symphony CD Companion*, 90
Wolosenko, Igor, 87-88, 137, 248
*Writing on the Edge (WOE)*, 17-18
writing techniques, 26, 50, 63, 130. See also individual techniques

Young, Stephanie, 114
YouTube, 116, 120

Zapata, Canek, 130; "La máquina distópica", 166-67
zapatistas, 175-77
Zappar, 97-98
Zelevansky, Paul: "Swallows", 10, 46, 259n25; *The Case for the Burial of Ancestors. Book 2. Genealogy*, 13, 43, 46

Zielinski, Siegfried, 142, 153
zine, 58, 62, 63, 263n40
zone of contact, 5-6, 20-21, 180-85, 205, 209; arts of the contact zone, 182; binding media as, 184; methodological approach, 185; as technocultural notion, 179-80, 215
Zúñiga, Carolina: Cartografía de literatura digital latinoamericana, 147

**STANFORD TEXT TECHNOLOGIES**

Paul Fyfe
*Digital Victorians: From Nineteenth-Century Media to Digital Humanities*

Martin Paul Eve
*Theses on the Metaphors of Digital-Textual History*

Geoffrey Turnovsky
*Reading Typographically: Immersed in Print in Early Modern France*

Collin Jennings
*Enlightenment Links: Theories of Mind and Media in Eighteenth-Century Britain*

Bridget Whearty
*Digital Codicology: Medieval Books and Modern Labor*

Michael Gavin
*Literary Mathematics: Quantitative Theory for Textual Studies*

Michelle Warren
*Holy Digital Grail: A Medieval Book on the Internet*

Blaine Greteman
*Networking Print in Shakespeare's England:
Influence, Agency, and Revolutionary Change*

Simon Reader
*Notework: Victorian Literature and Nonlinear Style*

Yohei Igarashi
*The Connected Condition: Romanticism
and the Dream of Communication*

Elaine Treharne and Claude Willan
*Text Technologies: A History*

The authorized representative in the EU for product safety and compliance is:
Mare Nostrum Group B.V.
Mauritskade 21D
1091 GC Amsterdam
The Netherlands
Email address: gpsr@mare-nostrum.co.uk

KVK chamber of commerce number: 96249943

www.ingramcontent.com/pod-product-compliance
Lightning Source LLC
LaVergne TN
LVHW051817060925
820435LV00002B/9